FOURTH EDITION

Working in Groups

Communication Principles and Strategies

Isa N. Engleberg
Prince George's Community College, Largo, Maryland

Dianna R. Wynn
Courtroom Intelligence, Raleigh, North Carolina

Houghton Mifflin Company   *Boston   New York*

Editor in Chief: Patricia Coryell
Executive Editor: Mary Finch
Developmental Editor: Julia Giannotti
Editorial Assistant: Amanda Nietzel
Project Editor: Nan Lewis-Schulz
Editorial Assistant: Katherine Roz
Senior Production/Design Coordinator: Jill Haber
Photo Editor: Jennifer Meyer Dare
Composition Buyer: Chuck Dutton
Manufacturing Coordinator: Brian Pieragostini
Marketing Manager: Elinor Gregory
Marketing Associate: Evelyn Yang

Cover image: © Julie Delton / Getty Images

Printed in the U.S.A.

Library of Congress Control Number: 2006922674

For orders, use student text ISBNs:
ISBN-10: 0-205-55487-3
ISBN-13: 978-0-205-55487-4

456789–DOC–10 09 08

Contents

CHAPTER 5 Verbal and Nonverbal Communication in Groups 121

Online Study Center ONLINE CHAPTERS

Preface

Since writing the first edition of *Working in Groups* more than a decade ago, the study of group communication has become more rigorous and more relevant to the everyday life of groups. Consequently, we have added new theories, advances in research, and innovations in teaching and learning to this fourth edition. At the same time, our research and writing continue to be guided by a central question: "What do students enrolled in an introductory group communication course *really* need to know?" We use two criteria to help us answer this question. First, we include both classic and current theories of group communication that focus on "how groups work." Second, we include practical information on group communication strategies and skills that emphasize "how to work in groups." These criteria help us select and balance the amount and types of theory and skills appropriate for an introductory college course in group communication.

We have been delighted by the positive response to each edition of *Working in Groups*, particularly its adoption in business management, psychology, and communication technology programs. We are gratified by enthusiastic endorsements from both instructors and students who praise the book for its academic rigor and sound practicality. In addition to updated textbook content, the fourth edition of *Working in Groups* introduces many new features. Two major additions are an introduction to group dialectics and a *Working in Groups* video.

WORKING IN GROUPS: MAJOR NEW FEATURES

Group Dialectics
***Working in Groups* Video**

GROUP DIALECTICS

Beginning with the first edition of *Working in Groups*, we have used the concept of **balance** as a central metaphor. The idea of balance explores how group communication theories, methods, and tools interact with group goals and member needs. A group that reaches a decision or completes a task is not in balance if group members end up disliking or mistrusting one another. A group that relies on two or three members to do all the work is not in balance. Effective groups balance factors such as task and social functions, individual and group needs, and leadership and followership. Achieving balance requires an understanding of the contradictory forces that operate in all groups.

The fourth edition of *Working in Groups* further develops the balance metaphor by introducing the concept of **group dialectics**—the interplay of opposing or contradictory forces inherent in group work. A dialectic approach examines how group members negotiate and resolve the conflicts and differences they encounter while working together to achieve a common goal. A dialectic approach also gives real-world significance to the experience and study of group communication. We offer nine group dialectics that characterize the delicate balance achieved by effective groups.

GROUP DIALECTICS

Individual Goals ■	Group Goals
Conflict ■	Cohesion
Conforming ■	Nonconforming
Task Dimensions ■	Social Dimensions
Homogeneous ■	Heterogeneous
Leadership ■	Followership
Structure ■	Spontaneity
Engaged ■	Disengaged
Open System ■	Closed System

These nine dialectics apply to traditional areas of group communication studies, such as group development, group conflict and cohesion, group leadership and participation, group decision making and problem solving, and group meetings. The nine dialectics also inform emerging areas of group communication studies: member diversity, listening in groups, group creativity, argumentation in groups, group goal setting, member motivation, and the use of advanced communication technologies.

Effective groups do not just happen; conscientious members use communication strategies and skills to make what happens in groups meaningful and productive. The key to successful group communication is achieving balance among the complex and competing dialectic tensions that arise any time three or more interdependent people work together to achieve a common goal.

WORKING IN GROUPS VIDEO CASES

The new *Working in Groups* Video Cases offers original case studies that highlight important group communication principles and strategies. Video clips can be used to supplement classroom lectures and discussions, as the basis for exam questions, or as cases for analysis in student papers. Video case studies include the following scenarios:

- *Planning a playground.* A group of community residents meets for the first time to discuss raising funds for a neighborhood playground.

- *The politics of sociology.* Members of a college's sociology department discuss possible course offerings for the next semester.

- *Helping Annie.* A school nurse has called a meeting with a psychiatrist and a social worker to discuss the best treatment plan for Annie, a high school student with possible depression and an eating disorder.

- *Virtual misunderstanding.* A project manager has organized a conference call with an offsite staff writer and designer to discuss a missed deadline for their sales brochure.

TEXTBOOK FORMAT AND CHAPTERS

Although some of the chapters have been reordered, the fourth edition of *Working in Groups* continues to be organized into four major sections. In addition, Web Chapter A and Web Chapter B have been added to provide readers with a practical reference for group research and parliamentary procedure.

- Part I, "Basic Group Concepts," provides an introduction to some of the most basic theories and principles of group communication, including the importance, nature, and dialectics of group communication; the formation, development, and norms of groups; and the theories and practices of effective communication in diverse groups.

- Part II, "Interaction Skills," examines communication principles and the competencies required of effective group members, including communication confidence, listening ability, verbal and nonverbal communication skills, and strategies for expressing differences, managing conflict, and fostering group cohesiveness.

- Part III, "Achieving Group Goals," focuses on task-specific competencies that are common to most work groups, including leadership, argumentation, decision making and problem solving, creativity, and group goal setting and motivation.

- Part IV, "Participation Tools," serves as a "how to" section, focusing on methods and tools that are essential for efficient and effective group action in a variety of contexts. Separate chapters address planning and conducting meetings; making presentations in, for, and by groups; and using communication technology in face-to-face and virtual groups.

- The Web chapters provide two important reference guides. "Web Chapter A: Informed Groups" offers research strategies and skills to help group members search for, collect, analyze, and use the information needed to achieve a group's goal. "Web Chapter B: Parliamentary Procedure" provides an introduction to the basic rules of parliamentary procedure as a method of ensuring that group decisions express the will of the majority while protecting the rights of minority members.

NEW AND IMPROVED CONTENT

The fourth edition of *Working in Groups* strengthens the textbook's scholarship and applicability. In addition to integrating group dialectics into the text, we have added goal setting to the chapter on group motivation, rewritten the chapter on group participation to focus on adapting to diverse group members, enhanced the section on creativity in the problem-solving process, and significantly updated the chapter on technology and virtual groups.

WORKING IN GROUPS:
NEW AND IMPROVED CONTENT

Member diversity
Group goal setting and motivation
Problem solving and creativity
Groups and technology

Member Diversity Chapter 3, "Group Member Diversity," is a new chapter that presents a framework for understanding and applying communication theory, methods, and tools to diverse groups. This chapter is unique in that it adds a section on personality differences to more traditional topics such as cultural, gender, and generational diversity. We strongly believe that all groups must strive to understand, respect, and adapt to members' differences. Groups that know how to balance and benefit from member diversity have the power to create a collaborative climate that enhances group excellence and teamwork.

Group Goal Setting and Motivation We have expanded the third edition's chapter on group motivation—a topic missing from most group communication textbooks—to include strategies and skills for group goal setting. Chapter 11, "Goal Setting and Motivation in Groups," acknowledges that effective communication is an absolute prerequisite for group success, but does not necessarily guarantee that the group will achieve a common goal or that the group experience will satisfy members' needs and expectations. Two additional elements, goal setting and motivation, are necessary to focus and fuel group performance. Effective goal setting helps group members identify a clear goal, understand what actions are needed to accomplish the goal, agree upon the criteria for judging whether the goal has been reached, and highlight how members' behavior contributes to achieving the goal.

Problem Solving and Creativity Chapter 9, "Structured and Creative Problem Solving in Groups," explores the structure–spontaneity dialectic and its importance in group decision-making and problem-solving. Group creativity in and of itself may lead nowhere if groups lack a clear purpose and an overall method for achieving their goals. Traditional decision-making and problem-solving procedures may lead to unsatisfactory outcomes if groups discourage spontaneity, originality, and creative thinking. This chapter strives to balance the practical benefits of structured and creative problem solving.

Groups and Technology Group interaction is no longer confined to face-to-face, real-time settings. Learning how to work in and lead virtual teams has become a fundamental skill for everyone working in groups. *Every* chapter in this edition includes GroupTech, a special boxed feature on the use of technology in face-to-face and virtual groups.

We have revised and updated Chapter 14, "Technology and Virtual Groups." This chapter examines how audio-, video-, and text-based media can enhance group effectiveness and how various forms of groupware can be utilized to improve productivity and member satisfaction. In addition to examining the methods and tools necessary to conduct effective audio- and videoconferences, we have expanded our discussion of text-based computer conferences and groupware to include the ways in which groups can benefit from using email, bulletin boards, electronic chat, blogs, and electronic meeting systems.

WEB CHAPTERS

Two chapters in the fourth edition of *Working in Groups* are presented exclusively as Web chapters. Depending on the needs of your students or your desire to include additional topics of study, you may assign, recommend, or bypass these chapters.

Web Chapter A: Informed Groups We devote an entire Web chapter, "Informed Groups," to the process of finding, analyzing, and using research to inform and support group goals. Researchers note that the amount and accuracy of information available to a group is a critical factor in predicting the group's success. "Informed Groups" covers various research methods and sources as well as methods for assessing the validity of information. The chapter also includes the Toolboxes, GroupTech, Ethical Groups, GroupWork, and GroupAssessment features as well as online test bank questions and group activities.

Web Chapter B: Parliamentary Procedure In Web Chapter B, "Parliamentary Procedure," we provide an introduction to parliamentary procedure and a summary of its rules. Given that the vast majority of corporate, professional, political, scientific, and civic groups use the rules of parliamentary procedure to conduct their official business, we believe that students should learn how to use this system to ensure that group decisions express the will of the majority while also protecting the rights of minority members. Toolboxes, GroupTech, Ethical Groups, GroupWork, and GroupAssessment features as well as online test bank questions and group activities are also included.

CONTINUED THEMES AND UNIQUE TOPICS

In addition to providing several new features, we have updated and strengthened the content of *every* chapter. We have made significant improvements in the standard treatments of group communication subjects and also cover the following topics, which are often neglected in group communication textbooks and courses:

CONTINUED THEMES AND UNIQUE TOPICS

Communication apprehension in groups
Listening in groups
Argumentation in groups
Planning and conducting meetings

Communication Apprehension in Groups Because so many people experience some level of speaking anxiety, we devote significant attention to the subjects of communication apprehension and member assertiveness as they relate to group processes and member confidence. Most group communication textbooks ignore these topics and their impact on members' productivity and satisfaction.

Listening in Groups An entire chapter is devoted to the difficult task of listening in a group setting, including ways to improve the listening behavior of a group by capitalizing on the relationship between listening abilities and member roles. Whereas most group communication textbooks devote only a few pages to listening and rarely discuss the unique challenge of listening in groups, Chapter 6, "Listening in Groups," links listening to group-specific topics such as group roles, note taking in meetings, self-listening during discussions, adapting to differences in members' listening styles, and listening in virtual groups.

Argumentation in Groups *Working in Groups* includes an entire chapter on argumentation. Chapter 10, "Argumentation in Groups," is designed to help group members advance their own viewpoints and analyze the viewpoints of others. Effective argumentation helps a group understand and analyze ideas, influence members, make informed and critical decisions, and achieve its goal. Thus, argumentation is both a significant factor in determining how group communication influences decision making *and* an essential skill for effective participation in groups.

Planning and Conducting Meetings Chapter 12, "Planning and Conducting Meetings," is devoted to running effective meetings. In addition to highlighting the important roles of chairpersons and responsible group members, we provide guidelines for dealing with many of the common duties and problems that arise before, during, and after meetings. The importance of using agendas and recording accurate minutes is emphasized.

GROUP COMMUNICATION LEARNING GUIDES

The fourth edition of *Working in Groups* adds several new features that link the theories of group communication (how groups work) with communication strategies and skills (how to work in groups). We emphasize that the best way to study groups is to balance an understanding of theories, methods, and tools with practical experience. Without theories, group members may not understand why certain methods and tools work in one situation and fail in others. Without the underlying theories, they may not appreciate the experiences and consequences of group communication and action.

GROUP COMMUNICATION LEARNING GUIDES

Toolboxes
Ethical Groups
GroupTech
GroupWork
GroupAssessment
Graphics as Study Aids
Expanded Glossary

Toolboxes In every chapter, there are Toolboxes that highlight significant group communication research and answer frequently asked questions about group communication. They provide practical tips for improving group effectiveness and describe special techniques for enhancing group productivity and member satisfaction. Toolboxes also offer guidelines for achieving a better understanding of group dialectics and the communication strategies and skills needed to manage the many challenges faced by groups. Some examples are "Strategies for Changing Norms" (Chapter 2) "Do Women Talk More than Men?" (Chapter 3), "Silence Speaks Volumes" (Chapter 5), "Know When to Apologize" (Chapter 7), "The Challenge of Young Leadership (Chapter 8), "The Hazards of Consensus" (Chapter 9), "Dealing with Apathy" (Chapter 10), "Choose an Appropriate Meeting Site" (Chapter 12), and "Cueless in Virtual Groups" (Chapter 14).

Ethical Groups Every chapter includes a new *Ethical Groups* feature that examines the ethical issues that frequently arise in group communication contexts.

Some examples are "The NCA Credo for Ethical Communication" (Chapter 1), "Balancing Individual and Group Needs" (Chapter 2), "The Ethics of Assertiveness" (Chapter 4), "Self-Centered Roles and Listening" (Chapter 6), "Leadership Integrity" (Chapter 8), "The Morality of Creative Outcomes" (Chapter 9), "Ethical Arguments in Groups" (Chapter 10), "Using Power and Punishment (Chapter 11), and "Ten Commandments for Computer Ethics" (Chapter 14).

GroupTech   In each chapter, the new *GroupTech* feature guides readers in the use of advanced technology to help achieve group goals. Some examples are "Virtual Group Development" (Chapter 2), "Cultural Diversity in Virtual Groups" (Chapter 3), "Listening in Virtual Groups" (Chapter 6), "Conflict in Virtual Groups" (Chapter 7), "Leadership in Virtual Groups" (Chapter 8), "Decision Making and Problem Solving in Virtual Groups" (Chapter 9), "Motivation in Virtual Groups" (Chapter 11), and "Group Blogs and Wikis" (Chapter 14).

GroupWork   The *GroupWork* feature at the end of every chapter provides a group-based exercise that is designed to demonstrate, illustrate, or practice a principle covered in the chapter. Although the *Instructor's Resource Manual* includes additional class exercises, in-text GroupWork provides a way for classroom groups to interact and function in a collaborative learning environment.

GroupAssessment   The end of every chapter includes a *GroupAssessment* feature that can be used to evaluate student and group understanding of concepts or mastery of skills. Other assessment instruments are provided in the *Instructor's Resource Manual.*

Graphics as Study Aids   Every chapter contains graphics (section previews, concept summaries, checklists, and figures) that illustrate group communication theories, methods, and/or tools. Checklists may be used to help readers chair a meeting, test the validity of evidence, or illustrate the steps in a problem-solving sequence. In many cases, figures serve as previews or summaries of major sections within a chapter. In all cases, the graphics have been designed to function as supplementary learning aids.

Expanded Glossary   An expanded glossary at the back of the book includes every significant term or phrase defined in the textbook. Words, phrases, and the names of theories printed in **bold** are defined within chapters as well as in the glossary.

A COMPLETE PACKAGE FOR INSTRUCTORS AND STUDENTS

We provide a full range of ancillary materials for instructors and students, including an online *Instructor's Resource Manual* and an Online Teaching Center.

Instructor's Resource Manual The comprehensive *Instructor's Resource Manual,* written by the authors, can be adapted to different types of students and course objectives as well as to a variety of course formats and teaching styles. In addition to content-based materials, the textbook and the *IRM* promote three essential and interrelated learning goals: active learning, critical thinking, and the integration of group communication theories, methods, and tools.

The *Instructor's Resource Manual* includes the following components:

- An introduction to group communication studies and pedagogy
- Sample syllabi
- A chapter-by-chapter test bank of objective and essay questions
- Ready-to-use group and writing assignments
- Ready-to-use assessment instruments
- Chapter-by-chapter exercises with accompanying teaching tips
- An instructor's resource library
- A guide to using the *Working in Groups* video

Online Teaching Center The Online Teaching Center features the online *IRM,* a Test Bank, and updated PowerPoint slides.

Online Study Center The *Online Study Center* includes student resources such as ACE Quizzes/Self-Tests, electronic versions of end-of-chapter activities, self-assessment quizzes, and the *Working in Groups* video cases. When you see the Online Study Center icon in the text, visit the textbook web site: college.hmco.com/pic/englebergWIG4e.com.

ACKNOWLEDGMENTS

At the top of our list of acknowledgments and thank-yous is Mary Finch, our executive editor at Houghton Mifflin Company. Mary's unflagging energy, willingness to take risks on our behalf, delightful sense of humor, and overall marketing savvy have made the development of *Working in Groups* an energizing and satisfying experience for two determined and highly opinionated coauthors. We also thank our diligent and patient development editor, Julia Giannotti; our marketing manager, Elinor Gregory; and our good friend George Hoffman, Houghton Mifflin's Editor-in-Chief for business, who sponsored our first edition and has valiantly endured our highly opinionated declarations.

As always and above all, we are indebted to our spouses, Allan Kennedy and Brian Holland. Their advice, support, and patience gave us the freedom to lock ourselves away with our text when deadlines were imminent. Again, we offer special thanks to Brian, corporate counsel at Global Knowledge, whose legal advice and technical expertise helped us make Chapter 14 a state-of-the-art contribution to the study of group communication.

In preparing the fourth edition of *Working in Groups,* we are particularly indebted to the students and faculty members who have shared their opinions and provided valuable suggestions and insights about the textbook. They are the measure of all things. We also extend thanks to the faculty participants in the group communication seminar at the 2005 NCA Institute for Faculty Development at Luther College in Iowa. Their enthusiastic response to group dialectics and their helpful contributions to developing the nine dialectics described in the textbook gave us both confidence and trust in this approach to studying group communication. In particular, we thank the following individuals, who personified the characteristics of an outstanding group: Pat Baker, Davidson College; Rich Briener, University of Great Falls; Joan Conners, Randolph-Macon College; Joe Dailey, Carroll College; Michele Egan, Lake Erie College; Alan Lerstrom, Luther College; Laughton Messmer, Eastern Tennessee State University; Darrell Mullins, Salisbury State University; Marilyn Reineck, Concordia College–St. Paul; Barbara Schmidt, Des Moines Area Community College; and Deb Uecker, Wisconsin Lutheran College.

We are particularly grateful to the following conscientious reviewers, whose excellent suggestions and comments enriched each edition of *Working in Groups:*

Mark G. Borzi, *Eastern Illinois University*
Diane Boynton, *Monterey Peninsula College*
David Browning, *University of Toledo*
Kurt A. Bruder, *Texas Tech University*
Stephanie J. Coopman, *San Jose State University*
Maurine Eckloff, *University of Nebraska at Kearney*
James J. Fernandes, *Gallaudet University*
Todd Holm, *Truman State University*
Ronda Knox, *University of Wisconsin-La Crosse*
Evelyn Plummer, *Seton Hall University*
L. Kristine Pond, *Kansas State University*
Cami Sanderson, *Ferris State University*
Denise Besson Silvia, *Gavilan College*
Debra L. Worthington, *Auburn University*
Kathryn Sue Young, *University of Central Arkansas*
Linda Zeuschner, *Cuesta College*

Isa Engleberg and Dianna Wynn
Working in Groups

PART I

Basic Group Concepts

© Walter Hodges/Stone/Getty images

CHAPTER 1

Introduction to Group Communication

CHAPTER OUTLINE

Succeeding in Groups

Defining Group Communication
Three or More People
Interaction
Common Goal
Interdependence
Working

The Process of Group Communication

Types of Groups
Primary Groups
Social Groups
Self-Help Groups
Learning Groups
Service Groups
Work Groups
Public Groups

Advantages and Disadvantages of Working in Groups
Advantages
Disadvantages

Balance: The Guiding Principle of Group Work
Group Dialectics
Ethics and Balance

GroupWork: It Was the Best of Groups; It Was the Worst of Groups

GroupAssessment: Essential Group Elements

SUCCEEDING IN GROUPS

A few hours after hearing that he had won the 2003 Nobel Prize in Chemistry, Dr. Peter Agre stepped up to a microphone at the Johns Hopkins University School of Medicine and made a startling announcement: "I didn't do this work." Agre said that he didn't deserve all the credit for his discovery of aquaportins, proteins that regulate the flow of water in all living cells. The real work, he stressed, was done by the young researchers in his laboratory, who put in long hours each day. "I made the coffee and sharpened the pencils," he said.

Dr. Agre's colleagues were not misled by his humility: Even the researcher's scientific rivals agree that he earned the honor. But Agre's remarks highlight an important point among scientists about the Nobel Prize and group work. In an age when most scientific breakthroughs are the result of the joint effort of many people over many years, who should get the credit? Unlike the situation at the turn of the last century, scientific discoveries are no longer made by lone geniuses locked in their laboratories. Today, collaborative, cross-disciplinary research is much more common.[1]

In 2004, the Detroit Pistons defeated the heavily favored Los Angeles Lakers in the National Basketball Association Finals. The Lakers had four probable Hall of Fame members (Shaquille O'Neal, Kobe Bryant, Karl Malone, and Gary Payton); the Pistons had only one second-team All-N.B.A. player (Ben Wallace). But the team of less-than-superstars defeated the team of champions, four games to one. Larry Brown, the victorious coach, said, "The sport is about players playing the right way and showing . . . that you can be a team and be successful."[2]

Scientific research teams and sports teams are just what their name implies: a team of people working together to achieve a shared goal. *Working in Groups* focuses on learning how to work effectively with others in many different group settings and circumstances—at school and at work, with family members and with friends, and in highly diverse arenas ranging from sports and science to courtrooms and classrooms. Whereas individual achievement was once the hallmark of personal success, we now live in an era in which success often depends on your ability to work in groups.

You may be surprised by the long list of groups to which you belong. College students typically list family, friends, study groups, class project groups, car pools, roommates, volunteer groups, sports teams, staff at work, campus clubs, religious groups, and neighborhood groups. After graduation, you may add service clubs, management teams, governing boards, political committees, and professional association memberships.

A report by the National Association of Colleges and Employers emphasizes the importance of group communication.[3] In a study identifying the skills that employers seek in college graduates, oral communication, motivation, teamwork, and leadership are the top-ranked skills on the list. Employers viewed group-related skills as more important than written communication skills, proficiency in the field of study, and computer skills. A survey of personnel directors asked to identify the most important skills for successful group participation concludes that members of work groups must be able to

- Listen effectively.

- Understand their roles within the group.

- Actively contribute to group problem solving.

- Ask clear questions to obtain information.

- Establish a professional rapport with other members.

- Communicate effectively with members from different cultures.

- Use language effectively.

- Convey a professional image nonverbally.

- Resolve group conflict.

- Demonstrate leadership.[4]

DEFINING GROUP COMMUNICATION

When does a collection of people become a group? Do people talking in an elevator or discussing the weather at an airport constitute a group? Are the members of a church congregation listening to a sermon or fans cheering at a baseball

TOOLBOX 1.1

 ### How to Use Toolboxes

Before you read any further in this textbook, we want to familiarize you with the functions and value of chapter Toolboxes. Toolboxes answer frequently asked questions about groups and group communication. They provide practical tips for improving your communication and effectiveness in groups. They tell stories about real-world groups and their members. And they describe special techniques for improving group productivity and member satisfaction. Our Toolboxes describe the theories, methods, resources, and skills needed to help you and your group interact and achieve a common goal.

We encourage you to read the Toolboxes when you encounter them. Their practical advice, "insider information," cautionary notes, and reminders will help you become a more effective group member and leader in a wide variety of situations and circumstances. The Toolboxes offer guidelines for achieving a better understanding of group complexity and the communication strategies and skills needed to manage the many challenges that groups face.

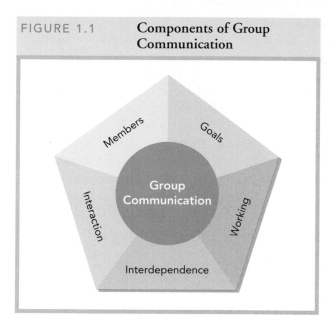

FIGURE 1.1   **Components of Group Communication**

game a group? Although the people in these examples may look like a group, they are not working for or with other members. Working in groups requires sustained and purposeful interaction.

We define **group communication** as the interaction of three or more interdependent people working to achieve a common goal. In order to better understand this definition, let's look at its essential components (see Figure 1.1).

Three or More People

A group consists of at least three people. The saying "two's company, three's a crowd" recognizes that a conversation between two people is quite different from a three-person discussion. When two people engage in a conversation, the interaction is limited to two possibilities: Eve communicates with Adam; Adam communicates with Eve. When a third person is added, the dynamics of the situation change. A third person can change a tie vote into a two-to-one decision. A third person can be the listener who judges and influences the content and style of the conversation. As the size of a group increases, the number of possible interactions (and potential misunderstandings) increases even faster. For example, a group with five members has the potential for 90 different types of interaction; a group of seven members has the potential for 966 different types of interaction.[5]

Although three is the minimum number of people needed for group communication, a maximum size is more difficult to recommend. In general, the ideal group size for a problem-solving discussion is five to seven members. To avoid ties, an odd number of members is usually better than an even number. Groups that have more than seven members tend to divide into subgroups. As groups grow larger, individual satisfaction with and commitment to the group often decrease.[6] Members may feel left out or inconsequential. On the other hand, groups with fewer than five members often lack the resources and diversity of opinions needed for effective problem solving.

A group size of five to seven members has proved its worth in many arenas, including successful evangelical megachurches in the United States. Megachurches may have thousands of members in their congregations, but small groups are the key to their success. Church members are encouraged to create or join tightly knit groups of five to seven people that meet in one another's homes to pray and support one another in times of need. Such groups are very personal, convenient, flexible, and supportive, and they cost nothing. Worshipers match their interests with those of other group members—new parents, retired accountants, mountain bike riders—and use their commonalities as the basis for religious discussions, member support, and voluntary actions. Thus, and ironically, the huge and highly successful megachurches are networks of small groups that share a common belief system, but rely on the motivation and comfort of small groups to strengthen their Christian faith.[7]

Obviously, many groups consist of more than seven members. Yet even in large groups, there is usually a core of five to seven members who do more work and take on leadership functions. In groups with more than fifteen members, coordination and control become difficult. Members may not know one another or be able to communicate directly with other members. Discussion often requires elaborate rules and procedures in order to organize group tasks and control the flow of communication.

Interaction

Interaction requires communication among group members, who use verbal and nonverbal messages to generate meanings and establish relationships.[8] Communication allows members to share information and opinions, make decisions and solve problems, and develop interpersonal relationships. The way in which group members communicate does more than reveal group dynamics; it creates them.[9] Members learn which behaviors are appropriate and which are inappropriate, and which communication rules govern the interaction among members. Regardless of whether group members are meeting face to face or in cyberspace, group communication requires interaction.

Common Goal

Group members come together for a reason. It is this collective reason or goal that defines and unifies a group. A **goal** is the purpose or objective toward which a group is directed. The label—goal, objective, purpose, mission, assignment, or vision—doesn't matter. Without a common goal, groups would wonder: Why are we meeting? Why should we care or work hard? Where are we going?

Often a group's goal is assigned. For example, a marketing instructor may assign a semester-long project to a group of students so that members of the group can demonstrate their ability to develop a marketing campaign. A chemical company may assemble a group of employees from various departments and ask them to make recommendations for more efficient and safer storage of hazardous chemicals.

Some groups may have the freedom to establish their own goals. A gathering of neighbors may meet to discuss ways to reduce crime in their neighborhood. Several nursing students may form a study group to review course materials for an anatomy exam. Whatever the circumstances, effective groups have a common goal and dedicate their efforts to the work needed to accomplish that goal.

The importance of a group's goal cannot be underestimated. If there is one single factor that separates successful from unsuccessful groups, it is having a clear goal. Why? Because goals guide action, set a standard for measuring success, provide a focus for resolving conflict, and motivate members. Thus, the first job of any group is to clarify and modify its goals until they are clear and accepted by everyone.[10] A well-known study by Carl Larson and Frank LaFasto concludes that "in every case, without exception, where an effectively functioning team was identified, it was described . . . as having a clear understanding of its objective."[11] In Chapter 11, "Goal Setting and Motivation in Groups," we look at several theories, methods, and tools for developing a clear and inspiring goal.

Interdependence

Interdependence means that each group member is affected and influenced by the actions of other members. A successful interdependent group functions as a team in which all members take responsibility for doing their part. The failure of a single group member can adversely affect the entire group. For example, if one student in a study group fails to read an assigned chapter, the entire group will be unprepared for questions related to the subject matter covered in that chapter. When a group strives to achieve a common goal, members exert influence on one another. Whether we like it or not, there are not many tasks that can be accomplished by a group without information, advice, support, and assistance from interdependent members.

Working

This textbook focuses on groups that work together in pursuit of a common goal. Working in groups, however, is not the same as groups at work. Certainly, many of the groups you have worked with have been at a job; however, groups that are unrelated to employment also engage in work. A school board discussing hiring practices is engaging in work. A family sitting around the kitchen table trying to come up with a way to divide household chores is working hard to find an equitable solution. However, friends meeting for dinner are not working. Friends who interact with the goal of meeting their social needs do not need to work in order to accomplish that goal. Being with friends is not the same thing as working with friends.

THE PROCESS OF GROUP COMMUNICATION

Central to our definition of *group communication* is the notion of *interaction*. That is, members must communicate with one another as they work together toward achieving a common goal. Communication is complex when just two people interact. However, the process becomes much more complicated when additional people are involved. At its most fundamental level, the group communication process includes the following basic elements common to all forms of human communication (see Figure 1.2):

- Members
- Messages
- Channels
- Feedback
- Context
- Noise

A **member** is any individual whom other members recognize as belonging to the group. Members bring distinctive skills, knowledge, experiences, personality traits, cultural backgrounds, and points of view to a group. As a member, you interact with other members by sending and receiving verbal and nonverbal messages. **Messages** consist of ideas, information, opinions, and/or feelings that generate meaning. For example, you may believe that your group has devoted a lot of time and effort to a project and has done an excellent job. How can you communicate this thought to the other members? You could thank members for a job well done, praise the group's commitment to excellence, share emails congratulating the group, or smile as you literally applaud the group's success.

Members send and receive messages through channels. **Channels** are the media through which group members share messages. You may send and receive messages through one or more of your five senses: hearing, seeing, touching, smelling, and tasting. For example, you could send group members an email thanking them for their hard work, or you could bring a box of cookies to the next meeting to show your appreciation. Many messages don't take the form of words. Group members may recognize that you appreciate their contributions when you nod, smile, or look attentive when they speak. They, in turn, may respond with a verbal message, such as, "Thanks; I'm pretty proud of the way we pulled together on this project." Or they may respond by becoming more motivated and productive. These verbal and nonverbal responses are feedback. **Feedback** is the response or reaction to a message. By recognizing and adapting to feedback, you can assess how well your messages are being received and interpreted.

To understand the communication process fully, you also must understand the critical role played by the context in which you and your group work. **Context** is the physical and psychological environment in which your group communicates. It includes the type and size of the group, the group's purpose and history, the physical setting, the group's role and status within an organization, and the characteristics of and relationships among group members. A newly formed study group meeting in the college cafeteria functions in a different

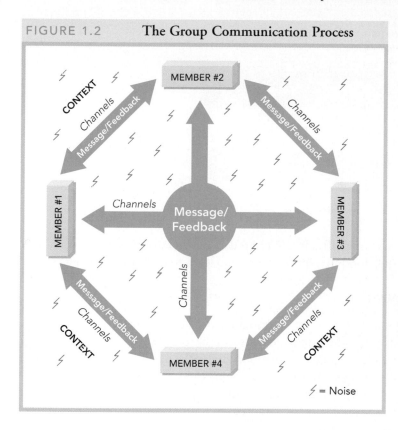

FIGURE 1.2   **The Group Communication Process**

context from a well-established corporate marketing team holding a videoconference meeting with international clients.

Communication is a complex and unpredictable process. Unfortunately, it does not always function as intended. We use the term **noise** to describe anything that interferes with or inhibits communication. Noise can be external—such as loud people in the hallway, an uncomfortable room, or a member walking in late to a meeting. Noise can also be internal and psychological. Biases, distracting thoughts about other activities, fatigue, and hunger all affect how well you express your thoughts or interpret the messages of other group members.

TYPES OF GROUPS

Groups, like their individual members, have many different characteristics and concerns. We have sorted the different types of groups into seven categories: primary groups, social groups, self-help groups, learning groups, service groups, work groups, and public groups (see Figure 1.3). These categories range from the most personal and informal types of groups to more formal types. Each type of group can be recognized by observing its setting (where and when the group meets) and its membership (who is in the group).

Primary Groups

Primary groups are made up of family members and friends; they provide affection, support, and a sense of belonging. Primary groups make us who we are. When families or close friends do not provide appropriate or sufficient support, the psychological scars can last a lifetime. When primary groups help us gain confidence, they make us better prepared for all the other types of groups we encounter. For example, as the first group among all the groups in your life,

FIGURE 1.3   Types of Groups

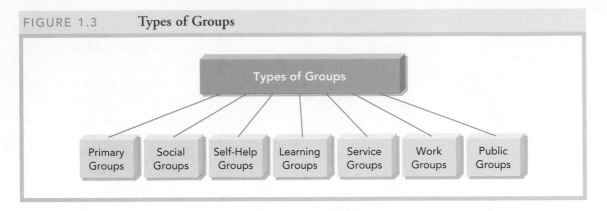

your family plays a significant role in how you learn to communicate using language and in relationships, and also how you learn to communicate in groups.[12]

Social Groups

Social groups share common interests in a friendly setting or participate in a common activity. These groups are formed by people who enjoy interacting with others while pursuing recreational or social goals. Examples of social groups include college sororities and fraternities, athletic teams, and hobby groups (for example, groups focusing on stamp collecting, gardening, classic cars, or videogames). For many children and young adults, peer groups have more influence on their development, behavior, and identity than parents do. Developmental psychologist Judith Rich Harris believes that parenting has almost *no* long-term effects on a child's personality, intelligence, or mental health. According to Harris, same-age peers, not parents, show children how to fit in and behave—in the classroom, on the ball field, or at parties.[13]

Self-Help Groups

Self-help groups offer support and encouragement to members who want or need assistance with personal problems. They are also referred to as support groups, therapy groups, personal growth groups, and encounter groups. People join self-help groups to meet and share their personal concerns with other people who are dealing with the same problems. In addition to private therapy groups, self-help groups include specialized organizations such as Parents Without Partners, Weight Watchers, and Alcoholics Anonymous.

Learning Groups

By sharing knowledge and experiences, **learning groups** help their members acquire information and develop skills. Learning groups can be designed to benefit individual members ("I want to improve my grade on the next exam.") or the

TOOLBOX 1.2

What Does It Mean to Be a Family?

There was a time when most people defined a family as a mother, a father, and their biological children. The *New York Times* reports that in 1960, about 45 percent of U.S. families could be described this way, but that by 2001, only 23 percent of U.S. families could be described as nuclear families.[1] So what *is* a family? A **family** is "a self-defined group of intimates who create and maintain themselves through their own interactions and their interactions with others."[2] A family may include both involuntary relationships (you don't get to choose your biological parents) and voluntary relationships (you choose your spouse or partner). Today we live among many types of families:[3]

1. *Nuclear family.* Wife, husband, and their biological children.
2. *Extended family.* Biological: Family includes other relatives, such as grandparents, aunts and uncles, cousins, and so on. Communal: Family includes close friends.
3. *Step family.* Two adults and children who are not the biological offspring of both parents.
4. *Adopted family.* One or two adults and an adopted child or children.
5. *Single-parent family.* One adult with a child or children.
6. *Couple.* Two adults living together in a romantic relationship with no children.
7. *Gay or lesbian family.* Two people of the same gender in an intimate relationship (who may have a child or children, either as biological offspring or adopted).
8. *Unmarried with children.* Unmarried couple with a biological child or children.

Regardless of the type of family you come from or belong to now, your family is a group in which interdependent people interact in order to achieve a common goal. Family goals include providing affection, protection, and a sense of belonging, and also guiding and supporting children as they grow to adulthood. Depending on the culture in which you live, your extended family may include only a few close relatives, or it can be as large as a village, tribe, or clan.

[1] Eric Schmidt, "For the First Time, Nuclear Families Drop Below 25% of Households," *New York Times*, May 15, 2001, pp. A1, A18.
[2] Lynn H. Turner and Richard West, *Perspectives on Family Communication*, 2nd ed. (Boston: McGraw-Hill, 2002), p. 8.
[3] Turner and West, p. 33.

group as a whole ("We must learn how to use our email system more effectively."). Learning groups can range from a postgraduate seminar at a university to a parenting class at the local hospital. Other examples include book discussion groups, religious study groups, class project groups, health and fitness classes, and professional workshops.

Service Groups

Like members of social groups, members of service groups may join these groups in order to socialize with others. In addition, however, **service groups** are dedicated to worthy causes that help other people both within and outside the group.

Many communities rely on service groups to fill the gap between self-help and government support. There are numerous examples of service groups, including the Kiwanis, labor unions, business and professional women's clubs, neighborhood associations, PTAs, the American Legion, and fire and police auxiliary groups.

Work Groups

If you are employed, you probably belong to several work groups. You may be a member of a production team or a work crew. You may be part of a sales staff, service department, management group, or research team. In almost every case, the **work groups** you belong to are responsible for achieving specific tasks or performing routine duties on behalf of a company, organization, association, agency, or institution. Among the many types of work groups, two deserve special attention: committees and work teams.

Committees.
Committees form when a group is given a specific assignment by a larger group or by a person in a position of authority. Although committees are most common in the work environment, they are often used by service groups when they have a specific task to accomplish. Committees can take several forms. An **ad hoc committee** is formed for a specific purpose and disbands once it has completed that assignment or task. For example, an ad hoc committee could plan a groundbreaking ceremony or high school reunion, organize a company's fund-raising campaign for a charity, or promote a community cleanup for a neighborhood.

Standing committees remain active in order to accomplish an ongoing task. Many businesses and organizations have ongoing social committees, membership committees, program committees, and finance committees. A **task force** is a type of committee appointed to gather information and make recommendations regarding a specific issue or problem. A corporation's marketing task force could recommend a package of promotional activities. A government task force could examine the health-care system or the reasons that test scores in a school system have declined.

Work Teams.
Work teams are groups that are given full responsibility and resources for their performance. Unlike committees, work teams are relatively permanent groups. They do not take time *from* work to meet—they unite *to* work. A health-care team attends to a specific patient or group of patients. A research team is assigned a specific research project. A legal team may form and work to defend or prosecute a specific case.

Public Groups

Primary, social, self-help, learning, service, and work groups usually function in private. Although a group and its product may be visible to the public, members often prefer to meet, discuss, and make decisions in private.

TOOLBOX 1.3

Are Groups Teams or Are Teams Groups?

Is there a difference between a *group* and a *team*? It depends on whom you ask and the situation requiring group work. Some people contend that teams are more structured than groups, take on more complex tasks, require higher levels of collaboration, and select members with task-specific skills.

We use the terms *groups* and *teams* interchangeably. Given our definition of group communication—the interaction of three or more interdependent people working to achieve a common goal—groups can and do vary in their formality, structure, complexity, membership, and title. Thus, a group of friends organizing a large annual block party can be just as diligent, structured, and productive as a corporate team

organizing a stockholders' meeting. In the aftermath of Hurricane Katrina, groups of local boat owners organized themselves into improvised fleets similar in purpose and operations to military search and rescue teams. Rather than worrying about fine distinctions between groups and teams, we are more interested in helping you learn about the group communication theories, methods, and tools that will help you interact effectively with group members in order to achieve a common goal. So although we don't call a football team a football group or a group of family members a team (unless they're playing a sport or game together), we can say that all of these people are interdependent and interact in order to achieve a common goal.

There is, however, one type of group that is seen and heard by nongroup members. **Public groups** interact and work through discussions in front of or for the benefit of the public. Their meetings usually occur in public settings, where they are judged by an audience of listeners. Although public groups may engage in information sharing, decision making, or problem solving, they are concerned with the impression they make on a public audience. Four different types of public groups (see Figure 1.4) illustrate how these groups function.

Panel Discussion.   A **panel discussion** involves several people who interact with one another on a common topic for the benefit of an audience. Panel discussions are very common on television shows such as *Oprah*, attracting huge audiences. Some of these programs present bizarre and controversial panel discussions, while more serious discussions are moderated on Sunday morning political discussion shows and on business programs such as *Wall $treet Week*. Regardless of whether a panel discussion is live or on television, there is usually a moderator who tries to control the flow of communication. Whatever the format, panel discussions are designed to educate, influence, or entertain an audience.

Symposium.   In a **symposium**, group members present short, uninterrupted speeches on different aspects of a topic for the benefit of an audience. For example, a local PTA may sponsor a drug symposium in which a physician, a psychologist,

FIGURE 1.4   **Types of Public Groups**

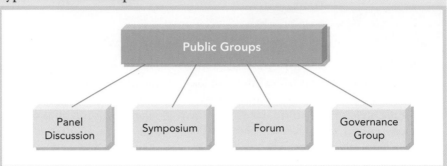

a police officer, and a former drug addict are given uninterrupted time to inform parents about the extent of the drug problem and to recommend strategies for prevention and treatment. At election time, the League of Women Voters or a group of politicians may organize a candidates' symposium at which each candidate is given five minutes to explain why he or she should be elected to public office. What makes a symposium unique is that group members give speeches to an audience rather than interact with other group members.

Forum.   Sometimes a panel or symposium is followed by a **forum**, which provides an opportunity for audience members to comment or ask questions. In some cases, a forum is an open discussion in which members of the public share their concerns about a specific issue with one another. In other cases, a forum is an opportunity for audience members to ask questions of and express concerns to elected officials and experts. A strong moderator is needed in a forum to make sure that audience members have an equal opportunity to speak.

Governance Group.   Public policy decisions are made in public by **governance groups**. State legislatures, city and county councils, and the governing boards of public agencies and educational institutions must conduct their meetings in public. The U.S. Congress cannot deny the public access to congressional debate. Unfortunately, as most government watchers know, "real" decisions are often made in private, and the public debate is just for show. At the same time, an elected or appointed official's vote is not a secret. Governance group members know that if their votes are different from their public positions, they may be accused of dishonesty or pandering to voters.

The seven types of groups are not absolute categories. Many forms of groups overlap. A Girl Scout belongs to both a social group and a learning group, whereas the adults who run a troop or form the national association would be classified as members of both a service group and a work group. Understanding the ways in which the types or forms of groups differ can help members work more efficiently and effectively.

GROUPTECH

Working in Virtual Groups

Instead of meeting face to face, many groups interact virtually. A **virtual group** uses technology to communicate synchronously and/or asynchronously, often across time, distance, and organizational boundaries. **Synchronous communication** occurs simultaneously and in real time. Electronic chat, audioconferences, and videoconferences allow for synchronous interaction. **Asynchronous communication** is electronic communication that does not occur simultaneously or in real time. Messages sent via email, voice mail, and electronic bulletin boards are asynchronous.

In their analysis of virtual groups, Deborah Duarte and Nancy Snyder point out that because virtual communication has become the way in which many companies function, "understanding how to work in or lead a virtual team is becoming a fundamental competency for people in many organizations."[1] Jon Katzenbach and Douglas Smith further observe that "today, organizations are no longer confined to team

efforts that assemble people from the same location or the same time zone. Indeed, small groups of people from two or more locations and time zones routinely convene for collaborative purposes."[2]

Virtual groups are complex. Members may come from different organizations, cultures, time zones, and geographic locations—not to mention that they interact via technology. As a result, virtual groups develop a different group dynamic from those meeting face to face.[3] Chapter 14, "Technology and Virtual Groups," discusses the unique issues these groups face. In addition, every chapter provides advice on adapting to the virtual group environment.

[1] Deborah L. Duarte and Nancy Tennant Snyder, *Mastering Virtual Teams: Strategies, Tools, and Techniques That Succeed*, 2nd ed. (San Francisco: Jossey-Bass, 2001), p. 4.
[2] Jon R. Katzenbach and Douglas K. Smith, *The Discipline of Teams: A Mindbook-Workbook for Delivering Small Group Performance* (New York: John Wiley & Sons, 2001), p. 23.
[3] Susan B. Barnes, *Online Connections: Internet Interpersonal Relationships* (Cresskill, NJ: Hampton Press, 2001), p. 41.

ADVANTAGES AND DISADVANTAGES OF WORKING IN GROUPS

If you are like most people, you have had to sit through long, boring meetings run by incompetent leaders. Perhaps you have lost patience with a group that couldn't accomplish a simple task that you could easily do all by yourself. In the long run, however, the advantages of working in effective groups outweigh the potential disadvantages.

Advantages

Although participating in groups can be time-consuming and even aggravating, the advantages are significant. In general, groups perform better than individuals working alone, members find the experience rewarding, participants learn

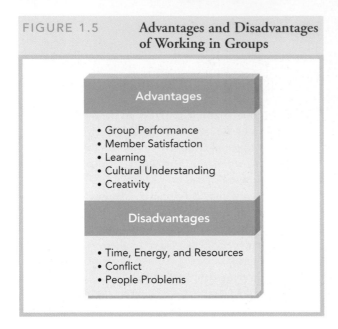

FIGURE 1.5   **Advantages and Disadvantages of Working in Groups**

Advantages

- Group Performance
- Member Satisfaction
- Learning
- Cultural Understanding
- Creativity

Disadvantages

- Time, Energy, and Resources
- Conflict
- People Problems

more, members gain cultural understanding, and group interaction enhances creativity.

Group Performance. Groups make decisions and solve problems. They decide how businesses compete, how staff members work, how governments rule, how instructors teach, and how doctors attend to patients' needs. The reason so many groups are doing so much that affects our daily lives is fairly simple: Groups can perform better and accomplish more than individuals working alone. As M.I.T. management professor Peter Senge writes, "If you want something really creative done, you ask a team to do it—instead of sending one person off to do it on his or her own."[14]

Despite such impressive claims about group performance, there are exceptions. If the task is fairly simple and routine (write a memo, mail a letter, total the receipts), it may be easier for an individual working alone to accomplish the task. If one person knows the answer to a question, or if the task requires a specialized expert, then a single person may be better equipped to get the job done. However, when the task is complex and the answers are unclear, an effective group will perform better.

Member Satisfaction. Even if groups didn't accomplish more than individuals working alone, many people would still join and work in groups. The social benefits can be just as important as task achievement. People belong to and work in groups because groups give them the opportunity to make friends, socialize, and feel part of a unified and successful team. After reviewing the literature on group member satisfaction, Charles Pavitt and Ellen Curtis conclude that "the greater the opportunity that people have to communicate in groups, the more satisfactory the group experience will be for them."[15]

Learning. An added advantage of working in groups is the amount of learning that occurs within an effective group. Groups can enhance learning by sharing collective information, stimulating critical thinking, challenging assumptions, and even raising standards of achievement. A review of 168 studies of college students comparing cooperative, group-based learning with traditional approaches indicates that collaborative learning promotes higher individual achievement in knowledge acquisition, retention, accuracy, creativity in problem solving, and higher-level reasoning.[16]

Why does working in groups enhance learning?
(© Gary Conner/ Photo Edit)

Working in groups gives us the opportunity to learn from and with other members. New members learn from veterans; amateurs learn from experts. Not only do members learn more about the topics they discuss, but they also learn more about how to work as a group.

Cultural Understanding. In most groups, there are differences in members' characteristics, life experiences, cultures, interests, and attitudes. Working effectively in groups requires that you understand, respect, and adapt to differences in members' skills, experiences, opinions, and behavior as well as differences in gender, age, race, nationality, ethnicity, religion, status, and worldviews. By recognizing, appreciating, and adapting to members' differences, you can become a more effective communicator in your group, and also in your community, your studies, your work, and your travels within this country or throughout the world. Chapter 3, "Group Member Diversity," provides a detailed examination of the ways in which member similarities and differences benefit groups.

Creativity. Not only do groups perform better than individuals working alone, but they can also generate more innovative ideas and creative solutions. Lee Towe, author of *Why Didn't I Think of That? Creativity in the Workplace*, writes that the "key to creativity is the mental flexibility required to mix thoughts from our many different experiences."[17] When you mix your thoughts with those of other group members, you increase the group's creative potential. Groups provide a creative multiplier effect by tapping more information, more brainpower, and more insights. Groups have "awesome superiority" when trying to unleash creativity and solve challenging problems.[18]

Disadvantages

The advantages of working in groups occur when groups are working efficiently and effectively. The disadvantages are more likely to occur when working in a group is not the appropriate way to achieve a goal, when members do not work to their full potential, or when problems interfere with group members' willingness and ability to communicate. The most common complaints about working in groups concern the amount of time, energy, and resources expended by groups and the conflict and people problems that can arise.

Time, Energy, and Resources. Working in groups costs time, energy, and resources. The 3M Corporation examined the many factors that affect the cost of meetings, including the hourly wages of group members, the wages of those who help prepare for meetings, the cost of materials used in meetings, and overhead costs. Here's its conclusion: The 3M corporation spends a staggering $78.8 million annually for meetings.[19] A Microsoft survey concludes that nonproductive meetings, poor communication, and hazy group objectives gobble up two of every five workdays. In another study, workers report that they spend an average of 5.6 hours a week in meetings and rate 69 percent of those meetings as "ineffective."[20] We spend a lot of time in groups; if that time is wasted, we are throwing away valuable resources and effort.

Conflict. Very few people enjoy or seek out conflict. However, when group members work together to achieve a common goal, there is always the potential for disagreement. Unfortunately, those who disagree are often seen as aggressive and disruptive. As a result, some people will do almost anything to avoid conflict and confrontation. They may even avoid working in groups. Most researchers and writers contend that "in a good discussion, arguing our different viewpoints might lead to clarifying and reconciling them."[21] Yet because of apprehension about conflict, some people avoid meetings in which controversial issues are scheduled for discussion, or are unwilling to express their opinions.

People Problems. As much as we may want others to share our interests, viewpoints, and willingness to work, there is always the potential for individual group members to create problems. Like anyone else in our daily lives, group members can be stubborn, lazy, and even cruel. When deciding whether to work in a group, we often consider whether we want to spend time working with certain members of that group.

Members who lack confidence or are unprepared may have little to contribute. In order to avoid conflict or extra work, some members may go along

TOOLBOX 1.4

Theories, Methods, and Tools Are Inseparable

Peter Senge, an influential management expert, contends that theories, methods, and tools are inseparable components of effective organizations. The interaction of theories, methods, and tools also lies at the heart of learning how to work in groups.[1] Throughout this textbook, we look at the theories, methods, and tools needed to promote group productivity and member satisfaction.

- **Theories** are statements that explain how the world works. They try to explain or predict events and behavior. Group communication theories have emerged from extensive observation and research. They help us understand what is occurring in a group and why a group succeeds or fails. Learning about such theories, however, will not make you a more effective group member. Theories do not necessarily tell you what to do or what is right or wrong. However, without theories, we would have difficulty understanding why or how a particular method or tool affects group performance.
- The word *method* comes from the Greek *methodos*—the means to pursue particular objectives. **Methods** are strategies, guidelines, procedures, and techniques for dealing with the issues and problems that arise in groups. Throughout this textbook, you will read about individual and group methods—from leadership strategies to participation guidelines, from conflict-management techniques to decision-making procedures. Learning about methods,

however, is not enough. Effective methods are based on theories. Without theories, you won't know why a particular method works in one situation and fails in another. Methods based on theories provide a way to understand when, where, why, and how to use methods effectively.

- Tools are devices used to perform work. Unlike handheld devices such as saws or hammers, the **tools** needed by groups are resources, rules, and skills that help the group carry out or achieve its common goal. Throughout this textbook, you will read about how to use agendas, minutes, parliamentary procedure, and even technology-based tools. You also will learn about the ways in which communication skills function as the most important tools available to all group members. Like methods, tools are most effective when their use is based on theories. Although a master carpenter can tell you what tool to use, you may have no idea how to use it or why it works. In our eagerness to solve problems or achieve a group's goal, we may grab ready-made, easy-to-use tools that do not address the causes of a problem or help us achieve the goal. Using tools without an understanding of methods and theories can make the process of working in groups inefficient, ineffective, and frustrating for all members.

[1] Peter M. Senge et al, *The Fifth Discipline Fieldbook: Strategies and Tools for Building a Learning Organization* (New York: Doubleday, 1994), pp. 28–31.

with the group or play "follow the leader" rather than search for the best solution to a problem. Strong, domineering members can put so much pressure on others that dissent is stifled. Although no one wants to work with a group of unpleasant members, there may be circumstances in which people problems cannot be avoided. When this situation occurs, the disadvantages of group work can overwhelm the advantages.

BALANCE: THE GUIDING PRINCIPLE OF GROUP WORK

At the heart of this book is a guiding principle that gives real-world significance to your experiences in and study of group communication. We believe that an ideal group succeeds because it has achieved *balance*.

The concept of **balance** is a way of relating group communication theories, methods, and tools to group goals and member needs. A clear goal is the point on which a group must balance many factors. A group that reaches a decision or completes an assigned task is not in balance if every person in the group ends up hating everyone else. A group that relies on one or two members to do all the work is not in balance. Effective groups balance factors such as the group's task and social functions, individual and group needs, and leadership and followership. Achieving balance requires an understanding of the interplay of the contradictory forces that operate in all groups.

Group Dialectics

The American Heritage Dictionary of the English Language defines **dialectics** as a method of argument or exposition that systematically weighs contradictory facts or ideas with a view of resolution of their real or apparent contradiction.[22] You encounter dialectic tensions all the time. Should you work or play? Should you spend or save? Should you eat or diet? Such dialectic tensions can often be resolved by taking a both/and approach rather than looking for either/or answers. If you find a job you love, it can be as exciting and rewarding as play. If you spend less and save more, you can look forward to a more secure financial situation. If you eat less food and exercise, you may have adopted a healthy diet. Higher-order dialectics—honesty or dishonesty, love or hate—ask more significant and complex questions. Here, too, a both/and approach rather than an either/or attitude can provide guidance and resolution. You may lie to protect someone from unnecessary harm and tell the truth when its importance outweighs the potential harms. You may hate what someone does and still love the person.

Communication scholars Leslie Baxter and Barbara Montgomery use the term *dialectics* to describe the complex and contradictory nature of *interpersonal* relationships.[23] Baxter and Montgomery's **Relational Dialectics Theory** claims that relationships are characterized by ongoing, dialectic tensions between the multiple contradictions, complexities, and changes in human experiences.[24] The following pairs of common folk proverbs illustrate such contradictory, dialectical tensions:

"Opposites attract" *but* "Birds of a feather flock together."

"Two's company; three's a crowd" *but* "The more, the merrier."[25]

"To know him is to love him" *but* "Familiarity breeds contempt."[26]

How does a cheerleading squad balance both the homogenous and heterogeneous characteristics of group members? (© Bob Daemmrich/The Image Works)

Rather than trying to prove that one of these contradictory proverbs is truer than the other—an either/or response—relational dialectics also takes a both/and approach. For example, in some groups, you may enjoy warm friendships with some members *and* endure cold relationships with others. You may want a stable, predictable group in some situations *and* the excitement of discovery and change in other circumstances. **Group dialectics** represent the balance between competing and contradictory components of group work by taking a both/and approach to resolving such tensions. In Figure 1.6 we present nine dialectical tensions that characterize the delicate balance required by groups that strive to epitomize the characteristics of effective groups.[27]

Individual Goals and Group Goals. In Chapter 2, we identify the many reasons for joining groups—to complete a task, to satisfy basic and interpersonal needs, and to seek social interactions. A group, however, will not function well—or at all—if members focus entirely on their individual goals rather than on the group's common goal. When a group agrees upon a clear and important goal, members can pursue both group *and* individual goals, as long as those personal goals do not undermine the group goal. For example, if you join a group because you're interested in forming a romantic attachment with another member, you may strongly support the group or its goal, in part, because it will impress the object of your desire.

In the best of groups, your personal goals support the group's common goal. If you do not share the group's goal, you may become frustrated or try to undermine the group. In ideal groups, members negotiate their needs and interests to achieve a balance between the dialectic tension of being independent and being part of an interdependent group.

Conflict and Cohesion. Conflict is unavoidable in effective groups. How else can members express disagreements that may lead to better solutions? How else can groups ensure that ethical standards are upheld? Groups without constructive conflict are groups without the means to analyze the wisdom of their decisions. At the same time, groups also benefit from cohesion—the mutual attraction that holds the members of a group together. All for one and one for all! Cohesive groups are committed, unified, and willing to engage in conflict. Chapter 7, "Conflict and Cohesion in Groups," examines the conflict–cohesiveness dialectic in detail.

FIGURE 1.6   **Group Dialectics**

Group Dialectics	Balancing Group Dialectics
Individual Goals ↔ Group Goals	Members' personal goals are *balanced* with the group's common goal.
Conflict ↔ Cohesion	The value of constructive conflict is *balanced* with the need for unity and cohesiveness.
Conforming ↔ Nonconforming	A commitment to group norms and standards is *balanced* with a willingness to differ and change.
Task Dimensions ↔ Social Dimensions	The responsibility and motivation to complete tasks are *balanced* with promoting member relationships.
Homogeneous ↔ Heterogeneous	Member similarities are *balanced* with member differences in skills, roles, personal characteristics, and cultural perspectives.
Leadership ↔ Followership	Effective and ethical leadership is *balanced* with loyal and responsible followership.
Structure ↔ Spontaneity	The need for structured procedures is *balanced* with the need for innovative and creative thinking.
Engaged ↔ Disengaged	Member energy and labor are *balanced* with the group's need for rest and renewal.
Open System ↔ Closed System	External support and recognition are *balanced* with internal group solidarity and rewards.

Conforming and Nonconforming. Group norms affect the quality and quantity of the work done by group members. Dialectic tensions can arise, however, when one or more members challenge the group's norms or achievement standards. When standards, methods, or norms are questioned, a group may benefit from reconsidering its position. Constructive criticism that also promotes a group's goal can contribute to group effectiveness. In Chapter 2, "Group Development," we explore the ways in which group norms address the need for both conformity and nonconformity.

Task Dimensions and Social Dimensions. In Chapter 2, "Group Development," we observe that people often join and work in groups because there's a job to do *and/or* because there are people with whom they want to work and socialize. The best groups negotiate the task–social dialectic by balancing work with pleasure. Members communicate in ways that allow the job to get done but that also make everyone feel valuable and well liked. Sociologists Rodney Napier and Matti Gershenfeld recognize the dialectic struggle within groups as the tensions between work efficiency and personal needs, between success measured in terms of getting the task done and success measured in terms of emotional fulfillment through friendships among members.[28] Achieving a both/and resolution is difficult because combining the two increases the complexity of existing relationships and the interpersonal risks for members. For example, imagine the hazard of criticizing poor work by a good friend in front of group members who are eager to complete a task that requires high standards of excellence.

Homogeneous and Heterogeneous. The prefixes *homo* and *hetero* come from the Greek language. *Homo* means *same* or *similar*; *hetero* means *different*. Thus a **homogeneous group** is composed of members who are all the same or very similar, and a **heterogeneous group** includes members who are different from one another. Not surprisingly, there is no such thing as a purely homogeneous group because no two people can be exactly the same. Certainly some groups are more homogeneous than heterogeneous. For example, the Black Caucus in the U.S. Congress will be more homogeneous than the Congress as a whole. The legal team representing a client will be more homogeneous in terms of education, income, professional experience, and lifestyle than the jury selected to hear the case. In Chapter 3, "Group Member Diversity," we emphasize that every person on this earth—and thus every member of a group—is different. And that's a good thing. If every member of a group were exactly alike, the group would not achieve much more than one member working alone. At the same time, similarities assure members that they share some common characteristics, traits, and attitudes.

Leadership and Followership. Chapter 8, "Group Leadership," examines the components and challenges of effective leadership. We note that effective leadership is not a solo task—it requires loyal, competent, and responsible followers. Effective leaders have the confidence to put their egos aside and bring out the leadership in others.[29] When different group members assume specific leadership functions, the group has achieved an optimum balance of leadership and followership.

Structure and Spontaneity. In Chapter 9, "Structured and Creative Problem Solving in Groups," we quote group communication scholar Marshall Scott

Poole, who notes that procedures are "the heart of group work [and] the most powerful tools we have to improve the conduct of meetings." Structured procedures help groups balance participation, resolve conflicts, organize discussions, and empower members. If, however, a group becomes obsessed with rigid procedures, it misses out on the benefits of spontaneity and creativity. Whether it's just "thinking outside the box" or organizing a creative problem-solving session, groups can reap enormous benefits by encouraging innovation and "what if" thinking. Effective groups balance the need for structure with time for spontaneous and creative thinking.

Engaged and Disengaged. The engaged–disengaged dialectic has two dimensions—one related to the amount of activity, and the other related to the level of commitment. Groups often experience two opposite types of activities: high-energy, nonstop action relieved by periods of relaxation and renewal. Effective groups understand that racing toward a distant finish line may only exhaust group members and leave some sitting on the sidelines. At the same time, low energy and inaction will accomplish nothing. Balancing the urge to run with the need for rest and renewal challenges most groups.

Sometimes, high-energy, nonstop action is unstoppable because group members are extremely motivated, personally committed, and appropriately rewarded for their work. Stopping to recharge or relax would only frustrate a group with pent-up energy. At the other end of the dialectic spectrum, groups that plod through problems with little enthusiasm may be unmotivated, uncaring, and unrewarded for their work. Asking them to pick up speed would only increase their resentment.

Open System and Closed System. *The American Heritage Dictionary of the English Language* defines system as "a group of interacting, interrelated, or interdependent elements forming a complex whole."[30] Sounds something like our definition of group communication, doesn't it? The only element we would add to this definition of a system is *a common goal*. Even your digestive system has a goal: ingesting and absorbing nutrients for survival. Most systems respond and adapt their environment in order to maintain an ideal balance. For example, if you eat too much, your digestive system responds by sending a signal that gives you the feeling of fullness—or even indigestion. Feeling hungry or full helps you moderate your food intake.

Most groups maintain a balance by moving between being open and closed systems. When a group functions as an open system, it welcomes input from and interchange with its environment. That input can be the opinions of nongroup members, information from outside research, or challenges from competing groups. When a group functions as a closed system, it guards its boundaries and discourages input from or interaction with the outside. Depending on the situation, a group may open its boundaries and welcome input

TOOLBOX 1.5

Unity Creates Synergy

When three or more interdependent people interact and work to achieve a common goal, they have the potential to be synergistic. **Synergy** is a term that describes the cooperative interaction of several factors that results in a combined effect greater than the total of all individual contributions. In other words, the whole is greater than the sum of its individual parts. The term *synergy* comes from the Greek word *sunergos,* meaning "working together." Synergy does not occur when people work alone; it occurs only when people work together.

Group communication, as we have defined it, is more than a collection of individuals who talk to one another. A group is a complex system. In such a system, the actions of individual members in the form of talk or behavior affect everyone in the group as well as the outcome of the group's

work. The analogy of a recipe illustrates this effect. Eggs, sugar, cream, and bourbon have very different and individual tastes, but when they are combined properly in a recipe, the result is an irresistible and intoxicating eggnog. In groups, people are the major ingredients; in the right combination, they can create a highly productive and satisfying experience.

Effective groups are synergistic. Baseball teams without superstars have won the World Series. Companies whose executives earn modest salaries have surpassed those companies in which the CEOs are paid millions of dollars. Ordinary groups have achieved extraordinary results. Synergy occurs when the knowledge, talents, and dedication of group members merge into a force that surpasses anything group members could have produced without cooperative interaction.

or close them to protect the group and its work. Effective groups understand that there are times when they must function as an open system and other times when they must close the door and work in private. For example, a hiring committee may function as an open system in order to recruit candidates and research their backgrounds. When the committee members have finished this process, they meet privately and confidentially to evaluate the candidates and make a hiring recommendation.

Ethics and Balance

Ethical questions—Are we doing the right thing? Are we fair? Is he dishonest? Is she tolerant of different viewpoints?—arise whenever we communicate because communication has consequences. What you say and do can help or hurt both group members and other people who are affected by the group's decisions and actions. Sadly, the theories, methods, and tools in this textbook can be and have been used for less-than-ethical purposes. For example, a group member may support a good but inexperienced friend for an important job, only to suffer the consequences when the friend botches the job or fails to meet the group's expectations.

Ethics requires an understanding of whether members' communication behaviors meet agreed-upon standards of right and wrong.[31] The National Communication Association (NCA) provides a credo for ethical communication.[32] In Latin, the word *credo* means "I believe." Thus, an ethics credo is a belief statement about what it means to be an ethical communicator. Notice how all the principles of ethical communication can be applied to working in groups.

The ancient Greek philosopher Aristotle offered the "doctrine of the mean" as a balanced approach to ethical behavior.[33] He suggested that when we face an ethical decision, we should engage our critical thinking ability to select an *appropriate* response somewhere between two extremes. For example, Aristotle

ETHICAL GROUPS

 ## The National Communication Association Credo for Ethical Communication

Questions of right and wrong arise whenever people communicate. Ethical communication is fundamental to responsible thinking, decision making, and the development of relationships and communities within and across contexts, cultures, channels, and media. Moreover, ethical communication enhances human worth and dignity by fostering truthfulness, fairness, responsibility, personal integrity, and respect for self and others. We believe that unethical communication threatens the well being of individuals and the society in which we live. Therefore we, the members of the National Communication Association, endorse and are committed to practicing the following principles of ethical communication:

- We advocate truthfulness, accuracy, honesty, and reason as essential to the integrity of communication.
- We endorse freedom of expression, diversity of perspective, and tolerance of dissent to achieve the informed and responsible decision making fundamental to a civic society.

- We strive to understand and respect other communicators before evaluating and responding to their messages.
- We promote access to communication resources and opportunities as necessary to fulfill human potential and contribute to the well being of families, communities, and society.
- We promote communication climates of caring and mutual understanding that respect the unique needs and characteristics of individual communicators.
- We condemn communication that degrades individuals and humanity through distortion, intimidation, coercion, and violence, and through the expression of intolerance and hatred.
- We are committed to the courageous expression of personal conviction in pursuit of fairness and justice.
- We advocate sharing information, opinions, and feelings when facing significant choices while also respecting privacy and confidentiality.
- We accept responsibility for the short- and long-term consequences of our own communication and expect the same of others.

maintained that anyone can become angry—that is easy. But to be angry at the right things, with the right people, to the right degree, at the right time, for the right purpose, and in the right way—that is worthy of praise.[34]

Keep Aristotle's doctrine of the mean in mind as you apply the ethics credo to group communication. If expressing your opinion has the potential to harm rather than help others, Aristotle would urge you to reconsider your decision to express it. And so would we. There are no "ten commandments" of ethics. In the end, you must decide whether you have communicated appropriately and ethically. Finding the golden mean requires an understanding of the dialectic tensions that operate in all groups as well as a desire to communicate in a way that meets agreed-upon standards of right and wrong.

GROUPWORK

It Was the Best of Groups; It Was the Worst of Groups

Goals
- To understand the advantages and disadvantages of working in groups
- To demonstrate the number and different types of groups to which students belong

Participants: Groups of 5–7 members

Procedure
1. Students should think about two groups to which they now belong or have belonged. One should be the "best of groups," that is, a group that is or was highly successful and/or personally satisfying. The other should be the "worst of groups"—one that is or was unsuccessful, disappointing, and/or frustrating. Students should consider what characteristics were unique to the best group and which were unique to the worst group. Then they should write down at least two unique characteristics of each type of group.

2. After students have completed their lists of characteristics, they should arrange themselves into groups of five to seven members. One member should record the best and worst characteristics noted by all members.

3. In turn, each member should explain one unique characteristic of a best group and one unique characteristic of a worst group. Students may use examples or tell stories about their good and bad group experiences. If there is enough time for a second round, each student can offer another characteristic of his or her best and worst groups.

4. As students explain their positive and negative experiences, the group's recorder should compile a list of the "best" and "worst" characteristics. A spokesperson

from each group should be selected to explain those characteristics to the rest of the class, and/or the recorder can write the two lists on a board or flip chart.

5. As a class, respond to the following questions:

- What are some of the most common characteristics of the best groups?
- What are some of the most common characteristics of the worst groups?
- Do any characteristics appear on both lists? Why would this happen?
- Which characteristics depended on communication skills?
- What dialectic tensions emerge from the list of characteristics?

GROUPASSESSMENT

Essential Group Elements

Directions. Group communication includes five basic elements: (1) group size, (2) interaction, (3) a common goal, (4) interdependence, and (5) working. Think about the groups you belong to or a group that has just formed in your class or at work. Answer the following questions to assess the extent to which your group contains the basic group elements. If you can answer *yes* to most of the questions, your group is likely to succeed.

Essential Elements of Group Communication

Group Size	Yes	No	Sometimes
1. Do group members communicate with one another directly?	☐	☐	☐
2. Does the group have enough people to achieve its goal?	☐	☐	☐
3. Can the group function effectively without forming subgroups?	☐	☐	☐

Interaction			
1. Do group members communicate with one another easily and frequently?	☐	☐	☐
2. Do members send, receive, and respond to messages in a way that enhances communication?	☐	☐	☐

Common Goal	Yes	No	Sometimes
1. Does the group have a clear goal?	☐	☐	☐
2. Do members understand and support the group's goal?	☐	☐	☐

Interdependence			
1. Do members feel responsible for the group's actions?	☐	☐	☐
2. Do members understand their individual and group responsibilities?	☐	☐	☐
3. Do members believe that "we're all in this together"?	☐	☐	☐

Working			
1. Are members ready, willing, and able to participate as active group members?	☐	☐	☐
2. Do members give the time and energy needed to achieve the group's goal?	☐	☐	☐

NOTES

1. Michael Stroh and Scott Shane, "Who Gets Credit Still a Nobel Issue," *The Sun*, October 12, 2003, p. A1.

2. Dean Robinson, "You Don't Need Superstars to Win," in "Year of Ideas," *New York Times Magazine*, December 12, 2004, p. 103.

3. National Association of Colleges and Employers, *Special Report: Job Outlook '96* (Bethlehem, PA: NACE,- November 1995).

4. Katherine W. Hawkins and Bryant P. Fillion, "Perceived Communication Needs for Work Groups," *Communication Research Reports*, 16, 1999, pp. 171–172.

5. Rodney W. Napier and Matti K. Gershenfeld, *Groups: Theory and Experience*, 7th ed. (Boston: Houghton Mifflin, 2004), pp. 42–43.

6. Joseph A. Bonito and Andrea Hollingshead, "Participation in Small Groups," in *Communication Yearbook 20,* ed. Brant R. Burleson (Thousand Oaks, CA: Sage, 1997), p. 236.

7. Malcolm Gladwell, "The Cellular Church," *The New Yorker*, September 12, 2005, pp. 61–63.

8. Based on the Association for Communication Administration's 1995 Conference on Defining the Discipline statement that "the field of communication *focuses* on how people use verbal and nonverbal messages to generate meanings within and across various contexts, cultures, channels, and media." See *Spectra,* the newsletter of the National Communication Association, October 1995, p. 12.

9. Anne Donnellon, *Team Talk: The Power of Language in Team Dynamics* (Boston: Harvard Business School Press, 1996), p. 28.

10. David W. Johnson and Frank P. Johnson, *Joining Together: Group Theory and Group Skills*, 2nd ed. (Englewood Cliffs, NJ: Prentice Hall, 1982), p. 173.

11. Carl E. Larson and Frank M. J. LaFasto, *TeamWork: What Must Go Right/What Can Go Wrong* (Newbury Park, CA: Sage, 1989), p. 27.

12. Thomas J. Socha, "Communication in Family Units: Studying the First 'Group,'" in *The Handbook of Group Communication Theory and Research*, ed.

Lawrence R. Frey, assoc. eds. Dennis S. Gouran and Marshall Scott Poole (Thousand Oaks, CA: Sage, 1999), p. 488.

13. *http://discuss.washingtonpost.com/wp-srv/zforum/98/harris093098.htm*; *Edge 58*, June 29, 1999, at *http://www.edge.org/documents/archive/edge58.html*; "Blame Your Peers, Not Your Parents, Authors Says," *APA Monitor*, October 1998, available at *http://www.snc.edu/psych/korshavn/peer01.htm*.

14. Peter M. Senge et al, *The Fifth Discipline Fieldbook: Strategies and Tools for Building a Learning Organization* (New York: Doubleday, 1994), p. 51.

15. Charles Pavitt and Ellen Curtis, *Small Group Discussion: A Theoretical Approach*, 2nd ed. (Scottsdale, AZ: Gorsuch, Scarisbrick, 1994), p. 54.

16. Quoted in David W. Johnson, R. T. Johnson, and K. A. Smith, "Cooperative Learning Returns to College," *Change*, July/August 1998, p. 31.

17. Lee Towe, *Why Didn't I Think of That? Creativity in the Workplace* (West Des Moines, IA: American Media Publishing, 1996), p. 8.

18. Donald J. Noone, *Creative Problem Solving*, 2nd ed. (Hauppauge, NY: Barron's, 1998), p. 132.

19. 3M Meeting Management Team with Jeannine Drew, *Mastering Meetings: Discovering the Hidden Potential of Effective Business Meetings* (New York: McGraw-Hill, 1994), p. 12.

20. *The Week,* April 1, 2005, p. 36.

21. Warren Bennis, Jagdish Parikh, and Ronnie Lessem, *Beyond Leadership: Balancing Economics, Ethics and Ecology* (Cambridge, MA: Blackwell, 1994), p. 139.

22. *The American Heritage Dictionary of the English Language*, 4th ed. (Boston: Houghton Mifflin, 2000), p. 501; Leslie A. Baxter and Barbara M. Montgomery, *Relating: Dialogues and Dialectics* (New York: Guilford Press, 1996), p. 19.

23. Baxter and Montgomery.

24. Richard West and Lynn H. Turner, *Introducing Communication Theory*, 2nd ed. (Boston: McGraw-Hill, 2004), p. 205. Also see Dominic A. Infante, Andrew S. Rancer, and Deanna F. Womack, *Building Communication Theory*, 4th ed. (Prospect Heights, IL: Waveland, 2003), p. 212.

25 Baxter and Montgomery, p. 3.

26. Em Griffin, *A First Look at Communication Theory*, 2nd ed. (New York: McGraw-Hill, 1994), p. 161.

27. The first edition of *Working in Groups* introduced the balance metaphor as a guiding principle for effective group communication. The nine dialectic tensions in this edition are an extension of this principle and are based on five major, contemporary sources: the dialectics of (1) autonomy and connectedness, (2) predictability and novelty, and (3) openness and closedness in Baxter and Montgomery; the dialectics of (1) affect and instrumentality and (2) judgment and acceptance in William K. Rawlins, *Friendship Matters: Communication, Dialectics, and the Life Course* (New York: Aldine De Gruyter, 1992); the dialectic of groups in Michael W. Kramer, "Toward a Communication Theory of Group Dialectics: An Ethnographic Study of Community Theater Groups," *Communication Monographs*, 71 (2004), pp. 311–332; Larry A. Erbert et al., "Perceptions of Turning Points and Dialectical Interpretations in Organizational Team Development," *Small Group Research*, 36 (2005), pp. 21–58; Scott D. Johnson and Lynette M. Long, "Being a Part and Being Apart," in *New Directions in Group Communication*, ed. Lawrence Frey (Thousand Oaks, CA: Sage, 2002), pp. 25–41. Special thanks are extended to the faculty members participating in the group communication seminar at the 2005 NCA Hope Institute for Faculty Development at Luther College in Iowa. Participants helped consolidate dozens of group tensions into nine dialectics that closely resemble those presented in this textbook.

28. Napier and Gershenfeld, p. 397.

29. Larson and LaFasto, p. 128.

30. *The American Heritage Dictionary of the English Language*, p. 1757.

31. Richard L. Johannesen, *Ethics in Human Communication*, 5th ed. (Prospect Heights, IL: Waveland, 2002), p. 1.

32. The NCA Credo for Ethical Communication was developed at the 1999 conference sponsored by the National Communication Association and facilitated by the authors of this textbook. The credo was adopted and endorsed by the Legislative Council of the National Communication Association in November 1999. *www.natcom.org/aboutNCA/Policies/Platform.html*.

33. D. S. Hutchinson, "Ethics," in *The Cambridge Companion to Aristotle*, ed. Jonathan Barnes (Cambridge: Cambridge University Press, 1995), p. 217–227.

34. Aristotle, *Nicomachean Ethics,* trans. W. D. Ross; revis. J. O. Urmson, in *The Complete Works of Aristotle: The Revised Oxford Translation*, ed. Jonathan Barnes (Princeton: Princeton University Press, 1984), p. 1776.

CHAPTER 2

Group Development

CHAPTER OUTLINE

THE LIFE CYCLE OF GROUPS

There are recognizable milestones in the life of most groups. Like individuals, groups move through stages as they develop and mature. An "infant" group behaves differently from a group that has worked together for a long time and has matured into an "adult." A group's ability to "grow up" directly affects whether and how well its members work together to achieve a common goal.

Group Development Stages

There are several theoretical models that describe how a group moves through several "passages" during its lifetime. In this textbook, we rely on Bruce W. Tuckman's stages—forming, storming, norming, performing, and adjourning—because they are well recognized and easy to remember. Tuckman, an educational psychologist, identifies five discrete phases in the life cycle of groups (see Figure 2.1). He claims that groups go through predictable stages of development, each of which contains both task and maintenance functions.[1]

- Stage 1: **Forming Stage.** Members cautiously explore their own goals in relation to the group and its goal. They may avoid controversy and conflict and be reluctant to express their personal opinions and feelings. Although little gets done during this orientation phase, members need this time to become acquainted with one another and think about the group's goal.

- Stage 2: **Storming Stage.** Members compete with one another to determine individual status and to establish group goals. Members may feel that they are becoming winners or losers and will look for structure and rules to reduce conflict.

- Stage 3: **Norming Stage.** Members resolve conflicts and work as a cohesive team to develop methods for achieving group goals and also "rules of engagement." In general, members feel more comfortable expressing personal opinions.

- Stage 4: **Performing Stage.** Members focus their energy on doing the work needed to achieve group goals. Roles and responsibilities change according to group needs, and group energy is channeled into the task. In this stage, group identity, loyalty, and morale are generally high.

- Stage 5: **Adjourning Stage.**[2] The group has achieved its common goal and may begin to disband. Generally, members are proud of what they've achieved, but they may feel a sense of loss when the group dissolves.

In order to demonstrate a group's passage through these five stages, we provide an example from the study of juries. One of us works as a legal communication consultant and routinely observes and analyzes mock juries.[3] In most cases, juries

FIGURE 2.1   **Forming, Storming, Norming, Performing, Adjourning**

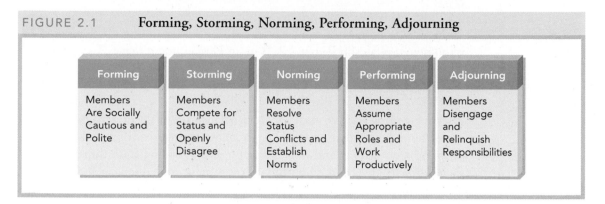

Forming	Storming	Norming	Performing	Adjourning
Members Are Socially Cautious and Polite	Members Compete for Status and Openly Disagree	Members Resolve Status Conflicts and Establish Norms	Members Assume Appropriate Roles and Work Productively	Members Disengage and Relinquish Responsibilities

progress through Tuckman's stages. The group experiences the forming stage upon entering the jury room. Members don't know one another, but they are aware that the issues in the case will probably cause conflict. Thus, interaction is initially strained and polite. This stage is typically spent exchanging personal information and engaging in small talk rather than talking about the case.

During the storming stage, jurors voice their opinions about the case and challenge one another's positions with comments such as "I thought the defendant was telling the truth," "He was too slick," or "Didn't you look at what their contract said?" During this stage, jurors form impressions of one another and begin to develop procedures and rules. A foreperson is usually selected to bring order to the group's deliberations.

During the norming stage, the jury usually settles into an orderly method for dealing with the issues. Norms might include listening respectfully to others, not interrupting, and voting in a certain order. At this point, the jury is ready to spend most of its time in the performing stage. Roles are now clear. For example, the jury may rely on one juror who recalls witnesses' testimony accurately, another who is good at asking jurors to express and justify their positions, and a third who conscientiously reviews documents that were presented in the courtroom. Members are comfortable with the group and have found ways to address personal differences. They are moving toward a consensus on the issues. In other words, they are doing the job they have been charged with doing. Finally, the jury reports its decision to the court and reaches the adjournment stage. After its decision has been recorded, the jury is dismissed, the group is disbanded, and even court is adjourned.

Keep in mind that Tuckman's stages represent only one of the many theories that attempt to explain the process of group development. While each theory uses different words to describe the process, the descriptions of group development in these theories are strikingly similar. Group development theories are useful for explaining how groups and their members behave at different points in their development and why. Notice the similarities among the theories of developmental phases in Figure 2.2, "Group Development Stages."

Characteristics of Effective Groups

Effective groups learn to negotiate and balance the dialectic tensions inherent in forming (individual and group goals), storming (conflict and cohesion), norming (conforming and nonconforming), performing (task dimensions and social dimensions), and adjourning (engagement and disengagement). When these tensions are resolved appropriately, the group that emerges possesses unique characteristics.

A major study by Carl E. Larson and Frank M. J. LaFasto asks one central question: What are the secrets of successful teams? To answer this question, Larson and LaFasto interviewed the leaders and members of various types of groups—from McDonald's Chicken McNuggets team and the space shuttle *Challenger* investigation team to cardiac surgery teams and a Notre Dame championship football team. They discovered that the most effective groups share the following eight characteristics:[4]

- *A clear, elevated goal.* Members understand and embrace the group's common goal.

- *A results-driven structure.* Members select an appropriate structure or system for solving problems, creating something, or implementing well-defined plans.

FIGURE 2.2	**Group Development Stages**

Bruce Tuckman[1]	B. Aubrey Fisher[2]	Susan Wheelan[3]	Yvonne Agazarian[4]
Forming	Orientation	Dependency and Inclusion	Authority—Flight
Storming	Conflict	Counterdependency and Fight	Authority—Fight
Norming	Emergence	Trust and Structure	Intimacy
Performing	Reinforcing	Work and Productivity	Interdependent Work
Adjourning		Termination	

[1] Bruce W. Tuckman and Mary Ann C. Jensen, "Stages of Small Group Development Revisited," *Group and Organizational Studies*, 2 (1977), pp. 419–427.
[2] B. Aubrey Fisher, "Decision Emergence: Phases in Group Decision Making," *Speech Monographs*, 37 (1970), pp. 53–66.
[3] Susan A. Wheelan, *Creating Effective Teams* (Thousand Oaks, CA: Sage, 1999), pp. 23–36; 93–132.
[4] Yvonne M. Agazarian, "Phases of Development in the Systems-Centered Psychotherapy Group," *Small Group Research*, 30 (1999), pp. 82–107.

- *Competent team members.* Members have the necessary technical, intellectual, and communication skills and the personal characteristics required to achieve excellence.

- *Unified commitment.* Members are loyal and dedicated to the group and its goal.

- *A collaborative climate.* Members work well together and create a climate that fosters honesty, openness, consistency, and respect for others.

- *Standards of excellence.* Members establish concrete standards for assessing group excellence and exert pressure on one another to achieve those standards.

- *External support and recognition.* Members are rewarded for excellence as a team and for behaving as a team.

- *Principled leadership.* Effective leaders suppress their own ego needs in favor of the group's goal by bringing out leadership in others and giving members the self-confidence to act and take responsibility.[5]

Think about the groups to which you have belonged. To what extent do Larson and LaFasto's characteristics describe the best of these groups? Did your group have standards for assessing excellence? Did the leader of your group put group goals ahead of ego-based goals? Were members consistently honest, open, and respectful of one another? Your answers to these questions say a great deal about what can go right and what can go wrong in groups as they move through the stages of group development. Learning about or trying to imitate the characteristics of effective groups, however, may not make your group any better if members do not work out how to balance the many conflicting forces that influence group success.

FORMING: BALANCING INDIVIDUAL AND GROUP NEEDS

During the **forming stage,** groups must balance individual goals and group goals. Members are cautious and somewhat uncomfortable about meeting a group of strangers. They try to understand their tasks and test personal relationships. During this stage, "the most important job for this team is not to build a better rocket or debug . . . a new software product or double sales—it is to orient itself to itself."[6] Often, members are hesitant to express strong opinions or assert their personal needs during this phase until they know more about how other members think and feel about the task and about one another.

The reasons we join and work in groups are not always based on a desire to achieve the group's goal. You may have a personal interest in the group's activities.

For example, you might join a volunteer fire department or participate in a neighborhood watch program to become involved in an activity you value. You also may join groups because you like the members. College students frequently join campus clubs and societies in order to be with or make new friends. Job applicants may decline an offer if they view members of the work team as unpleasant. You may join groups to satisfy a need. That is, membership in a group may be a way to fulfill a personal need or goal that is separate from the group's goal. For instance, a young attorney might join a local civic organization in an effort to meet prospective clients. A retiree may volunteer as a teacher's aide to feel productive and appreciated.[7]

Two psychological theories—Maslow's hierarchy of needs and Schutz's theory of interpersonal behavior—have made significant contributions to understanding why we join, stay in, and leave groups.

Maslow's Hierarchy of Needs

Abraham H. Maslow claims that as we move through life, some needs are more important than others. Basic survival needs must be satisfied before we can fulfill higher psychological needs. In other words, we cannot achieve personal success or meet our emotional needs if we are homeless and hungry. **Maslow's Hierarchy of Needs** ranks critical needs in the following order: physiological, safety, belongingness, esteem, and self-actualization (see Figure 2.3).[8] Although Maslow's hierarchy describes individual needs, it can be applied to group members' needs. At the most basic level, people join groups in order to survive; at the highest level, people join groups in order to reach their own full potential.

| FIGURE 2.3 | **Maslow's Hierarchy of Needs** |

Physiological Needs. Physiological needs are the needs of the body. A hunting/gathering clan cannot survive if its members fail to work together. Families provide food, water, and shelter for both young and aging relatives. Family farms and businesses still depend on everyone's cooperative effort.

As Hurricane Katrina approached the Gulf Coast in 2005, people banded together in impromptu groups to prepare and evacuate. The devastation following the hurricane prompted the formation of groups to meet the victims' need for water, food, and shelter. Stranded neighbors and groups of trapped strangers shared supplies and improvised shelters as they waited for rescue.

Safety Needs. Safety needs are met by groups when people join together to shelter and protect themselves. People join forces to establish police and fire departments. Unions were created to protect members from unfair labor practices. Military forces stand ready to protect our national security. Neighborhood watch groups are formed to deter crime in a community. Think of all the groups that were mobilized to protect Gulf Coast communities ravaged by Hurricane Katrina. In addition, neighbors joined forces to protect their homes and belongings from water, fire, and looters. Medical groups set up makeshift clinics to care for the sick and injured, while others supervised the removal of dead bodies.

Belongingness Needs. Once our physical and safety needs are satisfied, belongingness needs emerge. Just about everyone wants to be liked. We create circles of friends by joining groups. Regardless of the group's purpose, people join groups to satisfy their need to belong and be loved. When teenagers try to fit in with their peers, they are pursuing a belongingness need. As some groups helped hurricane survivors meet their physiological and safety needs, other groups were formed to help displaced people find their loved ones. Stories about mothers being separated from their children and older relatives left in deplorable shelters galvanized rescue workers to reunite families. And in the midst of chaos, we saw tearful family reunions as well as the warm embraces of caring relief workers.

Esteem Needs. Esteem needs reflect our desire to feel important and valued. People who strive for group leadership are often motivated by esteem needs. Membership in certain groups can enhance a person's esteem. Being invited to join an exclusive club, being asked to serve on a prestigious task force, and being honored by a group for exceptional service are common ways in which groups satisfy our need for personal success and esteem. At first, esteem needs may seem irrelevant to human needs after a hurricane. Yet, television and newspapers carried stories about unlikely individuals who took on leadership roles. One article highlighted a resident of a homeless shelter who emerged as the group's leader by salvaging "treasures" such as pudding cups, clothing and shoes, portable fans and blankets, and even gasoline for the one car that was still running.[9] He explained how good it felt to serve in a leadership role for the first time in his life.

Self-Actualization Needs. Our ultimate goal is what Maslow calls **self-actualization**, the need to fulfill our own human potential, the personal reward of becoming the best that we can be. Although self-actualization is an individual process, groups can enhance our ability to achieve this goal. We often join groups that we believe will help us become better individuals. Volunteering to serve meals to the needy, participating in church activities, and joining a professional organization to advance its goals demonstrate how groups can help individuals fulfill their self-actualization needs. Personal satisfaction comes from participating in a group that allows and encourages self-actualizing behavior. The tragedy of Hurricane Katrina was compounded by the fact that local and federal emergency services failed to mobilize and rescue those who were in need of immediate help. As is often the case in catastrophes, volunteers came forward to help. People with boats set their course for homes surrounded by deep water. In addition to medical units, fire and rescue teams, and law enforcement groups, individuals and groups volunteered to help. In San Antonio, the staff of a hair studio set up shop in a large shelter and gave free haircuts and shaves to evacuees. Many of these volunteers were rewarded with the personal satisfaction that comes from helping others.

Using Maslow's theory to improve a group's performance requires the translation of need satisfaction into action. For example, if members are preoccupied with issues related to job security or personal health, it may be difficult to get them to concentrate on the group's goal. If members' belongingness needs are unmet, they are likely to become more cooperative if they feel welcome and well liked. Praising and rewarding effective group behavior can satisfy esteem needs while encouraging a group to coordinate its talents and efforts toward a common goal.

Schutz's Theory of Interpersonal Needs

William Schutz developed a theory of interpersonal behavior called the **Fundamental Interpersonal Relationship Orientation (FIRO)**.[10] Unlike Maslow's hierarchy of needs, FIRO concentrates on three *interpersonal* needs that most people share to some degree: the needs for inclusion, for control, and for affection (see Figure 2.4). Schutz maintains that people join groups in order to satisfy one or more of these needs.

Inclusion. The **inclusion need** represents our need to belong, to be involved, to be accepted. For some group members, the need for inclusion is strong—they want to fit in and be appreciated by other members. For other group members, the need for inclusion may be less important—they are quite content to work without significant involvement in the group. When a group meets a member's inclusion needs, the result is what Schutz calls a **social member**—a person who enjoys working with people but is also comfortable working alone.

When inclusion needs are not met, members do not feel accepted; they do not fit in with the group and may engage in undersocial behavior or oversocial behavior. **Undersocial members** feel unworthy or undervalued by the group.

FIGURE 2.4   **Schutz's Fundamental Interpersonal Relationship Orientation Theory**

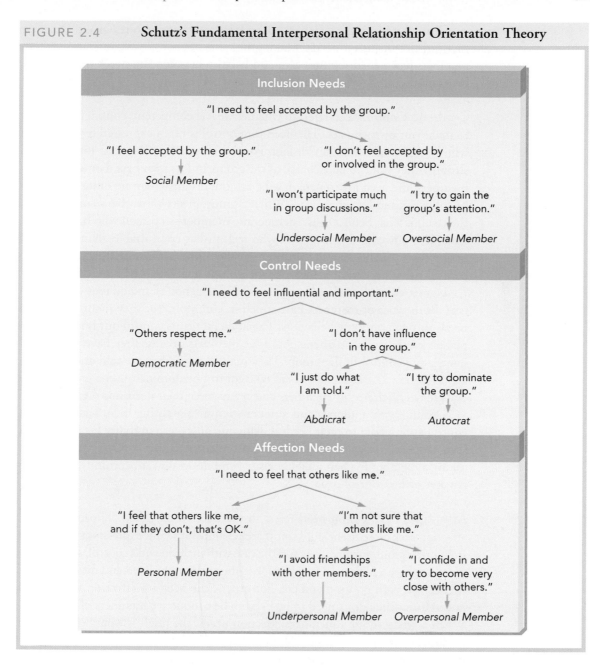

They may withdraw and become loners. Because they believe that no one values them, they avoid being hurt by trying not to be noticed. A quiet or unproductive member may be someone whose inclusion needs are unmet. **Oversocial members** try to attract attention to compensate for feelings of inadequacy. They seek companionship for all activities because they can't stand being alone. They try to impress other members with what and whom they know.

Dealing with undersocial and oversocial members requires group behavior that satisfies inclusion needs. Making new members feel welcome and veteran members feel valued requires a careful balance between the needs of the members and the needs of the group.

Control.   **Control need** refers to whether we feel competent, confident, and free to make our own choices. The need for control is often expressed by a member who wants to be the group's leader. For some members, the need for control is strong—they want to take charge of the group and its members. For other group members, the need for control may be less important—they are quite content to be followers and let others lead. When a group meets a member's control need, the result is what Schutz calls a **democratic member**—a person who has no problems with power and control and who feels just as comfortable giving orders as taking them. Such members are often excellent leaders because they can exercise control when needed, but they put the group's goal ahead of their own needs.

Unmet control needs can result in the emergence of an abdicrat or an autocrat. Both types of members have much in common, but they manifest control needs through opposite behaviors. The **abdicrat** wants control but is reluctant to pursue it. Abdicrats are often submissive members because they have no hope of having any control in the group. They may do what they are told and avoid responsibilities. The **autocrat** tries to take control by dominating the group. Autocrats may criticize other members and try to force their decisions on the group.

Dealing with abdicrats and autocrats requires granting members a sense of control appropriate to their needs. Giving members responsibility for and leadership of special projects or tasks may satisfy their need for control. For example, asking a member to chair a highly visible and important subcommittee may satisfy her or his control need.

Affection.[11]   **Affection need** refers to the need to feel liked. Those who need affection seek close friendships, intimate relationships, and expressions of warmth from other group members. As was the case with inclusion and control, some group members have a high need for affection—they want to be liked and develop strong friendships with group members. For others, the need for affection may be less important—they don't need to be liked to be productive members of the group. When a group meets a member's affection needs, the result is what Schutz calls a **personal member**—a person who has no emotional problems dealing with group members. While preferring to be liked, an ideal personal member is secure enough to function in a group where social interaction and affection are not high priorities.

When affection needs are not met, members do not feel liked; they become uncomfortable in the group setting. Reactions to this deficit fall into two categories: underpersonal behavior and overpersonal behavior. **Underpersonal members** believe that they are not liked and may establish only superficial relationships with other members. When pressed, they rarely share their honest feelings or opinions and may appear aloof and uninvolved. **Overpersonal members** try to get close to everyone. They seek intimate friendships despite the disinterest of other members. They may be too talkative, too personal, and too confiding.

Dealing with underpersonal and overpersonal members requires expressions of fondness and friendliness to those who need affection. Expressing liking to new members and taking the time to communicate affection to long-standing members can take extra time but have the potential to convert unsatisfied participants into ideal personal members.

Implications of FIRO Theory.

Using Schutz's theory to improve a group's performance requires adapting to members' inclusion, control, and affection needs. For example, a member who seeks attention or tries to impress other members may have a strong inclusion need. This need can be satisfied by praising that member's good work. When members have strong control needs but are not capable enough or eligible to lead a group, there may be value in assigning them to head up a special project. Just as praising and rewarding effective group behavior can satisfy esteem needs, such reinforcement can help group members feel included, competent, and well liked.

There are, however, reasons to be cautious about using FIRO theory to explain and predict group behavior. Undersocial behavior may not reflect unmet inclusion needs; the member may be quite comfortable and happy working alone. Overpersonal behavior may not reflect unmet affection needs; such behavior may be an enthusiastic attempt to create a positive social climate for the group.

Forming Tensions

Group members experience two common tensions unique to the forming phase of group development. In the first case, the tension is quite natural and characteristic of most new groups. In the second case, tension is created when a member's personal goals conflict with the group's goals.

Primary Tension.

Group communication scholar Ernest G. Bormann describes a general type of tension common to most new groups: primary tension.[12] As we note in our initial discussion of the forming stage, when you join a group and attend its first meeting, you don't know what to expect. Will everyone get along together and work hard? Will you make a good first impression? Will this be a positive experience or a nightmare? Most people enter a new group with caution. Bormann describes **primary tension** as the social unease and stiffness that accompanies the getting-acquainted stage in a new group.

Because most members of a new group want to create a good first impression, they tend to be overly polite with one another. Members don't interrupt one another, and there may be long, awkward pauses between comments. When members do speak, they often speak softly and avoid expressing strong opinions.

TOOLBOX 2.1

How Newcomers Become Socialized

Regardless of how many groups you belong to, you are a newcomer every time you join a new group. Not surprisingly, your experiences in other groups affect how you adapt to and communicate with new group members. Understanding the socialization process can help you reduce the uncertainty that accompanies every new group experience.

The socialization process is very important in groups because "positive socialization creates stronger commitments to confront and balance the multiple issues and tensions involved in participating in group activities."[1] Much like Tuckman, with his stages of group development, Carolyn Anderson and her colleagues view socialization as a passage through five phases:

1. *Antecedent phase.* As a newcomer, you bring your beliefs and attitudes, culture, needs and motives, communication skills, personality traits, knowledge, and prior group experiences to a new group. These factors influence how well you are accepted into a group. If you bring factors that are valued and needed by the group, socialization will be faster and easier.
2. *Anticipatory phase.* Members of an established group have expectations about newcomers. They may be looking for someone with certain types of knowledge or certain communication skills. They may have heard that you share their beliefs and attitudes. Socialization is more likely to succeed if a group's expectations match your characteristics and motives.
3. *Encounter phase.* During the encounter phase, newcomers try to fit in. You can do this by adjusting to group expectations, assuming

needed roles, communicating effectively, and finding an appropriate balance between your individual goals and the group's group goals.
4. *Assimilation phase.* During this phase, newcomers become fully integrated into the group's culture. Established members and newcomers blend into a comfortable state of working together to achieve shared goals.
5. *Exit phase.* Some groups, such as families, may never disband, although they change as new members join and others leave. Some groups manage this process by giving departing members a warm send-off and welcoming new members who take their place. Regardless of the reason (whether positive or negative), leaving an established group can be a traumatic experience.[2]

Socialization in groups is a give-and-take process in which members and groups come together to satisfy needs and accomplish goals. During the socialization process, newcomers, established members, and the group as a whole adjust and adapt to one another through verbal and nonverbal communication. When socialization is successful, the group creates a unique culture and group structure, engages in relevant activities, and pursues individual and group goals.[3] In short, socialization is the way in which newcomers become an integral part of a group.

[1] The definition of socialization is based on Carolyn M. Anderson, Bruce L. Riddle, and Matthew M. Martin, "Socialization Process in Groups," in *The Handbook of Group Communication Theory and Research,* ed. Lawrence R. Frey, assoc. eds. Dennis S. Gouran and Marshall Scott Poole (Thousand Oaks, CA: Sage, 1999), p. 155.
[2] Anderson, Riddle, and Martin, p. 139.
[3] Anderson, Riddle, and Martin, p. 142.

Although laughter may occur, it is often strained, inappropriate, or awkward. When the group starts its discussion, the topic may be small talk about sports, the weather, or a recent news event.

A group that is experiencing primary tension may talk less, provide little in the way of content, and be perceived as ineffective. Before a group can work efficiently and effectively, primary tension must be reduced. Usually, this initial tension decreases as members come to feel more comfortable with one another. In some groups, primary tension lasts for only a few minutes. In less fortunate groups, primary tension may continue for months. The group may fail to become a cohesive and productive team.

In many groups, primary tension will disappear quickly and naturally as group members gain confidence and become better acquainted. In other groups, direct intervention is needed to relieve this early form of tension. Recognizing and discussing primary tension is one way of breaking its cycle. A perceptive leader or participant can purposely exhibit behavior that counteracts primary tension, such as talking in a strong voice, looking involved and energized, sticking to the group's topic, and expressing an opinion. Usually, with each group meeting, the amount of primary tension decreases. However, if primary tension remains, a group can stall and never get beyond the forming stage. Here are some suggestions for resolving primary tension:

- Be positive and energetic. Smile. Nod in agreement. Laugh. Exhibit enthusiasm.

- Be patient and open-minded, knowing that primary tension should decrease with time.

- Be prepared and informed before your first meeting, so that you're well equipped to help the group focus on its task.

Hidden Agendas. Tensions also arise during the forming stage when hidden agendas interfere with a group's progress. Most groups know what they want and how they intend to go about achieving their goals. The same is true of individuals within a group. Individual members may have private goals and preferred methods for achieving those goals. A **hidden agenda** is a member's private goals that conflict with the group's goals. Hidden agendas represent what people really want rather than what they say they want. When hidden agendas become more important than a group's public agenda or goal, the result can be group frustration, unresolved conflict, and failure. Hidden agendas disrupt the flow of communication. Real issues and concerns may be buried while pseudoarguments dominate the discussion.

A student reported the following incident in which a hidden agenda disrupted a group's deliberations:

> I was on a student government board that decides how college activities funds are distributed to student clubs and intramural teams. About halfway

through the process, I became aware that several members were active in intramural sports. By the time I noticed their pro-sports voting pattern, they'd gotten most of what they wanted. You wouldn't believe the bizarre reasons they came up with to cut academic clubs while fully supporting the budgets of athletic teams. What made me mad was that they didn't care about what most students wanted; they only wanted to make sure that *their* favorite teams were funded.

If unrecognized and unresolved during the forming stage, hidden agendas can permeate and infect *all* stages of group development. Effective groups deal with hidden agendas by recognizing them and trying to resolve them whenever they occur.

When a group member is hesitant to get involved with other members and the group process or if the group's progress is unusually slow, look for hidden agendas. A question such as "What seems to be hanging us up here?" may encourage members to reveal some of their private concerns. Recognizing the existence of hidden agendas may be sufficient to keep a group moving from stage to stage in its development.

Even when you recognize the existence of hidden agendas, some of them cannot and should not be shared because they may create an atmosphere of distrust. Not many people would want to deal with the following revelation during a group discussion: "The reason I don't want to be here is that I don't want to work with Kenneth, who isn't trustworthy or competent." Recognizing hidden agendas means knowing that some of them can and should be confronted, whereas others cannot and should not be shared with the group.

Groups can resolve some of the problems caused by hidden agendas through early agreement on the group's goal and careful planning of the group's process. Sociologists Rodney Napier and Matti Gershenfeld suggest that discussing hidden agendas during the early stages of group development can counteract their blocking power.[13] Initial discussion could include some of the following questions:

- What are the group's goals?

- Does the leader have any personal concerns or goals that differ from these?

- Do any members have any personal concerns or goals that differ from these?

- What outcomes do members expect?

Discussing these questions openly can be productive if a group recognizes and respects the inevitability and function of hidden agendas. Hidden agendas do not necessarily cause problems or prevent a group from achieving its goal. Understanding them can help explain why members are or are not willing to participate fully in the work of a group.

STORMING: BALANCING CONFLICT AND COHESION

During the **storming stage,** groups become more argumentative and emotional as they discuss important issues and ideas. Many groups are tempted to skip this stage in an effort to avoid conflict. However, storming is a necessary part of a group's development. Without it, the group may be unsure of individual members' roles, who's in charge, or even what the group's goal is. Conflict is also necessary to establish a climate in which members feel free to disagree with one another.[14]

A group in the storming stage has overcome primary tension and is trying to get down to business. As soon as the group engages in this process, though, a different kind of social tension can develop. The most confident members now begin to compete for social acceptance and leadership. They openly disagree on issues of substance. It is still too early in the group's existence to predict the outcome of such competition. The frustrations and personality conflicts experienced by group members as they compete for acceptance and achievement within a group are the source of what Ernest G. Bormann calls **secondary tension.**

Whereas primary tension arises from lack of confidence, secondary tension emerges when members have gained enough confidence to become assertive and even aggressive as they pursue positions of power and influence. Conflicts can result from disagreements over issues, conflicts in values, or an inability to deal with disruptive members. Regardless of the causes, a group cannot hope to achieve its goals if secondary tension is not managed. The signs of secondary tension are almost the direct opposite of those of primary tension. There is a high level of energy and agitation. The group is noisier, more dynamic, and physically active. Members speak in louder voices, interrupting and overlapping one another so that two or three people may be speaking at the same time. Members sit up straight, lean forward, or squirm in their seats. Everyone is alert and listening intently.

Members of successful groups develop ways to handle this phase in a group's development. Often, one or two members will joke about the tension. The resulting laughter is likely to ease the stress. Sometimes individual members will work outside the group setting to discuss the personal difficulties and anxieties of group members. Dealing with secondary tension can be difficult, and even painful. However, if a group fails to resolve human relations problems, it will not become an effective and cohesive work group.

Most groups experience some form of primary and secondary tension during the forming and storming stages. In fact, a little bit of tension is advantageous. It can motivate a group toward action and increase a group's sensitivity to feedback. In fact, as Donald Ellis and Aubrey Fisher point out, "the successful and socially healthy group is not characterized by an absence of social tension, but by successful management of social tension."[15]

NORMING: BALANCING CONFORMITY AND NONCONFORMITY

When a group reaches the **norming stage,** primary and secondary tensions should have been resolved. The group is ready and even eager to begin working as a committed and unified team. There is more order and direction during this third stage of group development. Feelings of trust and clear goals emerge as members become more comfortable with one another and agree upon group procedures.[16]

One factor that influences a group's passage from forming to performing is the creation of norms. Patricia Andrews defines **norms** as "sets of expectations held by group members concerning what kinds of behavior or opinion are acceptable or unacceptable, good or bad, right or wrong, appropriate or inappropriate."[17] Norms are the group's rules. They determine how members behave, dress, speak, and work. For example, the norms for the members of a company's sales team might include meeting before lunch, applauding one another's successes, and wearing suits to work. Without norms, accomplishing group goals would be difficult. There would be no agreed-upon way to organize and perform work.

Some norms, however, can work against a group and its goals. If group norms place a premium on friendly and peaceful discussions, then the members of the group may be reluctant to voice disagreement or share bad news. If group norms permit members to arrive late and leave early, there may be times when a meeting lacks enough members to make important decisions. Norms that do not support a group's goal can prevent the group from succeeding.

Types of Norms

There are two general types of group norms—explicit and implicit. Because **explicit norms** are put in writing or are stated verbally, they are easy to recognize. Explicit norms are often imposed on a group. The group leader may have the authority to determine rules. A large group or organization may have standard procedures that it expects everyone to follow; for example, the workers in a customer services department may be required to wear name badges. The staff may have recommended this rule, the supervisor may have ordered this "custom," or the company may have established a policy regarding employee identification.

Because **implicit norms** are rarely discussed or openly communicated, they are not as easy to recognize. Generally they are the result of group interaction. For example, it may take new group members several weeks to learn that meetings begin fifteen minutes later than scheduled. Even seating arrangements may be governed by implicit norms. Group members often learn about an implicit norm when it has been violated. Almost all of us have been unsettled when we walked into a classroom and discovered someone sitting at "our" desk. Although groups rarely discuss such rules, offending members soon sense that an implicit norm has been violated.

FIGURE 2.5   **Types of Norms**

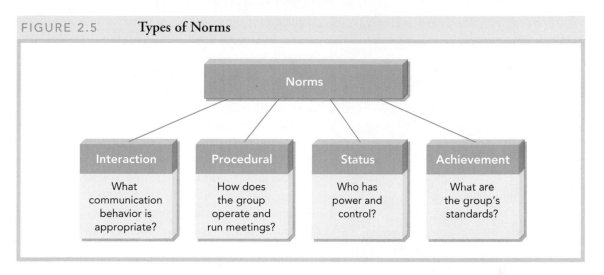

Regardless of whether they are openly communicated or implicitly understood, norms can be divided into four categories: interaction norms, procedural norms, status norms, and achievement norms (see Figure 2.5). **Interaction norms** determine how group members communicate with one another and will help you determine what types of communication behavior are appropriate in a group. **Procedural norms** dictate how the group will operate and will help you adapt to the rules and procedures that the group typically follows. Status refers to the degree of prestige, respect, or influence that a person possesses. **Status norms** identify the levels of influence among group members and will help you understand how status is determined. **Achievement norms** determine the quality and quantity of work expected from group members. They can help you make decisions about how much time and energy must be devoted to working with a particular group.

Conformity

Group norms function only to the extent that members conform to them. **Conformity** requires choosing "a course of action that a majority favors or that is socially acceptable."[18] We learn the value of conformity at a young age. In the classroom, children learn that standing in line and raising their hands are expected behaviors. On the playground, children who refuse to play by the rules may find themselves playing alone.

Groups can exert enormous pressure to conform. Two classic (and disturbing) studies illustrate our tendency to conform to unreasonable norms.[19] During the 1960s, Stanley Milgram of Yale University designed a series of experiments in which subjects were asked to administer painful electric shocks to research

Why is conforming to norms important for this group of Texas state police cadets? (© Bob Daemmrich/The Image Works)

associates if the associate answered a question incorrectly. In fact, *no* shock was given; the associates were trained to writhe in pain, scream, and pound on walls. Even though the subjects thought they were causing enormous pain, very few subjects refused to increase the shocks as directed by an experimenter. Pressure from an authority figure outweighed individual judgment and morality.

In another famous study conducted in the early 1970s, Philip Zimbardo created a realistic-looking prison in a Stanford University basement in which student subjects were assigned to play the role of prison guard or prisoner for several days. Very quickly, the prison guards used their power and became increasingly abusive and cruel. After a brief period of rebellion, the prisoners became passive, demoralized, and depressed. The experiment was halted to minimize psychological and physical damage to the subjects.

Although some group members may have reasons for ignoring or wanting to change norms, most groups pressure their members to conform. According to Rodney Napier and Matti Gershenfeld, you are more likely to conform to norms when one or more of the following factors are present:

- You want to continue your membership in the group.

- You have a lower status than other group members and don't want to risk being seen as an upstart.

- You feel obligated to conform.

- You get along with and like working with the other group members.

- You may be punished for violating norms and/or rewarded for compliance.[20]

Nonconformity

Members decide whether they will or will not conform to group norms. **Nonconformity** occurs when a member does not meet the expectations of the group. Although conformity to norms is essential to the functioning of a group, nonconformity can, in some cases, improve group performance. For example, members may deviate from the group when they have legitimate concerns and alternative suggestions. **Constructive nonconformity** occurs when a member resists a norm while still working to promote a group goal.

ETHICAL GROUPS

 ## Balancing Individual and Group Needs

Throughout the forming, storming, norming, performing, and adjourning stages of group development, effective members make ethical decisions. Group communication scholar Ernest G. Bormann contends that ethical dilemmas surface whenever groups face unavoidable dialectic tensions. Very often group members must choose between their personal goals and the goals of the group.[1] As we note previously, hidden agendas arise when these two goals conflict. As a result, a member may fake support and respect for others, be willing to lie or withhold vital information, or stir up conflict and suspicions in order to achieve a personal goal. These behaviors defy most principles in the NCA Credo for Ethical Communication and will impair the group's ability to achieve its goals.

Norms can present ethical dilemmas when they serve unethical purposes. In some groups, norms exclude people on the basis of race, gender, age, or personal philosophy. Roles can be counterproductive if, for example, a member functioning as the group's harmonizer stifles disagreement and debate rather than seeking ways of reducing tension. When group norms restrict individual rights or freedom of expression, an ethical member should object to the norm and try to change it, and, if all else fails, publicly renounce the group or quit in protest.

A group and its members have ethical responsibilities. We offer some conclusions based on Bormann's advice and urge you to meet these standards as you interact with group members to achieve a common goal:[2]

- When you join a group, you should make the group's goals your own, and that may mean pursuing the group's goals instead of your own goals.
- If you are asked to take on an unethical task, you should object or decline the assignment—and make the rest of the group aware of the ethical issues and consequences.
- If a group adopts unethical norms, such as restricting the free flow of information or diverse membership, you have a responsibility to push for changes in such restrictive norms.
- You should work for a group climate in which all members can develop their full potential as individuals of worth and dignity.
- You should build group cohesiveness, raise the status of others, volunteer to help the group, and release social tensions.
- Whatever the status of members, you should communicate to reflect the values of trust, respect, and honesty.
- As you become more knowledgeable about group communication, you should develop a well-thought-out code of ethics.

[1] Ernest G. Bormann, *Small Group Communication: Theory and Practice*, 3rd ed. (Edina, MN: Burgess, 1996), pp. 270–274.
[2] Bormann, pp. 286–288.

There are times when constructive nonconformity is needed and valuable. Movies, television shows, and books have championed the holdout juror, the stubbornly honest politician, and the principled but disobedient soldier or crew member. Sometimes there is so much pressure for group members to conform that they need a deviant to shake up the process, to provide critical feedback, and to create doubt about what had been a confident but wrong decision. Nonconformity can serve a group well if it prevents members from ignoring important information or making a hasty decision. The following statements are examples of constructive deviation:

- "I know we always ask the newest group member to take minutes during the meeting, but we may be losing the insight of an experienced member and skilled note taker by continuing this practice."

- "I can't attend any more meetings if they're going to last for three hours."

When a member voices concerns or objections, the other members are forced to defend their positions, address important issues, and explore alternatives. Thus, constructive nonconformity contributes to more effective group decisions and more creative solutions.[21] In contrast, **destructive nonconformity** occurs when a member resists conforming to norms without regard for the best interests of the group and its goal.

Nonconformity of either type provides a group with an opportunity to examine its norms. When members deviate, the group may have to discuss the value of a particular norm and subsequently choose to change it, clarify it, or continue to accept it. At the very least, nonconforming behavior helps members recognize and understand the norms of the group. For instance, if a member is reprimanded for criticizing an office policy, other members will learn that the boss should not be challenged. Some groups will attempt to correct deviating members or may change their norms as a result of constructive nonconformity.

While most groups can handle an occasional encounter with a renegade, dealing with highly disruptive members is another story. Fortunately, there are several strategies that can help a group deal with a member whose disruptive behavior becomes destructive. The group can accept, confront, or even exclude the troublesome member.

Accept. One strategy for dealing with disruptive nonconformity is to accept the behavior. Acceptance is not the same as approval; it involves learning to live with the disruptive behavior. When the deviation is not critical to the group's ultimate success, or when the member's positive contributions far outweigh the inconvenience and annoyance of putting up with the behavior, a group may allow the disruptive behavior to continue. For example, a member who is always late for meetings but puts in more than her fair share of work may find her tardy behavior accepted as an unavoidable idiosyncrasy.

Confront. Another strategy for dealing with disruptive nonconformity is confrontation. Disruptive behavior is impossible to accept or ignore when it threatens the group and its members. When a member becomes "impossible," groups may confront the perpetrator in several ways. At first, members may direct a lot of attention to the wayward member in an attempt to reason with him or her. They may even talk about him or her during the course of the discussion: "Barry, it's distracting and disrupts our discussion every time you choose to answer your cell phone. We need you to turn off your phone during meetings." Although such attention can be intimidating and uncomfortable for the nonconforming member, it may not be sufficient to overcome the problem.

As an alternative to a public confrontation, there may be value in discussing the problem with the disruptive member outside the group setting. A frank and open conversation between the disruptive member and the leader or a trusted member of the group may uncover the causes of the problem as well as solutions for it. Some nonconforming members may not see their behavior as disruptive and, as a result, may not understand why the group is ignoring, confronting, or excluding them. Taking time to talk with a disruptive member in a nonthreatening setting can solve both a personal and a group problem.

Exclude. When all else fails, a group may exclude disruptive members. Exclusion can take several forms. During discussions, group members can turn away from problem members, ignore their comments, or refuse to make eye contact. Exclusion might mean assigning disruptive members to unimportant, solo tasks or ones that will drive them away. Finally, a group may be able to expel unwanted members from the group and be rid of the troublemakers. Being asked to leave a group or being barred from participating is a humiliating experience that all but the most stubborn deviants would prefer to avoid.

Once, one of us had to ask a group member to leave a work group. For a variety of reasons, the person's behavior had become highly disruptive. Everyone was frustrated and often angry. Attempts to accept the behavior were unsuccessful. On various occasions, members had confronted or talked with the disruptive person. The member's behavior did not improve. Instead, it became more hostile and problematic. The group decided to expel the member. Although the exclusion caused a great deal of anxiety for everyone, the result was astonishing. Within a few weeks, the group became much more cohesive and was producing twice as much work. The difficult decision was the right decision.

Rather than covering up for disrupters and noncontributors, effective groups deal with such members. "Sometimes that requires replacing members, sometimes it requires punishing them, and sometimes it requires working with them. The real team does whatever it takes to eliminate disruptive behavior and ensure productive contributions from all of its members."[22]

PERFORMING: BALANCING TASK AND MAINTENANCE DIMENSIONS

When groups reach the **performing stage,** members focus their energies on group productivity and effectiveness. Decisions are reached, and solutions are agreed upon. Just about everyone shares in and supports a unified effort to achieve a common goal. During this final phase, "interaction patterns reflect virtually no

TOOLBOX 2.2

Strategies for Changing Norms

When norms no longer meet the needs of a group or its members, new ones should be established. Some norms may be too rigid or too vague. Other norms may have outlived their usefulness. Norms can be difficult to change, especially when they are implicit or unspoken. Changes in group norms typically occur in the following ways:

- Through contagious behavior, as in dress style and speech patterns
- Through the suggestions or actions of high-status members
- Through the suggestions or actions of highly confident members
- Through the suggestions of consultants

- Through group discussion and decision making (for explicit norms)
- Through continued interaction (for implicit norms)[1]

Some members will resist changes in norms because change can be disruptive and threatening. However, norms that are no longer useful can impede a group's progress. The natural development of most groups requires changes in goals, membership, and norms.

[1] Rodney W. Napier and Matti K Gershenfeld, *Groups: Theory and Experience*, 7th ed. (Boston: Houghton Mifflin, 2004), pp. 147–148.

tension; rather, the members are jovial, loud, boisterous, laughing, and verbally backslapping each other."[23]

During the performing phase of group development, members find a way to get a job done with congenial and cooperative people by balancing task and social needs. A group's **task dimension** focuses on the job—the goal or product of group effort. The **social dimension** is concerned with people—the interpersonal relationships among group members. For example, a group that is discussing a department's budget is primarily focused on its task, or issues directly related to doing the work of the group. However, if, at the end of the meeting, the group surprises a member with a cake in celebration of her birthday, the group's focus shifts to the social dimension. More often, a group exhibits both task- and social-oriented behaviors throughout its interactions. That is, as we engage in communication that allows the group to get the job done, we do it in a way that makes others feel socially accepted and valued. The task and social dimensions of a group "exert mutual and reciprocal influences on each other and are thus virtually inseparable in practice."[24]

All work and no play makes you dull. All play and no work can make you unemployed. A coordinated balance makes you more productive. It can be equally difficult and frustrating to work on a task when the participants do not get along with one another and to work with friends who don't take the task seriously. While both teamwork and "social" work are essential to team success, getting the whole team in sync is important.[25] One way of understanding how task and social dimensions are balanced is to appreciate the importance and diversity of members' roles.

Group members differ in terms of the roles they play. Unlike a theatrical role assigned to an actor, group roles are real and serve important group functions. When a group member exhibits a unique set of skills or behavioral patterns that serve specific functions within the group, that member has assumed a **role**.[26] For example, a group may rely on Portia to create enthusiasm for the group's work and promote teamwork, whereas Will is best at reconciling disagreements, reducing tension, and calming anxious members. Portia's role is that of energizer; Will is the group's harmonizer. Both of these roles serve valuable group functions.

Depending on your characteristics, attitudes, and skills, you will probably assume one or more group roles. Successful groups are made up of members who know how to define appropriate roles for themselves and how to work with the roles that other group members have adopted.[27]

A classic essay by Kenneth D. Benne and Paul Sheats identifies and describes the functional roles of group members.[28] We have modified the original Benne and Sheats list by adding or combining functional behaviors that we have observed in groups and roles identified by other writers and researchers. The following sections divide twenty-five participant roles into three functional categories: group task roles, group maintenance roles, and self-centered roles (see Figure 2.6).

Group **task roles** affect a group's ability to achieve its common goal by focusing on behaviors that help get the job done. Group **maintenance roles** affect how group members get along with one another while pursuing a shared goal. They are concerned with building relationships and keeping the group cohesive and cooperative. **Self-centered roles** put individual needs ahead of the group's

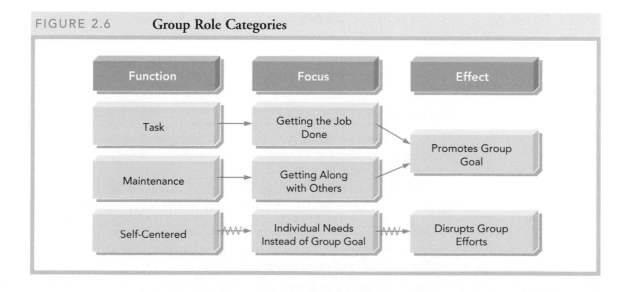

FIGURE 2.6   **Group Role Categories**

goal and other members' needs. In the following section, each functional role is categorized, named, described, and illustrated with a statement that might be heard from a member assuming such a role.

Group Task Roles

1. *Initiator.* Proposes ideas and suggestions; provides direction for the group; gets the group started.

    "Let's begin by trying to look at the problem from the client's point of view."

2. *Information seeker.* Asks for needed facts and figures; requests explanations and clarification of ideas; makes the group aware of information gaps.

    "How can we decide on a policy for disabled students without knowing more about the new federal laws and regulations?"

3. *Information giver.* Provides the group with relevant information; researches, organizes, and presents needed information.

    "I checked with our minority affairs officer, and she said . . ."

4. *Opinion seeker.* Asks for others' opinions; tests for group opinions and consensus; tries to discover what others believe or feel about an issue.

    "Lyle, what do you think? Will it work?"

5. *Opinion giver.* States personal beliefs and interpretations; shares feelings; offers analysis and arguments.

    "I don't agree that radio ads are the answer because they'll use up our entire promotional budget."

6. *Clarifier-summarizer.* Explains ideas and their consequences; reduces confusion; sums up group progress and conclusions.

    "We've been trying to analyze this problem for the last hour. Let me see if I can list the three causes we've identified so far."

7. *Evaluator-critic.* Assesses ideas, arguments, and suggestions; functions as the group's critical thinker; diagnoses task and procedural problems.

    "I think we've forgotten something here. The building figures don't take into account monthly operating costs, such as utilities and maintenance."

8. *Energizer.* Motivates group members to do their best; helps create enthusiasm for the task and, if needed, a sense of urgency; serves as the group's "cheerleader."

    "This is incredible! We may be the first department to come up with such a unique and workable solution to this problem."

9. *Procedural technician.* Assists with preparation for meetings, including suggesting agenda items, making room arrangements, and providing needed materials and equipment.

"Before our next meeting, let me know whether any of you will need an overhead projector or a flip chart."

10. *Recorder-secretary.* Keeps and provides accurate written records of a group's major ideas, suggestions, and decisions.

"Maggie, please repeat your two deadline dates so I can get them into the minutes."

Group Maintenance Roles

1. *Encourager-supporter.* Praises and agrees with group members; provides recognition and person-to-person encouragement; listens empathetically.

"The information you found has been a big help. Thanks for taking all that time to find it."

2. *Harmonizer.* Helps resolve conflicts; mediates differences among group members; emphasizes teamwork and the importance of everyone getting along.

"I know we're starting to get on each other's nerves, but we're almost done. Let's put aside our differences and finish up."

3. *Compromiser.* Offers suggestions that minimize differences; helps the group reach consensus; searches for solutions that are acceptable to everyone.

"It looks as though no one is going to agree on this one. Maybe we can improve the old system rather than trying to come up with a brand new way of doing it."

4. *Tension releaser.* Alleviates tension with friendly humor; breaks the ice and cools hot tempers; monitors tension levels and tries to relax the group.

"Can Karen and I arm wrestle to decide who gets the assignment?"

5. *Gatekeeper.* Monitors participation; encourages quiet members to speak and talkative members to stop speaking; tries to control the flow of communication.

"I think we've heard from everyone except Sophie, and I know she has strong feelings on this issue."

6. *Observer-interpreter.* Explains what others are trying to say; monitors and interprets feelings and nonverbal communication; expresses group feelings; paraphrases other members.

"I sense that you two are not really disagreeing. Tell me if I'm wrong, but I think that both of you are saying that we should . . ."

7. *Follower.* Supports the group and its members; accepts others' ideas and assignments; serves as an attentive audience member.

"That's fine with me. Just tell me when it's due."

Self-Centered Roles

1. *Aggressor.* Puts down members to get what he or she wants; is sarcastic toward and critical of others; may take credit for someone else's work or idea.

    "It's a good thing I had time to rewrite our report. There were so many mistakes in it, we would have been embarrassed by it."

2. *Blocker.* Stands in the way of progress; presents negative, disagreeable, and uncompromising positions; uses delaying tactics to derail an idea or proposal.

    "There's no way I'm signing off on this idea if you insist on putting Gabriel in charge of the project."

3. *Dominator.* Prevents others from participating; asserts authority and tries to manipulate others; interrupts others and monopolizes discussion.

    "That's crazy, Wanda. Right off the top of my head I can think of at least four major reasons why we can't do it your way. The first reason is . . ."

4. *Recognition seeker.* Boasts about personal accomplishments; tries to impress others and become the center of attention; pouts or disrupts the discussion if not getting enough attention.

    "As the only person here to have ever won the company's prestigious top achiever award, I personally suggest that . . ."

5. *Clown.* Injects inappropriate humor or commentary into the group; seems more interested in goofing off than in working; distracts the group.

    "Listen—I've been working on this outrageous impersonation of the boss. I've even got his funny walk down."

6. *Deserter.* Withdraws from the group; appears "above it all" and bored or annoyed with the discussion; remains aloof or stops contributing.

    "I'm leaving now because I have to go to an important meeting."

7. *Confessor.* Seeks emotional support from the group; shares very personal feelings and problems with members; uses the group for emotional support rather than contributing to the group's goal.

    "I had an argument with my boyfriend yesterday. I could really use some advice. Let me start at the beginning."

8. *Special interest pleader.* Speaks on behalf of an outside group or a personal interest; tries to influence group members to support nongroup interests.

    "Let's hire my brother-in-law to cater our annual dinner. We'd get better food than the usual rubber chicken."

Depending on your group's goal, the nature of its task, and the attitudes or abilities of other members, you could function in several different roles. If you know the most about the topic being discussed, your primary function might be that of information giver. If two members are locked in a serious disagreement, you might help your group by functioning as a harmonizer. And, if you strongly believe that the group is heading toward a disastrous decision, you might even decide to take on the function of a blocker in order to prevent the group from making a mistake. Moreover, when some group members perform critical task and maintenance roles effectively, they are more likely to be viewed as leaders.[29]

Group members must be "very clear about their roles," but they also must avoid the temptation of establishing inflexible roles.[30] If, for example, a member is a skilled information giver, the group should take advantage of that role and rely on the member to provide relevant, well-organized research and information. At the same time, confining a member to the role of information giver can decrease group effectiveness, particularly if that member is willing and able to take on other task and maintenance roles. One of the reasons groups are more productive than individuals is their potential to use different talents and skill

TOOLBOX 2.3

 ### Every Member Can Play an Important Role

Larson and LaFasto list "competent members" as one of the eight characteristics of effective groups. So what happens if your group includes one or more incompetent members? Is incompetence a self-centered role or just an insoluble problem? If a member behaves incompetently in order to get out of work, then incompetence is a self-centered role. In most cases, however, incompetent members haven't found the *right* role—one that matches their interests and abilities. Imagine the absurdity of casting a muscular, six-foot-tall man as the female love interest in a play unless you were casting a comedy that makes fun of that ridiculous situation. Asking group members to perform roles that do not suit their talents or interests can be just as absurd.

For example, just because everyone likes Greg does not necessarily mean that he will succeed in the important role of initiator, a person who proposes new ideas and suggestions, provides direction for the group, and gets the group moving toward its goal. Maybe the reason members

like Greg is that he's better suited to the role of encourager-supporter. He has a natural talent for praising and encouraging group members and is proud to be seen as a good listener. If Greg is trapped in the role of initiator, whether by appointment or by members' expectations, he may soon be viewed as incompetent. Members who once liked Greg may become frustrated and annoyed with his apparent lack of ability.

We encourage you to consider and even change the roles that you assume in groups as well as the roles that others perform. Are your roles a good match for your abilities? And, equally important, do you *like* serving in this role? For example, you may lack the organizational skills to serve as a group's procedural technician. Not only might you lack the skills, but you may hate the task. You see yourself as stuck in a dead-end role that satisfies none of your interests or needs. When members are stuck in roles they can't do or dislike, they may also assume negative, self-centered roles. The result: They are seen as incompetent.

sets in multiple ways. Don't lock your members into inflexible roles. Instead, seek balance. Create ways to use their multiple talents.[31] In the best of all possible groups, all the task and maintenance functions should be available as strategies to mobilize a group toward its goal.

ADJOURNING: BALANCING ENGAGEMENT AND DISENGAGEMENT

Groups end their work and their existence for many reasons. When a group is assigned a specific task, the completion of that task ends the need for the group. In other cases, individual members may leave a group for personal or professional reasons or to search out and join another group. When an entire group disbands, however, most members experience the tensions produced by relinquishing group responsibilities. They also confront relational issues, such as how to retain friendships with other members.[32] Group communication scholar Joann Keyton suggests that when a group ends, members should devote a final meeting to evaluating the group experience and to giving themselves a chance to say good-bye.[33]

BALANCING NEEDS, NORMS, AND ROLES

Throughout the group development process, members must work to balance the dialectic tensions of both individual and group needs, conflict and cohesion, conformity and nonconformity, task and social dimensions, and engagement and disengagement.

An effective group balances its members' individual needs with the work needed to accomplish the group's goal. When a group is forming, the social dimension may require more attention than the task dimension. However, once a group has moved beyond the early stages of development, it can reduce its concentration on social needs in order to focus its time and energy on the task dimension. At the same time, a group must appreciate the need for both conflict and cohesion in order to fulfill the personal needs of members, promote positive working relationships, foster member commitment and loyalty, and accomplish the group goal.

As a group matures, the costs and benefits of adhering to group norms must also be balanced. If members recklessly deviate from norms or assume self-centered roles, the group's equilibrium will be upset. If, on the other hand, members place too much value on conformity or inflexible roles, the group may fail to make effective decisions. As a group develops, it changes. Those changes represent the natural phases of group development. Effective groups monitor and adapt to change in order to negotiate the dialectics of group development.

GROUPTECH

Virtual Group Development

Virtual groups go through many of the same developmental stages as face-to-face groups. There are, however, several factors that are unique to the development of virtual groups. During the forming stage, many virtual groups find that a face-to-face or videoconference meeting is necessary for effective team inter-action at the beginning of the group's life cycle, especially when members have not previously worked together virtually.[1] This first stage of group development should familiarize members with the group's goal, its schedule for inter-action, and the expectations for individual and group performance. The forming stage is an excellent opportunity to introduce mem-bers to one another, to go over team norms and codes of virtual conduct, to review soft-ware and hardware requirements, and to answer questions.

During the storming stage, virtual groups must deal with an added level of problem solving imposed by the virtual environment. In addition to expressing opinions and debat-ing substantive issues, the group may have to address technical issues. What should the group do if technical systems are not compatible or if some members are technically unskilled or apprehensive about using advanced technology? What is the best way to assign responsibilities, given the group's inability to meet face to face? Virtual groups must solve technical problems if they hope to address task-related issues.

As virtual groups enter the norming stage, they will have defined members' roles, resolved conflicts, solved most technical problems, and accepted the group's norms for interaction; they

will be ready to focus on the task. They will have resolved issues related to differences in time, distance, technology, member cultures, and organizational environments. At this point, the group knows how to work virtually and effectively.

Once a virtual group reaches the performing stage, members engage in ongoing virtual inter-action and encourage equal participation by all members. They have learned to address technical roadblocks and have become comfortable with the virtual media used by the group.

And finally, a group may rely on virtual com-munication to blunt the separation anxiety that comes with the adjourning stage. If a group has matured and performed well, members will be reluctant to give up their relationships with their colleagues.

Depending on the circumstances, some virtual groups may be able to skip one or more stages.[2] For example, highly successful, expe-rienced virtual groups may move directly from stage 1 to stage 3 or 4 when they're working on routine tasks or tasks that they have success-fully completed many times before. Members know the rules and expectations and can con-centrate on performing the task. On the other hand, virtual groups addressing new or unique problems, the redistribution of resources, or the addition of new members may have to devote more time and attention to the second and third stages.

[1] Deborah L. Duarte and Nancy Tennant Snyder, *Mastering Virtual Teams*, 2nd ed. (San Francisco: Jossey-Bass, 1999), pp. 116–117.
[2] Duarte and Snyder, p. 183.

Classroom Norms

Goal: To understand the purpose and impact of implicit and explicit norms

Participants: Groups of 5–7 members

Procedure

1. The members of each group should generate a list of the implicit and explicit norms that operate in many of their classes.

   - *Implicit norm:* When students come in late, they tiptoe to the closest available seat near the door.
   - *Explicit norm:* The syllabus states that no makeup work will be allowed if students do not have legitimate, written excuses.

2. Each group should rank the norms on each list in terms of their usefulness in ensuring quality instruction and effective learning.

3. Groups should post their lists and compare them with the norms generated by other groups. The class should then discuss the following questions:

   - Do any norms appear on all or most of the lists?
   - Which norms are most important?
   - Are there more implicit than explicit norms?
   - Should any of the norms of this class be changed, strengthened, or abolished?

Group Attraction Survey

Directions: Think of an effective group in which you currently work or in which you have worked in the past. Try to keep the group you select in mind as you complete this assessment instrument. The following fifteen statements describe the possible reasons you joined or were attracted to your group. Indicate the degree to which each statement applies to you by marking whether you (5) strongly agree, (4) agree, (3) are undecided, (2) disagree, or (1) strongly disagree. Work quickly and record your first impression.

_____ 1. I like having authority and high status in the group.

_____ 2. I want the other group members to act friendly toward me.

_____ 3. Group members help one another solve personal problems.

_____ 4. I am proud when the group achieves a goal or an objective.

_____ 5. I try to be an active participant in group activities.

_____ 6. Some group members are close friends.

_____ 7. I become upset if group members waste time and effort.

_____ 8. I like to do things with group members outside the group.

_____ 9. Group members are excellent decision makers and problem solvers.

_____ 10. Group members like me.

_____ 11. I work hard to be a valuable group member.

_____ 12. I try to influence the opinions and actions of group members.

_____ 13. I like it when group members invite me to join their activities.

_____ 14. I enjoy talking to group members, even when the conversation is unrelated to the group's goal.

_____ 15. I try to get group members to do things the way I want them done.

Scoring

Seek Task Achievement   Add your responses to items 4, 7, and 9:

Seek Social Goals   Add your responses to items 3, 8, and 14:

Seek Inclusion   Add your responses to items 5, 11, and 13:

Seek Control   Add your responses to items 1, 12, and 15:

Seek Affection   Add your responses to items 2, 6, and 10:

A score of 12 or above in any category indicates that this source of attraction is an important reason that you joined and stay in this group. A score of 6 or below indicates that this source of attraction was not an important factor in your joining this group and not a major reason for your staying in it. Examining your attraction to other groups in which you work may result in different scores.

NOTES

1. Bruce W. Tuckman, "Developmental Sequence in Small Groups," *Psychological Bulletin,* 63 (1965), pp. 384–399. Tuckman's 1965 article is reprinted in *Group Facilitation: A Research and Applications Journal,* 3 (Spring 2001) and is available as a Word document at http://dennislearningcenter.osu.edu/references/Group%20DEV%ARTICLE.doc. See also Mark K. Smith, "Bruce W. Tuckman—Forming, Storming, Norming, and Performing in Groups," *The Encyclopaedia of Informal Education,* www.infed.org/thinkers/tuckman.htm, updated March 14, 2005; "Famous Models: Stages of Group Development" (Chimaera Consulting Limited) http://www.chimaeraconsulting.com/tuckman.htm, 2001.

2. In 1997, Tuckman and Jensen proposed an updated model that includes a fifth stage: adjourning. Bruce W. Tuckman and Mary Ann C. Jensen, "Stages of Small Group Development Revisited," *Group and Organizational Studies,* 2 (1977), pp. 419–427.

3. Dianna R. Wynn, coauthor of *Working in Groups,* is a trial consultant for Courtroom Intelligence and Jury Logic.

4. Mark L. Knapp, "Introduction," in Carl E. Larson and Frank M. J. LaFasto, *TeamWork: What Must Go*

Right/What Can Go Wrong (Thousand Oaks, CA: Sage, 1989), pp. 7–8.

5. Carl E. Larson and Frank M. J. LaFasto, *TeamWork: What Must Go Right/What Can Go Wrong* (Thousand Oaks, CA: Sage, 1989).

6. Harvey Robbins and Michael Finley, *Why Teams Don't Work: What Goes Wrong and How to Make It Right* (Princeton, NJ: Peterson's/Pacesetter Books, 1995), p. 26.

7. Rodney W. Napier and Matti K. Gershenfeld, *Groups: Theory and Experience*, 7th ed. (Boston: Houghton Mifflin, 2004), pp. 72–74.

8. Abraham H. Maslow, *Motivation and Personality* (New York: Harper & Row, 1954).

9. Abigail Tucker, "Shelter Residents Find Sense of Community," *The Sun*, September 6, 2005, p. 8A.

10. Will Schutz, *The Human Element: Productivity, Self-Esteem, and the Bottom Line* (San Francisco: Jossey-Bass, 1994).

11. In his more recent works, Schutz uses the term *openness* instead of *affection*. However, we find that students understand the third need better when we use Schutz's original term—*affection*.

12. Ernest G. Bormann, *Small Group Communication: Theory and Practice*, 3rd ed. (Edina, MN: Burgess, 1996), pp. 132–135, 181–183.

13. Napier and Gershenfeld, p. 182.

14. Susan A. Wheelan and Nancy Brewer Danganan, "The Relationship Between the Internal Dynamics of Student Affairs Leadership Teams and Campus Leaders' Perceptions of the Effectiveness of Student Affairs Divisions," *NASPA Journal*, 40 (Spring 2003), p. 96.

15. Donald G. Ellis and B. Aubrey Fisher, *Small Group Decision Making: Communication and the Group Process*, 4th ed. (New York: McGraw-Hill, 1994), pp. 43–44.

16. Susan A. Wheelan, *Group Process: A Developmental Perspective* (Boston: Allyn & Bacon, 1994), pp. 14–19.

17. Patricia H. Andrews, "Group Conformity," in *Small Group Communication: Theory and Practice,* 7th ed., ed. Robert S. Cathcart, Larry A. Samovar, and Linda D. Henman (Madison, WI: Brown & Benchmark, 1996), p. 185.

18. Charles Pavitt and Ellen Curtis, *Small Group Discussion: A Theoretical Approach*, 2nd ed. (Scottsdale, AZ: Gorsuch, Scarisbrick, 1994), p. 178.

19. For detailed descriptions of these classic studies, see Sharon S. Brehm, Saul M. Kassin, and Steven Fein, *Social Psychology*, 6th ed. (Boston: Houghton Mifflin, 2005), pp. 250–255, 472–475. Today, neither experiment would be conducted because all academic research using human subjects must be approved by an institution's research board to certify that the experimentation will not cause harm.

20. Napier and Gershenfeld, pp. 137–140.

21. Carole A. Barbato, "An Integrated Model of Group Decision-Making," paper presented at the meeting of the National Communication Association, Chicago, IL, November 1997, p. 19.

22. Jon R. Katzenbach and Douglas K. Smith, *The Discipline of Teams: A Mindbook-Workbook for Delivering Small Group Performance* (New York: Wiley, 2001), pp. 141–142.

23. B. Aubrey Fisher, "Decision Emergence: Phases in Group Decision Making," *Speech Monographs*, 37 (1970), p. 160.

24. Ellis and Fisher, p. 51.

25. Robbins and Finley, p. 26. See also Harvey Robbins and Michael Finley, *The New Why Teams Don't Work: What Went Wrong and How to Make It Right* (Princeton, NJ: Peterson's/Pacesetter Books, 2000), pp. 27–29.

26. Scott D. Johnson and Lynette M. Long, "Being a Part of Being Apart: Dialectics in Groups Communication," in *New Directions in Group Communication,* ed. Lawrence R. Frey (Thousand Oaks, CA: Sage, 2002), p. 35.

27. Jeanne M. Plas, *Person-Centered Leadership: An American Approach to Participator Management* (Thousand Oaks, CA: Sage, 2000), p. 88.

28. Kenneth D. Benne and Paul Sheats, "Functional Roles of Group Members," *Journal of Social Issues*, 4 (1948), pp. 41–49.

29. Michael Z. Hackman and Craig E. Johnson, *Leadership: A Communication Perspective*, 4th ed. (Long Grove, IL: Waveland, 2004), p. 82.

30. Katzenbach and Smith, pp. 20, 138.

31. Katzenbach and Smith, p. 138.

32. Carolyn M. Anderson, Bruce L. Riddle, and Matthew M. Martin, "Socialization Process in Groups," in *The Handbook of Group Communication Theory and Research*, ed. Lawrence R. Frey, assoc. eds. Dennis S. Gouran and Marshall Scott Poole (Thousand Oaks, CA: Sage, 1999), p 155.

CHAPTER 3

Group Member Diversity

HETEROGENEOUS GROUPS

When you read or hear the word *diversity*, you may think about race or about people from other countries. The concept of diversity, however, involves much more than country of origin, skin color, or ethnic heritage. When discussing group communication, we use the term *diversity* in its most general sense—the quality of being different. *The American Heritage Dictionary of the English Language* defines *diverse* as "made up of distinct characteristics, qualities, or elements."[1]

The homogeneous–heterogeneous dialectic is particularly applicable to the study of group membership. As we note in Chapter 1, the prefix *homo* comes from the Greek language and means "same" or "similar"; *hetero* means "different." Thus, a homogeneous group is composed of members who are the same or similar, and a heterogeneous group is composed of members who are not the same. And remember. there is no such thing as a purely homogeneous group because no two members can be *exactly* the same. Diversity exists in all groups.

Every person on this earth—and thus every member of a group—is different. Even identical twins have different experiences as well as different characteristics, abilities, and beliefs. Think about the many ways in which you differ from others by asking the following questions:

- Where did you grow up, and how did that influence who you are now?

- What aspects of your culture do you most appreciate and are not likely to give up?[2]

- Which of your physical characteristics do you like or dislike?

- What are your interpersonal, intellectual, and physical skills?

- When you have free time from work or studies, what do you like to do?

- What are your most obvious personality traits?

As a member of a group, you join a diverse collection of people. Although you may share similar backgrounds, interests, and talents with the other members, you rely on differences to establish your unique identity and value to the group. James Surowiecki, author of *The Wisdom of Crowds*, explains that member diversity helps groups make better decisions because it "adds perspectives that would otherwise be absent and because it takes away . . . some of the destructive characteristics" of poor group decision making.[3] James G. Marsh, an organizational theorist, contends that groups that are too much alike find it harder to keep learning, because each member is bringing less and less new information to the table."[4] Groups benefit when their members have distinct characteristics and qualities.

Lee Gardenswartz and Anita Rowe, authors of *Diverse Teams at Work*, note that "individual differences and uniqueness make every group diverse. . . . [In addition to race], gender, ethnicity, variations in age, education level, parental status, geographic location, sexual orientation, and work experience are a few of the many ways in which people can be different."[5]

Why should groups strive to understand, respect, and adapt to member diversity? (© Bob Daemmrich/The Image Works)

Figure 3.1 displays the three layers of diversity within every group member. Your core personality—which permeates all the other layers—is at the center and represents your unique ways of experiencing, interpreting, and behaving in the world around you. The second layer represents internal dimensions over which you have little or no control. The outer layer represents societal and experiential factors such as religion, marital status, and educational background. Not only do these three layers of diversity distinguish you from others, but they also form the screen through which you see yourself and those around you.[6]

In this chapter, we examine how all three layers of diversity influence your interaction in groups as well as overall group productivity and member satisfaction.

PERSONALITY DIMENSIONS

When diverse personalities join together in pursuit of a common goal, the resulting combination of personality traits may be compatible or conflicting. Each of us has a unique way of interacting with others. How would you rate yourself in terms of the following personality traits?

- Serious————————————Humorous

- Relaxed————————————Tense

- Rational————————————Emotional

Now consider this question: Which of these traits make someone an effective group member? Depending on the circumstances, these traits can help or hinder

FIGURE 3.1   **Three Layers of Diversity**

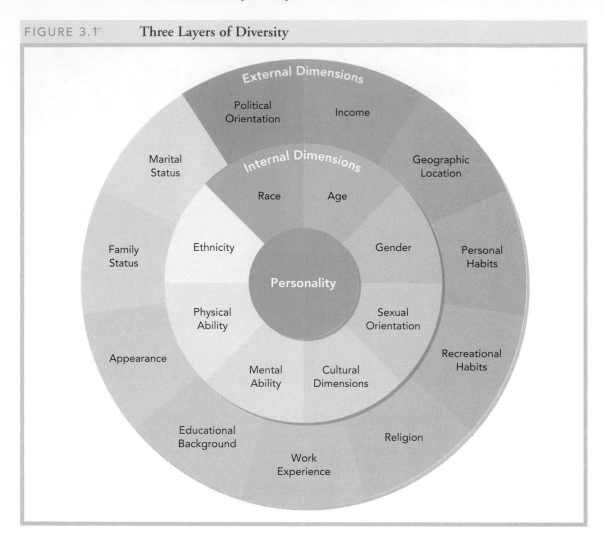

a group's interaction and progress toward a common goal.[7] Understanding personality theories can help a group balance its collection of unique temperaments, traits, and talents.

Personality Theory

There are many personality theories available for study. Here we examine the **Myers-Briggs Type Indicator®**, a personality theory that demonstrates why and how certain group members react to group tasks and social interactions in different ways.[8] Isabel Briggs Myers and her mother, Katherine Briggs, developed a personality type measure that examines the different ways in which people see and understand the world around them and also the different ways in which people reach conclusions and make decisions about what they have experienced.[9]

FIGURE 3.2   **Myers-Briggs Type Indicator® Preferences**

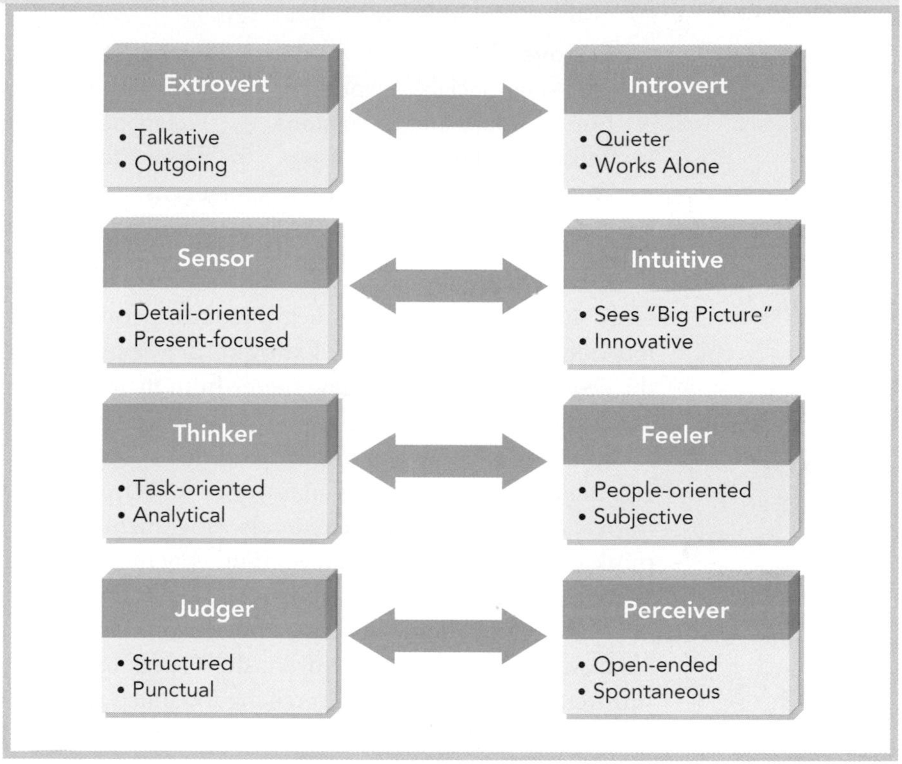

The Myers-Briggs Type Indicator®, as the measure is known, looks at the different ways in which "people *prefer* to use their minds, specifically, the way they perceive and the way they make judgments."[10] All of us have preferences of thought and behavior that can be divided into four dialectic categories, with two opposite preferences in each category (see Figure 3.2). As you read about the following categories and traits, ask yourself which preferences best describe the reasons you choose one way of reacting or behaving over another.

Extrovert–Introvert. These two traits relate to where you like to focus your attention—outward or inward. **Extroverts** are outgoing, talkative, and enthusiastic; they enjoy interaction with others. Extroverts get their energy by being with people. They like solving problems in groups and involving others in projects. In a group setting, extroverts may have a tendency to dominate the discussion without listening to others. At the same time, they can be terrific energizers and contributors. **Introverts** are more reserved, quiet, and private. They also need more time to themselves to think and reenergize. Although they may have a great deal to offer in a group discussion, they can find the experience exhausting. In general, introverts prefer to work by themselves rather than in groups. Notice how the differences between extroverts and introverts represent dialectic tensions:

Extrovert[11]	**Introvert**
Outgoing, sociable, expressive	Reserved, private, contained
Enjoys groups and discussions	Prefers one-to-one interactions
Talks first, then thinks	Thinks first, then talks
Does many things at once	Focuses on one thing at a time
Thinks out loud	Thinks to him- or herself

Extroverts are not necessarily wild and crazy talkers, nor are introverts necessarily shy and withdrawn. Rather, these two personality preferences refer to how individuals become energized. Extroverts draw energy from the outside world and the people in it. Introverts draw energy from their inner world of ideas, emotions, and impressions.

Knowing whether you or another group member is an extrovert or an introvert can be valuable. Whereas an extrovert is likely to prefer working on a subcommittee, an introvert may prefer a solo assignment. Introverts need more time to think before they speak or act. A group may miss out on good ideas and needed analysis if it rushes into solutions proposed by enthusiastic extroverts.

Misunderstandings between extroverts and introverts are common in groups. "Extroverts complain that introverts don't speak up at the right time in meetings. Introverts criticize extroverts for talking too much and not listening well."[12] Effective groups try to balance the needs of both personality types by accommodating the differences in communication style and tapping the best ideas from all members.

Sensor–Intuitive. These two traits focus on the way you look at the world around you—whether you see the trees or the forest. **Sensors** focus on details and prefer to concentrate on one task at a time. In groups, they may uncover minor flaws in an idea and request detailed instructions for completing a task. **Intuitives** look for connections and concepts rather than rules and flaws. They like to come up with big ideas but become bored with details. Notice how the differences between sensors and intuitives exemplify a dialectic tension:

Sensor	**Intuitive**
Focuses on details	Focuses on the big picture
Practical and realistic	Theoretical
Likes concrete information	Likes abstract information
Likes facts	Gets bored with facts and details
Trusts experience	Trusts inspiration and intuition
Values common sense	Values creativity and innovation

In a group, sensors and intuitives often see things quite differently. Sensors focus on regulations, step-by-step explanations, and facts, whereas intuitives focus on outwitting regulations, supplying theoretical explanations, and ignoring details.[13]

TOOLBOX 3.1

Group Survival Guide for Introverts

In *The Introvert Advantage: How to Thrive in an Extrovert World*, psychologist Marti Olsen Laney discusses the many pitfalls awaiting introverts in group settings. She writes that "introverts are often surprised when they are not valued for their considerable contributions" to a group, in part because they don't speak up and because "they usually find it hard to both absorb all the information *and* formulate an opinion about it. They need time away from meetings to sift and sort data." Some introverts can become "brainlocked" because they can't find the right words to express their meaning.[1] Given the inherent challenges facing introverts in group settings, Laney offers a list of strategies for letting other group members know that they are present, interested, and involved in a group and its work:

- Don't schedule too many meetings on the same day.
- Say hello and smile when you enter a room.

- Sit near the door in case you need a quick break.
- Take notes to help you focus your thoughts and avoid becoming overloaded with information.
- Use nonverbal signals like nodding your head, smiling, and eye contact to let others know that you are paying attention.
- Say *something*. Ask a question, or restate what someone else has said.
- Let people know that you will continue to think about the topic and get back to them with a reaction.
- Email or jot a note to other group members to ask for and provide feedback about issues discussed in a meeting.[2]

[1] Marti Olsen Laney, *The Introvert Advantage: How to Thrive in an Extrovert World* (New York: Workman, 2002), pp. 190 and 191–192.
[2] Laney, pp. 193–194.

Communication between sensors and intuitives can be difficult "because they see things so differently, and each believes that his or her information is more accurate, valid, and real."[14] Thus, intuitives should appreciate how much sensors accomplish by being realistic, down-to-earth, and practical, while sensors should appreciate the intuitive's inventive mind, original ideas, and ability to solve problems creatively.

Groups need both kinds of members in order to function effectively and efficiently. The example that follows emphasizes the importance of having a balance between the "nuts and bolts types" and those individuals who are capable of being creative and conceptual: "In the construction business it's important to have the 'big picture' people who can see the conceptual side of a project and know when major changes are necessary. This needs to be balanced, however, by people who are at the job site supervising the very detail-oriented portions of the work. Both are necessary members of a good project team."[15]

Thinker–Feeler. These two traits explain how you go about making decisions. **Thinkers** are task-oriented. They take pride in their ability to think objectively and logically. Thinkers often enjoy arguing and making difficult decisions; they want to get the job done, even if the cost is bad feelings among some group members. **Feelers** are people-oriented. They want everyone to get along. Feelers will spend time and effort helping other members.

Thinker	Feeler
Task-oriented	People-oriented
Objective, firm, analytical	Subjective, humane, appreciative
Enjoys arguing	Thinks arguing is disruptive
Prefers businesslike meetings	Prefers social interchange in meetings
Values competence, reason, and justice	Values relationships and harmony
Direct and firm-minded	Tactful and tenderhearted
Thinks with the head	Thinks with the heart

When thinkers and feelers work together in groups, there is a potential for misunderstanding. Thinkers may appear unemotional and aggressive. Feelers may annoy others by "wasting" time with social chitchat. Thinkers should try to modify their criticism of others—what's intended as good advice may be seen as cruel. Feelers should learn not to take criticism so personally and to speak up if they feel they're being treated unfairly.[16] When thinkers and feelers appreciate their differences as decision makers, they can form an unbeatable team. While the thinkers make decisions and move the group forward, feelers make sure that the group is working harmoniously.

Judger–Perceiver. The last two traits focus on how you deal with the outer world and its problems. **Judgers** are highly structured and well organized. They plan ahead, follow lengthy "to do" lists, and like closure. Judgers are very punctual and can become impatient with people who show up late or waste time. **Perceivers** are less rigid than judgers. Because they like open-endedness, being on time is less important to them than being flexible and adaptable. Perceivers are risk takers who are willing to try new options. However, they often procrastinate and end up in a frenzy to complete a task on time. Consider how the following dialectical differences can affect group interaction:

Judger	Perceiver
Values organization and structure	Values flexibility and spontaneity
In control and definite	Goes with the flow
Likes deadlines	Dislikes deadlines
Work now/play later	Play now/work later
Needs standards and expectations	Feels constrained by rules
Adjusts schedules to complete work	Works at the last minute

Judgers and perceivers often have difficulty working together. To a judger, a perceiver may appear scatterbrained. To a perceiver, a judger may appear rigid and controlling. Whereas judgers come prepared to make decisions and solve problems, perceivers "aren't comfortable with things being 'decided'; [they] want to reopen, discuss, rework, argue for the sake of arguing."[17] As difficult as it is for them, judgers should try to stop "doing" and take time to relax with others. Perceivers should try to respect deadlines and keep promises that they make to judgers.

Implications of Personality Dimensions

Just as it is desirable to achieve a balance between members' task and maintenance roles, the same is true for personality traits. A group without judgers can miss deadlines and fail to achieve its goal. A group without a sensor can overlook important details or critical flaws in a proposal. Although it is tempting to choose members who are just like you, a group will perform better with representatives of every type. According to Otto Kroeger and Janet Thuesen, in an ideal group, "we would have a smattering of Extroverts, Introverts, Sensors, Intuitives, Thinkers, Feelers, Judgers, and Perceivers—and we would put them together in such a way that they would not only understand their differences but could also draw upon them."[18]

We often see Myers-Briggs preferences in our students' behavior. For example, judgers tell us that they usually finish class assignments well in advance, whereas perceivers may pull all-nighters to get their work done. Judgers often describe perceivers as irresponsible and disorganized, whereas perceivers describe judgers as

TOOLBOX 3.2

Intelligent Groups Can Make Dumb Decisions

Group diversity improves group performance and member satisfaction in many ways—even in terms of how well a group makes "smart" decisions. Scott Page, a political scientist at the University of Michigan, studies groups and problem solving. He concludes that "on the group level, intelligence alone is not enough, because intelligence alone cannot guarantee you different perspectives on a problem. . . . Grouping only smart people together doesn't work that well because the smart people (whatever that means) tend to resemble each other in what they can do. . . . Adding in a few people who know less, but have different skills, actually improves the group's performance."[1]

Think about the many intelligent people on a U.S. president's staff—and then consider some of the poor decisions made within the White House, e.g., the U.S. invasion of Cuba, Watergate, and, some would say, the war in Iraq. Then think about the well-educated, intelligent people who run U.S. corporations and consider some of their poor decisions—from useless or defective consumer products to "creative" bookkeeping. In Chapter 7, "Conflict and Cohesion in Groups," we examine Irving Janis's concept of groupthink, a phenomenon that describes the deterioration of group effectiveness that results from in-group pressure. As you will see, it takes a lot more than collective intelligence to avoid the pitfalls of poor decision making.

[1] James Surowiecki, *The Wisdom of Crowds: Why the Many Are Smarter than the Few and How Collective Wisdom Shapes Business, Economics, Societies, and Nations* (New York: Doubleday, 2004), p. 30.

critical and compulsive workaholics. Nevertheless, both judgers and perceivers get their work done and do it well.

Students who are extroverts love to participate in heated class discussions, whereas the introverts don't like being put on the spot. Sensors like learning "the facts," and intuitives like "playing with theories." Thinkers become impatient with the social chitchat of feelers, and the feelers wonder whether the thinkers have hearts. Rather than criticizing others, Myers-Briggs helps group members learn how to accommodate and capitalize on differences in personality types and preferences, how to build on personal strengths, and—as a result—how to foster group productivity and cohesiveness.

CULTURAL DIMENSIONS

The cultural diversity of group members plays a critical role in whether a group achieves its common goal.

Respecting and adapting to cultural diversity begins with an understanding of different cultures. **Culture** can be viewed as "a learned set of shared interpretations about beliefs, values, and norms which affect the behaviors of a relatively large group of people."[19] Within most cultures, there are also groups of people— members of **co-cultures**—who coexist within the mainstream society, yet remain connected to one another through their cultural heritage.[20] In the United States, American Indian tribes are co-cultures, as are African Americans, Hispanic/Latino Americans, Asian Americans, Arab Americans, Irish Americans, and members of large and small religious groups. Given our broad definition of culture, a Nebraska rancher and a Boston professor can have very different cultural perspectives, as would a native Egyptian, Brazilian, Indonesian Muslim, and member of the Chippewa tribe.

According to the 2000 Census, the population of the United States has changed significantly. Not only are there many more people, but the color and characteristics of their faces have changed as well.[21] During the 1990s, the Hispanic population increased 58 percent, and the Asian population increased 48 percent. Between 1990 and 2000, more than 13 million people immigrated to the United States, the largest number of immigrants in a ten-year period in the country's history.

The 2000 Census also reports that three-quarters of the people in this country are white. But more than half of the people living in California are non-white, as are the majority of individuals living in several large American cities. Moreover, the population of Hispanic, Asian, and other immigrant groups is growing and will continue to grow, so that soon after the middle of this century, whites will become one of the many minority groups living in America.[22] In short, all groups will need to understand, respect, and adapt to cultures that are not their own.

We owe a great deal to a psychologist and an anthropologist for identifying several significant dimensions of culture. Dutch social psychologist Geert Hofstede's groundbreaking research on cultural characteristics has transformed our understanding of others. He defines an **intercultural dimension** as "an aspect of a culture that can be measured relative to other cultures."[23] His work on cultural differences identifies four dimensions that characterize cultural groups: individualism–collectivism, power distance, uncertainty avoidance, and masculine–feminine values. Anthropologist Edward T. Hall adds two more dimensions: high-context and low-context cultures and monochronic–polychronic time.[24] When group members with different cultural perspectives interact, they must find ways to negotiate the dialectic tensions that accompany cultural interactions. Figure 3.3 provides an overview of these six cultural dimensions and how they can be used to recognize and adapt to group member diversity.

FIGURE 3.3   Cultural Dimensions of Group Members

Cultural Dimension	Definition and Example	Group Member Behavior	Recommended Adaptations
INDIVIDUALISM-COLLECTIVISM	Prefer to act independently or interdependently. *Individualism:* Value individual achievement and freedom. **United States, Australia, Canada** *Collectivism:* Emphasize group identity. **Asian and Latin American Countries**	**Individualistic** members will work alone and seek credit for their own work; **collectivist** members will work in groups and try to help each other. Collectivist members may prefer face-to-face discussions instead of virtual discussion.	Encourage collectivism. Make sure that individualistic members understand that they are part of a larger group that needs their input and participation to achieve a shared goal.
POWER DISTANCE	Extent of equity or status among members. *High Power:* Inequity between high- and low-status members. **Mexico, India, Singapore** *Low Power:* Equity and interdependence among group members. **Israel, New Zealand, Denmark**	**High power-distance** members try to take charge and make decisions; **low power-distance** members seek consultation and consensus.	Establish clear norms for member behavior. To what extent will members participate in decision making? How will specific tasks be assigned? How and by whom will members be evaluated? Who will serve as leader(s)?
UNCERTAINTY AVOIDANCE	Extent of comfort in uncertain situations. *High Uncertainty:* Prefer rules, plans, and routines. **Japan, Belgium, Greece** *Low Uncertainty:* Comfortable with ambiguity and unpredictability. **Jamaica, Hong Kong**	**High-uncertainty** members require structured tasks and spend more time on details; **low-uncertainty** members want less structure and can work independently with little supervision.	Provide clear instructions to the high-uncertainty members while giving low-uncertainty members opportunities to function unaided. *(continued)*

FIGURE 3.3   **Cultural Dimensions of Group Members** (continued)

Cultural Dimension	Definition and Example	Group Member Behavior	Recommended Adaptations
MASCULINITY-FEMININITY	Concern for self and success versus a focus on caring and sharing. *Masculine:* Assertive, decisive, dominant. **Japan, Venezuela, Italy** *Feminine:* Nurturing, cooperative. **Sweden, Norway, Denmark**	**Masculine-oriented** members focus on the task and personal success; **feminine-oriented** members focus on member relations and respect for others.	Balance masculine and feminine values in order to achieve task and social goals. Do not forgo action in order to achieve total cooperation and consensus.
HIGH CONTEXT-LOW CONTEXT	Directness of communication in specific circumstances. *High Context:* Messages are implied and context-sensitive. **Japan, China, Greece, Mexico** *Low Context:* Messages are explicit, factual, and objective. **England, United States, Germany**	**High-context** members consider background, nonverbal cues, and interpersonal history when communicating; **low-context** members want facts and clear, direct, explicit communication.	Give high-context members time to review information and react; demonstrate the value of going beyond "just facts" to low-context members.
MONOCHRONIC-POLYCHRONIC	How people organize and value time. *Monochronic:* Adhere to plans, schedules, and deadlines because time is valuable. **North America and Northern European.** *Polychronic:* Not obsessed with promptness or schedules because time is not highly valued. **Kenya, Argentina, African Americans**	**Monochronic** members focus on one task at a time and work hard to meet deadlines; **polychronic** members are frequently late, do many things at once, are easily distracted and tolerant of interruptions.	Encourage monochronic members to take responsibility for time-sensitive tasks while accepting that polychronic members will vary promptness based on the nature and importance of a situation or relationship.

Individualism–Collectivism

According to Hofstede and many contemporary researchers, most of us in the United States accept **individualism** as a cultural value. As a whole, we believe that the individual is important, that independence is worth pursuing, that personal achievement should be rewarded, and that individual uniqueness is an important value.[25] In the United States, an "I" orientation prevails. However, the value of individualism is not shared by most other cultures. As much as 70 percent of the world's population regards interdependence or **collectivism** as a more important value.[26] In these cultures, "we" is much more important than "I." The following behaviors are characteristic of collectivist cultures:

* There is greater emphasis on the views, needs, and goals of the group than on the individual's views, needs, and goals.

- Social norms and duty are defined by the group rather than by the individual's personal pleasure or personal benefits.

- Beliefs that are shared with the group are more important than beliefs that distinguish an individual from the group.

- There is greater readiness to cooperate with group members.[27]

At first, a collectivist perspective may appear ideally suited for group work. Yet, the opinions of individualistic members may be essential to ensure that a group recognizes and adapts to a variety of useful perspectives.

You should not assume that *all* Americans are individualistic just because the United States is ranked first among individualistic cultures. Many Americans are not highly individualistic. For example, African Americans often have the characteristics of collective societies, as do Mexican Americans and other Hispanic/Latino co-cultures. Even so, the United States's focus on individual achievement and personal rewards can make interaction with group members from collectivist cultures quite difficult. People from these cultures may view a highly individualistic communication style and behavior as selfish, arrogant, antagonistic, power-hungry, ruthless, and impatient.

Power Distance

Can you walk into your boss's office, or do you have to navigate your way through an army of secretaries and administrative assistants? Is it easy to make a personal appointment with the president of your college or university? Does our society truly believe in the sentiments expressed in the U.S. Declaration of

How do cultures demonstrate power distance among members? (© Fujifotos/The Image Works

Independence that all people are created equal? These are the questions addressed in Hofstede's power distance dimension. **Power distance** refers to the physical and psychological distance between those who have power and those who do not have power in relationships, institutions, and organizations. It also represents "the extent to which the less powerful person in society accepts inequality in power and considers it normal."[28]

In cultures with **high power distance**, individuals accept major differences in power as normal, assuming that all people are *not* created equal. In a high-power-distance culture, you accept and do not challenge authority. Parents, for example, may have total control over their children, and men may have total control over the women in their family. The government, corporate officers, and religious or legal authorities may dictate rules of behavior and have the power to ensure compliance.

In cultures with **low power distance**, power distinctions are minimized: Supervisors work with subordinates; professors work with students; elected officials work with constituents. Despite the fact that the United States claims to be the greatest democracy on earth and an equal opportunity society, Hofstede ranks the United States sixteenth on the list of low-power-distance cultures—after Finland, Switzerland, Great Britain, Germany, Costa Rica, Australia, the Netherlands, and Canada.[29]

Power distance has enormous implications for groups, particularly given the strong correlation between collectivism and high power distance and between individualism and low power distance. If you are individualistic and are strongly encouraged to express your own opinion, you are more willing to challenge group members and leaders. If, on the other hand, your culture is collectivist and your personal opinion is subordinate to the welfare of others, you are less likely to challenge the collective authority of the group.

Uncertainty Avoidance

How well do you handle unexpected changes or uncertainty? Do you feel more comfortable if your future is predictable? Hofstede defines **uncertainty avoidance** as the extent to which people within a culture are made nervous by situations that they perceive as unstructured, unclear, or unpredictable. If uncertainty makes them very nervous, they avoid these situations by maintaining strict codes of behavior and a belief in absolute truths.[30]

In cultures with **high uncertainty avoidance**, members "feel threatened by uncertain or unknown situations. This feeling is expressed through nervous stress and in a need for predictability: a need for written and unwritten rules."[31]Hofstede puts it this way: "What is different, is dangerous."[32] Cultures with **low uncertainty avoidance** accept change as part of life, tolerate nonconformity, take risks, and view rules and regulations as restricting and counterproductive. Members of low-uncertainty-avoidance cultures "tend to live day to day. . . . Conflict and competition are natural, dissent is acceptable, deviance is not threatening, and individual achievement is regarded as beneficial."[33]

The United States is eleventh on the list of countries that feel comfortable with uncertainty. More highly ranked countries include Malaysia, India, and the Philippines. Imagine the communication challenge you face if you are comfortable with change and ambiguity, but you have to work with group members who have a strong desire to avoid uncertainty. While you are willing to take risks, other members find your attitude unconventional and even threatening. At the same time, you may see the other member as rigid, uncompromising, and fearful to break or bend rules.

Masculine–Feminine

Hofstede uses the terms *masculine* and *feminine* to describe whether masculine or feminine traits are valued by a culture. In **masculine societies**, men are supposed to be assertive, tough, and focused on material success, whereas women are supposed to be more modest, tender, and concerned with the quality of life. In **feminine societies**, gender roles overlap: Both men and women are supposed to be modest, tender, and concerned with the quality of life.[34]

Hofstede ranks the United States as fifteenth in terms of masculine values, but less masculine than Australia, New Zealand, and Greece.[35] In masculine societies, personal success, competition, assertiveness, and strength are admired. Unselfishness and nurturing may be seen as weaknesses or "women's work." Although women have come a long way from the rigid roles of past centuries, they have miles to go before they achieve genuine equality in a masculine-oriented culture.

Think of the challenges groups face when there is a mix of masculine and feminine values. Members with masculine perspectives may compete for leadership positions and exhibit highly assertive behavior. Members with more feminine values may be highly effective and supportive but never achieve a real voice or influence in the group.

High Context–Low Context

All communication occurs in a **context**, a physical and psychosocial environment. Anthropologist Edward T. Hall sees context as the information that surrounds an event and is inextricably bound up with the meaning of the event.[36] He claims that context—in and of itself—may hold more meaning than the actual words in a message. As with Hofstede's dimensions, we can place cultures on a continuum from high context to low context.

In a **high-context culture**, very little meaning is expressed through words. Gestures, silence, and facial expressions as well as the relationships among communicators have meaning. In high-context cultures, meaning can be conveyed through status (age, gender, education, family background, title, and affiliations) and through an individual's informal network of friends and associates.[37]

In a **low-context culture**, meaning is expressed primarily through language. As members of a low-context culture, people in North America tend to speak more, speak louder, and speak more rapidly than people from a high-context culture. We "speak up," "spell it out," "tell it like it is," and "speak our mind." Figure 3.4 contrasts the characteristics of high- and low-context cultures.

High-context communication usually occurs in collectivist cultures where members share similar attitudes, beliefs, and values. As a result, spoken communication can be indirect and implied because everyone *gets* the meaning by understanding the context, the person's nonverbal behavior, and the significance of the communicator's relationships with others. Notice how the following sayings capture the nature of high-context communication:

Seeing is better than hearing. (Nigeria)

It is the duck that squawks that gets shot. (Japan)

Once you preach, the point is gone. (Zen phrase)

Group members from high- and low-context cultures express and interpret messages in different ways. For example, suppose everyone knows that Allison and Philip have a close personal relationship. During a group discussion, Allison scowls every time Philip expresses his opinion or makes a suggestion. However, when asked whether she agrees with Philip, she says yes. Group members with high-context perspectives would pay more attention to Allison's nonverbal behavior and decide that she may be angry with Philip and disapproves of his ideas, whereas members with low-context perspectives may only hear the "yes" and assume that Allison and Philip are in total agreement.

Monochronic Time–Polychronic Time

In northern European and North American cultures, time is a very valuable commodity. As a result, we fill our time with multiple commitments and live a fast-paced life. However, the pace of life in countries such as India, Kenya, and Argentina is driven less by a need to "get things done" than by a sense of participation in events that create their own rhythm.[38]

FIGURE 3.4   **Characteristics of High- and Low-Context Cultures**

Characteristics of High- and Low-Context Cultures	
HIGH-CONTEXT CHARACTERISTICS	**LOW-CONTEXT CHARACTERISTICS**
• Rely on Nonverbal Meanings • Reserved Reactions • Strong In-group Bonds • High Level of Group Commitment	• Rely on Verbal Meanings • Reactions on the Surface • Flexible Group Membership • Lower Level of Group Commitment

Anthropologist Edward T. Hall classifies time as a form of communication. He claims that cultures organize time in one of two ways: either monochronic or polychronic.[39] In **monochronic time (M time)**, events are scheduled as separate items—one thing at a time. M-time people like to concentrate on one job before moving to another and may become irritated when someone in a meeting brings up a personal topic that is not related to the purpose of the meeting.

In **polychronic time (P time)**, schedules are not as important and are frequently broken. People in polychronic cultures are not slaves to time and are easily distracted and tolerant of interruptions. P-time people are frequently late for appointments or may not show up at all.[40] If you are a P-time person, you probably like doing several tasks at one time, find it stimulating to think about several different problems at the same time, and feel comfortable holding two or three conversations at the same time. In polychronic-time cultures—such as the Spanish-speaking cultures in Spain and Latin America—relationships are far more important than schedules. "Appointments will be quickly broken, schedules readily set aside, and deadlines unmet without guilt or apology when friends or family members require attention."[41]

When monochronic- and polychronic-time people interact in group settings, the results can be frustrating. Hall notes that monochronic Americans become distressed by how polychronic people treat schedules. For P-time people, schedules and commitments, particularly plans for the future, are not firm, and even important plans may change right up to the last minute.[42]

If you are an M-time person, you can try to modify and relax your obsession with time and scheduling. If you are a P-time person, you can do your best to respect and adapt to a monochronic member's need for careful scheduling and promptness.

Barriers to Cultural Understanding

Learning to communicate effectively in the global village that characterizes life in the twenty-first century can be a significant challenge. Culturally sensitive group members develop strategies and skills for interacting with others from diverse backgrounds. Yet simply learning about other cultures will not make you a more effective group member. You must also avoid four obstacles to understanding others: ethnocentrism, stereotyping, prejudice, and discrimination.

Ethnocentrism. **Ethnocentrism** is a belief that your culture is superior to others. Ethnocentrism is not just about patriotism or pride; it is a mistaken belief that your culture is a superior culture, with special rights and privileges that are or should be denied to others. An ethnocentric communicator believes that

- My culture should be the role model for other cultures.

- People would be happier if they lived like people in my culture.

- Most other cultures are backward when compared with my culture.

GROUPTECH

Cultural Diversity in Virtual Groups

In their book *Mastering Virtual Teams*, Deborah L. Duarte and Nancy Tennant Snyder contend that culture has an impact on how we use communication technology based on Hofstede's dimensions and Hall's research on context.[1]

- *Individualism–collectivism.* Members from highly collectivist cultures may prefer face-to-face interactions, whereas individualistic communicators may like having the screen to themselves as they share ideas and opinions.
- *Power distance.* Members from high-power-distance cultures may communicate more freely when technologies are asynchronous (do not occur in real time) and when they allow anonymous input.
- *Uncertainty avoidance.* Members from cultures with high uncertainty avoidance may be slower to adopt technology. They may also prefer technology that produces permanent records of discussions and decisions.
- *Masculinity–femininity.* Members from cultures with more feminine values may use technology in a nurturing way, that is, as a way of encouraging, supporting, and motivating others.
- *High context–low context.* People from high-context cultures may prefer more information-rich technologies (such as videoconferences), as well as those that offer the feeling of social presence. People from low-context cultures may prefer more asynchronous communication.
- *Monochronic–polychronic.* Monochronic members may become frustrated by polychronic members who are late to join a teleconference. Polychronic members may become distracted during an online meeting and interrupt the group to discuss unrelated issues.

[1] Based on Deborah L. Duarte and Nancy Tennant Snyder, *Mastering Virtual Teams* (San Francisco: Jossey-Bass, 1999), p. 60.

Ethnocentric group members offend others when they imply that they represent a superior culture with superior values. For example, have you ever been insulted by someone who implies that her religious beliefs are "true," whereas yours are not? Have you been disrespected by someone who believes that his traditions, language, or music preferences are "better" than yours? If so, you may have seen ethnocentrism in action. Group members with ethnocentric attitudes can derail group progress before it begins.

Stereotyping.   **Stereotypes** are generalizations about a group of people that oversimplify their characteristics. When we stereotype others, we rely on exaggerated beliefs to make judgments about a group of people. Unfortunately, stereotyping usually attributes negative traits to an entire group when, in reality, only a few people in that group may possess those traits. A study of college students found that, even in the mid-1990s, African Americans were stereotyped as lazy and loud, and Jews were described as shrewd and intelligent. In addition to negative stereotypes, we may hold positive ones. Comments such as "Asian students excel in math and science" or "Females are more compassionate than males" make positive but all-inclusive generalizations. While positive stereotypes may not seem harmful, they can lead to unfair judgments. Stereotyping other group members does more than derail progress; it prevents members from contributing their best skills and creates long-lasting resentment and anger. Too often, female group members are asked to chair a social committee or take notes because "women are better at that."

Prejudice. Stereotypes lead to **prejudices**—"negative attitudes about other people that are based on faulty and inflexible stereotypes."[43] Prejudices about an individual or cultural group often arise when we have no direct experience with that person or group. The word *prejudice* has two parts: *pre,* meaning "before," and *judice,* as in *judge*. When you believe or express a prejudice, you are making a judgment about someone before you have taken time to get to know that person and see whether your opinions and feelings are justified. Although prejudices can be positive—"He must be brilliant if he went to Yale"—most prejudices are negative. Statements such as "I don't want a disabled person working on our group project," "I'm not putting someone that old on the team," and "I'm not voting for a pregnant woman to lead this group" are all examples of prejudging someone based on stereotypes about people with disabilities, older people, and pregnant women. These kinds of prejudices have several characteristics:

- Biased perceptions and beliefs about group members that are not based on direct experience and firsthand knowledge

- Irrational feelings of dislike and even hatred for certain groups

- A readiness to behave in negative and unjust ways toward members of the group[44]

Discrimination. The word *discrimination* has many definitions. People with acute hearing can discriminate (that is, differentiate) one sound or tone from another. We also use the term **discrimination** to describe how we act out and express prejudice. When we discriminate, we exclude groups of people from opportunities granted to others: employment, promotion, housing, political expression, and equal rights.

Sadly, discrimination comes in many forms: racial discrimination; ethnic discrimination; religious discrimination; gender discrimination; sexual harassment; discrimination based on sexual orientation, disability, or age; and discrimination against people from different social classes and political ideologies. Discrimination has no place in groups.

You are surrounded by and dependent on diverse groups of people who deserve the same understanding and respect that you bestow on your own culture. The sooner you learn about the people around you, the better you will communicate with the range of people in our pluralistic society.

TOOLBOX 3.3

There Is *No* Such Thing as Race

The statement "There is *no* such thing as race" may seem dimwitted. Of course there's such a thing as race. After all, the U.S. Census asks questions about race, and we have laws prohibiting discrimination on the basis of race. We've witnessed race riots, seen an increasing number of interracial marriages, and debated the fairness of race-based grants and scholarships. No wonder most Americans believe that there *is* such a thing as race.

Race is a socially constructed concept that classifies people into separate value-based categories.[1] Unfortunately, many people see races as subdivisions of the human species based on significant genetic differences. Even in ancient times, the Egyptians, Greeks, and Romans left paintings, sculptures, and writings depicting people with perceived racial differences.[2] But ideas about race as we know it today did not exist until the eighteenth century, when a German scientist named Johann Friedrich Blumenbach classified humans based on geography and observed physical difference by using Caucasians as the ideal. The result was a racial ranking of Europeans first (white), Africans and Asians last, and Malays and Native Americans between them. These classifications led to the separation of people based on skin color: white (highest), yellow (middle), and black (lowest).

Modern anthropologists, biologists, geneticists, and ethicists, however, do not share these historical or popular beliefs about the nature of race. Despite countless studies searching for proof of biological differences among racial groups, scientists have come up empty-handed. Furthermore, geneticists have not turned up a single group of people that can be distinguished from outsiders by their chromosomes. The most sophisticated genetic tests cannot determine whether you are purely European, African, Asian, South/Central American, or from an indigenous people. In fact, 99.9 percent of DNA sequences are common to all humans.[3] Extensive research indicates that pure races have never existed and that all humans belong to the same species,[4] *Homo sapiens*, which had its origins in Africa. The characteristics on which we base our ideas of "race," such as skin color, are entirely superficial.

GENDER DIMENSIONS

In our discussion of cultural differences, the terms *masculine* and *feminine* describe whether masculine or feminine traits are valued by a culture. Hofstede uses the terms to describe a societal perspective, rather than male or female individuals. Here we take a look at individual gender differences. However, keep in mind that Hofstede ranks the United States as a more masculine-oriented culture—one in which men are assertive, tough, and focused on material success, whereas women are supposed to be more modest, tender, and concerned with the quality of life.

Numerous studies conclude that boys and girls grow up in what are essentially different cultures, making talk between men and women a cross-cultural experience. In *You Just Don't Understand*, Deborah Tannen makes a strong case for this two-world hypothesis. She concludes that men seek status and women

TOOLBOX 3.3 *(continued)*

A recent study at Pennsylvania State University helped dispel the notion of race. A group of students who thought of themselves as "100 percent" white or black or something else took complex genetic screening tests. It turned out that very few fell into any such category. Most learned that they shared genetic markers with people of other skin colors. One "white" student learned that 14 percent of his DNA was African—and 6 percent was East Asian.[5]

In 2006, Dr. Henry Louis Gates, Jr hosted a public television program which analyzed the DNA tests of famous African Americans such as Oprah Winfrey, Whoopi Goldberg, Quincy Jones, and surgeon Ben Carson. Professor Gates had believed that a white slave owner was his great-great-grandfather, but found no evidence to verify that claim. Oprah Winfrey had mistakenly believed she was descended from Zulu people. Almost all of the DNA tests conducted on the program's participants revealed evidence of Asian, European, or American Indian heredity.[6] In another case, an African American reporter for the

New York Times learned from a genetic screening test that half of his genetic material came from sub-Saharan Africa, one-quarter from Europe, and (which shocked him *and* his family) one-fifth from Asia![7]

Even though there is no genetically justified reason to classify people by race, we continue to do so. We do it because we were brought up doing it, because textbooks do it, because the media do it, and because people of different "races" continue to do it.

[1] Mark P. Orbe and Tina M. Harris, *Interracial Communication: Theory into Practice* (Belmont, CA: Wadsworth, 2001), p. 6.
[2] Marcel Danesi and Paul Perron, *Analyzing Cultures: An Introduction and Handbook* (Bloomington: Indiana University Press, 1999), p. 25.
[3] Danesi and Perron, p. 25.
[4] Orbe and Harris, p. 31.
[5] Editorial, "Debunking the Concept of Race," *New York Times*, July 30, 2005, p. A28.
[6] Virginia Heffernan, "Taking Black Family Trees Out of Slavery's Shadow," *New York Times*, February 1, 2006, available at http://www.nytimes.com/2006/02/01/arts/television/01heff.html
[7] Brent Staples, "Why Race Isn't as 'Black' and 'White' as We Think," *New York Times*, October 31, 2005, p. A20.

seek connection. Men seek independence; women prefer interdependence. In *Diverse Teams at Work*, Gardenswartz and Rowe summarize male and female differences as follows:

> Men use communication as a means of establishing a hierarchy of order and power in which they can solve problems. Women, on the other hand, interact to form relationships and share feelings and reactions. This difference can lead to subtle barriers in transmitting information and even subtler unconscious assumptions. She may be seen as wasting time; he may be seen as cold and insensitive. Her comments may be taken as nagging or an attempt to control; while the solutions he offers may be rejected as proof that "he didn't hear what I was saying."[45]

Given the potential clash of gender-based cultures in groups, all members should monitor and adapt to differences in the ways in which women and men interpret the world and express their opinions. Unfortunately, many women feel undervalued or even invisible in groups. William Sonnenschein, a diversity

TOOLBOX 3.4

Do Women Talk More than Men?

Many people believe that women talk too much. Yet, most women experience just the opposite, particularly when they're working in groups. Social scientists Rodney Napier and Matti Gershenfeld provide a brief history of this myth and a summary of research studies:

> Throughout history, women have been punished for talking too much or in the wrong way. In colonial America, there were a variety of physical punishments: women were strapped to dunking stools and held under water; they had to wear signs declaring their misconduct in public; they were gagged and silenced with a cleft stick applied to their tongues. . . . Yet study after study shows that it is men who talk more—at meetings, in mixed-group discussions held in classrooms where girls or young women sit next to boys or young men. . . . And not only did men speak for a longer time, but the women's longest turns were shorter than the men's shortest turns."[1]

[1] Rodney W. Napier and Matti K. Gershenfeld, *Groups: Theory and Experience*, 7th ed. (Boston: Houghton Mifflin, 2004), p. 29.

consultant and university professor, often hears working women complain that when they say something in a meeting, no one responds, yet a few minutes later a man makes the same suggestion and is praised for the quality of his input. Sonnenschein offers a list of common complaints voiced by men and women in work groups:

Women's Complaints:

- Men have low expectations of women.
- Women are misunderstood, underutilized, and unrecognized.
- Men do not accept a broad range of communication styles.
- Men focus too much on women's physical appearance.

Men's Complaints:

- Men do not see cross-gender communication as being as great a problem as women do.
- Men have to be cautious about what they say and do around women coworkers.
- Women want both to be provided for and to have equality.
- Women dress and act in ways that draw attention to their sexuality.[46]

Clearly, women and men share frustrations and confusion about how to act in mixed company. Such unresolved dialectic tensions between men and women can prevent a group from working collaboratively to achieve a common goal. So, are men really from Mars and women from Venus? Absolutely not! We're all from Earth—the planet positioned between Mars and Venus.

Group members should consider any differences between female and male members as differences in personality preferences—even though many men classify themselves as thinkers and many women see themselves as feelers. Here's some additional advice for adapting to both thinkers and feelers:

Thinkers (men):

- Don't use sarcasm or tell women they're illogical.

- Don't tell them they're too sensitive or too emotional.

- Listen to their concerns, but unless they ask for advice, don't try to solve their problems for them.

- Let women know that you appreciate their warmth, understanding, and compassion.

Feelers (women):

- Don't expect or force men to talk about or display their emotions.

- Ask men what they think, rather than what they feel.

- Express your disagreements without worrying about being unkind or starting an argument.

- Let men know that you appreciate their insightful analysis and their ability to remain calm and detached.[47]

We cannot end this section on gender differences without a few words on the risk of reaching erroneous or oversimplified conclusions about the characteristics of a group of people. Are all men thinkers and all women feelers? No. Do some women talk more than some men? Yes. Are some men more sympathetic, gentle-hearted, tactful, and emotional than some women? Yes. Unfortunately, assertive, thinking women may be viewed as unfeminine, while caring, feeling men are dismissed as effeminate "girly-men." Both labels are absurd and counterproductive to the work of good groups.

GENERATIONAL DIMENSIONS

Given the amazing advances in technology, improvements in health care, and significant increases in career opportunities for women and minority groups in the last half century, there are more pronounced differences between the generations today than there ever have been. Just think about the ways in which different generations use language differently. For example, to people from an older generation, the term *communication skills* means writing and speaking abilities, but it means email and instant messaging to a young college student.[48] Toolbox 3.5 describes the four major generational classifications.

The mixing of generations in families, communities, college classrooms, and work settings adds diversity *and* potential difficulties to the challenge of communicating in groups. Of all the generational mixes, the interaction of Baby Boomers and Generation Xers may be the most problematic. Several communication strategies can help Baby Boomers and Generation Xers interact more effectively.[49]

TOOLBOX 3.5

Generational Labels

Once upon a time, we classified people based on their age by putting them into one of two categories: the older generation and the younger generation. Today—probably because of marketing and advertising research—we are cataloged, graded, and pigeonholed based on our potential as buyers and voters. Labeling any group, however, allows members to identify with their contemporaries and to view other generations with some level of suspicion and even disapproval. After all, how can "they" be as good and as smart as "us"? Thus, we offer this unofficial list of generational descriptions with the understanding that these are only generalizations:[1]

- *Traditionalists or the Builder Generation, born 1900 to 1945.* Experiencing two world wars and the Great Depression taught this generation how to live within limited means. Traditionalists are loyal, hardworking, financially conservative, and faithful to institutions.
- *Baby Boomers or the Boomer Generation, born 1946 to 1964.* This is the generation that grew up with television and experienced the Vietnam War. Many of them bravely challenged the status quo and are responsible for many of the rights and opportunities that are now taken for granted. As a whole, this generation is politically adept when it comes to navigating political minefields in the workplace. Its

members often believe that they are always right, but are willing to work hard to get what they want. The term *workaholic* was coined to describe Baby Boomers.
- *Generation Xers or the X Generation, born 1965 to 1980.* Generation Xers are technologically savvy in the era of video games and personal computers. Because they witnessed skyrocketing divorce rates, employment layoffs, and challenges to the presidency, organized religion, and big corporations, they are often skeptical and distrustful of institutions. Generation Xers believe that work isn't the most important thing in their lives.
- *Millennials, the Net Generation, Generation Yers, or Nexters, born 1981 to 1999.* Many Millennials are still in school or just graduating from college. These are kids who've grown up with cell phones, pagers, and personal computers. Generally, they're confident and have high self-esteem. They're collaborators and favor teamwork, having functioned in groups in school, organized sports, and extracurricular activities from a very young age. They like keeping their career options open.

[1] Mayo Clinic, "Workplace Generation Gap: Understand Differences Among Colleagues," Special to CNN.com, *http://www.cnn.com/HEALTH/library/WL/00045.html*, July 6, 2005.

If you belong to Generation X, you should

- Show respect to Baby Boomers and acknowledge that you have less experience than the Baby Boomers and can learn from them.

- Communicate face to face rather than relying totally on email. Many Baby Boomers prefer speaking with someone face to face.

- Learn to play the political game. Baby Boomers are often diplomatic and can help Generation Xers navigate politically charged environments.

- Learn the corporate history and culture. Nothing bothers Baby Boomers more than a new employee who wants to change things, with seemingly no thought given to what's gone on before.

As a Baby Boomer, you should

- Get to the point. State your objectives clearly when communicating with Generation Xers.

- Avoid micromanaging Generation Xers who need autonomy.

- Get over the notion of dues paying. Although Baby Boomers may have worked 60 hours a week to get ahead, don't expect members of younger generations to do the same. Generation Xers—who value a healthy work-life balance—rarely spend that many hours at work, and they're getting ahead anyway.

- Lighten up. Remind yourself that it's OK for work to be fun. Generation Xers tend to think that Baby Boomers are too intense and set in their ways.

In general, the need to feel part of a group or team is a common value among Baby Boomers, but is less important to Generation Xers and Millennials. Whereas many Baby Boomers see group work as being more like football, in which all members act in concert and according to a plan, the younger generations see group work as more like a relay race: "I'll give it all I've got—when and where I'm supposed to."[50]

Not surprisingly, the American Association of Retired People points to research studies showing that older adults are better at solving problems, more flexible in their strategies, and better able to keep their cool during a crisis than are younger people. They also tend to bounce back from a bad mood more quickly. As one neurobiologist notes, in the old days, you called it wisdom.[51] Of course, in the not too distant future, young people will be older (and hopefully just as wise), and researchers will probably make the same claims about them.

 BALANCED DIVERSITY

As an effective group member, you must perform a difficult balancing act. You must balance your own needs and interests with those of the group. You must analyze your own personality traits as well as those of others to determine the different ways in which members understand and make decisions about the world around them. And certainly you must understand, respect, and adapt to the cultural, gender, and generational differences that shape every group.

William Sonnenschein writes that "we can be equal and still acknowledge our differences. . . . Embracing differences does not mean that all differences are acceptable. . . Yet, we need to discover those differences, acknowledge their

ETHICAL GROUPS

 ## Does the Golden Rule Apply to Groups?

The well-known Golden Rule—"Do unto others as you would have them do unto you"—may not work in groups with diverse members. Intercultural communication scholars Judith Martin and Thomas Nakayama note that "ethical principles are often culture-bound, and intercultural conflicts arise from varying notions of what constitutes ethical behavior."[1] For example, someone from an individualistic culture may see self-serving ambition as appropriate and ethical behavior—after all, that's how you get ahead. In collectivist cultures, however, the same behavior may be viewed as unethical, because the individual is not putting group interests ahead of personal interests.

Ethical group members should learn about cultural differences—the differences between their own culture and those of others. Martin and Nakayama recommend three strategies:[2]

1. *Practice self-reflection.* When you learn about other cultures, you also learn more about your own intercultural beliefs—and your prejudices. For example, you may believe that arranged marriage is unethical because it denies individuals the right to choose a spouse that they love. If, however, you meet someone who is in a successful arranged marriage, you may discover that there are some advantages, including a much lower divorce rate compared with traditional romantic marriages.

2. *Interact with others.* Ethical group members learn about others by interacting with them and talking about differences. Although you can read about differences in white and black perspectives or western European and Asian values, talking about such differences can help you understand group members as individuals rather than as stereotypical representatives of a different culture.

3. *Listen to others' voices.* Listening to the experiences of others has the power to transform your understanding of cultures and realize how their voices may be stifled. When, for example, Catholic priests from Spain established missions in what is now Texas, they imposed conditions on native people who sought the food, water, shelter, protection, and medical care offered in those missions. Native people had to give up their language and learn Spanish, change many of their customs and dress, and convert to Catholicism. Whether you believe the Catholic priests were ethical or unethical depends, in large part, on how you view the value of diversity and the sanctity of diverse cultures. Ethical group members should listen carefully to different voices as a way of integrating the contributions and perspectives of all members into the group process.

[1] Judith N. Martin and Thomas K. Nakayama, *Experiencing Intercultural Communication*, 2nd ed. (New York: McGraw-Hill, 2005), p. 18.
[2] Martin and Nakayama, pp. 20–22.

existence, and learn how to best utilize whichever ones we can to create a good team."[52] As we note in Chapter 2, some behaviors and values are detrimental to a group and must be resolved. At the same time, we must understand, respect, and adapt to differences that can make a group more effective. Groups that learn how to balance and benefit from the diversity within the group have the power to create a collaborative climate. This kind of climate is the essence of group excellence and teamwork.[53]

GROUPWORK

Personality Preferences

Directions. Read the two sets of descriptions for each personality type. For each pair of personality preferences, put a check mark next to the phrases that *best* describe you. Note the personality type with the most check marks—extrovert or introvert; sensing or intuitive; thinking or feeing; judging or perceiving. Answer as you really are, not as you wish you were or wish you could be in the future.

1. Are you an extrovert or an introvert?

Extrovert	Introvert
_____ I am outgoing, sociable, expressive	_____ I am reserved, private, contained
_____ I enjoy groups and discussions	_____ I prefer one-to-one interactions
_____ I talk first, think later	_____ I think first, then talk
_____ I can do many things at once	_____ I focus on one thing at a time
_____ I think out loud	_____ I think to myself
_____ Other people give me energy	_____ Other people often exhaust me
_____ Total	_____ Total

2. Are you a sensor or an intuitive?

Sensor	Intuitive
_____ I focus on details	_____ I focus on the big picture
_____ I am practical and realistic	_____ I am theoretical
_____ I like concrete information	_____ I like abstract information
_____ I like facts	_____ I get bored with facts and details
_____ I trust experience	_____ I trust inspiration and intuition

Sensor	Intuitive
_____ I value common sense	_____ I value creativity and innovation
_____ I want clear, realistic goals	_____ I want to pursue a vision
_____ **Total**	_____ **Total**

3. Are you a thinker or a feeler?

Thinker	Feeler
_____ I am task-oriented	_____ I am people-oriented
_____ I am objective, firm, analytical	_____ I am subjective, humane, appreciative
_____ I enjoy arguing	_____ I think arguing is disruptive
_____ I prefer businesslike meetings	_____ I prefer social interchange in meetings
_____ I value competence, reason, justice	_____ I value relationships and harmony
_____ I am direct and firm-minded	_____ I am tactful and tenderhearted
_____ I think with my head	_____ I think with my heart
_____ **Total**	_____ **Total**

4. Are you a judger or a perceiver?

Judger	Perceiver
_____ I value organization and structure	_____ I value flexibility and spontaneity
_____ I am in control and definite	_____ I go with the flow
_____ I like having deadlines	_____ I dislike deadlines
_____ I will work now, play later	_____ I will play now, work later
_____ I like standards and expectations	_____ I feel constrained by rules
_____ I adjust my schedule to complete work	_____ I do work at the last minute
_____ I plan ahead	_____ I adapt as I go
_____ **Total**	_____ **Total**

Summarize your decisions by indicating the letter that best describes your personality traits and preferences:

_____	_____	_____	_____
E or I	S or N	T or F	J or P

Considering the type of group member you are *based on your four-letter personality type*, answer the following questions:

1. Name two of your most effective personality traits as a group member. (Example: I am tactful and considerate of other group members.)

   • _____

   • _____

2. Name two ways in which group members see you as a group member. (Example: Other group members see me as objective and fair.)

   • _____

   • _____

3. Name two ways in which you can improve your effectiveness as a group member in light of your personality traits and preferences. (Example: I need to put more focus on the group's task rather than using so much time socializing with members.)

   • _____

   • _____

   Note: The Myers-Briggs Type Indicator® is for licensed use only by qualified professionals whose qualifications are on file and have been accepted by Consulting Psychologists Press, Inc. The exercise is only a quick self-test and is not a licensed instrument.

GroupAssessment

Identifying Cultural Dialectics

Directions. Your textbook identifies six dialectical dimensions that explain many cultural differences. The 20 statements listed here represent a group member's attitude or behavior. Match each statement with the appropriate cultural dimension or dimensions. Use the blank space before each statement and place the appropriate letter (A through F) in that space to indicate which dimension best explains the cultural perspective of the member. In some cases, more than one answer may be appropriate.

Cultural Dimensions

A. Individualism–Collectivism

B. High Power–Low Power Distance

C. Uncertainty Avoidance–Uncertainty Acceptance

D. Masculine–Feminine

E.   High Context–Low Context

F.   Polychronic–Monochronic

Statements

_____ 1. When a member of my group wins a prize, I feel proud.

_____ 2. I function best in a group when I can organize my responsibilities and put them on a schedule.

_____ 3. I prefer a leader who makes decisions promptly, communicates them to the group, and expects us to carry out the task.

_____ 4. I rely on a member's nonverbal behavior to tell me what he or she is really thinking.

_____ 5. I am good at figuring out what other members think about me and my ideas.

_____ 6. Groups don't function effectively if members are emotional and sensitive.

_____ 7. I am confident in my ability to predict how other group members will behave.

_____ 8. I enjoy "doing my own thing" in a group.

_____ 9. I prefer working in groups in which members are appreciative, curious, forgiving, kind, and understanding.

_____ 10. I become frustrated when someone in a meeting brings up a personal topic that is unrelated to the purpose of the meeting.

_____ 11. Group norms should be followed—even when I disagree with them.

_____ 12. Groups don't function effectively when members are aggressive, hardheaded, and opinionated.

_____ 13. My satisfaction in a group depends very much on the feelings of other members.

_____ 14. I don't like to focus my attention on only one thing at a time because I may be missing something important or interesting.

_____ 15. I prefer a leader who calls a meeting when an important issue comes up, gives us the problem to discuss, and seeks a group decision.

_____ 16. I can sit with another group member, not say anything, and still be comfortable.

_____ 17. I find silence awkward in conversations and group discussions.

_____ 18. I like to be clear and accurate when I speak to other group members.

_____ 19. I like doing several tasks at one time.

_____ 20. I like working in groups where I can compete with other members.

NOTES

1. *The American Heritage Dictionary of the English Language,* 4th ed. (Boston: Houghton Mifflin, 2000), p. 527.
2. William Sonnenschein, *The Diversity Toolkit* (Chicago: Contemporary Books, 1997), p. 101.
3 James Surowiecki, *The Wisdom of Crowds: Why the Many Are Smarter than the Few and How Collective Wisdom Shapes Business, Economics, Societies, and Nations* (New York: Doubleday, 2004), p. 29.
4. Quoted in Surowiecki, p. 31.
5. Lee Gardenswartz and Anita Rowe, *Diverse Teams at Work: Capitalizing on the Power of Diversity* (New York: McGraw-Hill, 1997), p. 18.
6. Diversity layers based on Gardenswartz and Rowe, pp. 31–80; Marilyn Loden and Judy R. Rosener, *Workforce America!* (New York: McGraw-Hill, 1990).
7. Gardenswartz and Rowe, pp. 34–35.
8. Hundreds of books and articles have been written about the Myers-Briggs Type Indicator®. The material in this chapter is based on Isa N. Engleberg's background and experience as a certified Myers-Briggs Type Indicator® trainer and a synthesis of materials from several MBTI resources: Isabel Briggs Myers (Revised by Linda K. Kirby and Katharine D. Myers), *Introduction to Type*, 7th ed. (Palo Alto, CA: Consulting Psychologists, 1998); Isabel Briggs Myers with Peter B. Myers, *Gifts Differing: Tenth Anniversary Edition* (Palo Alto, CA: Consulting Psychologists, 1990); Otto Kroeger and Janet M. Thuesen, *Type Talk* (New York: Delacorte, 1988); Otto Kroeger and Janet M. Thuesen, *Type Talk at Work: How the 16 Personality Types Determine Your Success on the Job* (New York: Delta/Tilden Press, 1992); David Keirsey, *Please Understand Me II* (Del Mar, CA: Prometheus Nemesis, 1998); S. K. Hirsh, *Introduction to Type and Teams* (Palo Alto, CA: Consulting Psychologists, 1992); Larry Demarest, *Looking at Type in the Workplace* (Gainesville, FL: Center for Applications of Psychological Type, 1997).
9. Note: The Myers-Briggs Type Indicator® is for licensed use only by qualified professionals whose qualifications are on file and have been accepted by Consulting Psychologists Press, Inc.
10. Myers with Myers, p. 1.
11. The Myers-Briggs Type Indicator® (MBTI) uses the word *extravert*—with an *a* in the middle of the word—to describe this personality preference rather than *extrovert*, the more common spelling. Dictionaries and psychology textbooks use *extrovert* as the preferred spelling but often note the alliterative similarities between *introvert* and *extrovert*. *Working in Groups* uses the term *extrovert*, but here acknowledges the MBTI preference for *extravert*.
12. Robert E. Levasseur, *Breakthrough Business Meetings: Shared Leadership in Action.* (Holbrook, MA: Bob Adams, 1994), p. 79.
13. J. M. Jaffe, "Of Different Minds," *Association Management*, 37 (1985), pp. 120–124.
14. Renee Baron, *What Type Am I?* (New York: Penguin, 1998), pp. 20–21.
15. Carl E. Larson and Frank M. J. LaFasto, *TeamWork: What Must Go Right/What Can Go Wrong* (Newbury Park, CA: Sage, 1989), p. 63.
16. Baron, pp. 29–30.
17. Kroeger and Thuesen, *Type Talk*, p. 80.
18. Kroeger and Thuesen, *Type Talk*, p. 114.
19. Myron W. Lustig and Jolene Koester, *Intercultural Competence: Interpersonal Communication Across Cultures*, 5th ed. (New York: Longman, 2006), p. 25.
20. Intercultural authors use a variety of terms (*co-cultures*, *microcultures*) to describe the cultural groups that coexist within a larger culture. Using either of these terms is preferable to using the older, somewhat derogatory term *subcultures*. The combined co-cultures living in the United States will, by mid-century, make up the majority population.
21. The statistics in this section come from two sources: *Encyclopedia Britannica Almanac 2004* (Chicago: Britannica Almanac, 2003), pp. 770–775; U.S. Census Bureau, Census 2000, *http://www.census.gov/population*.
22. U.S. Census Bureau, *http://www.census.gov/population*.
23. Geert Hofstede, *Cultures and Organizations: Software of the Mind* (New York: McGraw-Hill, 1997), p. 14. Also see Geert Hofstede, *Culture's Consequences*, 2nd ed. (Thousand Oaks, CA: Sage, 2001), p. 29. Hofstede identifies a fifth dimension: long-term versus short-term orientation, which relates to the choice of focus for people's efforts—either the future or the present. Cultures in Asia rank at the top of the list on long-term orientation, whereas those with a shorter-term orientation include English-speaking countries as well as Zimbabwe, Philippines, Nigeria, and Pakistan. We have not included this fifth dimension in the textbook because fewer cultures have been thoroughly studied on this dimension.
24. See Edward T. Hall, *The Silent Language* (Greenwich, CT: Fawcett, 1959); Edward T. Hall, *Beyond Culture*

(New York: Anchor, 1976); Edward T. Hall, *The Dance of Life: The Other Dimension of Time* (New York: Doubleday, 1983); Edward T. Hall and M. R. Hall, *Understanding Cultural Differences: Germans, French and Americans* (Yarmouth, ME: Intercultural Press, 1990).

25. Harry C. Triandis, *Individualism and Collectivism* (Boulder, CO: Westview, 1995).

26. Harry C. Triandis, "The Self and Social Behavior in Different Cultural Contexts," *Psychological Review*, 96 (1994), pp. 506–520. Also see Triandis, *Individualism and Collectivism.*

27. Harry C. Triandis, "The Cross-Cultural Studies of Individualism and Collectivism," in *Cross-Cultural Perspectives,* ed. J. J. Berman (Lincoln, University of Nebraska Press, 1990), p. 52.

28. Geert Hofstede, "The Cultural Relativity of the Quality of Life Concept," in *Cultural Communication and Conflict: Readings in Intercultural Relations*, 2nd ed., ed. G. R. Weaver (Boston: Pearson, 2000), p. 139.

29. Hofstede, *Culture's Consequences,* quoted in Larry A. Samovar and Richard Porter, *Communication Between Cultures*, 5th ed (Belmont, CA: Wadsworth, 2004), p. 65.

30. Hofstede, *Cultures and Organizations,* p. 113.

31. Hofstede, *Cultures and Organizations.*

32. Hofstede, *Cultures and Organizations,* p. 119.

33. Hofstede, *Cultures and Organizations,* p. 118.

34. Hofstede, *Cultures and Organizations,* p. 84.

35. Hofstede, *Cultures and Organizations.*

36. Hall and Hall, p. 6.

37. Dean Allen Foster, *Bargaining Across Borders* (New York: McGraw-Hill, 1992), p. 280.

38. Myron W. Lustig and Jolene Koester, *Intercultural Competence: Interpersonal Communication across Cultures*, 4th ed. (New York: Longman, 2003), p. 101.

39. Edward T. Hall, *The Dance of Life,* p. 42.

40. James W. Neuliep, *Intercultural Communication: A Contextual Approach*, 2nd ed. (Boston: Houghton Mifflin, 2003), pp. 132–133.

41. Lustig and Koester, *Intercultural Competence,* 5th ed., p. 226.

42. Edward T. Hall, "Monochronic and Polychronic Time," in *Intercultural Communication: A Reader*, 10th ed., ed. Larry A. Samovar and Richard E. Porter (Belmont, CA: Wadsworth, 2002), p. 263.

43. Lustig and Koester, *Intercultural Competence,* 5th ed., p. 151.

44. Lustig and Koester, *Intercultural Competence,* 4th ed., p. 153.

45. Gardenswartz and Rowe, pp. 39–40.

46. Sonnenschein, pp. 19–20.

47. Baron, p. 28.

48. Dennis Kersten, "Today's Generations Face New Communication Gaps," *www.usatoday.com/money/jobcenter/workplace/communication/2002-11-15-communication-gap_x.htm*, posted 11/15/2002, 10:03 a.m.

49. Mayo Clinic, "Workplace Generation Gap: Understand Differences among Colleagues," special to CNN.com, *http://www.cnn.com/HEALTH/library/WL/00045.html*, July 6, 2005.

50. David Stauffer, "Motivating Across Generations," in Harvard Business School Press, *Teams That Click* (Boston: Harvard Business School, 2004), p. 119.

51. Kelly Griffin, "You're Wiser Now," September/October 2005, p. 77.

52. Sonnenschein, p. 100.

53. Larson and LaFasto, p. 94.

Interaction Skills

© Bob Daemmrich/Photo Edit

CHAPTER 4

Confidence in Groups

CHAPTER OUTLINE

GROUP AND MEMBER CONFIDENCE

Regardless of what you know, think, experience, or need, your level of confidence has a direct effect on both the amount of talking you do in a group and the usefulness of that talk. Members who lack confidence are less likely to share what they know or voice their opinions. Confidence is often the major factor that separates effective group members from those who have difficulty fulfilling their responsibilities. If you feel good about yourself, you can enter a group discussion with confidence and confront controversial issues with competence and conviction.

Most of us see ourselves as bright and hard-working team players. At the same time, all of us have occasional doubts. We know people who seem smarter or more interesting than we are. We've seen natural leaders take over groups with assurance. Given that becoming a leader often depends on talking early and often as well as on expressing an opinion in the face of disagreement, members who are sure of themselves are more likely to emerge as leaders.[1]

Confident groups are more likely to succeed. They cope with unexpected events, problematic people, and challenging assignments effectively because their members have a positive, "can do" attitude. Fostering group and member confidence is much more than the power of positive thinking—it helps groups commit to ambitious goals and believe in their ability to succeed.[2] In this chapter, we look at the ways in which communication apprehension and assertiveness affect member and group confidence.

COMMUNICATION APPREHENSION

The anxiety that we sometimes experience when speaking to others is referred to by many names: stage fright, speech anxiety, and communication apprehension. James C. McCroskey and his colleagues have investigated the anxieties that people feel when they are asked to speak to others in a variety of contexts. The result of this study is a large body of research that has important implications for working in groups.

James McCroskey defines **communication apprehension** as "an individual's level of fear or anxiety associated with either real or anticipated communication with another person or persons."[3] About 20 percent of the general population experiences very high levels of communication apprehension. About 75 to 85 percent of the U.S. population experiences apprehension when faced with the prospect of making a presentation.[4] For several decades, researchers noted that when asked about "common" anxieties such as fear of snakes, death, and heights, Americans report that they are more afraid of public speaking than of anything else.[5] More recently, a Gallup Poll found that fear of public speaking is now second to fear of snakes.[6] However, communication apprehension includes more

How does this photograph reveal the speaker's confidence and control? (© Kathy McLaughlin/The Image Works)

than public speaking anxiety; it also encompasses fear of speaking in conversations, meetings, or group settings.

There are different levels of communication apprehension, depending on several factors, such as the personality of the speaker, the nature of the audience, and the characteristics of the occasion or setting. In other words, a person may have no fears when talking to a friend or colleagues, but may experience high levels of anxiety when asked to address a group of strangers in a large auditorium. Talking at a weekly staff meeting may be easy, but defending a department's actions at a meeting of company executives may generate high levels of anxiety.

Sources of Anxiety

There are many sources of communication apprehension. Heredity, biology, family background, stressful life events, and personal beliefs are just a few of the factors that may contribute to an individual's level of anxiety.[7] For instance, research indicates that in certain families, communication patterns are associated with the development of communication apprehension.[8] Children from families in which communication is met with criticism, rejection, or simply a lack of supportiveness are more likely to become apprehensive communicators. "Parents in such families are less open about their emotions and less likely to encourage their children to express their own feelings."[9] On the other hand, if our families encourage conversation and the expression of ideas, we may experience lower levels of communication apprehension.

Communication apprehension is associated with certain personality traits. In Chapter 3, "Group Member Diversity," we examine the differences between extroverts and introverts. Extroverts tend to be more outgoing and talkative group members, whereas introverts often prefer to work alone rather than in groups. Not surprisingly, many introverts experience higher levels of communication apprehension than extroverts do. As we note in Chapter 3, some introverts find it difficult to be articulate during a group discussion and experience what Dr. Marti Laney refers to as brainlock.[10] During group conflict or a lively discussion, an apprehensive introvert may become overstimulated and struggle to find the right words to express an idea or opinion. It is important to keep in mind, however, that not all introverts experience high levels of communication apprehension, and not all extroverts are confident group members.

Negative past experiences in groups or unfamiliar situations may also produce communication apprehension. Some members experience **grouphate**—an intense aversion to working in groups—which is often the result of poor group communication skills.[11] An individual who lacks the skills to function as a competent and effective group member may dread group meetings and discussions. Grouphate also results from negative past experiences. Unfortunately, you may have been part of groups that were unproductive, wasted time, managed conflict poorly, or had members that derailed the group's efforts. These poor group experiences create negative attitudes and beliefs about the value of working in groups. Fortunately, learning effective group communication skills can improve your group experiences and minimize feelings of anxiety and grouphate.

Communication apprehension often occurs when we work in unfamiliar circumstances or with unfamiliar people. For example, some level of apprehension is natural when you are joining an already established group and you are unfamiliar with the group's norms, members' roles, or status differences within the group. Communication apprehension may also increase when you are working with group members from different cultures. The less you are aware of and understand other members' cultures, the more communication apprehension you may experience while working in groups.[12] Becoming more aware of other members' cultures can increase your confidence when working with diverse group members.

The causes and sources of anxiety are complex. Rarely will a single negative experience result in significant levels of communication apprehension. However, a number of negative experiences can perpetuate communication apprehension and result in physical tension, irrational beliefs about yourself and others, negative self-talk, and avoidance of fearful situations.[13] This chapter provides several strategies that can help you manage communication apprehension, regardless of its source.

Apprehension in Groups

James McCroskey and Virginia Richmond write that "it is not an exaggeration to suggest that CA [Communication Apprehension] may be the single most important factor in predicting communication behavior in a small group."[14] Consequently, it is not surprising that highly apprehensive people may avoid small group communication or sit quietly in a group if they must be present.[15] Interestingly, both low and high apprehensives seem to have an innate ability to figure out where to sit in a small-group setting in order to either facilitate or avoid communication. For example, highly apprehensive group members with a low willingness to communicate often choose seats that inhibit communication and denote low status and power.[16] Figure 4.1 lists some of the basic characteristics of high and low apprehensives in groups. And, as you will read in the following section, communication apprehension has significant effects on the amount of talk, the content of communication, and the resulting perceptions of other group members.

Quantity of Talk.   If you are fearful about doing something, you probably will avoid that experience. In groups, anxious members are less likely to talk than confident members. Very often, highly apprehensive members will talk only when called upon. When they must speak, they say less or answer questions by agreeing rather than by voicing their concerns and opinions. Moreover, members who speak infrequently tend to perceive the group and its processes negatively.[17]

Quality of Talk.   If you are fearful about communicating, a lot of your attention and energy will be focused on how you feel rather than on what you say. When highly apprehensive participants are required to talk, their speech is often awkward. Sentences may be loaded with filler phrases such as "you know," "well, uh," "like," and "okay." The tone of voice may communicate distress or may be mistaken for disinterest.

Equally significant, apprehensive group members may talk about things that have little to do with the topic being discussed. They are so focused on their internal feelings that they may be unaware of the direction or focus of the discussion. There is also a tendency for apprehensive speakers to avoid disagreement or

FIGURE 4.1   **Effects of Communication Apprehension in Groups**

High Apprehensives May...	Low Apprehensives May...
• avoid group participation. • talk less often. • simply agree with others. • smile or giggle inappropriately. • fidget. • use awkward phrases and fillers, e.g. "well, uh." • have difficulty focusing on the discussion.	• initiate the discussion. • speak more often. • assert themselves. • become group leaders. • strategically choose when to remain silent. • appear more competent. • dominate a discussion or talk compulsively.

TOOLBOX 4.1

Don't Be a Compulsive Talker

Group members who talk too much can be just as much of a problem as members who don't speak up during a discussion. Compulsive talkers tend to dominate a discussion, speak more frequently than others, feel less inhibited, and experience lower levels of communication apprehension.[1] Compulsive talkers focus on expressing their own ideas and fail to listen to what others have to say. Unfortunately, compulsive talkers are often unaware that their behavior is a problem. If you answer *yes* to several of the following questions, you may be a compulsive talker.[2] Do you . . .

* Speak significantly more than other group members?
* Direct the course of a group's discussion?
* Immediately take charge of a group?
* Forcefully express opinions on even minor issues?
* Speak for long periods of time without pausing?

A compulsive talker can frustrate group members who never get a chance to express or respond to ideas during a discussion. One way to rein in a compulsive talker is to set ground rules or time limits for discussion. For example, "In order for us all to have a say, let's limit our comments on this issue to two minutes each." In other instances, it may simply be necessary to interrupt: "Sean, I appreciate your comments, but I would like to hear what others have to say on the matter."

[1] Robert N. Bostrom and Nancy Grant Harrington, "An Exploratory Investigation of Characteristics of Compulsive Talkers," *Communication Education,* 48 (1999), pp. 73–80.
[2] Bostrom and Harrington, p. 76.

conflict. They may go along with the majority, whether they agree or not. Expressing disagreement is too risky. Someone might challenge their position or, even worse, ask them to explain or justify their disagreement. For a highly apprehensive group member, it's much easier to become a silent member of the majority.

Perception of Others. As a result of talking less, apprehensive group members are viewed as less confident, less assertive, and even less responsible. Furthermore, members who speak more are often better liked than those who speak infrequently.[18] Given that leadership is often granted to members who talk early and often, rarely will a reluctant communicator be seen as a potential leader.

As real as communication apprehension is, it is not an insurmountable obstacle. Highly apprehensive speakers do not wear signs declaring their lack of confidence. Neither are they less intelligent, less hard working, or less competent than their more confident colleagues.

Whether your score on the Personal Report of Communication Apprehension (PRCA) at the end of this chapter is high or low, there are ways to improve your level of communication confidence. As you consider your scores on the PRCA, keep in mind that it is impossible to predict what is going to happen in a group solely on the basis of members' communication apprehension scores. Even though someone is anxious, she or he may still speak or express an opinion. On the other hand, the fact that someone is a confident speaker doesn't necessarily mean that this person is the group's natural leader. Stereotyping group members on the basis of their feelings about communicating will not help your group become more productive.

STRATEGIES FOR HIGH APPREHENSIVES

If your PRCA score classifies you as an apprehensive speaker or if you believe that your level of anxiety associated with talking in groups is unusually high, the following four strategies (see Figure 4.2) may help you reduce your level of fear:

- Realize that you are not alone.
- Be well prepared.
- Learn communication skills.
- Re-lax; re-think; re-vision.

You Are Not Alone

Everyone has experienced communication apprehension in certain settings. According to Richmond and McCroskey, "almost 95 percent of the population reports being scared about communicating with a person or group at some point in their lives."[19] If you dread the thought of communicating in a group or public setting, you are one of millions of people who feel the same way. Such feelings are normal. As you listen to other group members, don't assume that it is easy for them to talk. Several of them are probably experiencing the same level of fear and anxiety that you are.

TOOLBOX 4.2

Complete the PRCA

At the end of this chapter, there is a self-test called the Personal Report of Communication Apprehension, or PRCA. You might want to complete this questionnaire and follow the scoring instructions before reading the rest of this section. Your PRCA scores, particularly those related to groups and meetings, will help you understand how communication apprehension can affect your participation in group discussions.

According to James C. McCroskey, the principal researcher and creator of the Personal

Report of Communication Apprehension instrument, the PRCA is the best available measure of traitlike communication apprehension; that is, it measures relatively enduring, personality-type orientations toward a given mode of communication across a wide variety of contexts.[1] In other words, your PRCA score is a relatively permanent trait that is unlikely to change unless there is some type of effective intervention or training.

[1] Virginia P. Richmond and James C. McCroskey, *Communication: Apprehension, Avoidance, and Effectiveness*, 4th ed. (Scottsdale, AZ: Gorsuch, Scarisbrick, 1995), p. 43.

FIGURE 4.2   **Coping with Communication Apprehension**

Coping with Communication Apprehension

High Apprehensives
- You Are Not Alone
- Be Well Prepared
- Learn Communication Skills
- Re-lax, Re-think, Re-vision

Low Apprehensives
- Be Supportive
- Provide Constructive Feedback
- Include Anxious Members
- Stop Talking

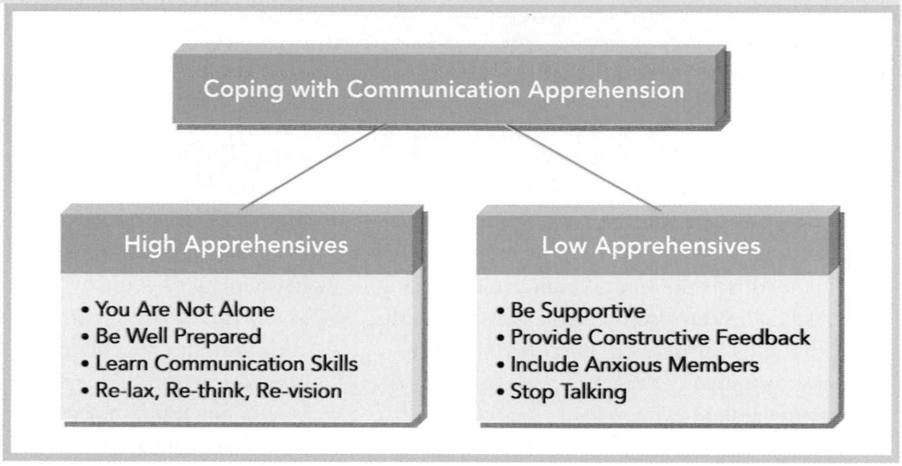

Be Well Prepared

Although you cannot totally eliminate communication apprehension, you can and should be well prepared for every group discussion. Being prepared can reduce your anxiety about participating. Many successful group members who also experience high levels of communication apprehension spend extra time making sure that they have prepared themselves for the topics scheduled for discussion. Well-prepared members know more about the topic and have a clear idea of the positions that they support. As a result, they are more confident when they are asked to participate. Being well prepared will not completely eliminate anxiety, but it can reduce a member's fear that he or she will be at a loss for relevant ideas and information when asked to contribute to the group discussion.

Learn Communication Skills

If you were trying to improve your tennis game, you would try to improve specific skills—perhaps your serve, your return, or your backhand shot. The same is true about communicating in groups. There are specific and learnable communication skills that can help you improve your ability to participate in groups. These skills are described throughout this textbook. Learning skills related to becoming sensitive to feedback, following a group's agenda, or serving as an effective group leader and participant can give you the tools you need to succeed in a group discussion. Improving your communication skills will not erase communication apprehension, but it can reduce your level of anxiety. So instead of telling yourself, "I can't participate; I'm not a skilled communicator," try telling yourself, "I'm learning."[20]

TOOLBOX 4.3

Confide in a Friend[1]

It's easy to believe that your anxiety is worse than anyone else's until you begin talking about it. When you discuss your fears with others, you may discover that you are not alone. Even the most confident-looking group members can have moments of self-doubt and even panic. Sharing your anxieties can also help you substitute positive thoughts for negative ones. If you tell another group member that you feel frustrated at not being able to express your ideas clearly, that person may assure you that he or she understood exactly what you meant.

Discussing your fears with another trusted group member can help correct misperceptions you may have about your own interaction in a group. If you tell a friend or your instructor that you stumble over words or that your voice shakes during a heated discussion, you may discover that that person has never noticed it. What seems inarticulate to you may be perceived by others as a natural pause. Furthermore, once you share your anxieties, a good group member can help ease your tension, be more supportive, and provide opportunities for you to participate in the group's meetings or discussions.

[1] Based on material previously published in Isa Engleberg and John Daly, *Presentations in Everyday Life: Strategies for Effective Speaking* (Boston: Houghton Mifflin, 2005), pp. 70–71.

Re-lax, Re-think, and Re-vision

Of all the methods for reducing communication apprehension, most communication researchers believe that combining physical relaxation with a positive mental attitude is the most effective strategy. The techniques for achieving these dual goals have a variety of names, such as *cognitive restructuring, visualization,* and *systematic desensitization.*[21]

Physical Relaxation.   One reason we experience communication apprehension is that our bodies feel tense. Our hearts beat faster, our hands shake, and we're short of breath. This response is a natural one and may reflect excitement and eagerness as much as anxiety and fear. By learning to relax your body, you may also reduce your level of communication apprehension. For example, break the word *relax* into two syllables: *re* and *lax.* Inhale slowly through your nose while saying the sound *re* ("ree") silently to yourself. Then breathe out slowly while thinking of the sound *lax* ("laks"). Inhale and exhale three or four times while thinking, "Reee-laaax." By the time you finish, your pulse should be slower, and, hopefully, you will also feel calmer.[22] Applying relaxation and meditation techniques can be the first step in reducing communication apprehension.

Cognitive Restructuring.   You may be able to reduce apprehension by changing the way you *think* about communicating. Rather than thinking, "They won't listen to me," try thinking, "Because I'm so well prepared, I'll make a valuable contribution." **Cognitive restructuring** assumes that communication anxiety is caused by worrisome, irrational, and nonproductive thoughts about speaking to and with others (cognitions) that need modifying (restructuring).[23] Researchers who study emotions contend that thinking happy or sad thoughts can make you *feel* happy or sad.[24] So think confident thoughts and feel confident! Next time you feel anxious, try telling yourself these positive statements: "My ideas are important." "I am well prepared." "Nervousness just gives me extra energy."[25]

Visualization.   Closely related to cognitive restructuring is **visualization,** a technique that encourages you to think positively about communicating in groups. Many professional athletes use visualization to improve their performance. They are told to find a quiet place where they can relax and visualize themselves competing and winning.[26] You can do the same thing. Take time—*before* you meet with your group—to visualize yourself communicating effectively. Mentally practice the skills you need in order to succeed while also building a positive image of your effectiveness. When you can visualize or imagine yourself succeeding in a group and you can maintain a relaxed state at the same time, you will have broken your fearful response to communicating in groups.

Systematic Desensitization.   The technique called **systematic desensitization** recognizes that we often associate fear with certain things or situations, such as snakes, heights, and speaking in groups. One way to break this fearful reaction is to learn a new, relaxed response to the same situation. You begin by learning to achieve deep muscle relaxation. In this relaxed state, you imagine yourself in a variety of communication situations, beginning with those that are very comfortable for you and going on to those that produce more anxiety. The more anxiety-producing the situation, the higher you are on what is called a desensitization hierarchy.

Toolbox 4.4 presents a hierarchy of anxiety-producing situations. As you practice physical relaxation techniques, visualize yourself behaving confidently and competently in each group situation. The more vividly you are able to imagine yourself as a confident group member, the more your communication apprehension will decrease.[27]

Everyone experiences communication apprehension differently. Some group members may have frightening mental images of communication. Others may be nervous because they lack effective communication skills. Even members who have a positive attitude and effective communication skills may nonetheless experience the physical symptoms of anxiety. Thus, it makes sense to choose a coping strategy based on the way in which you experience communication apprehension. For instance, focus on visualization techniques if negative mental images interfere with your confidence. Figure 4.3 matches coping strategies to six dimensions of apprehension.

TOOLBOX 4.4

Practice Systematic Desensitization

Relax your body and think about the first situation in the following list. In all likelihood, you won't experience the symptoms of nervousness. Even anxious group members generally feel comfortable thinking about the first few items in this hierarchy of experiences. As the list progresses, however, the situations become more anxiety-producing. By trying to relax when visualizing these situations, you can slowly learn to associate these communication experiences with relaxation rather than with nervousness.

1. You are having a casual conversation with a group member before a meeting.
2. Your group is scheduled to meet tomorrow, and you have not had time to prepare.
3. You are introducing yourself to a group in which you are the only new member.
4. Group members are taking turns presenting their opinions on an issue. Your turn is next.
5. You are trying to make a point in a group discussion, and you feel that everyone is looking at you.
6. Another group member has just asked you a difficult question.
7. The group's leader has unexpectedly called on you to present some information.
8. You have raised a controversial issue, and members have begun arguing.
9. You have been appointed the chairperson of a meeting.
10. You are a member of a group doing a panel presentation for a large audience.

STRATEGIES FOR LOW APPREHENSIVES

If your PRCA score classifies you as a low apprehensive, you may be able to help group members whose anxieties hinder their ability to participate in a group discussion. The following four strategies may reduce other members' level of communication apprehension:

- Be supportive.
- Provide constructive feedback.
- Include anxious members.
- Stop talking.

Be Supportive

Members who experience very little communication anxiety should be patient with and supportive of those who lack confidence. For those who are fearless in groups, it is fairly easy to interrupt a speaker or make a point in a strong, confident voice. Such interruptions may devastate a reluctant group member who is struggling to participate but is overlooked by more assertive members. Without support and encouragement, "even seasoned team members may never develop the confidence required to make their views known."[28]

FIGURE 4.3   **Match the Symptom to the Strategy**

Dimensions of Apprehension	Coping Strategies
Behavior: Inappropriate behavior or lack of skills	Learn communication skills. Be well prepared.
Affect: Negative emotions, moods, and feelings	Use systematic desensitization to relax when thinking about anxiety-producing situations.
Sensation: Negative or nervous bodily sensations	Practice relaxation and breathing techniques.
Imagery: Negative mental images	Practice visualization.
Cognition: Negative attitudes and opinions or irrational beliefs	Use cognitive restructuring to rethink and change your attitudes and beliefs.
Interpersonal Relationships: Lack of social skill or support system	Learn and practice effective communication skills. Confide in a trusted friend or group member.

Source: Based on Karen Kangas Dwyer, "The Multidimensional Model: Teaching Students to Self-Manage High Communication Apprehension by Self-Selecting Treatments," *Communication Education*, 49. (January 2000), pp. 75–76; Also see "A Multidimensional Plan for Conquering Speech Anxiety," in Karen Kangas Dwyer, *Conquer Your Speech Anxiety*, 2nd ed. (Belmont, CA: Thomas Wadsworth, 2005), pp. 43–46.

Provide Constructive Feedback

All group members work more effectively when they know how to give and interpret constructive feedback. Constructive feedback also boosts members' confidence and reduces communication apprehension. When apprehensive group members speak, you should smile and nod, listen patiently, and not interrupt or let other members interrupt them.

Constructive feedback should identify your feelings, thoughts, and wants: "I'm a little frustrated with this discussion (feeling), because we seem to be avoiding the real issue (thought). Let's talk about what's really hanging us up (want)."[29] Expressing feedback constructively can increase your own credibility and other members' confidence, while also moving the group forward. The following guidelines can help you provide constructive feedback that enhances members' confidence, facilitates interpersonal understanding, and improves discussion:

• Focus on the behavior (rather than on the person).

• Describe the behavior (rather than judge it).

• Provide observations (rather than assumptions).

- Choose an appropriate time and place to contribute feedback (rather than ignoring the circumstances).

- Give feedback to help others (rather than to meet your own needs).[30]

Include Anxious Members

Patience and understanding alone may not be enough to encourage a member who is too frightened to join in a discussion. Members who experience low levels of communication apprehension should try to include their nervous colleagues. Quiet members often have important information and good ideas. Encouraging anxious members to speak up contributes to the group's overall success.[31] There are, however, both effective and counterproductive ways to include someone. Confronting a reluctant speaker with a direct challenge, such as "Why in the world do you disagree with the rest of us?" is not very helpful. Asking a question that you know the apprehensive person is able to answer and taking turns speaking are much more effective ways to include all members.

Stop Talking

Finally, the most obvious thing you can do to help those who have difficulty participating is to stop talking. If you know that other members have difficulty entering the discussion or interrupting someone who is speaking, try to curb your own comments so that others have a chance to contribute. It is helpful to keep a careful eye on less-than-confident participants. Often you will see members take a breath as though they want to speak, only to be stifled by your continued comments or by the comments of others. When that happens, conclude your remarks and turn to the person who was trying to contribute in order to give that person an opportunity to speak.

ASSERTIVENESS

Assertiveness—speaking up and acting in your own best interests without denying the rights and interests of others[32]—has the potential to enhance the confidence and effectiveness of a group and its members. When expressed appropriately, assertive communication can raise your level of confidence and reduce communication apprehension.

Assertiveness seeks balance between passivity and aggression, and it applies to both groups and their members. Assertive group members have characteristics and skills that give them the confidence to stand up for themselves while interacting with others to achieve a group goal. Assertive group members tend to

- Appear confident, honest, open, and cooperative.

- Volunteer their ideas and opinions.

Chapter 4 Confidence in Groups

GROUPTECH

Confidence in Virtual Groups

When groups engage in teleconferences, video-conferences, and online or computer-mediated discussions, members' confidence may erode or improve, depending on the electronic medium used and the personal preferences of members. Three factors can contribute to the erosion of confidence:

- Communication apprehension
- Writing apprehension
- Computer apprehension

In a videoconference, members who experience high levels of communication apprehension may find themselves more nervous because they are "on television." Every word and movement is captured for all to see and hear. When a conference moves online, two other kinds of anxiety come into play. The first is writing apprehension.[1] Because online interaction depends on *written* words, poor writers and those who experience writing apprehension find themselves anxious about and preoccupied with the task of writing rather than being focused on the group's goal.

Computer anxiety—a condition affecting as many as 55 percent of all Americans—can complicate matters even further when members have negative attitudes about computers or express doubts about their technological skills. Fortunately, researchers have found that the more experience people have with computers, the less anxious they are.[2] The solution? Help anxious members in your group acquire and master computer skills, and their anxiety is likely to decrease.

There is, however, a flip side to the confidence coin when it's applied to online conferences and computer-mediated discussions. Some people are *more* confident when communicating via computer. A theory called **hyperpersonal communication** explains why some group members express themselves more competently and confidently in mediated settings than they do in face-to-face discussions.[3] One reason is that you have greater control over how you present yourself online. An added confidence booster is the fact that your written message is separate from your appearance, your gender and race, your status, and your accent or dialect. None of these nonverbal factors are displayed in your message unless you choose to include remarks about them. A second reason some participants prefer online communication is that other group members may overestimate the qualities of a member's online conversation. We tend to like cooperative and responsive online partners, and there's nothing comparable to being liked to boost one's confidence. A third reason is that the online channel allows members to take the time to construct suitable replies. For example, depending on how soon you have been asked to reply to a question, you can consult a report or do research and come off sounding like an expert. Finally, online communication usually provides you with feedback and lets you know whether your message was received and interpreted as you intended. Confirming feedback reinforces confidence.

[1] Andrew F. Wood and Matthew J. Smith, *Online Communication: Linking Technology, Identity, and Culture* (Mahwah, NJ: Erlbaum, 2001), p. 15. For more information about writing apprehension, see Virginia P. Richmond and James C. McCroskey, *Communication: Apprehension, Avoidance, and Effectiveness,* 4th ed. (Scottsdale, AZ: Gorsuch, Scarisbrick, 1995).

[2] Craig R. Scott and Steven C. Rockwell, "The Effect of Communication, Writing, and Technology Apprehension on Likelihood to Use New Communication Technologies," *Communication Education,* 46 (1997), pp. 29–43.

[3] Wood and Smith, p. 80.

[4] Wood and Smith, p. 81. Also see Andrew F. Wood and Matthew J. Smith, *Online Communication: Linking Technology, Identity, and Culture*, 2nd ed. (Mahwah, NJ: Erlbaum, 2005), pp. 88–90.

How can assertiveness help group members achieve a common goal?
(© Bob Daemmrich/The Image Works)

- Ask and answer questions without fear or hostility.
- Stand up for their beliefs, even when others disagree.
- Express their feelings openly.
- Respect and defend the rights and opinions of other group members.

Assertive members may choose to behave passively when an issue is unimportant or when the cost of getting their way is too high to achieve any benefits. In other situations, assertive members may express themselves aggressively when an issue is very important and the benefits of achieving a particular goal outweigh the cost of interpersonal conflict. Such members seek a golden mean between the dialectic tensions of passivity and aggression.

Balancing Passivity and Aggression

Passive group members often lack confidence. They are reluctant to express their opinions and feelings, may experience high levels of communication apprehension, fear criticism from others, and do what they're told to do, even when they disagree with or dislike the order. Passive group members are rarely satisfied with their group experiences because they feel powerless and put-upon.

Entire groups may behave passively. They may be stuck in primary tension or be unwilling to make decisions and take risks. Nonassertive groups may spend hours meeting and talking but fail to resolve an issue or achieve a goal. Members go through the motions of working in groups, but have little faith in themselves as a productive team.

Aggressive members act in their own self-interest at the expense of others. They are critical, insensitive, combative, and even abusive. They get what they want by taking over or by bullying other members into submission. As a consequence, they are often disliked and disrespected. In many cases, aggressive members behave this way because they don't know how to express themselves assertively. As is the case with passivity, entire groups may behave aggressively. In competitive situations, an aggressive reputation—whether real or pretended—may be an asset. Professional sports teams often benefit from an aggressive image. Sales teams may intimidate competitors by appearing aggressive. For most groups, however, aggression breeds resentment and defensiveness in others. Highly aggressive teams may not achieve their goal, for no other reason than that important nonteam members dislike them and obstruct their progress.

ETHICAL GROUPS

 ## The Ethics of Assertiveness

Psychologists Robert Alberti and Michael Emmons call attention to the fact that the principle of assertive action is embedded in our culture and even addressed in the U.S. Constitution.[1] Americans enjoy the constitutional rights of free speech, free press, and the right to peaceably assemble in the furtherance of asserting their convictions. Assertive communication is often culturally accepted, but in some instances it may also be ethically expected.

The National Communication Association's Credo for Ethical Communication calls for a commitment to the "courageous expression of personal conviction in pursuit of fairness and justice."[2] Ethical communicators have an obligation to assert themselves, not only to pursue their own goals, but to prevent unjust or unethical group action. For instance, members of a medical team must have the courage to speak up if they believe that a patient is being given the wrong medication. Whistle-blowers must have the courage to

report unethical or illegal corporate actions. Whether your group is deciding how to trim a budget, determining the best candidate to hire, or developing a marketing campaign, each group member has an ethical responsibility to act assertively in expressing opposition to group decisions that are potentially unethical.

Being assertive requires a willingness to speak out even in the face of other group members' disapproval or hostility. It requires candid expressions of opinion when facing difficult group decisions. Psychotherapist and best-selling author Nathaniel Branden contends that "to practice self-assertiveness is to live authentically, to speak and act from [your] innermost convictions and feelings."[3]

[1] Robert Alberti and Michael Emmons, *Your Perfect Right,* 8th ed. (Atascadero, CA: Impact Publishers, 2001), p. 222.
[2] The complete credo is available on the National Communication Association web site at *www.natcom.org/policies/External/EthicalComm.htm.*
[3] Nathaniel Branden, *The Six Pillars of Self-Esteem* (New York: Bantam, 1995), p. 119.

In some cases, passivity and aggression combine to create a third type of behavior—**passive-aggressive.** Passive-aggressives rarely exhibit aggressive behavior, even though they have little or no respect for the rights of others. They also may appear confident rather than passive because they speak up and contribute. However, beneath the façade of effective participation lies an insecure member. Passive-aggressives often get their way by undermining other members behind their backs, by behaving cooperatively but rarely following through with promised contributions, and by appearing to agree while privately planning an opposite action.

Occasionally, confident group members may exhibit passive, aggressive, or passive-aggressive behavior in frustrating situations. For the most part, however, confident group members have acquired assertiveness skills as a way of at least *appearing* confident. Assertive members are trusted because they do not violate the rights and interests of others. Instead, they establish strong interpersonal relationships with other group members. Assertive members speak up and help a group make decisions and solve problems. They enjoy working in groups and take great satisfaction in achieving a group goal.

The graph pictured in Figure 4.4 demonstrates how group or member assertiveness represents a balance between passivity and aggression.[33] Group or member effectiveness increases as you move from passivity to assertiveness and then decreases as you move beyond assertiveness into aggressiveness.

Assertiveness and Diversity

What is appropriate assertive behavior may differ depending on the situation you are in and the people with whom you are communicating. For example, in many Asian cultures, politeness is a key virtue, and communication is indirect in order to avoid confrontation or offense. "Assertiveness, in the Western sense of direct self-expression, is generally not considered appropriate" by those who value a less direct communication style.[34] As in all group communication situations, you must take into account the values, backgrounds, and experiences of other communicators.

Gender can also affect a member's ability to communicate assertively. According to **Muted Group Theory,** many women are less comfortable expressing themselves assertively, particularly in group and public settings.[35] For some women, assertive language seems inconsiderate and harsh. As a result, some female members may become a muted group. This muted group phenomenon even occurs in virtual groups. For example, female faculty members are rarely included in developing technology policy on college campuses, and masculine values and interests are still predominant in video games.

Dr. Rosabeth Moss Kanter, a professor at Harvard Business School, believes that fear of speaking in groups prevents many women from being leaders. She

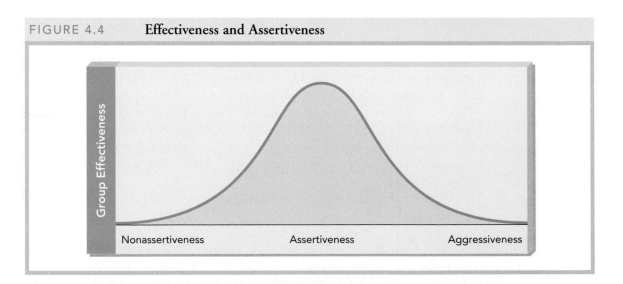

FIGURE 4.4   Effectiveness and Assertiveness

Group Effectiveness

Nonassertiveness   Assertiveness   Aggressiveness

notes that in business classes, "men seem to feel that they can start talking and eventually they'll have a point to make. The women are slightly more likely to feel that they ought to have something valuable to say before they say it."[36] The lesson for effective group members and would-be leaders is clear—female group members must have enough confidence in themselves and their own ideas and enough courage to speak up during discussions. As when dealing with group members from non-Western cultures, an effective group should understand and adapt to the different ways in which members express their ideas, opinions, and needs.

Assertiveness Skill Building

Regardless of how assertive you think you are, you can always improve your assertiveness skills. Building assertiveness skills incrementally can help you and your group increase in confidence while reducing social tensions. The following list includes both simple and complex skills for enhancing your assertiveness:

- Devote a significant amount of time to preparing for meetings.
- Enlist an assertive colleague who will make sure that you are recognized and given time to speak at meetings.
- Express your opinions clearly. Don't talk around the issue or ramble.
- Establish and maintain direct eye contact with individual group members.
- Assume an assertive body posture. Your body should be alert and focused in the direction of other speakers.
- Express your feelings as well as your thoughts. If you let group members see your emotions, your recommendations may be taken more seriously.
- Speak expressively—use volume, pitch, and rate to help your statements stand out.

Memorizing a list of skills for enhancing your assertiveness is not the same thing as becoming more assertive. As is the case with many communication methods and tools, you must choose the strategy that is best suited to your purpose. In some cases, a simple statement may serve your purpose. In other cases, you will have to describe a situation, share your feelings, and state your intentions. Selecting from among the following four options can ensure that your assertive behaviors are appropriate and effective:[37]

- Basic assertion
- Empathetic assertion
- Escalating assertion
- Three-part assertion

Basic Assertion. This technique is the simplest and most straightforward way of expressing your beliefs, feelings, or opinions. It usually involves a simple "I want" or "I feel" statement. Examples:

> "I feel uncomfortable about asking Deirdre to participate in this discussion."

> "I want us to be more open about our private agendas as we talk about this project."

Empathetic Assertion. An empathetic assertion conveys your sensitivity to and understanding of another person. It usually contains two parts—a recognition of the other person's situation or feelings, followed by a statement in which you stand up for your rights. Examples:

> "I know you've really been busy, but I want to feel that our group is important to you. I want you to make more time for the project."

TOOLBOX 4.5

Just Say *No*

One of the most basic but difficult assertiveness skills is having the ability and confidence to say *no*. Randy Paterson, author of *The Assertiveness Workbook*, puts it this way: "If you cannot say *no*, you are not in charge of your own life."[1] Why, then, do so many people believe that if someone asks us to do something, we have to do it? Paterson offers several reasons:

- They won't accept my *no* and will expect me to do it anyway.
- They won't accept or like *me* if I say *no*.
- Given our relationship, I don't have the right or the courage to say *no*.[2]

Think of it this way. If someone said, "Can I have your car?" you'd say *no*, wouldn't you? What about, "Would you write this paper and put my name on it?" or "Will you drive me to the gym? I go three times a week."

Certainly there's nothing wrong with saying *yes* when the request is reasonable and you want to do it or to help someone. But what if you want to say *no*? Fortunately, there are several communication strategies and skills you can use to say *no*:

- Use assertive body posture. If you say *no* with your words, but signal *maybe* with your body, people will believe that you can be persuaded to do what they want.
- Wait for the question. Don't say *yes* or *no* until you hear a request. For example, if someone says, "I can't ask the group to stay late and help me," don't say, "I'll do it for you."
- Decide on your wording. Use a clear statement, such as "No, I'm not willing to do that," rather than "Gee, I'm not sure . . . maybe another time."
- Don't apologize or make an excuse when it isn't necessary. Avoid statements such as "I'm sorry but I really can't . . ." or "I wish I could but . . ."
- Don't ask permission to say *no*. Avoid saying, "Would it be okay if I didn't . . . ?" or "Will you be upset if I say *no*?"
- Accept the consequences. Just as you have the right to say *no*, others have the right not to like it.[3]

[1] Randy J. Paterson, *The Assertiveness Workbook* (Oakland, CA: New Harbinger, 2000), p. 149.
[2] Peterson, p. 150.
[3] Peterson, pp. 151–153.

"I appreciate your concern for achieving a unanimous vote. At the same
time, I strongly believe that this decision could backfire and cause serious
problems in the future."

Escalating Assertion. When basic and empathetic assertions do not work,
or when the other person fails to respond to your basic assertion and continues
to violate your rights, consider using an escalating assertion. Gradually escalate
the force of your assertion and become increasingly firm. You may even mention
some type of resulting action on your part, but only after making several basic
assertive statements. Examples:

"If you don't finish your portion of the project by tomorrow, I'll be forced
to call an emergency group meeting."

"We spent a lot of time agreeing to complete this project by December 1,
but you haven't begun working on it. Unless I see some action on your
part, I will deny your request for personal leave in order to make sure
that we complete the project on time."

Three-Part Assertion. This assertion technique is especially useful for expressing negative feelings and involves the following three-part statement:

1. When you do _____ (describe the behavior).

2. The effects are _____ (describe how the behavior concretely affects you).

3. I'd prefer _____ (describe what you want).

The real focus of a three-part assertion is on the "I feel" and "I want" parts of
the statement. When expressing anger, the tendency is to blame the other person, fly off the handle, or get caught up in the emotion. The three-part assertion
provides a way of turning your emotional reaction into an assertive statement.
Examples:

"When you didn't give me the data I requested, I couldn't complete my
report on time. I feel hurt, and I'm frustrated. Next time, I'd like you to
do what you say you'll do."

"When you forgot to forward Bruce's email to me, I didn't know that he
had canceled the meeting. I'm angry because I wasted my entire morning driving across town, only to find out that there was no meeting.
I wish you would be more responsible and conscientious."

Assertive group members reap many rewards. Generally, they are more satisfied with and proud of the work they do in groups. They are also more likely to
become group leaders. Because assertive members respect the rights of others,
they are well liked. There is much to be gained from exhibiting assertive behavior in groups, and first among those benefits is increased confidence.

BALANCING ABILITY AND CONFIDENCE

Mature groups have two characteristics—their members are able to *do* the work needed to achieve a goal, and their members are *confident* that they will succeed. When group members are both very capable and very confident, a leader may have little to do other than help the group as it steamrolls its way to a goal.[38]

When groups are not mature, problems may arise. Group members with outstanding abilities may not interact with other members because they lack confidence or are unwilling to be assertive. Other group members with great confidence and strong opinions may lack the skills needed to help a group achieve its goal.

Successful groups understand that group effectiveness and members' confidence are inseparable and must be balanced. Balancing the quantity and quality of group communication means understanding how confidence affects group interaction. Group leaders and members should try to balance the amount of talk in a group by providing opportunities for quiet members while restraining members who may tend to dominate a discussion. In addition, members should learn to value assertiveness as a means of expressing opinions and feelings. By finding the golden mean between passivity and aggression, assertive members become more productive and confident.

When individual team members are confident, the group as a whole becomes more sure of itself, its goals, and the ability of its members to achieve those goals. Carl Larson and Frank LaFasto believe that this kind of confidence "translates into the ability of a team to be self-correcting in its capacity to adjust to unexpected adversity and emergent challenges."[39] In other words, a confident group is highly adaptive and welcomes challenge.

GROUPWORK

Sorting the Symptoms

Goal: To summarize and understand the symptoms of communication apprehension

Participants: Groups of 5–7 members

Procedure

1. Make a list of the symptoms of communication apprehension (increased heart rate, excessive perspiration, use of filler phrases such as "you know" and "OK") that *you* experience when speaking to a group or giving a public presentation.

2. Create a master list of symptoms by combining the lists of all group members.

3. Identify the symptoms that are more likely to occur during a group discussion.

4. Discuss the following questions:
- How can the type of group or topic of discussion affect the number and severity of symptoms?
- Which symptoms can or cannot be seen or heard by other group members?
- What is the relationship, if any, between the number and type of symptoms and a person's PRCA score for groups, meetings, interpersonal communication, and public speaking?
- How can you alleviate some of the causes and symptoms of communication apprehension in groups?

GroupAssessment

Personal Report of Communication Apprehension (PRCA-24)

Directions. This instrument is composed of twenty-four statements concerning feelings about communication with other people. Please indicate the degree to which each statement applies to you by marking whether you (1) strongly agree, (2) agree, (3) are undecided, (4) disagree, or (5) strongly disagree. Work quickly; record your first impression.

_____ 1. I dislike participating in group discussions.

_____ 2. Generally, I am comfortable while participating in group discussions.

_____ 3. I am tense and nervous while participating in group discussions.

_____ 4. I like to get involved in group discussions.

_____ 5. Engaging in a group discussion with new people makes me tense and nervous.

_____ 6. I am calm and relaxed while participating in a group discussion.

_____ 7. Generally, I am nervous when I have to participate in a meeting.

_____ 8. Usually I am calm and relaxed while participating in a meeting.

_____ 9. I am very calm and relaxed when I am called upon to express an opinion at a meeting.

_____ 10. I am afraid to express myself at meetings.

_____ 11. Communicating at meetings usually makes me feel uncomfortable.

_____ 12. I am very relaxed when answering questions at a meeting.

_____ 13. While participating in a conversation with a new acquaintance, I feel very nervous.

_____ 14. I have no fear of speaking up in conversations.

_____ 15. Ordinarily I am very tense and nervous in conversations.

_____ 16. Ordinarily I am very calm and relaxed in conversations.

_____ 17. While conversing with a new acquaintance, I feel very relaxed.

_____ 18. I'm afraid to speak up in conversations.

_____ 19. I have no fear of giving a speech.

_____ 20. Certain parts of my body feel very tense and rigid while I am giving a speech.

_____ 21. I feel relaxed while giving a speech.

_____ 22. My thoughts become confused and jumbled when I am giving a speech.

_____ 23. I face the prospect of giving a speech with confidence.

_____ 24. While giving a speech, I get so nervous that I forget facts I really know.

Scoring: The PRCA permits computation of one total score and four subscores. The subscores are related to communication apprehension in each of four common communication contexts: group discussions, meetings, interpersonal conversations, and public speaking. To compute your scores, merely add or subtract your scores for each item as indicated here.

To obtain your total score for the PRCA, simply add your four subscores together. Your score should be between 24 and 120. If your score is below 24 or above 120, you have made a mistake in computing the score. Scores for each of the four contexts (groups, meetings, interpersonal conversations, and public speaking) can range from a low of 6 to a high of 30. Any score above 18 indicates some degree of apprehension. If your score is above 18 for the public speaking context, you are like the overwhelming majority of Americans.

Scoring Formula

Group Discussions: 18 + scores for items 2, 4, and 6; − scores for items 1, 3, and 5.

Meetings: 18 + scores for items 8, 9, and 12; − scores for items 7, 10, and 11.

Interpersonal Conversations: 18 + scores for items 14, 16, and 17; − scores for items 13, 15, and 18.

Public Speaking: 18 + scores for items 19, 21, and 23; − scores for items 20, 22, and 24.

Subscores

_____ Group Discussions

_____ Meetings

_____ Interpersonal Conversations

_____ Public Speaking

Norms for PRCA-24:

	Mean	Standard Deviation
Total Score	65.5	15.3
Group	15.4	4.8
Meetings	16.4	4.8
Interpersonal	14.5	4.2
Public Speaking	19.3	5.1

Source: PRCA-24 reprinted with permission from the author. See James C. McCroskey, *An Intro-duction to Rhetorical Communication,* 6th ed. (Englewood Cliffs, NJ: Prentice Hall, 1993), p. 37.

NOTES

1. Edwin P. Hollander, *Leadership Dynamics: A Practical Guide to Effective Relationships* (New York: Macmillan, 1978), p. 53; Chapter 8 of this book, "Group Leadership," devotes an entire section to strategies for becoming a leader.

2. James M. Kouzes and Barry Z. Posner, *The Leadership Challenge*, 3rd ed. (San Francisco: Jossey-Bass, 2002), p. 296. Also see the discussion of a leader's role in building group confidence in Frank M. J. LaFasto and Carl Larson, *When Teams Work Best* (Thousand Oaks, CA: Sage, 2001), pp. 121–130.

3. Virginia P. Richmond and James C. McCroskey, *Communication: Apprehension, Avoidance, and Effectiveness,* 4th ed. (Scottsdale, AZ: Gorsuch, Scarisbrick, 1995), p. 41.

4. Michael T. Motley, *Overcoming Your Fear of Public Speaking: A Proven Method* (Boston: Houghton Mifflin, 1997), p. 3; Virginia P. Richmond and James C. McCroskey, *Communication: Apprehension, Avoidance, and Effectiveness*, 5th ed. (Boston: Allyn & Bacon/Longman, 1998).

5. In Karen Kangas Dwyer, *Conquer Your Speech Anxiety,* 2nd ed. (Belmont, CA: Thomson Wadsworth, 2005), Dwyer cites *The Book of Lists* by David Wallenchinsky, Irving Wallace, and Amy Wallace (New York: Bantam Books, 1997), in which fear of public speaking ranks as the number one "common fear" in America. Similar data can be found in The Bruskin Report, *What Are Americans Afraid Of?* (Research Report No. 53, 1973).

6. See *http://www.gallup.com/poll/releases/pr013119.asp*, "Snakes Top List of Americans' Fears," March 19, 2001. Please note that surveys of the top "common" fears do not include much bigger, event-related fears such as terrorism, war, or epidemics.

7. Edmund J. Bourne and Lorna Garano, *Coping with Anxiety: 10 Simple Ways to Relieve Anxiety, Fear and Worry* (Oakland, CA: New Harbinger Publications, 2003), p. 7. Also see Richmond and McCroskey, 4th ed., pp. 29–32.

8. Lynne Kelly et al., "Family Communication Patterns and the Development of Reticence," *Communication Education,* 51 (2002), pp. 202–209.

9. Kelly et al, p. 207.

10. Marti Olsen Laney, *The Introvert Advantage: How to Thrive in an Extrovert World.* (New York: Workman, 2002), p. 193.

11. S. M. Sorensen, "Grouphate: A Negative Reaction to Group Work," paper presented at the annual meeting of the International Communication Association, Minneapolis, MN, 1981.

12. Chintawa Monthienvichienchai, Sirintorn Bhibulbhanuwat, Chintawee Kasemsuk, and Mark Speece, "Cultural Awareness, Communication Apprehension, and Communication Competence: A Case Study of Saint John's International School," *International Journal of Educational Management,* 16 (2002), pp. 288–296.

13. Bourne and Garano, p. 9.

14. James C. McCroskey and Virginia P. Richmond, "Communication Apprehension and Small Group Communication," in *Small Group Communication: A Reader*, 6th ed., ed. Robert S. Cathcart and Larry A. Samovar (Dubuque, IA: Wm. C. Brown, 1992), p. 368. Also see Beth Bonniwell Haslett and Jenn Ruebush, "What Differences Do Individual Differences in Groups Make?" in *The Handbook of Group Communication Theory and Research*, ed. Lawrence R. Frey, assoc. eds. Dennis S. Gouran and Marshall Scott Poole (Thousand Oaks, CA: Sage, 1999), p. 124.

15. Richmond and McCroskey, 4th ed. p. 57.

16. Richmond and McCroskey, 4th ed. p. 58.

17. Joseph A. Bonito and Andrea B. Hollingshead, "Participation in Small Groups," in *Communication Yearbook,* 20, ed. Brant R. Burleson (Thousand Oaks, CA: Sage, 1997), p. 245.

18. Bonito and Hollingshead, p. 245.

19. Richmond and McCroskey, 4th ed. p. 46.

20. Diane Dreher, *The Tao of Personal Leadership* (New York: HarperCollins, 1996), p. 75.

21. The following books describe a variety of techniques designed to reduce communication apprehension: Dwyer; Michael T. Motley, *Overcoming Your Fear of Public Speaking* (Boston: Houghton Mifflin, 1997); Richmond and McCroskey, *Communication,* 5th ed.

22. Isa N. Engleberg and John A. Daly, *Presentations in Everyday Life: Strategies for Effective Speaking*, 2nd ed. (Boston: Houghton Mifflin, 2005), p. 68.

23. Dwyer, pp. 72–94; Richmond and McCroskey, 4th ed., pp. 102–105.

24. See Chapter 2, "Listening to the Cries and Whispers of the Articulate Body," in Randolph R. Cornelius, *The Science of Emotions: Research and Tradition in the Psychology of Emotions* (Upper Saddle River, NJ: Prentice Hall, 1996).

25. Delaine Fragnoli, "Fear of Lying," *Bicycling*, 38 (1997), pp. 46–47.

26. Joe Ayres, Tim Hopf, and Debbie M. Ayres, "An Examination of Whether Imaging Ability Enhances the Effectiveness of an Intervention Designed to Reduce Speech Anxiety," *Communication Education,* 43 (1994), pp. 252–258; Joe Ayres, B. Heuett, and D. A. Sonandre, "Testing a Refinement in an Intervention for Communication Apprehension," *Communication Reports,* 11 (1998), pp. 73–84.

27. Joe Ayres, Tim Hopf, and Patricia A. Edwards, "Vividness and Control: Factors in the Effectiveness of Performance Visualization?" *Communication Education,* 48 (1999), pp. 287–293.

28. Mattison Crowe, "Why the Members of Your Group Won't Speak Up, and What You Can Do

About It," *Harvard Management Update,* 1 (November 1996), p. 8.

29. Ron Short, *A Special Kind of Leadership: The Key to Learning Organizations* (Seattle, WA: The Leadership Group, 1991), pp. 17, 26.

30. Sam R. Lloyd, *Leading Teams: The Skills for Success* (West Des Moines, IA: American Media, 1996), p. 57.

31. Bonito and Hollingshead, p. 249.

32. A more detailed definition and explanation of assertiveness can be found in Robert E. Alberti and Michael L. Emmons, *Your Perfect Right: Assertiveness and Equality in Your Life and Personal Relationships*, 8th ed. (Atascadero, CA: AImpact, 2001).

33. Joshua D. Guilar, *The Interpersonal Communication Skills Workshop* (New York: AMACOM, 2001), p. 70.

34. Alberti and Emmons, p. 41.

35. For more information on Muted Group Theory, see Cheris Kramarae, *Women and Men Speaking: Frameworks for Analysis* (Rowley, MA: Newbury House, 1981); Shirley Ardener, "The 'Problem' Revisited," in Shirley E. Ardener, *Perceiving Women* (London: Malaby, 1975); Shirley Ardener, *Defining Females: The Nature of Women in Society* (New York: Wiley, 1978). A useful summary of Muted Group Theory can be found in Richard West and Lynn H. Turner, *Introducing Communication Theory: Analysis and Application* (Boston: McGraw-Hill, 2004), pp. 476–492.

36. Barbara Kantrowitz, "When Women Lead," *Newsweek*, October 24, 2005, p. 67.

37. Counseling and Mental Health Center, University of Texas at Austin, *Learning to Be Assertive*, http://www.utexas.edu/student/cmhc/booklets/assert/assertive.html, updated 10/10/02.

38. Chapter 8, "Group Leadership," reviews Hersey and Blanchard's Situational Leadership Theory. See Paul Hersey and Kenneth Blanchard, *Management of Organizational Behavior Utilizing Human Resources*, 5th ed. (Englewood Cliffs, NJ: Prentice Hall, 1988).

39. Carl E. Larson and Frank M. J. LaFasto, *TeamWork: What Must Go Right/What Can Go Wrong* (Newbury Park, CA: Sage, 1989), p. 71.

CHAPTER 5

Verbal and Nonverbal Communication in Groups

CHAPTER OUTLINE

TWO ESSENTIAL TOOLS

Verbal and nonverbal communication are the means you use to generate meaning in group settings. **Verbal communication** focuses on how you use the words in our language. Communication may be "face to face, fax to fax, over the phone, or through electronic mail, but regardless of the channel used, groups do their work through language."[1] Without spoken and written language, you cannot have a group discussion; you cannot follow an agenda, take minutes, read a report, or interact effectively with other group members. Linguists Victoria Fromkin and Robert Rodman note, "Whatever else people do when they come together—whether they play, fight, make love, or make automobiles, they talk. We live in a world of language."[2]

The other essential communication tool, nonverbal communication, is just as important as language. Without the nonverbal component, it would be difficult to interpret the meaning of spoken language. The tone of voice, directness of eye contact, and physical proximity of group members can reveal at least as much about their thoughts and feelings as the words they speak. Generally, group members use words to express the content of a message and use nonverbal behavior to express the emotional element of a message.[3]

In dialectic terms, effective group members rely on *both* verbal *and* nonverbal communication to generate meaning. For example, as you know from Chapter 3, "Group Member Diversity," people in high-context cultures place emphasis on nonverbal codes and the nature of interpersonal relationships to generate and interpret meaning. In low-context cultures, people generate and interpret the meaning of messages that are clearly and explicitly expressed in words. Thus in a diverse group, African American and Latino members may be more sensitive to the nonverbal components of messages, whereas European Americans may rely on and trust a member's words to convey meaning.[4] Effective groups recognize that this dialectic tension provides a richer basis for effective and ethical communication.

LANGUAGE AND MEANING

Your ability to use language helps to determine the extent to which you successfully express your ideas and influence the actions of other group members. Several basic principles of language address the complex relationship between words and meaning.

Denotation and Connotation

When communicating in groups, you will encounter different meanings for and reactions to words, depending on the type of group, its goal, its history of interaction, and the background and experience of its members. The multiple meanings of words can be further understood by examining two major types of meaning: denotative and connotative.

Denotation refers to the objective, dictionary-based meaning of a word. However, words usually have more than one definition. For example, the *minutes* taken in a meeting are not the same as the *minutes* it may take to get a meeting started. **Connotation** refers to the personal feelings connected to the meaning of a word. Semanticist S. I. Hayakawa refers to connotation as "the aura of feelings, pleasant or unpleasant, that surround practically all words."[5] We evaluate the extent to which we like or dislike the thing or idea that the word represents.

Connotation is more likely than denotation to influence how you respond to words. For example, the denotative meaning or dictionary definition of a *meeting* is "an assembly or gathering of people, as for a business, social, or religious purpose."[6] However, the word *meeting* can connote hours of wasted time to some members or the best way to solve a complex problem to others. When the word *meeting* comes to mean a dreaded event at which unpleasant people argue over trivial issues, you are letting the word influence your feelings about the event it symbolizes.

Levels of Meaning

Group members can minimize the misinterpretation of words by recognizing the ways in which different levels of meaning affect communication. Some words are more abstract than others. An **abstract word** refers to an idea or concept that cannot be observed or touched. Words such as *fairness* and *freedom* may not have the same meaning for everyone. Total reliance on abstract words increases the chances of misunderstanding. The more abstract your language is, the more likely it is that group members will interpret your meaning in some way other than the way you intended. **Concrete words** refer to specific things that can be perceived by our senses. They narrow the number of possible meanings and decrease the likelihood of misinterpretation.

There are three levels of abstraction, ranging from the most abstract to the most concrete.[7] **Superordinate terms** are words in which objects and ideas are grouped together very generally, e.g., *vehicle*. **Basic terms** are words that immediately come to mind when you see an object, e.g., *car, van,* or *truck*. **Subordinate terms** are more concrete and specialized. The vehicle parked outside is not just a *car*. It is a *red Mercedes sports car*.

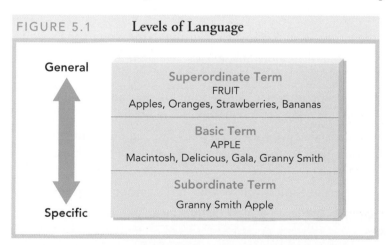

FIGURE 5.1   **Levels of Language**

General ↕ Specific

Superordinate Term
FRUIT
Apples, Oranges, Strawberries, Bananas

Basic Term
APPLE
Macintosh, Delicious, Gala, Granny Smith

Subordinate Term
Granny Smith Apple

Avoid using overly abstract words when working in groups. Use words that refer directly to observable objects, people, or behavior. For example, stating that "Greg's behavior was disruptive" could imply many things. Did he yell at a group member, use profanity, refuse to participate, or insist that his ideas were superior? Stating that "Greg arrived fifteen minutes late to the meeting" is more descriptive. Clarifying what you mean by using concrete words prevents inaccurate inferences and misunderstandings.

TEAM TALK

Team Talk, the title of a book by Anne Donnellon, examines the power of language in team dynamics. Donnellon uses the term **team talk** to describe the nature of the language that group members use as they work together. Not only does team talk enable group members to share information and express opinions, but analysis of team talk also "reveals where the team is coming from and where it is headed. More importantly, talk is a tool for changing a team's destination" and achieving success.[8] Team talk is the means we use to achieve group goals, the stimulus we use to build group relationships, and the evidence we use to assess group work.

Group members should listen carefully for words, sentences, and patterns of speech that are used repetitively during discussions and meetings. By listening to one another talk and analyzing how the group uses language, group members can discover how the group's language fosters or inhibits success. Figure 5.2 illustrates six dimensions of team talk and provides examples of successful and unsuccessful language use.

Language is more than the verbal medium through which groups communicate. Language also "creates thoughts, feelings, and behavior in team members which affect the way the team uses power, manages conflict, and negotiates."[10] Once group members analyze the nature of team talk, they can take steps to modify the way they interact and work with one another. The following suggestions can help produce a stronger and more cooperative group:

- Use the pronouns *we, us,* and *our* when referring to the group and its work.
- Express shared rather than individual needs: "We need to . . ." rather than "I want . . ."
- If you are in a position of power, refrain from talking and interrupting more than others and asking more questions than others.
- Speak in a specific and active voice ("I haven't finished the report due next week") rather than an abstract and passive voice ("The task hasn't been completed").
- Ask group members to address you by your first name or nickname.
- Encourage group members to express disagreement and listen patiently to dissenters.

FIGURE 5.2   **The Dimensions of Team Talk[9]**

Team Talk Dimensions	Successful Examples	Unsuccessful Examples
1. Identification. Members use plural pronouns rather than singular ones when talking about the group and its work.	"Let's keep working on this until we're ready for lunch."	"I don't think you should quit until you've finished."
2. Interdependence. Members use language that acknowledges shared needs, solicits opinions, and expresses the need for cooperation.	"If we can develop a plan, our work will be much easier to schedule. What do you think?"	"We can develop this plan without input from the group. I'll tell the boss that Fred and I will do it on our own."
3. Power Differentiation. Members talk to one another on equal terms.	"Sorry. My other meeting ran overtime. Is there a way I can catch up?" "Fred, could you tell me more about that? Thanks."	"Stop and tell me what's happened so far." "I don't like this. If you can't do it, we'll have to assign this to someone else."
4. Social Distance. Members use casual language, nicknames, slang. Members express empathy and liking and avoid titles.	"What's up, Doc?" "Fred, try to find out where Bob stands on this." "Hey, guys!"	"Let us review our progress thus far." "Mr. Nunez, contact Dr. Ford after the meeting." "Ladies and gentlemen . . . ."
5. Conflict Management Techniques. Members express interest in solving problems and use a nonthreatening tone and nonjudgmental language. Members paraphrase others.	"What do you need to know from us to do this?" "Could we back up and look at this from a different angle?"	"How many of you think that Fred is right?" "We're not getting anywhere, so I'll take it up with Dr. Ford after the meeting."
6. Negotiation Process. Members ask "what if" questions, propose objective criteria for solutions, and summarize areas of agreement.	"What if we wrote up a justification for the cost?" "Does this meet our standard?" "What else could persuade us to do this?"	"We've always done it this way." "Why? Because I just don't like it, that's why."

- Ask more "what if" questions and make fewer "we can't do it" statements.

- When in doubt, rephrase or ask questions about what someone else has said to ensure understanding.

LANGUAGE DIFFICULTIES

Many misunderstandings in group discussions can be avoided by overcoming language-based barriers to communication. Among the most common language difficulties are bypassing, offensive language, and jargon.

Bypassing

When group members have different meanings for the same words and phrases, they risk engaging in **bypassing,** a form of miscommunication that occurs when people "miss each other with their meanings."[11] An entire group project can be compromised if there are differences in the interpretation of a single word or phrase. Note the problems created by the following example of bypassing:

> At a routine staff meeting, a vice president asks her managers to "survey the members of your department to find out whether they are satisfied with the new email system." During the following week, the vice president receives a copy of a memo from one manager requesting that everyone in his department fill out a two-page questionnaire about the email system. The vice president telephones the manager and asks, "What's this questionnaire all about?" The manager replies, "I thought you said I have to survey everyone in my department."

What the vice president had in mind was for the manager to informally ask staff members for their initial impressions rather than ask for a detailed analysis of the new system. Although the manager heard the vice president's words, the communicators "missed" each other's meaning.

"Communicators who habitually look for meanings in the people using words, rather than in the words themselves, are much less prone to bypass or to be bypassed."[12] In other words, it's not what words mean but what speakers mean when they use words that is most important.

Offensive Language

Offensive language employs terminology that demeans, inappropriately excludes, or stereotypes people. For example, using sexist language in a group may alienate and offend both male and female members of that group. Referring to women as "girls" implies that women are childlike and not capable of adult thought and responsibilities. Refer to female group members as "girls" only if you also refer to male members as "boys." Avoid words that specify the gender of individuals in particular roles or occupations. Instead, use words that refer to both men and women. For example, instead of referring to the *chairman,* use the term *chair* or *chairperson.*

You should also avoid language that stereotypes people based on their culture, race, religion, or lifestyle. Language perpetuates discrimination. Therefore, avoiding language that stereotypes people in this way can help prevent discrimination.[13] Words such as *nigger, trailer trash,* and *faggot* are offensive and demeaning. Is it OK to use these words if none of your group members would be targeted by them? Absolutely not! This type of language can offend and alienate everyone in the group. A member of an insurance investigation team recounted the following experience:

> We were meeting to discuss ways to better recognize fraudulent claims. At one point, another member said, "I'm working on a claim now involving a carload of wetbacks." I couldn't believe he used that term. He obviously didn't know that my husband is Latino. I was insulted. Other group members were offended, too.

Two problems occur when you label someone or accept a label that you hear or see. First, you reduce an entire person to a label—black doctor, dumb blonde, deaf cousin, or rich uncle. Second, the label can affect your perceptions of or relationship with that person. For example, if you label a person as inconsiderate, you may question the motives behind an act of kindness: "I wonder what prompted her to do that?" When you label someone as near perfect, you may go to great lengths to justify or explain less-than-perfect behavior: "Tiger Woods is still the best player in golf; he's just having an off year." Labels also influence how we interpret the same behavior:

- I'm energetic; you're overexcited; he's out of control.

- I'm laid back; you're untidy; she's a slob.

- I'm smart; you're intelligent; Chris is brilliant!

Jargon

Jargon is the specialized or technical language of a profession. Groups use jargon as "verbal shorthand that allows members to communicate with each other clearly, efficiently, and quickly."[14] In some groups, the ability to use jargon properly is a sign of team membership. In other groups, jargon can make ideas difficult to understand and may be used to conceal the truth. Members who are unfamiliar with a group's jargon are easily intimidated and frustrated. Consider the experience of the vice president of a large technology corporation:

> When I first joined the company, I had to learn the lingo of the various groups in which I worked. I remember attending my first CMG meeting (I didn't even know what that meant at the time) and listening to people talk about red files and green files. Do we color-code files? No, there is no such thing

ETHICAL GROUPS

 ## Sticks and Stones May Break Your Bones, but Words Can Hurt Forever

In his book on toxic language, Arthur Bell examines the ways in which abusive words hurt groups and their members. When under assault by abusive language, group members can become discouraged, withdrawn, and isolated or can be provoked into shouting matches with their attacker. Abusive language has the "immediate result of spoiling relationships (and productivity based on such relationships), and the long-term effect of ruining morale, teamwork, and loyalty."[1]

The following list depicts several characteristics of verbal abuse:

- *Tone of voice:* Harsh, sarcastic, angry, or belittling
- *Content:* Sexual references, racial slurs, cruel comments about someone's appearance
- *Language choice:* Foul or obscene words
- *Nonverbal cues:* Insulting facial expressions, gross gestures, threatening movements
- *Speaking volume:* Loud, screaming voice or hissed messages[2]

Ethical communicators *both* take responsibility for what they say *and* take action when others use abusive language. Here we offer several techniques for avoiding, interrupting, challenging, and stopping verbal abuse:

1. *Express your objections.* At the first sign of verbal abuse, calmly explain that you feel abused, but you are willing to continue the discussion if the language becomes less inflammatory.
2. *Ask for repetition.* Ask the person to repeat what he or she has just said, as in, "Please

repeat that. I want to make sure I heard what you said."
3. *Step back.* When someone is verbally abusive, step back four or five steps, as if to say that you want to talk about the problem, but you don't want to be yelled at or insulted. If the abuse continues, walk away.
4. *Quote the law.* When a discussion becomes abusive, quote the law or group norms: "That kind of language is illegal in the workplace" or "that word violates company policies."
5. *Take a time-out:* Say "Time out" when a discussion becomes uncomfortable or abusive. Follow that with "Let's take a minute to calm down before we continue."
6. *Practice what you preach.* If you take action against others, make sure that you avoid all forms of verbal abuse:

   - Do not raise your voice.
   - Do not swear.
   - Do not call members insulting names.
   - Do not use sarcasm to wound others.

7. *Listen.* Listen more than you speak when you're upset, particularly if you're so mad that you're afraid of what you might say. As you listen, try to calm down physically and mentally.[3]

[1] Thomas J. Housel, "Foreword," in Arthur H. Bell, *You Can't Talk to Me That Way!* (Franklin Lakes, NJ: Career Press, 2005), p. 11.
[2] Based on Arthur H. Bell, *You Can't Talk to Me That Way!* (Franklin Lakes, NJ: Career Press, 2005), pp. 24–25.
[3] Based on Bell, pp. 192–200.

as an actual red or green file. Rather, the terms *red file* and *green file* refer to different pricing structures for our products. I also discovered that the same term might be used differently from one group to another. For instance, in some meetings *IP* refers to Internet provider. However, in other groups, it's short for information professional. As an attorney, I use the term to refer to intellectual property. I'm now familiar with the language of our company, but I know how confusing it can be when you're new to the team.

Some people use jargon to impress others with their specialized knowledge. Such tactics usually fail to inform others and often result in misunderstandings and resentment. Use jargon only when you are sure that all the members of your group will understand it and that it's absolutely necessary. If some of the jargon or technical terms of a field are important, take the time to explain those words to new members.

ADAPTING TO LANGUAGE DIFFERENCES

Most groups include diverse members who influence how we use and listen to language. Although there is nothing right or wrong about the different ways in which people use language, these differences can create misunderstandings among group members.

Language and Gender

As we explain in Chapter 3, "Group Member Diversity," men and women inhabit gender-based cultures that account for differences in perspectives and communication styles. We recommend that all group members monitor and adapt to the different ways in which women and men interpret the world and express their opinions.

Linguist Deborah Tannen maintains that men and women use language quite differently.[15] Women tend to use language to maintain relationships and cooperate with others. Many women speak tentatively. Their speech is more likely to contain qualifiers and tag questions. A qualifier is a word that conveys uncertainty, such as *maybe* and *perhaps*. Tag questions are questions connected to a statement. For instance, "It may be time to move on to our next point, don't you think so?" is a statement made tentatively with a tag question. This tentative style does not necessarily represent a lack of confidence. Instead, it can be viewed as a cooperative approach that encourages others to respond.

In general, men tend to use language to assert their ideas and compete with others. Men are less likely to express themselves tentatively. Male speech is generally characterized as direct and forceful. One style of communication is not better than the other. The two are simply different. Effective group members use elements from both male and female approaches to language.

Language and Culture

For most groups, a single language is the medium of interaction, even though members from different backgrounds, generations, and geographic areas may speak the same language quite differently. Variations in vocabulary, pronunciation, syntax, and style that distinguish speakers from different ethnic groups, geographic areas, and social classes are referred to as **dialects.** Dialects are distinct from the commonly accepted form of a particular language. In the United States, there are southern dialects, New England dialects, Brooklyn dialects, and a whole range of foreign accents. Approximately 80 to 90 percent of all African Americans use a distinct dialect at least some of the time.[16]

No one dialect is superior to another. However, Standard American English is the most commonly accepted dialect and is spoken by as much as 60 percent of the U.S. population. If, however, you enjoy *pizzer* and *beah* instead of pizza and beer, you may be from Massachusetts. If you say, *"Ah nevah go theyuh,"* you could be from Alabama or parts of Texas. Unfortunately, studies repeatedly find that "accented speech and dialects provoke stereotyped reactions in listeners so that the speakers are usually perceived as having less status, prestige, and overall competence."[17] Moreover, people with Appalachian dialects and "those who speak Black Standard English, are sometimes unfairly assumed to be less reliable, less intelligent, and of lower status than those who speak General American Speech."[18] The implications of such research are clear: Group members who do not use Standard American English in business and academic settings may be viewed as less articulate or less competent.

Because dialects have the potential to influence the perceptions of group members, speakers may engage in codeswitching as a way to avoid negative stereotypes related to language. **Codeswitching** refers to the ability to change from the dialect of your own cultural setting and adopt the language of the majority in particular situations. In other words, the dialect you speak at home may not be the best way to communicate in a business meeting. In reviewing the research on dialects, Carley Dodd concludes "that: (1) people judge others by their speech, (2) upward mobility and social aspirations influence whether people change their speech to the accepted norms, (3) general American speech is most accepted by the majority of the American culture, and (4) people should be aware of these prejudices and attempt to look beyond the surface."[19] Thus, you should try to understand, respect, and adapt to the dialects you hear in group communication contexts.

IMPROVING VERBAL COMMUNICATION

Without intelligent and appropriate use of language, groups cannot achieve their goals. As Suzanne Beyea, director of nursing research at Dartmouth-Hitchcock Medical Center, aptly observes, "Imagine an OR [operating room] in which members of the team never talk to each other."[20] Quality health care depends on a medical team's effective use of language.

TOOLBOX 5.1

An Accent and a Dialect Are Not the Same Thing

Accents and dialects are not the same thing. An **accent** is the sound of one language imposed on another. For example, some Asian speakers have difficulty producing the "r" and "v" sounds in English. **Dialects** differ from accents in that they represent regional and cultural differences within the same language. What people call a southern accent is really a southern dialect.[1] In general, dialects refer to the use of different words for a similar object or idea as well as variations in the pronunciation of common words.

Linguists have identified eighteen regional dialects of American English. For example, a carbonated soft drink is called *soda* in the Northeast; *pop* in the inland and Northwest; *tonic* in eastern New England; and *soda pop* in parts of southern West Virginia, eastern Kentucky, western Carolina, and eastern Tennessee.

Dialects may also have a distinctive sound. Northeast dialects, for example, range from the unique sound of New York City residents to the loss of "r" sounds in New England (in words such as *park, car, Harvard*, and *yard*). Southern dialects are also marked by the loss of the "r" sound as well as by distinctive phrases such as *y'all*.

A consistent finding across several studies is that speakers of Standard American English are judged as more intelligent, ambitious, and successful, even when the judges themselves speak a nonstandard American dialect.[2] However, having an accent or dialect does not stop anyone from being an effective communicator. What matters is that you speak loudly enough and clearly enough for others to hear and understand—and that is true no matter what language or dialect you speak.

[1] Isa Engleberg and John Daly, *Presentations in Everyday Life: Strategies for Effective Speaking* (Boston: Houghton Mifflin, 2005), pp. 347–349; William O'Grady et al., *Contemporary Linguistics*, 5th ed. (Boston: Bedford/St. Martin's, 2005), pp. 627, 635.
[2] Ethel C. Glenn, Phillip J. Glenn, and Sandra Forman, *Your Voice and Articulation*, 4th ed. (Boston: Allyn & Bacon, 1998), p. 10.

The previous section emphasizes what *not* to do if you want to be understood and respected by the other members of your group. Fortunately, there also are positive steps you can take to improve your use of language.

Improve Your Vocabulary

Although words have great power, they also pose many challenges. As Mark Twain, the great American humorist, observed, "The difference between the almost right word and the right word is really a large matter—'tis the difference between the lightning bug and the lightning."[21] Finding the "right" word is a lot easier if you have a lot of words to choose from.

As you learn more words, make sure you understand their meaning and usage. For example, you should be able to make distinctions in meaning among the words in each of the following groups.[22]

- absurd, silly, dumb, preposterous, ridiculous, ludicrous, idiotic

- abnormal, odd, eccentric, foreign, strange, peculiar, weird

- pretty, attractive, gorgeous, elegant, lovely, cute, beautiful

The difference between the almost right word and the right word really *is* a very large matter. Although you learn the basic grammar of language before you start school, you must work on improving your vocabulary throughout your life.

Usually, there is a big difference between the words we use for written documents or formal presentations and the words we use when working in groups. Our advice: *Say what you mean by speaking the way you talk, not the way you write.* This is the language of team talk.

- Use shorter, familiar words. For example, say *home* rather than *residence.*

- Use shorter, simpler sentences. For example, say *He came back* rather than *He returned from his point of departure.*

- Use more informal colloquial expressions. For example, say *Give it a try* rather than *You should attempt it.*

Use "I," "You," and "We" Language

When you use the word *I*, you take responsibility for your own feelings and actions: *I* feel great; *I* am a straight A student; *I* am not pleased with the team's work on this project. Some people avoid using the word *I* because they think they're showing off, being selfish, or bragging. Other people use the word *I* too much and appear self-centered or oblivious to those around them.

Unfortunately, some people avoid "I" language when it is most important. Instead, they shift responsibility from themselves to others by using the word *you*. "You" language can be used to express judgments about others. When the judgments are positive—"You did a great job," or "You look marvelous!"—there's rarely a problem. When *you* is used to accuse, blame, or criticize, you can arouse defensiveness, anger, and even revenge. Consider the following statements: "You make me angry." "You embarrass me." "You drive too fast." Sometimes, the word *you* is implied, as in "Stop telling me what to do." and "What a stupid thing to do."

Successful teams use the plural pronouns *we* and *you* when talking to one another.[23] Plural pronouns are inclusive. They announce that the group depends on everyone rather than on a single member. Plural pronouns also share credit for team achievements. Successful teams use pronouns in specific ways.[24] Members say *we*, *us*, and *our* when talking about the group and its work. When members say *you*, they are usually addressing the whole group.

Use Appropriate Grammar

Do you ever say to yourself, "Because I don't know if I should use *who* or *whom*, I won't even ask the question?" Probably not. If you're like most people, when you're talking, 98 percent of the time your grammar is fine and is not an issue. As for the 2 percent of time your grammar is a problem, many of your listeners won't even notice your mistakes.[25]

Your ability to use grammar correctly makes a public statement about your education, your social class, and even your intelligence. Think about the television shows and films you've seen. What do many scriptwriters do when they put words in the mouth of a dumb character? They break grammatical rules. "Him and I was out partying." "I don't know nothin'." "She know better."

Grammar is important. However, worrying about it all the time may make it impossible for you to write or speak. If you have questions about grammar, consult a good writing handbook.[26] Although most listeners will miss or forgive a few grammatical errors, consistent grammatical problems can distract listeners and seriously harm your credibility.

THE IMPORTANCE OF NONVERBAL COMMUNICATION

Nonverbal communication refers to the behavioral elements of messages other than the actual words spoken. Your appearance, posture, and facial expressions also send messages. Research has suggested that between 60 and 70 percent of all meaning is derived from nonverbal behavior.[27] That is, people base their understanding of what you mean not only on what you say, but also on what you do.

In their anthology of group communication research, Robert Cathcart and colleagues note that "groups provide a rich source of nonverbal messages because so many behaviors occur simultaneously."[28] Using and interpreting nonverbal behavior are critical to effective communication in groups. Unfortunately, we often put more thought into choosing the best words than into selecting the most appropriate behavior for conveying our ideas.

TOOLBOX 5.2

Silence Speaks Volumes

The well-known phrase "silence is golden" may be based on a Swiss saying "Sprechen ist silbern, Schweigen ist golden," which means "speech is silver; silence is golden." This metaphor contrasts the value of speech and that of silence. Speech is important, but silence may be even more significant. The power of silence is recognized and embraced in many cultures:

- Those who know do not speak. Those who speak do not know. (*Tao Te Ching*)
- Silence is also speech. (African proverb)
- Silence is a friend who will not betray. (Confucius)

- A loud voice shows an empty head. (Finnish proverb)
- The cat that does not meow catches rats. (Japanese proverb)

Understanding the communicative value of silence is important for several reasons. We use silence to communicate many things: to establish interpersonal distance, to put our thoughts together, to show respect for another person, or to modify others' behaviors.[1]

[1] Virginia P. Richmond and James C. McCroskey, *Nonverbal Behavior in Interpersonal Relationships*, 5th ed. (Boston: Allyn & Bacon, 2004), p. 103.

NONVERBAL BEHAVIOR

Group members send messages through their personal appearance as well as through their facial, vocal, and physical expression. When all of these nonverbal elements are combined, they add enormous complexity and subtlety to group interaction.

Personal Appearance

When group members meet for the first time, they know very little about one another beyond what they see. Physical appearance is influential in forming first impressions. Based on physical appearance, we draw conclusions about someone's education, level of success, moral character, social position, and trustworthiness.[29] For better or worse, attractive people tend to be perceived as friendlier and more credible than those who are considered less attractive. Older people may be viewed as more knowledgeable and experienced than younger people. Men may seem more assertive than women. One study found that good-looking people tend to make more money and get promoted more often than those with average looks.[30]

Even the clothes you wear send messages to other group members. Peter Andersen maintains that "effective small group members should view clothes and hair styles as an important silent statement made to the group. Dress that is appropriate is perhaps most important."[31] Thus, casual attire is more acceptable in informal groups, whereas a professional appearance is expected in business settings and important group presentations. Your appearance should communicate that you respect the group and take its work seriously.

How does the nonverbal environment promote or inhibit group interaction?
(© Bob Daemmrich/Stock, Boston)

Facial Expression

Your face is composed of a complex set of muscles and can produce over a thousand different expressions.[32] Facial expressions allow listeners to continuously contribute to an ongoing group discussion.[33] The facial expressions of group members let you know if they are interested in, agree with, or understand what you have said. Generally, women tend to be more facially expressive, while men are more likely to limit the amount of emotion

TOOLBOX 5.3

Tattoos and Body Piercing Can Damage Credibility

In many cultures—both past and present—people have pierced and tattooed their bodies. These markings often commemorate a rite of passage, such as puberty, marriage, or a successful hunt. However, in most Western cultures, tattoos have been associated with people of lower social status and members of groups such as gangs, "bikers," and lower-ranked military.

Today, pierced ears on women—and a few men—are fairly common. In the past, piercing the nose, tongue, eyebrow, lip, navel, and other body parts was virtually unheard of in mainstream society. However, that too has changed. Tattooing and body piercing have become a popular trend, especially among adolescents and younger adults. Yet, professional men and women in corporate settings rarely display tattoos.

Tattoos and body piercing create an impression that may not serve you well or be what you intend. In one survey, 42 percent of people polled said that they have negative perceptions of employees who display tattoos or body piercing. More than 50 percent of employees with tattoos or body piercing conceal it on the job.[1] Public perception may change as a younger generation of tattooed and pierced college graduates rises to leadership positions in companies and communities. In the meantime, recognize that a tattoo or body piercing can distract from and misrepresent the impression that you want to create. As many young job seekers have learned, you may have to conceal tattoos and remove body piercings for job interviews and in many professional settings.[2]

[1] "Tattoos, Body Art and Piercing" (February 2003). Available from FindArticles, Inc., San Francisco, CA. Copyright National Recreation and Park Association and Gale Group.
[2] Mark Hickson, III, Don W. Stacks, and Nina-Jo Moore, *Nonverbal Communication: Studies and Applications*, 4th ed. (Los Angeles: Roxbury Publishing, 2004), p. 187.

they reveal. Good listening requires that you look at a speaker's facial expressions in order to comprehend the full message.

Of all your facial features, your eyes are the most revealing. Generally, North Americans perceive eye contact as an indicator of attitude. Lack of eye contact is frequently perceived as signifying rudeness, indifference, nervousness, or dishonesty. However, perceptions of eye contact are culturally based. According to Guo-Ming Chen and William Starosta, "direct eye contact is a taboo or an insult in many Asian cultures. Cambodians consider direct eye contact as an invasion of one's privacy."[34]

Eye contact influences interaction in groups. A seating arrangement that allows group members to face one another and establish eye contact helps to maintain interaction. Eye contact also tells others when you want to speak. Returning eye contact to a group leader indicates that you are ready to respond, whereas avoiding eye contact is perceived as an attempt to avoid interaction.

Vocal Expression

Vocal expression is the way you say a word rather than the word itself. Some of the most important vocal characteristics are pitch, volume, rate, and word stress. Variations in these elements can result in different messages. For example, a group

GROUPTECH

Nonverbal Emoticons

When groups meet face to face, members can listen to how words are said and observe nonverbal behavior. However, most virtual groups rely on technologies that don't allow the members to hear or see one another. Participants can't see the facial expressions, head nods, gestures, or posture of other group members. As a result, early users of computer-mediated communication developed emoticons to function in place of nonverbal cues. An **emoticon** is the use of ordinary typographical characters to convey a nonverbal expression. For example, ☺, :-), ;-), :-(, and <g> are commonly used emoticons that convey smiles, winks, frowns, or grins.

In theory, emoticons serve as substitutes for nonverbal behavior. However, research suggests that emoticons have become less and less useful as nonverbal cues. Joseph Walther and K. P. D'Addario found that emoticons have little or no effect on the interpretation of a typed message.[1] Thus, virtual group members are more likely to rely on your words than on your emoticons when interpreting the intention of your message.

Walther and D'Addario also suggest that "the emoticon is now over-used, and the impact that it is supposed to have diminished, either culturally/historically, or as an individual user is first entertained, and later bored, with the cuteness of them all."[2] In their book *Rules of the Net,* Thomas Mandel and Gerard Van der Leun offer the following suggestion: "Nothing—especially the symbols on the top row of your keyboard—can substitute for a clear idea simply expressed. Avoid :-) and all associated emoticons as you would avoid clichés, e.g., like the plague."[3]

Generally, we advise you to avoid emoticons. However, if using emoticons is a norm within your group, ☺ away.

[1] Joseph B. Walther and K. P. D'Addario, *"The Impacts of Emoticons on Message Interpretation in Computer-Mediated Communication."* Paper presented at the meeting of the International Communication Association, Washington, D.C., May 2001.
[2] Walther and D'Addario, p. 13.
[3] Thomas Mandel and Gerard Van der Leun, *Rules of the Net: Online Operating Instructions for Human Beings* (New York: Hyperion, 1996), p. 92.

may find it difficult or unpleasant to listen to a member with a very high-pitched or a monotone voice. A loud voice can convey anger, excitement, or dominance. Group members speaking quietly may signal that the information is confidential. Your volume should be adjusted to the group setting and type of activity. A group may be bored by or stop listening to a member who speaks too slowly. A speaking rate that is too fast makes it difficult to understand the message.

When pitch, volume, and rate are combined, they can be used to vary the stress you give to a word or phrase. **Word stress** refers to the "degree of prominence given to a syllable within a word or a word within a phrase or sentence."[35] Notice the differences in meaning as you stress the italicized words in the following three sentences: Is *that* the report you want me to read? Is that the report you want *me* to read? Is that the report you want me to *read*? Although the same words are used in all three sentences, the meaning of each question is quite different.

Physical Expression

The study of body movement and physical expression is referred to as **kinesics.** Gestures are one of the most animated forms of kinesics. They can emphasize or stress parts of a message, reveal discomfort with the group situation, or convey a message without the use of words. For example, Jeff points to his watch to let the chairperson know that time is running short. At the end of a discussion, a thumbs-up gesture from several group members signals that everyone is satisfied with the group's progress. Many people have difficulty expressing their thoughts without using gestures. Why else would we gesture when we are speaking to someone on the phone? Research suggests that gesturing helps ease the mental effort when communication is difficult.[36]

Even your posture can convey moods and emotions. For example, slouching back in your chair may be perceived as lack of interest or dislike for the group. On the other hand, sitting upright and leaning forward communicates interest and is a sign of attentive listening.

One of the most potent forms of physical expression is touch. Touch can convey a wide range of meanings. In groups, touch is typically used to express encouragement, support, or happiness. Peter Andersen points out that "touch in a small group may establish greater teamwork, solidarity, or sharing."[37] Some group members, however, are more comfortable with touch than others. At one end of a continuum are touch avoiders; at the other end are touch approachers. Misunderstandings can occur between these two kinds of people. Approachers may view avoiders as cold and unfriendly. However, avoiders may perceive approachers as invasive and rude. It is important to remember that gender and culture influence touch avoidance. Women are more likely to avoid opposite-sex touch, whereas men often avoid same-sex touch. In particular, Far Eastern women exhibit more touch avoidance than individuals from other cultures.[38]

THE NONVERBAL ENVIRONMENT

Nonverbal communication extends beyond the behavior of group members; it also includes the group's environment. Two important aspects of a group's nonverbal environment are the arrangement of space and perceptions of personal space.

Arrangement of Space

The way members are seated in relation to one another significantly affects group interaction. Arrangements that physically separate group members make group interaction difficult. For example, the traditional classroom arrangement of rows facing the teacher promotes interaction between the students and the teacher, but it does not encourage communication among the students. Arrangements that bring people closer together and permit direct eye contact among all members promote group interaction. Group members arranged in a circle or around a table can more easily interact with one another.

Your choice of seating position in groups has a direct effect on interaction and influence.[39] A number of studies have demonstrated that group members prefer corner-to-corner or side-by-side seating for cooperative activities. Such an arrangement allows them to be close enough to share materials. Members who anticipate competition or disagreement often choose seats across from each other.

Leadership and group dominance often can be determined by seating positions. Group leaders are more likely to choose or be assigned a seat at the head of a table. Task-oriented leaders are attracted to the head of a table, while the middle position at the side of a table attracts more socially oriented leaders—members who are more concerned about group relationships and encouraging everyone to participate.[40] These two locations place the leader in a position to see and be seen by everyone in the group. Choosing one of these centrally located positions also makes it easier for a member to gain speaking opportunities.

Even the arrangement of a room or the shape of a conference table sends a message to group members. A long, rectangular table gives a group's leader a special place of prominence at its head. A round table allows all members to sit in equally important positions. The Paris peace talks that helped end the war in Vietnam were bogged down for eight months until delegates from South Vietnam, the National Liberation Front, and the United States agreed to a round table as the setting for negotiation. When the leaders of Bosnia, Croatia, and Serbia met at Wright-Patterson Air Force Base in Ohio, the United States made sure that each party had equal seating space around a modest but perfectly round table. The arrangement of space is not a trivial matter when the success of a group is so consequential.

In addition to seating arrangement, the décor of a room can have a direct influence on a group and its work. A New England advertising agency learned this lesson the hard way when a fistfight broke out during a focus group session.[41] Facilitators reported that regardless of the topic being

How does the group's seating arrangement affect the group's interaction?
(© Masterfile)

FIGURE 5.3   **Seating Arrangements**

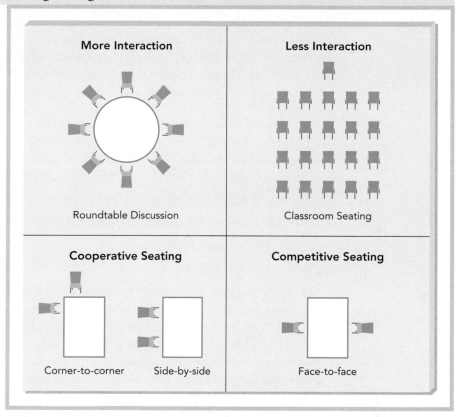

discussed, no one ever seemed happy in the room. Participants were grumpy, negative, and resistant to new ideas. The company discovered that the problem was the room itself: It was cramped, stifling, and forbidding—a cross between a hospital room and a police interrogation room. The solution: a total redesign and redecoration. The room was expanded and given long, gently curved walls. Soft, indirect light filtered in through curved windows. Participants were given seating choices of armchairs or small couches surrounding circular coffee tables. The results were better than expected. There were no more fistfights. Instead, focus group participants became much more cooperative and positive.

Perceptions of Personal Space

Groups and their members may function quite differently depending on how they perceive the space and people around them. The study of how we perceive and use personal space is referred to as **proxemics**. Within groups, two important proxemic variables are territoriality and interpersonal space.

Territoriality.   **Territoriality** is the sense of personal ownership that is attached to a particular space. For instance, in most classrooms, students sit in the same place every day. If you have ever walked into a classroom and found another person in *your* seat, you may have felt that your territory had been violated. Ownership of space is often designated by objects acting as markers of territory. Placing a coat or books on a chair lets others know that that space is taken. As a group develops, members often establish their individual territory. They may sit in the same place near the same people during every meeting. Individuals who fail to respect the territory of others are violating an important group norm.

Interpersonal Space. **Interpersonal space** can be thought of as an invisible, psychological "bubble" surrounding each person that expands or shrinks depending on the communicators and the context. Anthropologist Edward T. Hall identifies four zones of interaction used by most North Americans.[42]

* Intimate distance: touching to eighteen inches
* Personal distance: eighteen inches to four feet
* Social distance: four to eight feet
* Public distance: eight or more feet

Intimate distance ranges from touching to approximately eighteen inches apart. Close friends, some family members, and lovers are normally permitted to come this close. Peter Andersen notes that "at such close distances group members will feel inhibited from interacting and will make an attempt to restore their personal space bubble by moving back even if that means leaving the group."[43]

Personal distance ranges from about eighteen inches to four feet apart. The typical distance is an arm's length away. This zone is used for conversations with friends and acquaintances. Members of most well-established groups interact with one another at this distance. They feel close enough to engage in discussion but far enough away to be comfortable.

FIGURE 5.4   **Zones of Personal Space**

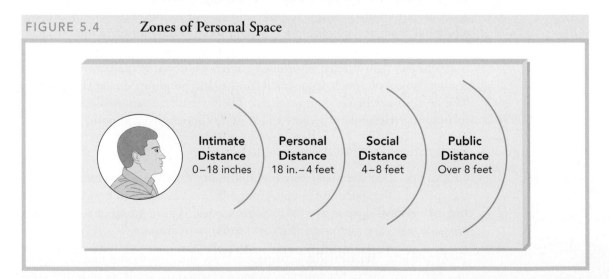

| | Intimate Distance 0–18 inches | Personal Distance 18 in.–4 feet | Social Distance 4–8 feet | Public Distance Over 8 feet |

Social distance encompasses a range of four to eight feet apart. We usually interact with new acquaintances and strangers in this zone. Groups in which members use the outer limits of this zone will find it difficult to maintain interaction.

Public distance extends beyond eight feet. Lectures and speeches are usually presented using this distance. Groups are unlikely to use this zone unless they are making a presentation to a larger audience.

NONVERBAL COMMUNICATION AND CULTURE

When we interact with group members from different cultural backgrounds, interpreting their nonverbal behavior may be as difficult as translating an unfamiliar foreign language. The multiple meanings of nonverbal communication in other cultures can be illustrated by focusing on two elements: personal space and eye contact. Research on personal space indicates that most Latin Americans, Arabs, and Greeks require less distance between people than North Americans do. Cultural differences also are evident when measuring the amount and directness of eye contact. If, for example, a white supervisor reprimands a young black male, the employee may respond by looking downward rather than looking at the supervisor. In some cases, the employee's response may anger the supervisor and be interpreted as inattention or defiance. Intercultural researchers report that "members of certain segments of black culture reportedly cast their eyes downward as a sign of respect; in white cultures, however, members expect direct eye contact as a sign of listening and showing respect for authority."[44]

There is a danger, however, of stereotyping people from different backgrounds and cultures on the basis of their nonverbal behavior. Latino, Arab, and Greek group members may not be comfortable with less personal space than a North American. Young black males may look directly at a white supervisor with respect. When interpreting nonverbal behavior, try to understand, respect, and adapt to individual differences rather than assuming that all people from a particular culture behave alike.

If you are unsure about the appropriate way to respond nonverbally, ask. Too often, we find out about the nonverbal rules of another culture only after we have broken them.

CREATING A SUPPORTIVE COMMUNICATION CLIMATE

Our use of and reaction to language and nonverbal communication establishes a unique group atmosphere or climate. Specifically, a group's **climate** is the degree to which the group's members feel comfortable interacting. In some groups, the climate is warm and supportive. Members like and trust one another as they work

FIGURE 5.5   **Group Communication Climates**

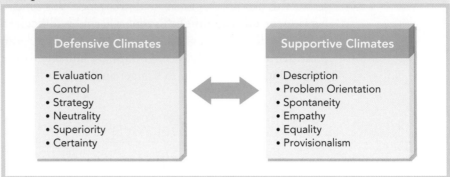

toward a common goal. In chillier group climates, defensiveness and tension pollute the atmosphere. Members may feel threatened by and suspicious of one another.

Jack Gibb has described six pairs of communication behavior that influence whether a group's climate is defensive or supportive.[45] When the group climate is defensive, members devote attention to defending themselves and defeating perceived opponents. Synergy occurs only when a group functions in a supportive climate.

Chapter 1, "Introduction to Group Communication," introduces the notion of dialectic tensions and the need to balance those tensions in effective groups. Gibb's dimensions constitute dialectic tensions that characterize a group's communication climate. Similarly, groups must effectively balance defensive and supportive behaviors. For instance, successful groups must balance the need to evaluate the group's work with the use of supportive behavior. The need to approach problems strategically must be balanced with the need for spontaneous communication. And, successful groups recognize when neutral behavior is needed and when expressions of empathy are more appropriate.

Evaluation and Description

Which of the following statements would you prefer to hear from a member of your group: "That's the dumbest idea you've ever come up with" or "I'd like to think we could do that, but I have some concerns"? The first statement evaluates the person and the idea, whereas the second begins a description of the speaker's reservations. Statements and behavior that evaluate or judge others elicit defensiveness. Nonverbal behavior such as laughter or groans can be as evaluative as the sharpest verbal criticism. Description includes neutral requests for information and statements that do not attack other people's opinions or actions. Although groups cannot and should not completely eliminate evaluative communication, highly judgmental remarks aimed at particular individuals should be avoided.

One of the best ways to move from evaluation to description is to substitute specific "I" statements for critical "you" statements. Beginning a statement with,

"You disappoint me when . . ." can promote defensiveness. "You" implies blame. "I" clarifies what you think and feel, while "you" can make a person feel criticized. "I am disappointed that the report isn't complete" acknowledges that you are responsible for your own thoughts and feelings while describing the situation that you find troublesome.

Control and Problem Orientation

Problem orientation implies that members are highly committed to the group and its goal. Control implies that some members are more interested in gaining power and achieving their own personal goals. For example, the overly aggressive salesperson or telephone solicitor is trying to separate you from your money rather than understanding and finding the solution that best meets your needs. If you think that someone is trying to manipulate or control you, you are likely to resist. Approaching communication from the perspective of problem orientation results in a message that indicates that you are not trying to control or impose a predetermined solution upon the group.

Strategy and Spontaneity

Strategic communication suggests that hidden agendas are operating within the group. Members suspect that their ideas are not being listened to fairly. Spontaneous communication implies the use of honest and open responses. How would you feel if, after what appears to be a sincere and spontaneous discussion, someone in your group says, "I just happen to have a proposal that George and I put together—it's written and ready to sign off on." Suspicion and defensiveness would be a natural reaction to such a strategic move by two group members.

Neutrality and Empathy

Neutral behaviors are impersonal and fail to express concern for another person's emotional needs. Empathic communication conveys an understanding of members' feelings. When your words and nonverbal behavior communicate a lack of concern or understanding, resentment and defensiveness can result. If you are explaining why you have not met a deadline and other group members sit stone-faced, they may be telling you that your personal problems are of no interest to them. If group members nod their heads and look concerned when you describe the difficulties you have encountered, their understanding and sympathy have created a much more supportive group climate.

Superiority and Equality

A meeting may be the worst place to show off and brag about your accomplishments and status. If your communication style and comments suggest that you are better than other members, your suggestions may be met with hostility and defensiveness. Arranging a meeting room so that some members have more prominent seats or better chairs than other members suggests that not all members are created equal. Conveying a willingness to cooperate with group members implies an attitude of equality. When all members are viewed equally, then loyalty, respect, and effort can be expected from everyone.

Certainty and Provisionalism

Members who insist that they are always right and focus on winning arguments produce a climate of certainty. As a result, other group members are inclined to make greater efforts to defend their own ideas. An attitude of provisionalism suggests a willingness to modify one's own attitudes and behaviors as a result of group feedback. If you are certain, you are less likely to listen to other members and less likely to alter your opinion. If you can be flexible and focus on achieving the group's goal, there is a greater likelihood that the group's performance and outcome will be successful.

BALANCING LANGUAGE AND NONVERBAL BEHAVIOR

There is an inseparable connection between language and nonverbal communication. When verbal and nonverbal behavior reinforce and complement each other, communication is enhanced. When verbal and nonverbal messages contradict each other, the group can become confused and defensive. If members put too much emphasis on the meanings of words, bypassing is more likely to occur.

In a supportive group climate, members are more likely to feel comfortable and confident. By avoiding statements and actions that are highly evaluative, controlling, strategic, neutral, superior, and certain, a group is more likely to succeed in working together toward the achievement of a shared goal.

Groups must achieve a balance of language and nonverbal behavior in order to maximize the effectiveness of both forms of communication. Although language and nonverbal behavior are powerful tools, they will be only as effective as the member who uses them.

GroupWork

Context, Context, Context

Goal: To demonstrate the extent to which the meanings of words and nonverbal behavior are dependent on social climate and group circumstances

Participants: Groups of at least three members

Procedure

1. Each group should create a situation in which the following sentence is uttered: "I don't think that's right." The group must

   - Decide what sentence came before and after "I don't think that's right."
   - Decide upon the physical setting and situation confronting the group in which a member would say, "I don't think that's right."

   Each group should then create and stage a "scene" in which at least two group members "act" the parts in an incident where "I don't think that's right" is part of the "script." The group may introduce the scene to the class by describing the "roles" and "setting" before the scene begins.

2. After all the groups have "performed" their scene, the class should discuss the following questions:

   - How did the context or situation change the meaning of "I don't think that's right"?
   - How did the nonverbal behavior and setting differ in each scene?
   - How could each group's "I don't think that's right" be paraphrased into a different sentence?
   - Which component communicated the most information about the meaning of the scene—the words, the nonverbal behavior, or the situation?

GROUPASSESSMENT

Auditing Team Talk

Directions: Circle the term that best describes the extent to which the members of your group engage in productive team talk.

When your group communicates . . .

1. Do members use plural pronouns rather than singular ones?	Very often	Sometimes	Rarely
2. Do members use language that acknowledges shared needs?	Very often	Sometimes	Rarely
3. Do members solicit opinions and express the need for cooperation?	Very often	Sometimes	Rarely
4. Do members talk to one another on equal terms?	Very often	Sometimes	Rarely
5. Do members use casual language, nicknames, slang?	Very often	Sometimes	Rarely

6. Do members express empathy and liking?	Very often	Sometimes	Rarely
7. Do members express interest in solving problems?	Very often	Sometimes	Rarely
8. Do members use a nonthreatening tone and nonjudgmental language?	Very often	Sometimes	Rarely
9. Do members paraphrase one another?	Very often	Sometimes	Rarely
10. Do members ask "what if" questions?	Very often	Sometimes	Rarely
11. Do members propose objective criteria for solutions?	Very often	Sometimes	Rarely
12. Do members summarize areas of agreement?	Very often	Sometimes	Rarely

Scoring: Analyze your group's team talk by looking at the number of times you circled *Very often, Sometimes,* and *Rarely.* The more times you circled *Very often,* the more likely it is that your group engages in productive team talk. The more times you circled *Rarely,* the more likely it is that team talk inhibits the progress and success of your group. To get a more accurate assessment of team talk for your entire group, everyone should complete the questionnaire and share their responses. Is there a consistent response to each question? If there are significant disagreements on several questions, the members of your group may benefit from a discussion about the nature of their team talk.

NOTES

1. Ann Donnellon, *Team Talk: The Power of Language in Team Dynamics (*Boston: Harvard Business School, 1996), p. 6.
2. Victoria Fromkin and Robert Rodman, *An Introduction to Language,* 6th ed. (Ft. Worth, TX: Harcourt Grace, 1998), p. 3.
3. Virginia P. Richmond and James C. McCroskey. *Nonverbal Behavior in Interpersonal Relations,* 5th ed. (Boston: Allyn & Bacon, 2004), p. 5.
4. Myron W. Lustig and Jolene Koester, *Intercultural Competence: Interpersonal Communication Across Cultures,* 5th ed. (Boston: Pearson/Allyn & Bacon, 2006), pp. 110, 111.
5. S. I. Hayakawa and Alan R. Hayakawa, *Language and Thought in Action,* 5th ed. (San Diego, CA: Harcourt Brace Jovanovich, 1990), p. 43.
6. *The American Heritage Dictionary of the English Language,* 4th ed. (Boston: Houghton Mifflin, 2000), p. 1093.
7. Vivian Cook, *Inside Language* (London: Arnold, 1997), p. 91.
8. Donnellon, p. 25.
9. Based on Donnellon, pp. 31–33.
10. Donnellon, p. 25.
11. William V. Haney, *Communication and Interpersonal Relations: Text and Cases, 6th ed. (*Homewood, IL: Irwin, 1992), p. 269.
12. Haney, p. 290.
13. Cook, p. 244.
14. William Lutz, *Doublespeak* (New York: HarperPerennial, 1990), p. 3.
15. Deborah Tannen, *You Just Don't Understand: Women and Men in Conversation* (New York: William Morrow, 1990).
16. Shirley N. Weber, "The Need to Be: The Sociocultural Significance of Black Language," in Kathleen S. Verderber, *Voices: A Selection of Multicultural Readings* (Belmont, CA: Wadsworth, 1995), p. 30.

17. Lustig and Koester, p. 200.

18. Lustig and Koester, p. 199.

19. Carley H. Dodd, *Dynamics of Intercultural Communication,* 4th ed. (Madison, WI: Brown & Benchmark, 1995), p. 151.

20. Suzanne C. Beyea, "Improving Verbal Communication in Clinical Care," *AORN Journal,* 79 (May 2004). Available at http://www.find/articles.com/p/articles/mi_,0FSL/is_5_79/ai_n6074289.

21. Mark Twain, Letter to George Bainton, October 15, 1888. http://www.twainquotes.com/Lightning.html.

22. Based on Melinda G. Kramer, Greg Leggett, and C. David Mead, *Prentice Hall Handbook for Writers,* 12th ed. (Englewood Cliffs, NJ: Prentice Hall, 1995), p. 272.

23. Donnellon, p. 33.

24. Donnellon, pp. 40–41.

25. Joel Saltzman, *If You Can Talk, You Can Write* (New York: Time Warner, 1993), pp. 48–49.

26. See Ann Raimes, *Keys for Writers: A Brief Handbook,* 3rd ed. (Boston: Houghton Mifflin, 2003), pp. 282–284. Also see Isa Engleberg and Ann Raimes, *Pocket Keys for Speakers* (Boston: Houghton Mifflin, 2004), Part 12, pp. 227–264.

27. See Mark Hickson, III, Don W. Stacks, and Nina-Jo Moore, *Nonverbal Communication: Studies and Applications, 4th ed.* (Los Angeles: Roxbury Publishing, 2004), p. 7; Albert Mehrabian, *Silent Messages: Implicit Communication of Emotions and Attitudes,* 2nd ed. (Belmont, CA: Wadsworth, 1981), p. 77.

28. Robert S. Cathcart, Larry A. Samovar, and Linda D. Henman, *Small Group Communication: Theory and Practice,* 7th ed. (Dubuque, IA: Brown & Benchmark, 1996), p. 236.

29. Hickson, Stacks, and Moore, p. 189.

30. From The Federal Reserve Bank of St. Louis, *The Regional Economist,* April 2005, quoted in "Good Looks Can Mean Good Pay, Study Says," *The Sun,* April 28, 2005, p. D1.

31. Peter A. Andersen, "Nonverbal Communication in the Small Group," in *Small Group Communication:* *A Reader,* 6th ed. ed. Robert S. Cathcart and Larry A. Samovar (Dubuque, IA: Wm. C. Brown, 1992), p. 273.

32. Martin S. Remland, *Nonverbal Communication in Everyday Life (*Boston: Houghton Mifflin, 2000), p. 169.

33. Nicole Chovil, "Measuring Conversational Facial Displays," in *The Sourcebook of Nonverbal Measures: Going Beyond Words*, ed. Valerie Manusov (Mahwah, NJ: Lawrence Erlbaum, 2005), p. 174.

34. Guo-Ming Chen and William J. Starosta, *Foundations of Intercultural Communication (*Boston: Allyn & Bacon, 1998), p. 91.

35. Lyle V. Mayer, *Fundamentals of Voice and Diction,* 13th ed. (Madison, WI: Brown & Benchmark, 2004), p. 229.

36. Sharon Begley, "Gesturing as You Talk Can Help You Take a Load Off Your Mind," *Wall Street Journal,* November 14, 2003.

37. Andersen, p. 267.

38. Peter A. Andersen, "The Touch Avoidance Measure," in *The Sourcebook of Nonverbal Measures: Going Beyond Words,* ed. Valerie Manusov (Mahwah, NJ: Lawrence Erlbaum, 2005), p. 62.

39. See Judith K. Burgoon, "Spatial Relationships in Small Groups," in Randy Y. Hirokawa, Robert S. Cathcart, Larry A. Samovar, and Linda D Henman, *Small Group Communication: Theory and Practice*, 8th ed. (Los Angeles: Roxbury, 2003), pp. 85–96.

40. Mark L. Knapp and Judith A. Hall, *Nonverbal Communication in Human Interaction,* 4th ed. (Fort Worth, TX: Harcourt Brace, 1997), p. 177.

41. Jeffrey Krasner, "Fistfights and Feng Shui," *Boston Globe* (July 21, 2001), pp. C1–C2.

42. Edward T. Hall, *The Hidden Dimension (*New York: Doubleday, 1982).

43. Andersen, p. 269.

44. Dodd, p. 160.

45. Jack R. Gibb, "Defensive Communication," in Robert S. Cathcart and Larry A. Samovar, *Small Group Communication: A Reader*, 2nd ed. (1974), pp. 327–333.

Listening in Groups

THE CHALLENGE OF LISTENING IN GROUPS

The ability to balance effective speaking with appropriate listening affects every facet of group life. When communication researchers ask experienced personnel managers to identify the communication skills that they consider important for employees working in group settings, effective listening often tops the list of critical communication skills.[1] Bonnie Jacobson, author of *If Only You Would Listen,* believes that "the main skill required to build an effective work team is keeping your mouth shut and giving your team members the chance to give you their point of view."[2]

Listening is more difficult in groups than it is in almost any other communication situation. There are multiple speakers, multiple perspectives, and multiple goals. You are expected to listen and, at the same time, to be able to respond, on the spot, to unexpected news, unusual ideas, and conflicting points of view. Instead of concentrating on what *one* person says and does, you must pay attention to *everyone's* reactions. In a group discussion, a short daydream, a side conversation, or thoughts about a personal problem can result in missed information, misinterpreted instructions, or inappropriate reactions. Complicating matters is the fact that the social pressure to listen is not as strong in groups as it would be in a two-person conversation. If one group member doesn't listen or respond, others usually will. Thus, group members may be poor listeners because they count on others to listen for them.[3]

Communication consultant Harry Chambers put it this way: "The challenge of effective listening is universal. It is the least practiced skill in America today; poor listening skills influence our professional lives and also play a major role in our personal relationships."[4] But unlike the case with many other influences, *you* control whether, when, and how you listen.

The Nature of Listening

Listening is the ability to understand, analyze, respect, and appropriately respond to the meaning of another person's spoken and nonverbal messages. At first, listening may appear to be as easy and natural as breathing. In fact, nothing could be farther from the truth. Although most of us can *hear*, we often fail to *listen* to what others say. Hearing requires only physical ability; listening requires complex thinking ability. People who are hearing-impaired may be better listeners than those who can hear the faintest sound.

Listening is our number one communication activity. A study of college students found that listening occupies more than half of their communicating time.[5] In the corporate world, studies estimate that managers spend the equivalent of two out of every five working days in meetings and may devote over 60 percent of their workday to listening to others.[6] Chief executives may spend as much as 75 percent of their communicating time listening.[7] This means that businesses

What nonverbal behaviors do these group members exhibit that suggest that they are listening effectively? (© Michael Newman/ Photo Edit)

are spending millions of dollars to pay people to listen, "and simply assuming (or hoping) that it's money well spent."[8] Although percentages vary from study to study, Figure 6.1 shows how most of us divide up our daily communicating time.

Yet, despite the enormous amount of time we spend listening, most of us are not very good listeners. In fact, we tend to think we're better listeners than we really are. Several studies report that immediately after listening to a short talk, most of us cannot accurately report 50 percent of what was said. Without training, we listen at only 25 percent efficiency.[9] And, of that 25 percent, most of what we remember is a distorted or inaccurate recollection.[10]

In surveys of business leaders, listening is often cited as the communication skill that is most lacking in new employees. When asked about the percentage of high school graduates with good listening skills, the answer was only 19 percent.[11] A study of Fortune 500 company training managers concludes that "poor listening performance is ranked as a serious problem during meetings, performance appraisals, and superior-subordinate communication."[12]

FIGURE 6.1   **Time Spent Communicating**

Communication Activity	Percent of Communicating Time
Listening	40–70%
Speaking	20–35%
Reading	10–20%
Writing	5–15%

The Dialectics of Listening

Speaking and listening are two sides of a single coin, twin competencies that rely on and reflect each other. Thus, the dialectics of speaking and listening affect how members become and succeed as leaders. As you will learn in Chapter 8, "Group Leadership," the member who speaks first and most often is more likely to emerge as the group's leader.[13] The number of contributions is even more important than the quality of those contributions. On the other hand, once a person becomes a leader, listening is much more important in determining his or her success. Effective leaders engage in listening more than talking and in asking more than telling.[14]

The vast majority of your time in groups will be spent listening. Even during a simple half-hour meeting of five people, it is unlikely that any member will talk more than a total of ten minutes—unless that person wants to be accused of monopolizing the discussion. Unfortunately, many of us place more emphasis on the roles and responsibilities of group members who talk rather than on those

TOOLBOX 6.1

You Must *Want* to Listen

Stephen R. Covey, author of *The 7 Habits of Highly Effective People*, provides a definition of *habit* that also describes effective communication. In Covey's opinion, habits require knowledge, skills, and desire. Knowledge plays a role similar to that of methods and theories by describing *what* to do and *why* to do it. Skills represent *how* to do it. And, most important of all, you must have the desire to communicate effectively and ethically. In order to make something a habit, you have to have all three. Effective listening relies as much on your attitude (*wanting* to do it) as it does on your knowledge and skills. Covey uses the challenge of listening to illustrate the three components of an effective habit:

1. *Knowledge.* I may be ineffective in my interaction with my work associates, my spouse, or my children because I constantly tell them what I think, but I never really listen to them. Unless I search out correct principles of human interaction, I may not even *know* I need to listen.

2. *Skills.* Even if I do know that to interact effectively with others, I really need to listen to them, I may not have the skill. I may not know how to really listen deeply to another human being.

3. *Desire.* But knowing I need to listen and knowing how to listen is not enough. Unless I *want* to listen, unless I have the desire, it won't be a habit in my life.[1]

The best listeners are motivated to listen; they let go of what's on their mind long enough to hear what's on the other person's mind. An appropriate listening attitude does not mean that you know exactly what another person thinks or feels. Instead, it is a genuine willingness and openness to listen and discover.[2]

[1] Stephen R. Covey, *The 7 Habits of Highly Effective People* (New York: Simon and Schuster, 1989), p. 48.
[2] Michael P. Nichols, *The Lost Art of Listening* (New York: Guilford, 1995), pp. 42, 43.

who listen. "This unbalanced emphasis, especially as it actually affects persons in real discussions, could be an important cause of the problems that speaking is supposed to cure."[15] In other words, if you are concerned only about what you are going to say in a group discussion, you can't give your full attention to what is being said by others.

TYPES OF LISTENING

Effective group members use different types of listening to advance group goals. For example, if your group is discussing a controversial issue or proposal, you may engage analytical listening skills. However, if you're celebrating a group member's birthday, you may put aside analytical listening to enjoy the festivities. Researchers have identified several types of listening, each of which calls upon unique listening skills.

Discriminative Listening

In Chapter 3, "Group Member Diversity," we define discrimination as the way in which people act out and express prejudice. The meaning of discriminative listening is very different. In fact, the first definition of *discriminate* in *The American Heritage Dictionary of the English Language* is "to make a clear distinction; distinguish," as in "Can you discriminate among the different sounds of orchestra instruments?"[16] Thus, **discriminative listening** is the ability "to distinguish auditory and/or visual stimuli."[17]

Discriminative listening answers the question: Do I hear accurately? At its simplest level, it involves the ability to make clear, aural distinctions among the sounds and words in a language. Discriminative listeners also notice nonverbal behavior, such as a smile, a groan, or the shrug of a shoulder.

Discriminative listening comes first among the five types of listening because it forms the basis for the other four. If you cannot hear the difference between an on-key and an off-key note, you may not be able to listen appreciatively to a singer. If you cannot hear or recognize the distress in a person's voice, you may not be able to listen empathically.

FIGURE 6.2   **Types of Listening**

Types of Listening

- Discriminative Listening
- Comprehensive Listening
- Empathic Listening
- Analytical Listening
- Appreciative Listening

Comprehensive Listening

Comprehensive listening in a group discussion requires an answer to the following question: What do group members mean? **Comprehensive listening** focuses on accurately understanding the meaning of group members' spoken and nonverbal messages. After all, if you don't understand what a person means, you can't be expected to respond in a reasonable way. For example, an after-class discussion might begin as follows: "Let's have a party on the last day of class," says Geneva. A comprehensive listener may wonder whether Geneva means that (1) we should have a party instead of an exam, (2) we should ask the instructor whether we can have a party, or (3) we should have a party after class. Misinterpreting the meaning of Geneva's comment could result in an inappropriate response.

Answering the following questions can help you understand several criteria for effective comprehensive listening:

- How well do you understand the words spoken by other group members?

- How well can you accurately identify the main ideas and the arguments and evidence used to support a group member's claim?

- How well does the message confirm what you already know or believe?

Empathic Listening

Empathic listening in a group discussion requires an answer to the following question: How do group members feel? **Empathic listening** goes beyond comprehending what a person means; it focuses on understanding and identifying with a member's situation, feelings, or motives. Can you see the situation through the other member's eyes? Put another way, how would you feel in a similar situation?

By not listening for feelings, you may overlook the most important part of a message. Even if you understand every word a person says, you can still miss the anger, enthusiasm, or frustration in a group member's voice. An empathic listener doesn't have to agree with other group members or feel the same way as they do, but the person does have to try to understand the type and intensity of feelings that those members are experiencing. For example, the after-class discussion might continue as follows: "A class party would be a waste of time," exclaims Kim. An empathic listener may wonder whether Kim means that (1) she has more important things to do during exam week, (2) she doesn't think the class or the instructor deserves a party, or (3) she doesn't want to be obligated to attend such a party.

Empathic listening is difficult, but it also is "the pinnacle of listening" because it demands "fine skill and exquisite tuning into another's mood and feeling."[18] You can improve your empathic listening ability by using one or more of the following strategies:

- Be conscious of your feedback. Are you showing interest and concern? Do your vocal tone, gestures, and posture communicate friendliness and trust?

- Avoid being judgmental.

- Focus on the speaker, not on yourself. Avoid talking about your own experiences and feelings.[19]

Analytical Listening

Analytical listening asks this question: What's my opinion? **Analytical listening** focuses on evaluating and forming appropriate opinions about the content of a message. It requires critical thinking and careful analysis. Once you comprehend and empathize with group members, you may ask yourself whether you think they are right or wrong, logical or illogical. Good analytical listeners understand why they accept or reject another member's ideas and suggestions.

Russell makes the following proposal: "Suppose we chip in and give Professor Hawkins a gift at the party?" An analytical listener might think that (1) the instructor could misinterpret the gift, (2) some class members won't want to make a contribution, or (3) there isn't enough time to collect money and buy an appropriate gift.

Recognizing that another group member is trying to persuade—rather than merely inform—is the first step in improving your analytical listening. The following strategies can help you improve this critical listening skill:[20]

- Learn to recognize persuasive strategies. Is the group member appealing to your emotions and/or to your critical thinking ability?

- Evaluate persuasive arguments and evidence. Are conclusions based on relevant and reliable evidence?

- Recognize any changes in your beliefs or attitudes. Have you changed your original position? Why or why not?

TOOLBOX 6.2

Critical Thinking and Listening

Analytical listening requires critical thinking. Some people, however, mistakenly believe that critical thinking means the same thing as criticizing. Definitions of the word *criticize* include "to find fault with" and "to judge the merits and faults of."[1] The word *critical* is a broader, less fault-finding term. *Critical* comes from the Greek word for critic (*kritikos*), which means to question, to make sense of, or to be able to analyze.[2]

Critical thinking is a way of analyzing what you read, see, hear, and experience in order to make intelligent decisions about what to believe or do. It is not the same as tearing down someone's argument or criticizing a person. Critical thinkers must identify what they are being asked to believe or accept and evaluate the evidence and reasoning given in support of the belief. Good critical thinkers develop and defend a position on an issue, ask probing questions, are open-minded, and draw reasonable conclusions.[3] And they are skilled analytical listeners.

[1] *The American Heritage Dictionary of the English Language*, 4th ed. (Boston: Houghton Mifflin, 2000), p. 432.
[2] John Chaffee, *Thinking Critically*, 7th ed. (Boston: Houghton Mifflin, 2003), p. 51.
[3] Robert H. Ennis, "Critical Thinking Assessment," *Theory into Practice*, 32 (1993), p. 180.

Appreciative Listening

Appreciative listening answers this question: Do I like or value what another member has said? **Appreciative listening** focuses on the *way* group members think and speak—the way they choose and use words; their ability to inject appropriate humor, argue persuasively, or demonstrate understanding. For example, if a group is struggling with the wording of a recommendation, appreciative listening can help identify the statement that best captures and eloquently expresses the central idea and spirit of the proposal. When we are pleased to hear a member find the right words to calm a frustrated member or energize an apathetic group, we are listening appreciatively. Appreciative listening skills help us enjoy and acknowledge good talk in groups.

"Well," suggests Paul, "why not buy a thank-you card, ask class members to sign it, and present it to Mr. Hawkins at the party?" An appreciative listener might think, (1) Paul always comes up with the best ideas, (2) a well-selected card may be able to express our appreciation better than we could, or (3) I will thank Paul for making a suggestion that doesn't obligate anyone to contribute to or attend the party.

Florence Wolff and Nadine Marsnik note that "listeners often devote a great part of their day to appreciative listening, but often without a conscious plan."[21] We listen appreciatively to a favorite radio station or CD. We appreciate a spellbinding or funny story. But when we are asked to listen to something new or challenging, we're often hard-pressed to listen appreciatively. Here are some suggestions for improving this type of listening:

- Set aside time for appreciative listening. For example, don't listen to a friend's story or problem while scanning a magazine.

- Welcome opportunities to hear something new or challenging.

- Prepare to listen appreciatively. For example, read about or discuss a play or composer before going to the theater or concert hall.

GROUP ROLES AND LISTENING

No one is a perfect listener. Certainly, it is unreasonable to expect that every group member will be an ideal discriminative, comprehensive, empathic, analytical, and appreciative listener. Fortunately, the group situation provides a way of balancing the strengths and weaknesses of listeners within a group. One way to assess and improve the listening behavior of a group as a whole is to understand the relationship between listening abilities and member roles.

Task Roles and Listening

Members who assume important task roles are often good comprehensive and analytical listeners. Clarifier-summarizers use comprehensive listening to accurately reexplain the ideas of others and summarize group conclusions. Evaluator-critics are usually effective analytical listeners who assess ideas and suggestions as well as the validity of arguments. An effective recorder-secretary, however, must be a comprehensive rather than an analytical listener when taking minutes. If several group members effectively assume most of the traditional task roles, the group, as a whole, is likely to be good at comprehensive and analytical listening.

Maintenance Roles and Listening

Maintenance roles affect how well a group gets along. They focus on building relationships and maintaining a friendly atmosphere. Members who assume important maintenance roles are often good empathic and appreciative listeners. Encourager-supporters and observer-interpreters use comprehensive, empathic, and appreciative listening to explain both how others feel and what others are trying to

ETHICAL GROUPS

 # Self-Centered Roles and Listening

As you know from Chapter 2, "Group Development," self-centered roles occur when members put their own needs ahead of the group's goal and other members' needs. Although members who assume self-centered roles may be excellent comprehensive and analytical listeners, their goals may be unethical. For example, aggressors and dominators may be analytical listeners who eagerly expose the weaknesses in other members' comments in order to get their own way. Blockers may be good listeners who purposely ignore what they hear or poor listeners who are incapable of comprehending or appreciating the comments of others. Recognition seekers, confessors, and special interest pleaders may be so preoccupied with their own needs that they are unable to listen to anyone else in the group.

In addition to the listening styles that reflect self-centered roles, unethical listening can take other forms that serve self-centered goals, as illustrated in the following situations:

- Listening behavior that shows no respect for the opinions of others
- Listening for the purpose of criticizing the ideas of others
- Listening for personal information that can be used to humiliate or criticize others
- Faking listening in order to curry favor with high-status members

Ethical listening is as important as ethical speaking, particularly because we spend most of our communicating time listening. Alexander Solzhenitsyn, winner of the Nobel Prize in Literature, lamented that "many hasty, immature, superficial, and misleading judgments are expressed every day . . . without any verification."[1] Ethical listeners have a responsibility to understand, analyze, and respond appropriately to messages that have personal, professional, political, and moral consequences for themselves and others.

[1] Alexander Solzhenitsyn, "A World Split Apart," *Vital Speeches*, September 1978, p. 680.

say. Harmonizers and tension releasers are often empathic listeners who understand when and how to resolve conflicts, mediate differences, and relax the group. If several group members effectively assume most maintenance roles, the group, as a whole, is likely to be good at empathic and appreciative listening.

Leadership Functions and Listening

Researchers have discovered strong links between listening skills and successful leadership.[22] Good leaders are good listeners. They know when to use comprehensive, empathic, analytical, and appreciative listening. Effective leaders are also proactive listeners. They don't wait to clear up misunderstandings; they try to make sure that every group member comprehends what is being said. They don't wait for misunderstandings to escalate into arguments; they intervene at the slightest hint of hostility. Proactive leaders try to find out what members think and feel by asking them rather than by guessing what is on their minds.

Leaders who are good listeners do not fake attention, pretend to comprehend, or ignore other group members. Instead, they work as hard as they can to better understand what members are saying and how their comments affect the group and its goals. In studying the characteristics of effective groups and their leaders, Larson and LaFasto share the comments of a successful aerospace leader: "The worst failing is a team leader who's a nonlistener. A guy who doesn't listen to his people—and that doesn't mean listening to them and doing whatever the hell he wants to do—can make a lot of mistakes."[23]

IMPROVING LISTENING

Two major listening principles balance the need for comprehensive and analytical listening with the need for empathic and appreciative listening. The two principles are (1) use your extra thought speed, and (2) apply the golden listening rule. Once these principles are understood and employed as overriding listening standards, group members can begin to work on specific listening methods and skills.

Use Your Extra Thought Speed

Most people talk at about 125 to 150 words per minute. According to Ralph Nichols, there is good evidence that if thought were measured in words per minute, most of us could think at three to four times the rate at which we speak.[24] Thus, we have about four hundred extra words of spare thinking time during every minute a person is talking to us.

Thought speed is the speed (in words per minute) at which most people can think compared to the speed at which others can speak. Ralph Nichols asks the obvious question: "What do we do with our excess thinking time while someone is speaking?"[25] Poor listeners use their extra thought speed to daydream, engage in side conversations, take unnecessary notes, or plan how to confront the speaker. Good listeners use their extra thought speed productively. They . . .

- identify and summarize main ideas.

- pay extra attention to nonverbal behavior.

- analyze arguments.

- assess the relevance of a speaker's comments.

Effective group members don't waste their extra thought speed—they use it to enhance comprehensive and analytical listening.

Apply the Golden Listening Rule

The **golden listening rule** is easy to remember: Listen to others as you would have them listen to you. Unfortunately, this rule can be difficult to follow. It asks you to suspend your own needs in order to listen to someone else's. Michael P. Nichols counsels, "Let go of what's on your mind long enough to hear what's on the other person's."[26]

The golden listening rule is not so much a "rule" as it is a positive listening attitude. If you aren't motivated to listen, you won't listen. If you aren't willing to stop talking, you won't listen. The following six positive listening attitudes have six negative counterparts:[27]

Positive Listening Attitudes	Negative Listening Attitudes
Interested	Uninterested
Responsible	Irresponsible
Other-oriented	Self-centered
Patient	Impatient
Equal	Superior
Open-minded	Close-minded

The key to playing by the golden listening rule is to understand that both "players" must have a positive listening attitude.

Listening Strategies

Although using your extra thought speed and applying the golden listening rule are critical listening goals, how to achieve them may not be obvious. The five strategies listed in Figure 6.3 can improve your listening ability and help you apply the two basic principles of effective listening.

Listen for Big Ideas.

Good listeners use their extra thought speed to identify a speaker's overall purpose. Poor listeners tend to listen for and remember isolated facts rather than identifying big ideas. Sometimes listening for big ideas can be very difficult when the fault lies with the speaker. For example, listeners may lose track

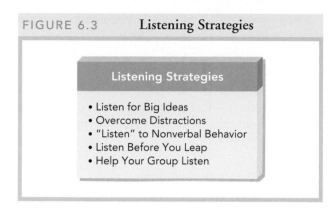

FIGURE 6.3   **Listening Strategies**

Listening Strategies

- Listen for Big Ideas
- Overcome Distractions
- "Listen" to Nonverbal Behavior
- Listen Before You Leap
- Help Your Group Listen

and drift off when listening to a speaker whose message lacks relevant content and a clear structure or whose voice lacks expressiveness. In a small-group setting, good listeners who sense such problems may interrupt a speaker and politely ask, "Could you help me out here and summarize your point in a couple of sentences?" Although it is tempting to blame poor speakers when you can't comprehend a person's message, good listeners try to cut through irrelevant facts and opinions in order to identify the most important ideas.

Overcome Distractions. Distractions can take many forms in a group discussion.[28] Loud and annoying noises, uncomfortable room temperature and seating, frequent interruptions, or distracting décor and outside activities are environmental distractions. Distractions can also be caused by members, such as someone talking too softly, too rapidly, or too slowly; someone speaking in a monotone or with an unfamiliar accent; or someone having unusual mannerisms or appearance. It is difficult to listen when someone is fidgeting, doodling, tapping a pencil, or openly reading or writing something unrelated to the discussion.

When a distraction is environmental, you can get up and shut the door, open the window, or turn on more lights. When another member's behavior is distracting, you can try to minimize or stop the disruption. If members speak too softly, have side conversations, or use visual aids that are too small, a conscientious listener will ask a member to speak up, request that side conversations be postponed, or move closer to a visual aid.

"Listen" to Nonverbal Behavior. Speakers don't always put everything that's important to them into words. Very often you can understand a speaker's meaning by observing his or her nonverbal behavior. A change in vocal tone or volume may be another way of saying, "Listen up—this is very important." A person's sustained eye contact may be a way of saying, "I'm talking to you!" Facial expressions can reveal whether a thought is painful, joyous, exciting, serious, or boring. Even gestures can be used to express a level of excitement that words cannot convey.

It is, however, easy to misinterpret nonverbal behavior. Effective listeners verbally confirm their interpretation of someone's nonverbal communication. A question as simple as "Do your nods indicate a *yes* vote?" can ensure that everyone is on the same nonverbal wavelength. If, as nonverbal research indicates, more than half of a speaker's meaning is conveyed nonverbally,[29] we are missing a lot of important information if we fail to "listen" to nonverbal behavior. Even Freud suggested that "he that has eyes to see and ears to hear may convince himself that no mortal can keep a secret. If his lips are silent, he chatters with his fingertips;

betrayal oozes out of him at every pore."[30] No wonder it is difficult for most people to conceal what they mean and feel in a face-to-face group discussion.

Correctly interpreting nonverbal responses can tell you as much as or more than spoken words. At the same time, the nonverbal reactions of listeners (head nods, smiles, frowns, eye contact, and gestures) can help you adjust what you say when you are speaking. Even the nonverbal setting of a group discussion can communicate a wealth of meaning about the status, power, and respect given to speakers and listeners.

Listen Before You Leap. One of the most often quoted pieces of listening advice coming from Ralph Nichols's writings is, "We must always withhold evaluation until our comprehension is complete."[31] This phrase counsels listeners to make sure that they understand a speaker before they respond.

When we become angry, friends may sometimes tell us to "count to ten" before reacting. This is also good advice when we listen. Counting to ten, however, implies more than withholding evaluation until comprehension is complete. You may comprehend a speaker perfectly, but be infuriated or offended by what you hear. If an insensitive leader asks that "one of you girls take minutes," it may take a count to twenty to collect your thoughts before you can respond to this sexist

TOOLBOX 6.3

Listening in High-Context Cultures

In Chapter 3, "Group Member Diversity," we explore the high-context–low-context dialectic and note that someone from a high-context culture goes well beyond a person's words to interpret meaning. High-context communicators also pay close attention to nonverbal cues when they listen. Interestingly, the Chinese symbol for listening includes characters for eyes, ears, and heart.

For the Chinese "it is impossible to listen . . . without using the eyes because you need to look for nonverbal communication. You certainly must listen with ears" because Chinese is a tonal language in which intonation determines meaning. "Finally, you listen with your heart because" you must sense the "emotional undertones expressed by the speaker." In Korean, there is a word, *nunchi*, that means that you communicate through your eyes. "Koreans believe that

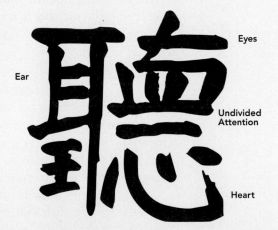

the environment supplies most of the information that we seek, so there is little need to speak."[1]

[1] Elizabeth A. Tuleja, *Intercultural Communication for Business* (Mason, OH: Thomson Higher Education, 2005), p. 43.

comment in a professional manner. If a group member tells an offensive joke, you may have a double reaction—anger at the speaker and disappointment with those who laughed. Listening before you leap gives you time to adjust your reaction in a way that will help rather than disrupt a group discussion.

Help Your Group Listen. In the most effective groups, members help one another listen. The most effective listeners may become the group's translators, explaining what other group members mean and interpreting their responses. One way to help a group listen is to do periodic group listening checks that ask for a confirmation of comprehension. By asking, "What is everyone's understanding of . . . ?" or "Am I right in saying that all of us agree to . . . ?" you are making sure that everyone understands and is responding to the same message.

You also can help a group listen when group members disagree or argue. When members' emotions are stirred up, their thoughts may be devoted to responding to the opposition rather than to applying the golden listening rule. You can help a group resolve such conflicts by summarizing different positions in accurate and neutral terms.

Try to keep good listening habits at the forefront of the group's attention. Remind members how important it is for everyone to improve her or his listening behavior. Such reminders can have powerful consequences. In fact, some experts claim that 50 percent of our potential improvement in listening can come simply from realizing that we have poor listening habits and are capable of listening much better.[32]

The Art of Paraphrasing

Paraphrasing (also called *reflective listening* or *mirror responses*) is the ability to restate what people say in a way that indicates that you understand them. When you paraphrase, you go beyond the words you hear to understand the feelings

TOOLBOX 6.4

Listening Is Hard Work

Effective listening is hard work and requires a great deal more than keeping quiet and recognizing individual words. Researchers note that "active listeners register an increase in blood pressure, a higher pulse rate, and even more perspiration. [Active listening] means concentrating on the other person rather than on yourself. As a result, a lot of people just don't do it."[1]

Listening requires the kind of preparation and concentration required of attorneys trying a case, psychologists counseling a client, and physicians seeking a diagnosis based on patients' reported symptoms. Intensive listening can be an exhausting experience. If you are not willing to work at listening, you will not be a good listener.

[1] Tony Alessandra and Phil Hunsaker, *Communicating at Work* (New York: Fireside, 1993), p. 55.

and underlying meanings that accompany the words. Too often, we jump to conclusions and incorrectly assume that we know what a speaker means and feels.

Paraphrasing is a form of feedback—a listening check—that asks, "Am I right—is this what you mean?" Paraphrasing is not repeating what a person says; it requires finding *new* words to describe what you have heard rather than repeating what you have heard. In addition to rephrasing another person's message, a paraphrase usually includes a request for confirmation.

Paraphrasing can be used for many purposes:

- To ensure comprehension before evaluation
- To reassure others that you want to understand them
- To clear up confusion and ask for clarification
- To summarize lengthy comments
- To help others uncover thoughts and feelings
- To provide a safe and supportive communication climate
- To help others reach their own conclusions[33]

If you want to clarify someone's meaning, you might say, "When you said you were not going to the conference, did you mean that you want one of us to go instead?" If you want to make sure that you understand a person's feelings, you might say, "I know you said you approve, but I sense that you're not happy with the outcome—am I way off?" If you are summarizing someone's lengthy comments, you might say, "What you seem to be saying is that it's not the best time to change this policy, right?"

Paraphrasing is difficult. Not only are you putting aside your own interests and opinions, but you are also finding *new* words that best match someone else's meaning. The phrasing of an effective paraphrase can vary in four critical ways: content, depth, meaning, and language.[34]

Paraphrasing Content.   Content refers to the words used. If all you do is repeat the exact same words you hear, you are not paraphrasing—you are parroting. "Repeating a person's words actually gets in the way of communicating an understanding of the essential meaning of a statement."[35] And, as depicted in the following example, it sounds foolish.

Susan: "I never seem to get anywhere on time, and I don't know why."

You: "Ah, so you don't know why you never seem to get anywhere on time?"

Susan: "Yeah, that's what I just said.

Paraphrasing Depth.   Depth refers to the degree to which you match the importance of and emotions in the speaker's message in your response. Try to avoid responding lightly to a serious problem, and vice versa. Responses that match a speaker's depth of feeling or that lead the person to a slightly greater depth of feeling are most effective.[36]

> Susan: "People, including my boss, bug me about being late, and sometimes I can tell that they're pretty angry."
>
> You: "In other words, you worry that other people are upset by your lateness."

Notice that you did not repeat the words *bug me* and *pretty angry*. Instead, you looked for comparable words—*worried* and *upset by*—that try to match the same depth of feeling.

Paraphrasing Meaning. Even experienced listeners may miss another person's meaning when paraphrasing. Sometimes we may add an unintended meaning to a person's message if we become impatient and complete a sentence or thought for the speaker. What if Susan tried to say, "I really don't know what to do to change," and you interrupted as follows:

> Susan: "I really don't know . . . "
>
> You: " . . . how to manage your time?"

In this case you would be denying Susan the opportunity to describe her own problem. We also may add meaning by responding to ideas that the speaker uses only as an example. Suppose Susan said, "I have an important project coming up at work, and I worry that I'll be late getting there and getting it done on time." Responding with, "You seem to be very upset about getting an important project done" would be an inaccurate paraphrase because it responds to only one specific example that Susan gives, instead of responding to her much larger lateness problem.

Paraphrasing Language. Finally, keep language simple to ensure accurate communication. If you doubt how important word choice can be, imagine Susan's perplexity and frustration if you responded to her as follows:

> Susan: "I never seem to get anywhere on time, and I don't know why."
>
> You: "Ahh, your importunate perplexities about punctuality are inextricably linked."
>
> Susan: "Huh?"

Effective paraphrasing requires mindful listening. Paraphrasing says, "I want to hear what you have to say, and I want to understand what you mean." If you paraphrase accurately, the other person will feel grateful for being understood. And if you don't quite get the paraphrase right, your feedback provides another opportunity for the speaker to explain.[37]

LISTENING TO DIFFERENCES

Just as there are differences among members' backgrounds, perceptions, and values, there are differences in the way people listen. Fortunately, a group provides a setting in which different listening abilities and styles can be an asset rather than a liability. If you have difficulty analyzing an argument, there may be someone else in the group who can be relied upon to serve as an analytical listener. If you know that several members pay attention only to the words they hear rather than observing the nonverbal behavior that accompanies those words, you may appoint yourself the group's empathic listener.

Listening behavior may also differ between male and female members. Deborah Tannen suggests that men are more likely to listen to the content of what is said, whereas women focus on the relationships among speakers.[38] In other words, men tend to focus on comprehensive and analytical listening, whereas women are more likely to be empathic and appreciative listeners. If "males tend to hear the facts while females are more aware of the mood of the communication," a group is fortunate to have both kinds of listeners contributing to the group process.[39]

Differences in personalities may also affect the way members listen. The Myers-Briggs Type Indicator® predicts that introverts will be better comprehensive listeners than extroverts, who are eager to speak out—even when they haven't understood all that is being said. Sensing members may listen for facts and figures, while intuitives listen for key ideas and overarching themes. Thinking members are often effective analytical listeners, whereas feeling members are more likely to be effective empathetic listeners. Judging listeners may drive the group to reach a decision, while perceivers take the time to appreciate what they hear without leaping to immediate conclusions.[40]

In addition to gender and personality-type distinctions, cultural differences can influence the ways in which group members listen and respond to one another. One study concludes that international students see U.S. students as being less willing and less patient as listeners than students from African, Asian, South American, or European cultures.[41] One way to explain such differences in perceived listening behavior is offered by Myron Lustig and Jolene Koester, who explain that English is a speaker-responsible language in which the speaker structures the message and relies primarily upon words to provide meaning. In Japanese, however, which is a listener-responsible language, speakers indirectly indicate what they want the listener to know. The listener must rely on nonverbal communication and an understanding of the relationship between the speaker and the listener to interpret meaning.[42] Thus, an English-speaking listener may feel that a Japanese speaker is leaving out important information; the Japanese listener, however, may think that the English speaker is overexplaining or talking down to him or her. Such misunderstandings and perceived discourtesies are the result of speaking and listening differences rather than of substantive disagreement.

TAKING NOTES IN GROUPS

If most of us listen at only 25 percent efficiency, why not take notes during a discussion? Why not write down important ideas and facts? Taking notes makes a great deal of sense, but only if it is done with skill.

The inclination to take notes is understandable. After all, that's what we do in a classroom when an instructor lectures. However, if you are like most listeners, only one-fourth of what is said will end up in your notes. Even if it were possible for you to copy down every word uttered in a group discussion, your notes would be missing the nonverbal clues that often tell you more about what a person means and feels. And if you spend all of your time taking notes, when will you put aside your pen and participate? Ralph Nichols summarized the dilemma of balancing note taking and listening when he concluded that "there is some evidence to indicate that the volume of notes taken and their value to the taker are inversely related."[43] Thus, the challenge for a group member is this: How do I obtain brief, meaningful records of a group discussion? Several methods can help, depending upon your needs and your role in the group.

If a member is assigned to take minutes, you can rely on the official record of the meeting. But here, too, there are potential problems. What if the secretary is a poor listener? What if you need the notes immediately and can't wait for the official minutes to be distributed and approved? Suppose you need personalized meeting notes that record your assignments and important information? In such cases, minutes may not be enough.

Flexibility is the key to taking useful and personalized meeting notes. Good listeners adjust their note-taking system to a group's agenda or impose a note-taking pattern on a disorganized discussion. In some cases, marginal notes on an agenda may be sufficient to highlight important information and actions. If you attend a lot of meetings, you may find it helpful to use a brief form that records important details and provides space for critical information and action. The form shown in Figure 6.4 is an example of the way in which vital information and actions can be recorded.

SELF-LISTENING IN GROUPS

As important as it is to listen to other members of your group, it is just as important to listen to yourself. Poor self-listening is often the cause of communication breakdowns. Rebecca Shafir, author of *The Zen of Listening*, maintains that "if we could hear our words . . . through the ears of our listeners, we would be appalled at the overgeneralizations, the inaccuracies, and the insensitive, negative comments we make about ourselves and others."[44] If you can monitor, understand, and modify the effects of what you say, you can become a more effective group member. Two strategies can enhance your ability to listen to yourself. The first is

FIGURE 6.4   **Sample Form for Meeting Notes**

Meeting Notes

Group: Goal/Topic:

Date and Time: Place:

Members Attending:

Members Absent:

Vital Information

1.

2.

3.

Decisions Reached

1.

2.

3.

Personal To-Do List   Date Due

1.

2.

3.

Date/Time/Place of Next Meeting:

to translate feedback into useful information about the way you speak and listen so that you can answer questions such as these:

- Do members listen to me, or do I seem to be talking to a blank wall?

- Do members seem to understand what I am saying, or are there frequent questions or confusion following my remarks?

- Do I feel my voice rising and my heart racing when I address a controversial issue or an argumentative member?

When you listen to yourself, "Whatever you have to say needs only to pass the simple test of teamwork: Are you saying something that is germane to the team as a whole—to its objectives, to its overriding vision, to the tasks it has set out for itself? . . . If not, fix your message so that it is direct, relevant, and respectful of others."[45]

A second way to listen to yourself is to become aware of your internal thought processes. This strategy recognizes that, in a group discussion, what you *want* to say may not be what you *should* say. In order to illustrate the usefulness of this strategy, consider the following hypothetical situation:

A professional facilitator has been hired to work with a student government council charged with rewriting the council's constitution and bylaws. Right from the start, the student government president and the facilitator do not hit it off. The situation has become so bad that the rest of the council is paralyzed. Nothing gets done, as everyone spends valuable meeting time watching the president and facilitator fight over every issue on the group's agenda.

If you were a member of this group, what would you say or do to help resolve such a problem? A lot depends on how well you listen to others and to yourself, how efficiently you use your extra thought speed, and how fairly you apply the golden listening rule. The following seven questions may help you assess your internal thought processes:

1. *What do I want to say?* "I wish you two would stop acting like babies. We're sick and tired of your bickering."

2. *What are the consequences of saying what I want to say?* Both of them will become angry or hurt, and what is left of group morale and cohesiveness could fall apart.

3. *Have I listened comprehensively?* What is each side trying to say? Is the president saying that the facilitator has no right to impose her will on the group? Is the facilitator saying that the president doesn't respect her as an expert?

4. *Have I listened analytically?* Is either side right or wrong? Both the president and the facilitator have legitimate complaints, but their arguments are becoming personal rather than substantive.

5. *Have I listened empathically?* How would I feel if someone treated me this way? I'd probably be just as angry.

6. *Have I listened appreciatively?* Do the president and the facilitator have positive contributions to make? The president should be commended for how well he has led our group. The facilitator should be thanked for sharing useful resources and helping us understand the scope of our assignment.

7. *So, what should I say?* I should speak on behalf of the group and tell the president and the facilitator how much we value both of them, but that the group, as a whole, is distressed by the conflict between them. I should ask whether there is something we can do to resolve the problem.

Taking the time to ask a series of self-listening questions can help you develop an appropriate and useful response. Analyzing your own thought processes lets you employ different types of listening to come up with a useful response that can help resolve a group problem.

BALANCED LISTENING

Groups lose their balance when many members want to talk rather than listen. If members fail to listen discriminatively, comprehensively, analytically, empathically, and appreciatively, a group will soon lose its ability to work together. In a well-balanced group, members spend more time listening than speaking; they try to balance their own needs with those of listeners. In fact, there may be no more difficult task in a group discussion than suspending your own needs and

GROUPTECH

Listening in Virtual Groups

Effective listening in virtual groups requires adapting to a different medium of expression. In a sophisticated teleconference, this adaptation is relatively easy—you can see and hear group members sitting at a conference table in another city or on another continent almost as clearly as you can see and hear the colleagues sitting across the table from you. Your only adaptation is making sure that your microphone is on or off at appropriate times. In an email discussion, however, you can neither see nor hear participants, but you still must "listen" to their messages.

Ironically, it may be easier to "listen" to group members in a virtual meeting than in a face-to-face setting. What makes it easier is the amount of time you have to listen and respond as well as the luxury of controlling the content and style of your responses. In a face-to-face discussion, you hear what members say and are expected to respond immediately. Members can see one another grimace, smile, or roll their eyes in disgust. In an email discussion—whether synchronous or asynchronous—you have more time to listen to others and control your reactions.

For example, you can read and reread what someone has written to make sure that you comprehend the message. In a virtual discussion, time also gives you the luxury of using all four listening styles. Because you have more than the few seconds given a listener in a face-to-face discussion, you can interpret and analyze a message, determine the content and tone of the response you want to make, and choose appropriate words. The downside of the time-to-listen advantage is that it is easier to fake attention in electronic meetings. You can pretend to participate online by typing an occasional comment. During a teleconference, you can stop listening completely and work on other tasks at your desk, but you can check in and respond with an "I agree" or "Good job, Fred" to feign participation. Although you can fake listening in a face-to-face discussion, your physical presence makes it difficult to "be elsewhere."

[1] Andrew F. Wood and Matthew J. Smith, *Online Communication: Linking Technology, Identity, and Culture,* 2nd ed. (Mahwah, NJ: Erlbaum, 2005), p. 82.

your desire to talk in order to listen to what someone else has to say. In 1961, Ralph Nichols contrasted the hard work of listening with faked attention:

> Listening is hard work. It is characterized by faster heart action, quicker circulation of the blood, a small rise in bodily temperature. The over-relaxed listener is merely appearing to tune-in and then feeling conscience-free to pursue any of a thousand mental tangents. . . . For selfish reasons alone, one of the best investments we can make is to give each speaker our conscious attention.[46]

As we note at the beginning of this chapter, effective listening is the counterpart of effective speaking. Effective group members both create messages *and* listen and respond to other members' messages appropriately during the course of group interaction. Engaging in both of these communication activities simultaneously is challenging *and* essential for groups working to achieve a common goal.

GROUPWORK

Practice Paraphrasing

Directions. Read the four statements made by group members and write the response you would make that best paraphrases their meaning. As a guide, we recommend that you include at least three components in your paraphrase:

- State your interest in understanding the other person, such as, "I sense that . . ." or "If I understand you correctly, you . . ." or "It sounds as if you . . ."
- Identify the other person's emotion or feeling, but make sure you find alternatives to the words the person uses. For example, if a person says, "I'm angry," you will need to decide whether this means that the person is annoyed, irritated, disgusted, or furious. Try to find a word that matches the person's meaning and emotion.
- Describe the situation, event, or facts using alternative words.[47]

Sample Situation and Paraphrase

Group Member: "I get really annoyed when André yells at one of us during a meeting."

Paraphrase 1: "It sounds as though you get pretty upset with André when he shouts at you or another group member. Am I right?"

1. Group Member: I have the worst luck with computers. Every single one I've ever used has problems. Just when the warranty runs out, something goes wrong and I have to spend a lot to get it fixed. The computer I have now has crashed twice, and I lost all of my documents. Maybe it's me—I mean maybe I'm doing something wrong. Why me? I must be cursed or something.

   Paraphrase: _____

   _____

   _____

2. Group Member: I hope Anita doesn't react too strongly to Chris and Mark's concerns about the scope of our project at today's meeting. She can be very emotional when she feels strongly about something she really believes in.

   Paraphrase: _____

   _____

   _____

3. Group Member: I dislike saying *no* to anyone in our group who asks for help, but then I have to rush or stay up late to get my own work done. I want to help, but I also want to do my own job—and do it well.

   Paraphrase: _____

   _____

   _____

4. How on earth are we going to get an A on this assignment if we can't even find time to meet?

Paraphrase: _____

_____

_____

GROUPASSESSMENT

Shafir's Self-Listening Test

Self-knowledge is the first step toward self-improvement. This assessment instrument looks at how you listen in a variety of situations and settings. Carefully consider each question and indicate whether or not you consistently demonstrate each behavior.

Do you

1. Think about what *you* are going to say while the speaker is talking?
   ☐ Yes, consistently   ☐ No, almost never   ☐ Sometimes

2. Tune out people who say things you don't agree with or don't want to hear?
   ☐ Yes, consistently   ☐ No, almost never   ☐ Sometimes

3. Learn something from each person you meet, even if it is ever so slight?
   ☐ Yes, consistently   ☐ No, almost never   ☐ Sometimes

4. Keep eye contact with the person who is speaking?
   ☐ Yes, consistently   ☐ No, almost never   ☐ Sometimes

5. Become self-conscious in one-on-one or small group conversations?
   ☐ Yes, consistently   ☐ No, almost never   ☐ Sometimes

6. Often interrupt the speaker?
   ☐ Yes, consistently   ☐ No, almost never   ☐ Sometimes

7. Fall asleep or daydream during meetings or presentations?
   ☐ Yes, consistently   ☐ No, almost never   ☐ Sometimes

8. Restate instructions or messages to be sure you understood correctly?
   ☐ Yes, consistently   ☐ No, almost never   ☐ Sometimes

9. Allow the speaker to vent negative feelings toward you without becoming defensive or physically tense?
   ☐ Yes, consistently   ☐ No, almost never   ☐ Sometimes

10. Listen for the meaning behind a speaker's words through gestures and facial expressions?
    ☐ Yes, consistently   ☐ No, almost never   ☐ Sometimes

11. Feel frustrated or impatient when communicating with persons from other cultures?
    ☐ Yes, consistently   ☐ No, almost never   ☐ Sometimes

12. Inquire about the meaning of unfamiliar words or jargon?
    ☐ Yes, consistently   ☐ No, almost never   ☐ Sometimes

13. Give the appearance of listening when you are not?
    ☐ Yes, consistently   ☐ No, almost never   ☐ Sometimes

14. Listen to the speaker without judging or criticizing?
    ☐ Yes, consistently   ☐ No, almost never   ☐ Sometimes

15. Start giving advice before you are asked?
    ☐ Yes, consistently   ☐ No, almost never   ☐ Sometimes

16. Ramble on before getting to the point?
    ☐ Yes, consistently   ☐ No, almost never   ☐ Sometimes

17. Take notes when necessary to help you remember?
    ☐ Yes, consistently   ☐ No, almost never   ☐ Sometimes

18. Consider the state of the person you are talking to (nervous, rushed, hearing-impaired, and so on)?
    ☐ Yes, consistently   ☐ No, almost never   ☐ Sometimes

19. Let a speaker's physical appearance or mannerisms distract you from listening?
    ☐ Yes, consistently   ☐ No, almost never   ☐ Sometimes

20. Remember a person's name after you have been introduced?
    ☐ Yes, consistently   ☐ No, almost never   ☐ Sometimes

21. Assume that you know what the speaker is going to say and stop listening?
    ☐ Yes, consistently   ☐ No, almost never   ☐ Sometimes

22. Feel uncomfortable allowing silence between you and your conversation partner?
    ☐ Yes, consistently   ☐ No, almost never   ☐ Sometimes

23. Ask for feedback to make sure you are getting across to the other person?
    ☐ Yes, consistently   ☐ No, almost never   ☐ Sometimes

24. Preface your statements with unflattering remarks about yourself?
    ☐ Yes, consistently   ☐ No, almost never   ☐ Sometimes

25. Think more about building warm working relationships with team members and customers than about bringing in revenue?
    ☐ Yes, consistently   ☐ No, almost never   ☐ Sometimes

Scoring: Compare your answers to those on the following chart. For every answer that matches the key, give yourself one point. If you answered *Sometimes* to any of the questions, score half a point. Total the number of points.

1. N	6. N	11. N	16. N	21. N
2. N	7. N	12. Y	17. Y	22. N
3. Y	8. Y	13. N	18. Y	23. Y
4. Y	9. Y	14. Y	19. N	24. N
5. N	10. Y	15. N	20. Y	25. Y

Total points:

Interpretation of Results

21+ points: You are an excellent listener in most settings and circumstances. Note which areas could use further improvement.

16–20 points: You usually absorb most of the main ideas, but you often miss a good portion of the rest of the message as a result of difficulties with sustained attention. You may feel detached from the speaker and start thinking about other things or about what you are going to say next.

10–15 points: You may be focusing more on your own agenda than on the speaker's needs. You easily become distracted, and you perceive listening as a task. Personal biases may get in the way of fully understanding a speaker.

9 points or less: Most of the time you experience listening as a boring activity. You might complain that your memory is poor and feel great frustration when trying to retain information and succeed in a classroom situation.

Note: If you answered *Sometimes* to many of the questions, then obviously you are a sometimes listener. Chances are that your ability to concentrate may be at fault and/or that you are a highly critical individual and quick to judge whether a listening opportunity is worthwhile. However, there have been times when you have experienced the satisfaction of being fully absorbed in what someone has to say.

Source: "Self-Listening Test" from Rebecca Z. Shafir, *The Zen of Listening: Mindful Communication in the Age of Distraction*, pp. 28–33. Copyright ©2000. Reprinted by permission of Quest Books/The Theosophical Publishing House, Wheaton, IL.

NOTES

1. Katherine W. Hawkins and Bryant P. Fillion, "Perceived Communication Skill Needs for Workgroups," *Communication Research Reports, 16* (1999), pp. 167–174.
2. Bonnie Jacobson, author of *If Only You Would Listen* (Boston: St. Martin's, 1995) cited in David Stauffer, "Yo, Listen Up: A Brief Hearing on the Most Neglected Communication Skill," *Harvard Management Update*, 3 (July 1998), p. 10.
3. Patrice Johnson and Kittie Watson, "Managing Interpersonal and Team Conflict: Listening Strategies," in *Listening in Everyday Life: A Personal and Professional Approach, 2nd* ed., ed. Michael Purdy and Deborah Borisoff (Lanham, MD: University

Press, 1997), pp. 121–132; also see Hawkins and Fillion, p. 168.

4. Harry E. Chambers, *Effective Communication Skills for Scientific and Technical Professionals* (Cambridge, MA: Perseus, 2001), p. 139.

5. Larry L. Barker et al., "An Investigation of Proportional Time Spent in Various Communication Activities by College Students," *Journal of Applied Communication Research*, 8 (1980), pp. 101–109.

6. Andrew D. Wolvin and Carolyn G. Coakley, *Listening*, 5th ed. (Madison, WI: Brown and Benchmark, 1996), p. 15.

7. Michael Purdy, "The Listener Wins"; available at http://featuredreports.monster.com/listen/overview.

8. Sandra D. Collins, *Listening and Responding* (Mason, OH: Thomson Higher Education, 2006), p. 2.

9. Ralph G. Nichols, "Listening Is a 10-Part Skill." *Nation's Business, 75* (September 1987), p. 40.

10. S. S. Benoit and J. W. Lee, "Listening: It Can Be Taught," *Journal of Education for Business, 63* (1986), pp. 229–232.

11. Donald Carstensen, vice president for education services at ACT, quoted in Michael Purdy, "The Listener Wins"; available at http://featuredreports.monster.com/listen/overview. Also see http/www.act.org/workkeys/assess/listen/levels.html for information about ACT's listening assessment criteria.

12. Florence I. Wolff and Nadine C. Marsnik, *Perceptive Listening*, 2nd ed. (Fort Worth, TX: Harcourt Brace Jovanovich, 1992), pp. 9–16.

13. Edwin P. Hollander, *Leadership Dynamics: A Practical Guide to Effective Relationships* (New York: Macmillan, 1978), p. 53.

14. Fran Rees, *How to Lead Work Teams*, 2nd ed. (San Francisco: Jossey-Bass, 2001), p. 41.

15. Charles M. Kelly, "Empathetic Listening," in *Small Group Communication: A Reader,* 2nd ed., ed. Robert S. Cathcart and Larry A. Samovar (Dubuque, IA: Wm. C. Brown, 1974), p. 340.

16. *The American Heritage Dictionary of the English Language*, 4th ed. (Boston: Houghton Mifflin, 2000), p. 517.

17. Wolvin and Coakley, p. 158.

18. Based on Wolff and Marsnik, p. 100.

19. Wolff and Marsnik, pp. 101–102.

20. Based on Wolff and Marsnik, pp. 94–95.

21. Wolff and Marsnik, p. 97.

22. Hawkins and Fillion, p. 172.

23. Carl E. Larson and Frank M. J. LaFasto, *TeamWork: What Must Go Right/What Can Go Wrong* (Newbury Park, CA: Sage, 1989), p. 90.

24. Ralph Nichols, p. 40.

25. Ralph Nichols, p. 40.

26. Michael P. Nichols, *The Lost Art of Listening* (New York: Guilford, 1995), p. 42.

27. Wolvin and Coakley, pp. 135–138.

28. Madelyn Burley-Allen, *Listening: The Forgotten Skill, 2nd ed.* (New York: Wiley, 1995), pp. 68–70.

29. See Peter A. Andersen, *Nonverbal Communication: Forms and Functions (*Mountain View, CA: Mayfield, 1999), pp. 1–2.

30. As cited in Mark L. Knapp and Judith A. Hall, *Nonverbal Communication in Human Interaction, 5th ed. (*Fort Worth, TX: Holt, Rinehart, and Winston, 1997), p. 466.

31. Ralph G. Nichols, "Do We Know How to Listen? Practical Helps in a Modern Age," *Speech Teacher, 10* (1961), p. 121.

32. David Stauffer, "Yo, Listen Up: A Brief Hearing on the Most Neglected Communication Skill," *Harvard Management Update*, 3 (July 1998), p. 11.

33. Adapted from Wolvin and Coakley, p. 299.

34. David W. Johnson's Questionnaire on Listening and Response Alternatives in *Reaching Out: Interpersonal Effectiveness and Self-Actualization*, 7th ed. (Boston: Allyn & Bacon, 2000), pp. 234–239.

35. Johnson, p. 234.

36. Johnson, p. 235.

37. Michael P. Nichols, p. 126.

38. Deborah Tannen, *You Just Don't Understand: Women and Men in Conversation (*New York: William Morrow, 1990), pp. 149–151.

39. Melanie Booth-Butterfield, "She Hears . . . He Hears: What They Hear and Why," *Personnel Journal, 44* (1984), p. 39.

40. See Chapter 3 for a discussion of the Myers-Briggs Type Indicator®.

41. Wolvin and Coakley, p. 125.

42. Myron W. Lustig and Jolene Koester, *Intercultural Competencies: Interpersonal Communication Across Cultures, 5th* ed. (New York: HarperCollins, 2006), pp. 238–239.

43. Ralph G. Nichols, "Listening Is a 10-Part Skill," p. 40.

44. Rebecca Z. Shafir, *The Zen of Listening: Mindful Communication in the Age of Distraction* (Wheaton, IL: Quest Books, 2003), p. 18.

45. Harvey Robbins and Michael Finley, *The New Why Teams Don't Work: What Went Wrong and How to Make It Right* (Princeton, NJ: Peterson's/Pacesetter Books, 1995), p. 142.

46. Ralph G. Nichols, "Do We Know How to Listen?" p. 122.

47. Recommendation based on the Listener's Summarization Model in Burley-Allen, p. 132.

CHAPTER 7

Conflict and Cohesion in Groups

CHAPTER OUTLINE

CONFLICT IN GROUPS

Conflict is unavoidable in effective groups. Rarely do conscientious group members work together for any length of time without expressing differences and disagreeing. Yet despite the inevitability of conflict, many of us go out of our way to avoid or suppress it. Too often, we believe that effective groups "are characterized by chumminess. Many effective teams look more like battlegrounds, it turns out. . . . Teams with vastly competent members embrace conflict as the price of synergy and set good idea against good idea to arrive at the best idea."[1]

The word *conflict* is frequently associated with quarreling, fighting, anger, and hostility. While these elements may be present in a group situation, conflict does not have to involve the expression of negative emotions. When it is treated as an expression of legitimate differences, conflict can improve group problem solving, promote cohesiveness, increase group knowledge, enhance creativity, and promote the group's goal.[2] We define **conflict** as the disagreement and disharmony that occur in groups when differences regarding ideas, members, and/or methods are expressed. The sources of conflict listed in this definition can be categorized as substantive, affective, and procedural conflict, as illustrated in Figure 7.1.[3]

Substantive Conflict

Substantive conflict occurs when members disagree about ideas, issue analysis, and potential solutions or actions. For example, when the members of a student government council try to answer the question "Should student activities fees be raised?" their conflict is substantive because it focuses on working toward the group's goal of serving students' cocurricular needs. In Chapter 10, "Argumentation in Groups," we examine the ways in which effective and ethical argumentation can help groups understand and analyze ideas, influence members, make informed and critical decisions, and achieve their goals.

Affective Conflict

The word *affective* means "influenced by or resulting from the emotions."[4] **Affective conflict** reflects the emotions stirred by interpersonal disagreements, differences in personalities and communication styles, and members' beliefs and feelings. Affective conflict may occur when a member does not feel valued or feels threatened by the group. Affective conflict also occurs when members believe that their ideas are not being judged fairly or when group members are struggling for power. Affective conflict is more difficult to resolve than substantive conflict because it involves people's feelings and the way members relate to one another.

Both substantive and affective conflict are often present when group members disagree. For example, Dee believes that student fees should be raised in order to fund more campus activities. Charles disagrees; he suggests that the existing funds should be used more efficiently rather than placing a larger financial burden on

FIGURE 7.1   **Sources of Group Conflict**

students. At this point in the discussion, the conflict is substantive; it is focused on issues. However, when responding to Dee, Charles rolls his eyes and states, "Only a political fool believes that higher fees are the answer to the problem." Not only does Dee disagree with Charles on the issues, but she is angered by his comment. Now the conflict has gone beyond its substance; it has become affective as well.

Procedural Conflict

Procedural conflict is disagreement among group members about the methods or process that the group should follow in its attempt to accomplish a goal. Some group members may want to begin a discussion by suggesting solutions to a problem, whereas others may want to start by gathering and discussing information. Some members may believe that a decision should be made by secret ballot, whereas others may want a show of hands.

Procedural conflicts often arise when groups have difficulty resolving substantive or affective conflict. Rather than facing the issues, they rely on procedures to get them through. "Procedures such as moving to the next agenda item, taking a vote, or changing the topic are ways of withdrawing from conflict." At the same time—as you will see in Chapter 9, "Structured and Creative Problem Solving in Groups"—constructive procedures can help a group "reduce uncertainty about group decisions" and create a more positive group climate.[5]

CONSTRUCTIVE AND DESTRUCTIVE CONFLICT

Conflict itself is neither good nor bad. However, the way in which a group deals with conflict can be either constructive or destructive. **Destructive conflict** results when groups engage in behaviors that create hostility and prevent achievement of the group's goal. Constant complaining, personal insults, conflict avoidance, and loud arguments or threats all contribute to destructive conflict.[6] The quality of group decision making deteriorates when members are inflexible and are not

FIGURE 7.2   **Constructive and Destructive Conflict**

Constructive Conflict	Destructive Conflict
• Focus on Issues • Respect for Others • Supportiveness • Flexibility • Cooperation • Commitment to Conflict Management	• Personal Attacks • Insults • Defensiveness • Inflexibility • Competition • Avoidance of Conflict

open to other points of view. Destructive conflict has the potential to permanently disable a group.

Constructive conflict results when group members express disagreement in a way that values everyone's contributions and promotes the group's goal. Figure 7.2 characterizes the differences between destructive and constructive conflict.

Groups that are committed to constructive conflict abide by the following principles:[7]

- Disagreement does not result in punishment.

  "I'm not afraid of being fired for disagreeing with other members."

- Members work with one another to achieve a mutually satisfying resolution of conflict.

  "We can work this out. After all, we're all after the same thing in the long run."

- Lower-status group members are free to disagree with higher-status members.

  "I know she's the CEO, but I think there are some disadvantages to the approach that she suggests."

- The group has an agreed-upon approach for conflict resolution and decision making.

  "Our group is using the Nominal Group Technique, so I know my ideas will be heard and included."

- Members can disagree and still respect one another.

  "The group may not like my idea, but the members would never personally attack me for expressing my opinion."

Constructive group conflict has many positive outcomes. Issues and people are better understood through an open exchange of ideas, opinions, and feelings.

TOOLBOX 7.1

Know When to Apologize

An apology can go a long way toward diffusing tension and hostility and opening the door to constructive conflict resolution. Research suggests that an apology may even deter lawsuits.[1] Studies conducted by Jennifer Robbennolt, a law professor at University of Missouri–Columbia, indicate that 73 percent of complainants will accept a settlement offer when a full apology is given. When there is no apology, only 52 percent are willing to accept a settlement and avoid escalating the conflict by going to court.

In spite of the importance and simplicity of an apology, we often find it difficult to say the words "I'm sorry." When you say you are sorry, you take responsibility for your behavior and the consequences of your actions. Although you may feel as though you've "lost" or sacrificed some of your pride, an effective apology can pave the way for mutual problem solving. A willingness to own up to your actions can earn the respect of other group members and help build trusting relationships. The following guidelines provide suggestions for making an effective apology:[2]

- *Take responsibility for your actions with "I" statements.* "*I* failed to put all the group members' names on the final report."

- *Clearly identify the behavior that was wrong.* "Everyone provided valuable input and should have been acknowledged."
- *Acknowledge how others might feel.* "I understand that most of you are probably annoyed with me."
- *Acknowledge that you could have acted differently.* "I should have asked the group about this first."
- *Express regret.* "I'm angry with myself for not thinking ahead."
- *Follow through on any promises to correct the situation.* "I'll send an email out tomorrow acknowledging that your names should have been included on the report."
- *Request, but don't demand, forgiveness.* "This group is important to me. I hope that you will forgive me."

[1] "Full Apologies Deter Lawsuits, New Studies Find," Newswise, www.newswise.com/articles/view/500630/?sc=wire, August 26, 2003.
[2] Kenneth Cloke and Joan Goldsmith, *Resolving Conflicts at Work: A Complete Guide for Everyone on the Job* (New York: Jossey-Bass, 2000), pp. 109–110; "When and How to Apologize," University of Nebraska Cooperative Extension and the Nebraska Health and Human Services System, http://extension.unl.edu/welfare/apology.htm.

The quality of decision making improves as opposing viewpoints and concerns are discussed. Expressing differences constructively can make a group discussion more interesting and promote participation.

CONFLICT STYLES

Research indicates that all of us have characteristic conflict-handling styles that we tend to apply regardless of the differences in situations.[8] Whereas some people will move heaven and earth to avoid conflict of any kind, others enjoy the competitive atmosphere and the exultation of "winning." In *Working Through Conflict,*

Joseph Folger and his colleagues recommend that group members work on mastering various styles of *doing* conflict.

There are five traditional conflict styles: avoidance, accommodation, competition, compromise, and collaboration.[9] These five styles reflect a dialectic tension between focusing on and asserting your personal goals and working cooperatively to achieve the group's goal. For example, if you are motivated to achieve your own goals, you may use a more competitive conflict style. If you are dedicated to achieving the group's goals, you may use a more accommodating or collaborative conflict style. Kenneth Thomas, whose research with Ralph Kilmann produced the five conflict-handling styles illustrated in Figure 7.3, acknowledges the dialectic nature of these dimensions. "They are *not* opposites," he writes. Collaborating, for example, is *both* assertive *and* cooperative.[10]

Avoidance

When members are unable or unwilling to accomplish their own goals or contribute to achieving the group's goal, they may adopt the **avoidance conflict style.** In some cases, members who care about the group and its goals may adopt the avoidance style because they are uncomfortable with or unskilled at asserting themselves. Group members who use this style may change the subject, avoid bringing up a controversial issue, and even deny that a conflict exists. Avoiding conflict in groups is usually counterproductive because it fails to address a problem and can increase group tensions. Furthermore, ignoring or avoiding conflict does not make it go away.

FIGURE 7.3   **Conflict Styles**

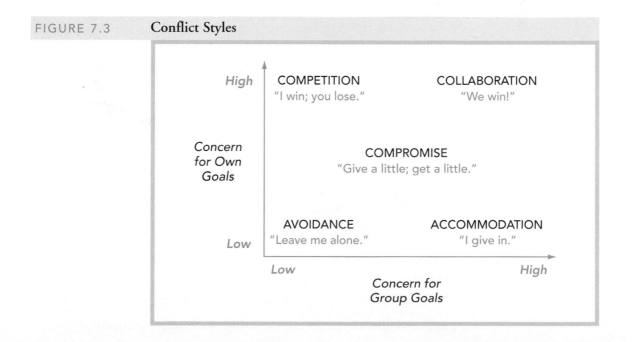

However, in some circumstances, avoidance of conflict can be an appropriate approach—specifically when

- The issue is not that important to you.

- You need to take time to collect your thoughts or control your emotions.

- Other group members are addressing the same concerns effectively.

- The consequences of confrontation are too risky.

Accommodation

Group members using the **accommodating conflict style** give in to other members at the expense of their own goals. Accommodators are often motivated by a genuine desire to get along with other group members. They believe that giving in to others serves the needs of the group, even when the group could benefit from further discussion. A group member who always approaches conflict by accommodating others may ultimately be perceived as being less powerful and have less influence in group decision making.

Accommodating during conflict can be an appropriate approach when

- The issue is very important to others but is not very important to you.

- It is more important to preserve group harmony than to resolve the current issue.

- You realize that you are wrong or you have changed your mind.

- You are unlikely to succeed in persuading the group to adopt your position.

Competition

The **competitive conflict style** occurs when group members are more concerned with their own goals than with meeting the needs of the group. Competitive members want to win; they argue that their ideas are superior to the alternatives suggested by others. When used inappropriately, the competitive style may be characterized by hostility, ridicule, and personal attacks against group members. Approaching conflict competitively tends to divide group members into winners and losers. Ultimately, this may damage the relationships among group members.

In certain group situations, however, the competitive approach may be the most appropriate style. Approach conflict competitively when

- You have strong beliefs about an important issue.

- The group must act immediately on an urgent issue or in an emergency situation.

- The consequences of the group's decision may be very serious or harmful.

- You believe that the group may be acting unethically or illegally.

Compromise

The **compromising conflict style** is a "middle ground" approach that involves conceding some goals in order to achieve others. When group members compromise, each member is willing to suffer some losses in exchange for gaining something else. Group members who approach conflict through compromise argue that it is a fair method of resolving problems, since everyone loses equally. "However, when each person gives up something in order to meet the others halfway, the result is only partial satisfaction for all concerned. Commitment to solutions will be questionable."[11]

The compromise approach should be used when the group has been unable to find a more constructive solution. Groups should consider compromising when

- Other methods of resolving the conflict will not be effective.
- The members have reached an impasse and are no longer progressing toward a reasonable solution.
- The group does not have enough time to explore more creative solutions.

Collaboration

The **collaborative conflict style** searches for new solutions that will achieve both the individual goals of group members and the goals of the group. Instead of arguing over who is right or wrong, the collaborative group seeks creative solutions that satisfy everyone's interests and needs.[12] Collaboration promotes synergy and resolves the dialectic tension between assertiveness and cooperation. It also "involves trying to find an 'integrative' (or win-win) solution" that allows the group to make progress toward achieving its common goal.[13]

There are, however, two important drawbacks to the collaborative approach. First, collaboration requires a lot of the group's time and energy. Some issues may not be important enough to justify such creative effort and extra time. Second, in order for collaboration to be successful, all group members must participate fully. Avoiders and accommodators can prevent a group from engaging in true collaboration.

Groups should approach conflict resolution collaboratively when

- They want to find a solution that will satisfy all group members.
- New and creative ideas are needed.
- A commitment to the final decision is needed from each group member.
- The group has enough time to commit to creative problem solving.

Choosing a Conflict Style

While individuals may be predisposed to a particular conflict style, effective group members choose the style that is most appropriate for a particular group in a particular situation. As situations change, so may the members' approach to conflict. One of us works as a legal communication consultant who routinely sees members of mock juries use various conflict styles while deliberating a case.[14] The following is an example:

During the first hour of deliberation, the jury engaged in a heated debate over a controversial, yet central, issue in the case. Tony was conspicuously silent throughout this discussion. He was asked his opinion several times. Each time, he indicated that he agreed with the arguments that Pam had presented. On a later issue, Tony was a central participant. He argued vehemently that one of the defendants should not be held liable. He even said, "I'm just not going to concede this point. It's not right for the man to go to jail over this." Eventually, one of the jurors suggested that Tony reexamine a document presented as evidence of the defendant's guilt. Tony was quiet for a few minutes and carefully reviewed the document for himself. He then looked up at the group and said, "Well, this changes everything for me. I guess he really was a part of the conspiracy."

Tony used several approaches to deal with conflict in the group. First, he avoided it altogether. He simply had nothing to add to the discussion. Tony then became competitive when he thought that a person might be unjustly imprisoned. However, he became accommodating when a review of the evidence convinced him that he had been wrong.

When selecting a conflict style, you should consider the following questions:

- How important is the issue to you?
- How important is the issue to other members?
- How important is it to maintain positive relationships within the group?
- How much time does the group have to address the issue?
- How fully do group members trust one another?[15]

Answers to these questions can suggest whether a particular conflict style is appropriate or inappropriate in a particular situation. For instance, if group members do not trust one another, the compromising style would be less appropriate. If the issue is very important, and the group has plenty of time to discuss it, collaboration should be explored. There is no single conflict style that will be effective in all group situations. The skilled member balances a variety of considerations and chooses an appropriate style.

CONFLICT MANAGEMENT STRATEGIES

Appropriate conflict styles can help resolve disagreements, particularly when group members understand the dialectic tension between assertiveness and cooperation. Sometimes, however, a group must set aside the substantive, affective, or procedural issue under discussion and address the nature or causes of the conflict directly. In short, groups need a strategy for analyzing the conflict.

GROUPTECH

Conflict in Virtual Groups

Conflicts in virtual groups arise for a variety of reasons and are difficult to resolve. Sometimes virtual groups become embroiled in an issue because members have misunderstood a message. In her book *The Argument Culture,* Deborah Tannen points out that "the potential for misunderstandings and mishaps with electronic communication expands in proportion to the potential for positive exchanges."[1] Have you ever received email messages that were not intended for you and that you found disturbing to read? Have you ever fired off an angry email, only to regret your action later? The efficiency of email makes it easy to forward messages without reading them carefully, reply to messages while you're still angry, and send a message to a lot of people without knowing if each will interpret it in the same way.

The time, distance, and possible anonymity that separate members of virtual groups can play a significant role in increasing conflict. Unfortunately, some group members feel less obligated to engage in polite behavior when the interaction isn't face to face. As a result, virtual groups tend to communicate more negative, insulting, and impolite messages than do face-to-face groups.[2] However, just because someone can't challenge or reprimand you in person is no reason to abandon civil behavior. Susan Barnes, author of *Online Connections,* notes that "challenging comments can quickly turn professional working adults into 'textual mud slingers.' Curt email messages are rapidly thrown back and forth as the electronic packs of digital data pulse through the Internet to reach their destinations."[3]

Some technologies are better suited for dealing with interpersonal and task-related conflict than others.[4] Using audio-only (e.g., the telephone) or data-only (e.g., email or bulletin boards) technology is a poor way to deal with conflict. Video-conferencing works slightly better. However, major conflicts are best resolved face to face.

[1] Deborah Tannen, *The Argument Culture: Moving from Debate to Dialogue* (New York: Random House, 1998), p. 242.
[2] Deborah L. Duarte and Nancy Tennant Snyder, *Mastering Virtual Teams,* 2nd ed. (San Francisco: Jossey-Bass, 2001), p. 154.
[3] Susan B. Barnes, *Online Connections: Internet Interpersonal Relationships* (Cresskill, NJ: Hampton Press, 2001), p. 46.
[4] Duarte and Snyder, p. 28.

The 4Rs Method

In order to choose the most appropriate conflict management strategy, you must understand your group's conflict. We suggest using the **4Rs method** to analyze the conflict in a particular situation. The four steps of the method are accompanied by these relevant questions:

- **Reasons.** What are the reasons for or causes of the conflict? Are the causes associated with expressed differences about issues, methods, and/or members? Do other concerned members agree with your assessment of the reasons for the conflict?

- **Reactions.** How are group members reacting to one another? Are the reactions constructive or destructive in nature? Can members' reactions be modified into more constructive behavior?

- **Results.** What are the consequences of the group's current approach to the conflict? Is the conflict serious enough to jeopardize the group's goal and members' morale?

- **Resolution.** What are the available methods for resolving the conflict? Which method best matches the nature of the group and its conflict?

Analyzing and understanding the nature of the disagreement will result in a better resolution. The 4Rs method provides a way of thinking about conflict and selecting an appropriate approach to conflict management.

The A-E-I-O-U Model

In order to resolve conflict, a group must fully understand its members' concerns. If members do not understand the problem, they cannot find effective solutions. Jerry Wisinski's **A-E-I-O-U Model** is a way to clearly communicate concerns and suggest alternative actions.[16] The steps in the A-E-I-O-U Model are as follows:

A—Assume that the other members mean well.

E—Express your feelings.

I—Identify what you would like to have happen.

O—Outcomes you expect are made clear.

U—Understanding on a mutual basis is achieved.

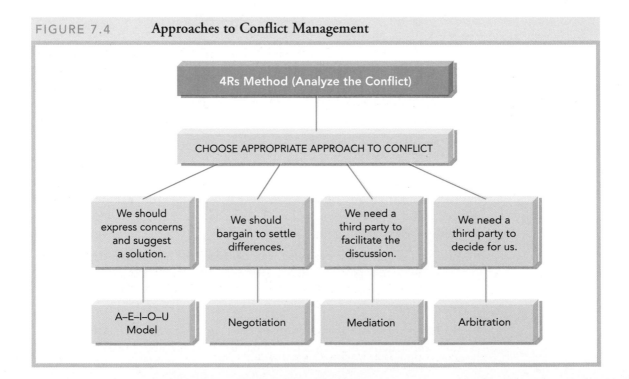

FIGURE 7.4   **Approaches to Conflict Management**

The first step, *A,* requires a belief that other group members are willing to cooperate. Such a belief could be expressed as follows: "I know that all of us want this project to be successful." If you or other members sense that some people are not willing to cooperate or that a hidden agenda is lurking below the surface, the group should spend as much time as needed on this step to ensure that members are committed to resolving the conflict.

The second step, *E,* identifies your feelings associated with a specific behavior or action: "But, I'm really worried, because it seems as though we're not putting in the work that's needed." Expressing your feelings and describing behavior helps the group interpret your reaction to the situation. Also, as you listen to others express their feelings, paraphrase what they've said to ensure that you and others understand their concerns.

The third step, *I,* requires that you not only express your concerns but also identify what you want to have happen: "I would like to be assured that all of you are as concerned about the success of this project as I am, and that you have been thinking about how we can make sure the work gets done on time." The group can now focus its discussion on solving the problem. As you listen to others share their recommendations, you may realize that group members are close to or far from agreement.

The fourth step, *O,* directs you to inform members of the potential outcomes of their behavior: "I sincerely believe that if we don't work late for the next couple of days, we will not be prepared to make an effective group presentation next week."

The final step, *U,* recognizes that your group may need more time to reach a mutual understanding: "Could we try staying late for the next few days to get ahead of the game? What do you think?" A group will frequently reject an initial suggestion but then go on to develop a more satisfactory solution. This final step requires that all group members understand the problem and agree to a solution. When all the steps in the A-E-I-O-U Model are combined, they become the essential ingredients in creating a constructive approach to conflict management.

Negotiation

Negotiation is a process of bargaining in order to settle differences or reach solutions. Normally, negotiation takes the form of compromise, with group members conceding some issues in order to achieve agreement on other points. Group members will be more willing to bargain if they believe that they will be no worse off and might even be better off by the end of the negotiation process.

Conflict can be resolved through a process of "principled negotiation."[17] The four principles are as follows:

- Separate the people from the problem.

- Focus on group interests, not positions.

- Generate a variety of possible solutions for mutual gain.

- Insist on objective criteria for choosing a solution.

When group members focus on defending their positions, the result is winners and losers. When the members focus on group interests, the entire group wins. However, group negotiation can become deadlocked when members are unable to appreciate the needs of others or are unwilling to make concessions. The following strategies can help break a deadlock:[18]

- Limit the scope of the problem by dividing it into manageable parts.

- Minimize defensive behavior by having members explain or paraphrase the other side's position.

- Summarize areas of agreement to promote further cooperation.

- Take a break to relieve group tensions.

- Ask for more information to avoid inaccurate assumptions.

Clearly, group members must balance a variety of needs during negotiation.[19] They must be willing to cooperate with others while attempting to meet as many of their own needs as possible. They must openly communicate what they are willing to concede, yet not sacrifice more than is necessary. Finally, members must balance the need to gain their own short-term goals against the benefits of mutually desirable long-term conflict resolution.

Mediation

In recent years, *mediation* has become a more commonly used tool for resolving disputes. **Mediation** is "facilitated negotiation [that] employs the services of impartial third parties only for the purpose of guiding, coaching, and encouraging the disputants through negotiation to successful resolution and agreement."[20] Mediation is an appropriate approach to conflict resolution when group members are unable to resolve the conflict by themselves and when everyone concerned is willing to participate in the process and abide by the final settlement. If group members cannot agree to these terms, then mediation is not an option.

Once a group has decided to use mediation, there are two basic requirements: an impartial mediator and a well-planned mediation session. The group must choose an impartial mediator who is not involved in the conflict. If a conflict involves all members of the group, a mediator from outside the group should be chosen. The group leader or another group member should be considered as a mediator only if he or she is not involved in the conflict. The mediator does not take sides in the dispute. Instead, he or she guides the group through the process and facilitates negotiation.

Effective mediators follow a well-established set of basic steps:[21]

- *Introduction.* Explain the mediation process and create a supportive climate by offering words of encouragement and asking for questions prior to beginning.

- *Storytelling.* Allow each member to tell his or her story without interruption. Use stories to identify issues and establish commonalities. Summarize each group member's perspective.

- *Agenda building.* List the issues to be negotiated and frame the goals of the session.

- *Negotiation and problem solving.* Guide the group members toward possible solutions.

- *Testing agreement.* After agreeing on a resolution to the conflict, discuss ways to implement the solution. Write a clear, unambiguous, and understood agreement. Group members should sign the agreement.

- *Closure.* Praise the group and provide copies of the agreement to all members. If possible, lead a discussion on ways in which the group can resolve future conflicts.[22]

An effective mediator establishes a rapport with disputing group members through empathic listening.[23] Listen to each member's concerns, acknowledge the legitimacy of those concerns, and assure members that you will try to help everyone discover a solution that will meet their needs.[24]

Arbitration

Groups often seek mediation when all other methods of resolving a conflict have failed. If, however, mediation does not work, a group may seek arbitration. **Arbitration,** like mediation, involves a third party. However, after considering all sides, the agreed-upon arbitrator decides how to resolve the conflict. The arbitrator may choose one person's solution or may develop a solution the group has not yet considered. Whatever the final decision, group members are obligated to accept and implement the solution, no matter what they think about the decision.

When turning to an arbitrator to make a decision, group members "have acknowledged that their own decision-making powers are insufficient to resolve the dispute. Their function, therefore, is to present their side of the case as fully and as capably as possible so that fairness and justice can prevail."[25] Despite the hope for a just outcome, professional arbitrators understand that their decisions may not satisfy or please everyone in a group. Yet, for groups that cannot resolve conflicts or solve problems on their own or with the help of a mediator, arbitration may be the only way to make a needed decision.

ETHICAL GROUPS

Ethical Conflict Resolution

Ethical conflict resolution respects differences, uses power positively, encourages collaboration, seeks constructive change, and promotes positive relationships. Mediation experts Stephen Little-john and Kathy Domenici suggest the following strategies for resolving conflict constructively:[1]

- Speak to be understood rather than to win.
- Focus on your own perspective rather than criticizing others' behavior.
- Speak in ways that are respectful rather then attacking or threatening another.
- Recognize that there are many perspectives rather than polarizing a dispute into only two points of view.

- Express uncertainties rather than blindly adhering to a position.
- Recognize the complexities of an issue rather than oversimplifying it.
- Explore ideas in new ways.

Engaging in ethical and constructive conflict resolution does not guarantee that you will get what you want, nor does it preclude that possibility. Rather, practicing ethical conflict resolution promotes respectful communication that encourages us to seek solutions that satisfy everyone involved.

[1] Stephen W. Littlejohn and Kathy Domenici, *Engaging Communication in Conflict: Systematic Practice* (Thousand Oaks, CA: Sage, 2001), pp. 44–45.

GROUP COHESION

Resolving conflict in groups does not guarantee success, nor does it ensure that group members will work together in pursuit of a common goal. Working in groups also requires cohesion. **Cohesion** is the mutual attraction that holds the members of a group together. Groups that are cohesive feel committed and unified; members develop a sense of teamwork and pride in the group. The following are characteristics of a cohesive group:

- High levels of interaction
- A friendly and supportive communication climate
- A desire to conform to group expectations
- The use of creative and productive approaches to achieving goals
- Satisfied members[26]

Enhancing Cohesion

Cohesive groups are happier and get more work done. Clearly, your group wants to strive for cohesion. We suggest four general strategies for developing group cohesion: establish a group identity and traditions, emphasize teamwork, recognize and reward participation, and respect group members.[27]

Establish a Group Identity and Traditions. Begin by referring to the group using terms such as *we* and *our* instead of *I* and *my*. The language that members use to refer to the group can influence the way they perceive their connection to it. Some groups create more obvious signs of identity, such as a group name, logo, or motto. As members continue to work and interact with one another, the group begins to develop its own history. Many groups develop rituals and ceremonies to reinforce their traditions.

Emphasize Teamwork. The members of cohesive groups believe that their contributions are essential to the success of the group. Group members feel responsibility for and take pride in both the work that they do and the work of other members. They frequently make statements that stress the importance of everyone's role. Rather than the individual members taking personal credit for success, a cohesive group will emphasize the group's accomplishments.

Recognize and Reward Contributions. Frequently, group members become so involved in their own work that they neglect to praise others for their contributions. In addition, members are often quick to criticize others' mistakes and poor work. While constructive criticism is important, members must feel that their efforts are appreciated. Cohesive groups establish a climate in which praise is encouraged. Many groups reward individual efforts and initiative. Celebration dinners, letters of appreciation, certificates, and gifts are all ways in which some groups reward themselves.

Respect Group Members. When strong interpersonal relationships are developed in groups, members become more sensitive to one another's needs. Groups that require members to do their part of the work without regard for individual concerns will develop little cohesion. Treating members with respect, showing concern for their personal needs, and appreciating diversity will promote a feeling of acceptance.

Groupthink

Groupthink is a term that describes the deterioration of group effectiveness that can result from in-group pressure.[28] Group pressure that produces too much conformity can have disastrous effects. The homogeneous–heterogeneous dialectic discussed in Chapter 1 is particularly important when dealing with groupthink. The more members have in common, the more cohesive they may become. Homogeneous groups run the risk of being "more insulated from outside opinions, and therefore more convinced that the group's judgment on important issues must be right."[29]

Symptoms of Groupthink. Irving Janis, a professor at Yale University, developed the theory of groupthink after recognizing patterns in what he termed policymaking fiascoes. He suggested that groupthink was a significant factor in several major policy decisions, including the Bay of Pigs invasion of Cuba, the escalation of both the Korean and Vietnam wars, the attack on Pearl Harbor, and the Watergate burglary and cover-up.[30] Groupthink may also have contributed to the explosion of the space shuttle *Challenger.*[31] After analyzing many of these policy decisions, Janis identified eight symptoms of groupthink. Figure 7.5 illustrates the symptoms and expressions of groupthink.

Dealing with Groupthink. The best way to deal with groupthink is to prevent it from happening in the first place. The following list provides practical

FIGURE 7.5　　**Groupthink**

Groupthink Symptoms	Expressions of Groupthink
Invulnerability: Is overly confident; willing to take big risks.	"We're right. We've done this many times, and nothing's gone wrong."
Rationalization: Makes excuses; discounts warnings.	"What does Lewis know? He's been here only three weeks."
Morality: Ignores ethical and moral consequences.	"Sometimes the end justifies the means."
Stereotyping Outsiders: Considers opposition too weak and stupid to make real trouble.	"Let's not worry about the subcommittee—they can't even get their own act together."
Self-Censorship: Doubts his or her own reservations; unwilling to disagree or dissent.	"I guess there's no harm in going along with the group—I'm the only one who disagrees."
Pressure on Dissent: Pressures members to agree.	"Why are you trying to hold this up? You'll ruin the project."
Illusion of Unanimity: Believes everyone agrees.	"Hearing no objections, the motion passes."
Mindguarding: Shields members from adverse information or opposition.	"Rhea wanted to come to this meeting, but I told her that wasn't necessary."

ways to minimize the potential of groupthink.[32] Choose the methods that are most appropriate for your group.

- Ask each member to serve in the role of critical evaluator.

- If possible, have more than one group member work on the same problem independently.

- Discuss the group's progress with someone outside the group. Report the feedback to the entire group.

- Periodically invite an expert to join your meeting and encourage constructive criticism.

- Discuss the potential negative consequences of any decision or action.

- Follow a formal decision-making procedure that encourages expression of disagreement and evaluation of ideas.

- Ask questions, offer reasons for positions, and demand justifications from others.

- Before finalizing the decision, give members a second chance to express doubts.

In the short term, groupthink decisions are easier. The group finishes early and doesn't have to deal with conflict. However, such decisions are often poor and sometimes result in harm. Spending the time and energy to work through differences will result in better decisions without sacrificing group cohesiveness.

ADAPTING TO DIFFERENCES

Conflict becomes more complex when group members are diverse. Differences in cultural and gender perspectives may result in misunderstandings, prejudices, and unintentionally offensive behavior. A group's failure to manage conflict among diverse members effectively can have serious consequences. Companies that fail to understand, respect, and adapt to differences are likely to have more strikes and lawsuits, low morale among workers, less productivity, and a higher turnover of employees.[33]

Cultural Responses to Conflict

The cultural values of individual members will greatly influence the degree to which they are comfortable with conflict and the way in which conflict is resolved. Members from cultures that value conformity are less likely to express disagreement than those from cultures that place a higher value on individualism. While people from Japanese, German, Mexican, and Brazilian cultures value group conformity, those from Swedish and French cultures are generally more comfortable expressing differences.[34] In addition, Chinese group members may feel uncomfortable with adversarial approaches to conflict.[35] It is also important to remember that cultural differences may be regional rather than international. For example, Franco-Canadians are often more cooperative during the negotiation of conflict, while Anglo-Canadians are slower to agree to a resolution.[36]

In Chapter 3, "Group Member Diversity," we note that the individualism–collectivism -cultural dimension strongly influences the ways in which group members communicate. Not surprisingly, this dialectic also explains why members define and respond to conflict differently. For example, collectivist members may merge substantive and affective concerns, making conflict much more personal. "To shout and scream publicly, thus displaying the conflict to others, threatens everyone's face to such an extreme degree that such behavior is usually avoided at all costs." In individualistic cultures, however, group members may express their anger about an issue and then joke and socialize with others once the disagreement is over. "It is almost as if once the conflict is resolved, it is completely forgotten."[37] Thus, when an individualistic member prefaces a critical or disparaging remark by saying, "Now don't take this personally . . . ," you can bet that a collectivist member will do just the opposite.

Gender Responses to Conflict

Groups must also be sensitive to how gender differences influence conflict. In general, women are more likely to avoid conflict or to leave a group when there is continuous conflict.[38] In addition, women are more likely to address conflict privately rather than in front of the entire group.[39] Men and women can learn from each other's perspectives as they work through a group's conflict.

TOOLBOX 7.2

Let Members Save Face

Collectivist cultures place a high value on "face." From a cultural perspective, **face** is the positive image that you wish to create or preserve. Thus, cultures that place a great deal of value on "saving face" discourage personal attacks and outcomes in which one person "loses." Keep in mind the following collectivist perspectives about conflict:[1]

• Conflict is understood within the context of relationships and the need to preserve "face."

• Conflict resolution requires that "face" issues be mutually managed before a discussion of other issues.

• Conflict resolution is considered successful when both parties are able to save "face" and when both can claim that they have "won."

[1] William R. Cupach and Daniel J. Canary, *Competencies in Interpersonal Conflict* (New York: McGraw-Hill, 1997), p. 133.

How must the "tribe" members on the reality show *Survivor* balance the need to work together while also competing against each other? (© CBS/Photofest)

Studies show that men and women from similar cultures do not differ significantly in terms of the conflict strategies and styles that they use. However, men and women do differ in terms of their expected focus and behavior in conflicts. Men tend to focus on substantive issues, while women tend to focus on the relationships among members. As a result, women tend to behave more cooperatively than men under ideal conditions. At the same time, research notes that women may compete more forcefully in reaction to what they perceive as betrayal or underhanded behavior by others.[40]

BALANCING CONFLICT AND COHESION

The management of conflict is "a delicate balancing act, like that of a tightrope walker, or a rock climber who must find just the right handholds or fall to sure death."[41] Effective groups must balance the conflict–cohesion dialectic. Having group members with different perspectives promotes critical thinking and creative problem solving. At the same time, "too many differences, or one difference that is so strong it dominates grouping resources, can overwhelm the group" and its ability to focus on the group goal.[42] Groups must balance the need to express differences with the need to achieve group consensus. Individual thought must be encouraged, yet collective group goals need to be achieved.

A group that lacks cohesion is less creative, productive, and satisfied. Extremely cohesive groups, however, risk engaging in groupthink. Yet fear of groupthink should not discourage efforts to promote cohesion. Groups that are characterized by too much or poorly managed conflict do not develop cohesion. However, groups that place too much emphasis on cohesion while avoiding conflict will often make bad decisions. Groups that engage in constructive conflict are able to successfully balance conflict and cohesion.

GROUPWORK

Win as Much as You Can

Goal: To demonstrate the merit of competitive and cooperative models of conflict styles within the context of small group communication

Participants: One or more groups of eight divided into four dyads (two-person subgroups)

Procedure

1. There are ten rounds in this exercise. During each round, you and your partner will have to choose an X or a Y. The payoff for each round is determined by the choices of all the dyads in your eight-person group.

2. There are three key rules:
   • Do not confer with other members of your group unless you are told to do so.
   • Each dyad must agree upon a single choice for each round.
   • Make sure that other members of your group do not know your dyad's choice until you are told to reveal it.

3. Confer with your partner on every round. Before rounds 5, 8, and 10, you can confer with the other pairs in your group.

Payoff Chart

4	Xs:	Lose	$1.00 each
3	Xs:	Win	$1.00 each
1	Y:	Lose	$3.00 each
2	Xs:	Win	$2.00 each
2	Ys:	Lose	$2.00 each
1	X:	Win	$3.00 each
3	Ys:	Lose	$1.00 each
4	Ys:	Win	$1.00 each

*The textbook's *Instructor's Resource Manual* explains how to conduct this GroupWork exercise.

Tally Sheet

Round	Time Allowed	Confer with	Choice	$ Won	$ Lost	Balance
1	2 min.	partner				
2	1 min.	partner				
3	1 min.	partner				
4	1 min.	partner				
5*	3 min. +1 min.	group partner				
6	1 min.	partner				
7	1 min.	partner				
8**	3 min. +1 min.	group partner				
9	1 min.	partner				
10***	3 min. +1 min.	group partner				

*Payoff is multiplied by 3.
**Payoff is multiplied by 5.
***Payoff is multiplied by 10.

Source: Based on W. Gellerman, "Win as Much as You Can," in *A Handbook of Structured Experiences for Human Relations Training*, Vol. 2, ed. J. William Pfeiffer and John E. Jones (La Jolla, CA: University Associates, 1970), pp. 66–69.

GROUPASSESSMENT

Ross-DeWine Conflict Management Message Style Instrument

Directions. Below you will find messages that have been delivered by persons in conflict situations. Consider each message separately, and decide how closely this message resembles the ones that you have used in conflict settings. The language may not be exactly the same as yours, but consider the messages in terms of their fundamental similarity to your messages in conflict situations. There are no right or wrong answers, nor are these messages designed to trick you. Answer in terms of the responses you actually make, not what you think you should say. Give each message a 1 to 5 rating on the answer sheet provided according to the following scale. Mark one answer only.

In conflict situations, I . . .

1	2	3	4	5
never say things like this	rarely say things like this	sometimes say things like this	often say things like this	usually say things like this

_____ 1. "Can't you see how foolish you're being with that thinking?"

_____ 2. "How can I make you feel happy again?"

_____ 3. "I'm really bothered by some things that are happening here; can we talk about these?"

_____ 4. "I really don't have any more to say on this . . . (silence)."

_____ 5. "What possible solutions can we come up with?"

_____ 6. "I'm really sorry that your feelings are hurt—maybe you're right."

_____ 7. "Let's talk this thing out and see how we can deal with this hassle."

_____ 8. "Shut up! You are wrong! I don't want to hear any more of what you have to say."

_____ 9. "It is your fault if I fail at this, and don't you ever expect any help from me when you're on the spot."

_____ 10. "You can't do (say) that to me—it's either my way or forget it."

_____ 11. "Let's try finding an answer that will give us both some of what we want."

_____ 12. "This is something we have to work out; we're always arguing about it."

_____ 13. "Whatever makes you feel happiest is OK by me."

_____ 14. "Let's just leave well enough alone."

_____ 15. "That's OK . . . it wasn't important anyway. . . . You feeling OK now?"

_____ 16. "If you're not going to cooperate, I'll just go to someone who will."

_____ 17. "I think we need to try to understand the problem."

_____ 18. "You might as well accept my decision; you can't do anything about it anyway."

Scoring Instructions: Next to each item, list the rating (from 1 to 5) that you gave that item. When you have entered all ratings, add the total ratings for each column and divide by 6. Enter the resulting score in the space provided.

SELF Items	ISSUE Items	OTHER Items
1. _____	3. _____	2. _____
8. _____	5. _____	4. _____
9. _____	7. _____	6. _____
10. _____	11. _____	13. _____
16. _____	12. _____	14. _____
18. _____	17. _____	15. _____

Your Total Score   _____   _____   _____

Average Score   (13.17)   (24.26)   (21.00)

All of us may use any one of these styles in different settings and under different circumstances. People do tend to have a predominant style, however, which is evidenced by the kinds of messages generally sent during conflict situations.

The SELF items deal with one's personal interests in the conflict situation. These messages suggest that one's primary concern is in resolving the conflict so that one's personal view of the conflict is accepted by the other. This is a "win" approach to conflict resolution.

The ISSUE items deal with an emphasis on both parties dealing with the problem. These message statements suggest an overriding concern with the content of the conflict rather than the personal relationship.

The OTHER items deal with neither the conflict issues nor personal interests, but emphasize maintaining the relationship, even at the cost of resolving the conflict. These statements suggest that one would rather ignore the problem to maintain a good relationship with the other person.

The averages are an indication of scores one might expect to receive. Scores that are higher or lower than these means indicate a higher or lower use of this message style than would normally be expected.

Source: Sue DeWine, The Consultant's Craft: Improving Organizational Communication (New York: St. Martin's, 1994), pp. 268–272; Rosanna Ross and Sue DeWine, "Communication Messages in Conflict: A Message-Focused Instrument to Assess Conflict Management Styles," *Management Communication Quarterly,* 1 (1988), pp. 389–413.

NOTES

1. Jim Billington, "The Three Essentials of an Effective Team," *Harvard Management Update, 2 (January 1997),* p. 3.

2. Peg Pickering, *How to Manage Conflict: Turn All Conflicts into Win-Win Outcomes,* 3rd ed. (Franklin Lakes, NJ: Career Press, 2000), p. 3.

3. Linda L. Putnam, "Conflict in Group Decision-Making," in *Communication and Group Decision-Making,* ed. Randy Y. Hirokawa and Marshall Scott Poole (Beverly Hills, CA: Sage, 1986), pp. 175–196. Also see Joseph P. Folger, Marshall Scott Poole, and Randall K. Stutman, *Working Through Conflict,* 5th ed. (Boston: Allyn & Bacon, 2005), pp. 19–20.

4. *The American Heritage Dictionary of the English Language,* 4th ed. (Boston: Houghton Mifflin, 2000), p. 28.

5. Putnam, p. 185.

6. Ronald T. Potter-Efron, *Work Rage: Preventing Anger and Resolving Conflict on the Job* (New York: Barnes & Noble Books, 2000), pp. 22–23.

7. Based on Stephen W. Littlejohn and Kathy Domenici, *Engaging Communication in Conflict: Systematic Practice* (Thousand Oaks, CA: Sage, 2001), pp. 94–103.

8. Folger, Poole, and Stutman, p. 213.

9. See Kenneth W. Thomas and Ralph H. Kilmann, "Developing a Forced-Choice Measure of Conflict-Handling Behavior: The MODE Instrument," *Educational and Psychological Measurement, 37* (1977), pp. 390–395; see also Pickering, pp. 35–41. Whereas Thomas and Kilmann classify conflict styles as avoidance, accommodation, competition, compromise, and collaboration, other researchers use different terms for similar categories, e.g., competing, avoiding, accommodating, compromising, and problem-solving, as in Robert R. Blake and Jane S. Mouton, *The Managerial Grid* (Houston: Gulf Publishing, 1964).

10. Kenneth W. Thomas, *Intrinsic Motivation at Work: Building Energy and Commitment* (San Francisco: Berret-Koehler, 2000), p. 94.

11. Littlejohn and Domenici, p. 181.

12. Gary Harper, *The Joy of Conflict Resolution: Transforming Victims, Villains and Heroes in the Workplace and at Home* (Gabriola Island, Canada: New Society Publishers, 2004), p. 121.

13. Thomas, p. 94.

14. Dianna Wynn is a trial consultant for *Courtroom Intelligence,* a consulting firm specializing in courtroom communication.

15. Folger, Poole, and Stutman, pp. 229–231.

16. Jerry Wisinski, *Resolving Conflicts on the Job* (New York: American Management Association, 1993), pp. 27–31.

17. Roger Fisher, William Ury, and Bruce Patton, *Getting to Yes: Negotiating Agreement Without Giving In* (Boston: Houghton Mifflin, 1991), p. 15.

18. Myra Warren Isenhart and Michael Spangle, *Collaborative Approaches to Resolving Conflict* (Thousand Oaks, CA: Sage, 2000), p. 58.

19. Jeffrey Z. Rubin, "Negotiation: An Introduction to Some Issues and Themes," in *Small Group Communication: A Reader,* 6th ed., ed. Robert S. Cathcart and Larry A. Samovar (Dubuque, IA: Wm. C. Brown, 1992), pp. 415–423.

20. William D. Kimsey, Rex M. Fuller, and Bruce C. McKinney, *Mediation and Conflict Management: General Mediation Manual* (Harrisonburg, VA: James Madison University Center for Mediation), p. 21.

21. Suzanne McCorkle and Melanie J. Reese, *Mediation Theory and Practice* (Boston: Allyn & Bacon, 2005), pp. 20–32; Bruce C. McKinney, William D. Kimsey, and Rex M. Fuller, *Mediator Communication Competencies: Interpersonal Communication and Alternative Dispute Resolution,* 4th ed. (Edina, MN: Burgess, 1995), pp. 67–98.

22. Dean Tjosvold and Evert van de Vliert, "Applying Cooperative and Competitive Conflict to Mediation," *Mediation Quarterly, 11* (1994), pp. 303–311.

23. Stephen B. Goldberg, "The Secrets of Successful Mediators," *Negotiation Journal, 3* (July 2005), p. 369.

24. Goldberg, p. 372.

25. John W. Keltner, The Management of Struggle: Elements of Dispute Resolution through Negotiation, Mediation, and Arbitration (Cresskill, NJ: Hampton, 1994), p. 168.

26. Marvin E. Shaw, "Group Composition and Group Cohesiveness," in *Small Group Communication: A Reader,* 6th ed., ed. Robert S. Cathcart and Larry A. Samovar (Dubuque, IA: Wm. C. Brown, 1992), pp. 214–220.

27. Based on Ernest G. Bormann and Nancy Bormann, *Effective Small Group Communication,* 6th ed. (Edina, MN: Burgess Publishing, 1996), pp. 137–139.

28. Irving L. Janis, *Groupthink: Psychological Studies of Policy Decisions and Fiascoes,* 2nd ed. (Boston: Houghton Mifflin, 1982), p. 9.

29. James Surowiecki, *The Wisdom of Crowds: Why the Many Are Smarter than the Few and How Collective Wisdom Shapes Business, Economies, Societies, and Nations* (New York: Doubleday, 2004), pp. 36–37.

30. Janis, pp. 174–175.

31. Gregory Moorhead, Richard Ference, and Christopher P. Neck, "Group Decision Fiascos Continue: Space Shuttle *Challenger* and a Groupthink Framework," *Human Relations, 44,* pp. 539–550, reprinted in *Small Group Communication: Theory and Practice,* 7th ed., ed. Robert S. Cathcart, Larry A. Samovar, and Linda D. Henman (Dubuque, IA: Brown and Benchmark, 1991), pp. 161–170. For a different perspective, see Diane Vaughan, *The Challenger Launch Decision: Risk*

Technology, Culture, and Deviance at NASA (Chicago: University of Chicago, 1996).

32. See Janis; R. J. W. Cline, "Groupthink and the Watergate Cover-Up: The Illusion of Unanimity," in *Group Communication in Context: Studies of Natural Groups,* ed. Lawrence R. Frey (Hillsdale, NJ: Erlbaum, 1994), pp. 199–223; 3M Meeting Management Team, *Mastering Meetings: Discovering the Hidden Potential of Effective Business Meetings* (New York: McGraw-Hill, 1994), p. 58.

33. Bren Ortega Murphy, "Promoting Dialogue in Culturally Diverse Workplace Environments," in *Innovation in Group Facilitation: Applications in Natural Settings,* ed. Lawrence R. Frey (Cresskill, NJ: Hampton, 1995), pp. 77–93.

34. Myron W. Lustig and Laura L. Cassotta, "Comparing Group Communication Across Cultures: Leadership, Conformity, and Discussion Processes," in *Small Group Communication: Theory and Practice,* 7th ed., ed. Robert S. Cathcart, Larry A. Samovar, and Linda D. Henman (Madison, WI: Brown & Benchmark, 1996), pp. 316–326.

35. Russell Copranzano, Herman Aguinis, Marshall Schminke, and Dina L. Denham, "Disputant Reactions to Managerial Conflict Resolution Tactics: A Comparison Among Argentina, the Dominican Republic, Mexico, and the United States," *Group and Organization Management, 24* (1999), p. 131.

36. Laura E. Drake, "The Culture–Negotiation Link: Integrative and Distributive Bargaining Through an Intercultural Communication Lens," *Human Communication Research, 27* (2001), p. 321.

37. Myron W. Lustig and Jolene Koester, *Intercultural Competence: Interpersonal Communication Across Cultures* (Boston: Allyn & Bacon, 2006), pp. 283–294. Lustig and Koester summarize research by Stella Ting-Toomey and John G. Oetzel, *Managing Interpersonal Conflict Effectively* (Thousand Oaks, CA: Sage, 2002).

38. William W. Wilmot and Joyce L. Hocker, *Interpersonal Conflict,* 6th ed. (New York: McGraw-Hill, 2001), p. 31.

39. Deborah Tannen, *The Argument Culture: Moving from Debate to Dialogue* (New York: Random House, 1998), p. 196.

40. Folger, Poole, and Stutman, p. 235.

41. Wilmot and Hocker, p. 22.

42. John O. Burtis and Paul D. Turman, *Group Communication Pitfalls: Overcoming Barriers to an Effective Group Experience* (Thousand Oaks, CA: Sage, 2006), p. 127.

Achieving Group Goals

© Strauss/Curtis/Corbis

CHAPTER 8

Group Leadership

CHAPTER OUTLINE

What Is Leadership?

Leadership and Power
Reward Power
Coercive Power
Legitimate Power
Expert Power
Referent Power

Becoming a Leader
Designated Leaders
Emergent Leaders
Strategies for Becoming a Leader

Leadership Theories
Trait Theory
Styles Theory
Situational Theory
Transformational Theory

The 4-M Model of Leadership Effectiveness
Model Leadership Behavior
Motivate Members
Manage Group Process
Make Decisions

Diversity and Leadership
Gender and Leadership
Cultural Diversity and Leadership

Balanced Leadership

GroupWork: The Least-Preferred-Coworker Scale

GroupAssessment: Are You Ready to Lead?

WHAT IS LEADERSHIP?

All groups need leadership. Without leadership, a group may be nothing more than a collection of individuals, lacking the coordination and motivation to achieve a common goal. Quite simply, "there are no successful groups without leaders. . . . Leaders lead because groups demand it and rely on leaders to satisfy needs."[1]

A leader and leadership are not the same thing. **Leadership** is the ability to make strategic decisions and use communication effectively to mobilize group members toward achieving a common goal. *Leader* is the title given to a person; *leadership* refers to the actions that a leader takes to help group members achieve shared goals. Even groups without official leaders may rely on several members to perform leadership functions.

Another way to understand the nature of leadership is to contrast it with the functions of management. Whereas managers concentrate on getting an assigned job done, leaders focus on the ultimate direction and goal of the group. Note how the employee in the following situation describes the difference between a manager and a leader:

> Lee is the manager of our department, so he's technically our leader. He always follows procedures and meets deadlines for paperwork, so I guess he's a good manager. But we don't get much guidance from him. I think that managing tasks and real leadership of people are somehow different. Allison supervises the other department. She seems to inspire her workers. They're more innovative, and they work closely with one another. We do our job, but they seem to be on a mission. I've always thought that working for Allison would be more rewarding and enjoyable.

LEADERSHIP AND POWER

It is impossible to understand effective leadership without understanding the importance of power. Leadership experts Warren Bennis and Bruce Nanus claim that power is "the quality without which leaders cannot lead."[2] In the hands of a just and wise leader, power is a positive force; in the hands of an unjust and foolish leader, power can be corrupting and destructive.

Power is the ability or authority to influence and motivate others. In their analysis of power in groups, John French and Bertram Raven classify power into five categories: reward power, coercive power, legitimate power, expert power, and referent power.

Reward Power

Reward power derives from a leader's authority to give group members something that they value. Whether the reward is a cash bonus, a promotion, or a convenient

FIGURE 8.1   **Power in Groups**

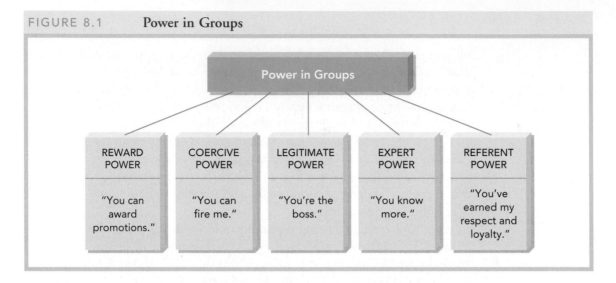

work schedule, its effectiveness depends on whether group members value the reward. Some leaders may think that they have power because they control group rewards, only to discover that those rewards have little value for members. Employees may not want a promotion if the new job is less appealing than their current job. Only when the reward is worthwhile will group members respond to a leader who uses this kind of power.

Coercive Power

If the carrot approach doesn't work, a leader may resort to using a stick: **coercive power.** Another way to describe coercive power is to call it punishment power. When leaders can discipline, demote, or dismiss group members, they have coercive power. In the extreme, highly coercive leaders can range from the "abusive tyrant, who bawls out and humiliates people, to the manipulative sociopath. Such leaders have an emotional impact a bit like the 'dementors' in the Harry Potter series, who 'drain peace, hope, and happiness out of the air around them.' At their worst, leaders who rely on coercive power have no idea how destructive they are—or they simply don't care."[3]

In *Leadership*, authors Michael Hackman and Craig Johnson contend that "coercion is most effective when those subject to this form of power are aware of expectations and are warned in advance about the penalties for failure to comply. Leaders using coercive power must consistently carry out threatened punishments."[4] A skillful leader uses coercive power sparingly, and only when all other means of influence have failed.

Legitimate Power

Legitimate power resides in a job, position, or assignment rather than in a person. For example, elected officials have the power to vote on the public's behalf;

As the Secretary of State, what types of leadership power might Dr. Condoleezza Rice possess? (© Bob Daemmrich/ Photo Edit)

committee chairpersons are authorized to take control of their assigned tasks; supervisors have authority over their workers. The word *legitimate* means "lawful" or "proper." Most people believe that it is lawful and proper for a judge to make decisions and keep order in a courtroom. Group leaders may call meetings, assign tasks, and evaluate members as part of their legitimate duties.

Expert Power

Expert power is assigned to someone who has demonstrated a particular skill or special knowledge. Just as we may accept the advice of a doctor when we're ill or that of an auto mechanic when our car has broken down on the highway, we are more likely to grant power to an expert. However, if the advice of a supposed expert proves incorrect, his or her power will fade and may even disappear. A leader can rely on expert power only if the group recognizes the leader as a well-informed and reliable authority.

Referent Power

Referent power is role model power—the ability to influence that arises when one person admires another.[5] Referent power is the personal power or influence held by people who are liked, admired, and respected. When certain members demonstrate that they are effective communicators, talented organizers, skilled problem solvers, and good listeners, we are more likely to be influenced by them. We often feel honored to work with someone who has strong referent power. Referent or personal power is influential because it is recognized and conferred by the group rather than by an outside source.

In most groups, a leader employs several kinds of power, depending on the needs of the group and the situation. Some leaders may have the power to reward and coerce as well as having legitimate, expert, and referent power. In other groups, a leader may depend entirely on one type of power to get a group to work cooperatively toward a goal. The more power a leader has, the more carefully the use of that power must be balanced with the needs of the group. If you exert too

ETHICAL GROUPS

 ## Leadership Integrity

In his book on leadership, Andrew DuBrin makes the case that ethical leaders do "the *right* thing as perceived by a consensus of *reasonable* people."[1] Doing the right thing requires honesty, trustworthiness, and integrity. Leaders with integrity honor their commitments and their promises. They practice what they preach, regardless of emotional or social pressure. For example, if a good friend in your group asks to chair a committee, and you've promised the position to someone with better skills, you should keep your promise even if it upsets your friend.[2]

Unethical leadership has enormous consequences, regardless of whether it affects a small study group or a global corporation. Unethical behavior has bankrupted companies, led to thousands of layoffs, and exposed the unrestrained spending of self-centered corporate executives. Executives such as Kenneth Lay (Enron), Bernard Ebbers (WorldCom), and Dennis Kozlowski (Tyco) exemplify unethical leadership that harmed thousands of trusting employees and investors.[3]

The Center for Business Ethics at Bentley College poses six questions to help you decide whether your leadership behaviors are ethical or unethical:[4]

- *Is it right?* Do you conform to universally accepted guiding principles of rightness and wrongness, such as "thou shalt not steal"?

- *Is it fair?* Would you overlook a competent person in order to promote a less competent relative or friend?
- *Who gets hurt?* Do you try to do the greatest good for the greatest number of people?
- *Would you be comfortable if the details of your decisions or actions were made public in the media or through email?*
- *What would you tell your child or a young relative to do?*
- *How does it smell?* If a reasonable person with good common sense were to look at your decision or action, would it "smell" suspicious or bad to that person? Would it seem wrong?

Leadership can become an ego trip—or, even worse, a power trip. Bennis and Goldsmith describe leadership as a three-legged stool—ambition, competence, and integrity—that must remain in balance if the leader is to be a constructive force rather than a destructive force, interested only in achieving her or his own goals.[5]

[1] Andrew J. DuBrin, *Leadership: Research Findings, Practice, and Skills*, 4th ed. (New York: Houghton Mifflin, 2004), p. 168.
[2] DuBrin, p. 168.
[3] DuBrin, pp. 175–176.
[4] Kris Maher, "Wanted: Ethical Employer," *Wall Street Journal*, July 9, 2002, p. B1, as quoted in DuBrin, pp. 172–173.
[5] Warren Bennis and Joan Goldsmith, *Learning to Lead: A Workbook on Becoming a Leader*, Updated Edition (Cambridge, MA: Perseus, 1997), p. 3.

much power, your group may lose its energy and enthusiasm. If you don't exert enough power, your group may flounder and fail.

BECOMING A LEADER

Anyone can become a leader. Abraham Lincoln and Harry S. Truman rose from humble beginnings and hardship to become U.S. presidents. Corporate executives have worked their way up from the sales force and the secretarial pool to become chief executive officers. Condoleezza Rice, the great-grandchild of slaves, was born in segregated Birmingham, Alabama, and became U.S. secretary of state and one of the most powerful women in U.S. history. Yet, as inspiring as such examples may be, the leaders you encounter on an everyday basis are not necessarily the hardest workers or the smartest employees. The path to a leadership position can be as easy as being in the right place at the right time or being the only person willing to take on a difficult job. Becoming the leader of a group primarily occurs in one of two ways: being chosen to lead or naturally emerging as leader of the group.

Designated Leaders

Designated leaders are selected by group members or by an outside authority. You may be hired for a job that gives you authority over others. You may be promoted or elected to a leadership position. You may be assigned to chair a special work team or subcommittee. In all these cases, the selection of the leader depends on an election or an appointment.

Sometimes, less-than-deserving people are appointed or elected to powerful positions. Electing a compromise candidate and appointing a politically connected group member as a leader are common practices, and neither is any guarantee of leadership ability. Is it possible, then, for a designated leader to be an effective leader? Of course it is, particularly when a leader's abilities match the needs of the group and its goal.

Designated leaders face unique challenges. When a newly appointed leader enters a well-established group, there can be a long and difficult period of adjustment for everyone. One student described this difficult process as follows:

> For five summers, I worked as a counselor at a county day camp for underprivileged children. Harry was our boss, and all of us liked him. We worked hard for Harry because we knew he'd look the other way if we showed up late or left early on a Friday. As long as the kids were safe and supervised, he didn't bother us. But when Harry was promoted into management at the county government office, we got Frank. The first few weeks were awful. Frank would dock us if we were late. No one could leave early. He demanded that we come up with more activities for the kids. Weekend pool parties were banned. He even made us attend a counselors' meeting every morning, rather than once every couple of weeks. But, in the end, most of us had to

admit that Frank was a better director. The camp did more for the kids, and that was the point.

Both Harry and Frank were leaders with legitimate power. What made them different was the various kinds of power available to them. Because Harry had earned the admiration and respect of the staff, he could rely on referent power. Frank, however, had to use coercive power to establish order and authority.

When a leader is elected or appointed from within a group, the problems can be as difficult as those faced by a leader from outside the group. If the person who once worked next to you becomes your boss, the adjustment can be problematic. Here is the way a business executive described how difficult it was when she was promoted to vice president:

> When I was promoted, I became responsible for making decisions that affected my colleagues, many of whom were close friends. I was given the authority to approve projects, recommend salary increases, and grant promotions. Colleagues who had always been open and honest with me were more cautious and careful about what they said. I had to deny requests from people I cared about, while approving requests from colleagues with whom I often disagreed. Even though I was the same person, I was treated differently, and, as a result, I behaved differently.

Being plucked from a group in order to lead it can present problems because it changes the nature of your relationship with the other members of the group.

TOOLBOX 8.1

The Challenges of Young Leadership

In 2005, Casey Durdiness, a 20-year-old college sophomore, was elected mayor of California, Pennsylvania.[1] How and why this happened is an interesting story. Here, however, we focus on the leadership challenges that Mr. Durdiness faces as the youngest-ever mayor of a college town with a population of 5,200 people.

When asked why he was elected, Durdiness said that what he lacked in experience, he would make up for in confidence: "I think I have the personality that is needed to be an effective leader." Although some of his friends joked that he would order police officers to stop arresting students for alcohol violations, he says that his peers should not expect any leniency. "It puts me in a tough position . . . but I have to uphold the laws of the borough whether or not it conflicts with the party schedules of students."[2]

Mr. Durdiness faces challenges inherent in the leadership–followership dialectic:

> Like all public officials, Mr. Durdiness knows he must find the proper balance between giving people what they want and doing what he thinks is right. If he takes too firm a stand on any issue, he could be perceived as immature. If he is too quick to concede to others, he could be viewed as easy to manipulate.[3]

[1] Elizabeth F. Farrell, "Meet the Mayor," *Chronicle of Higher Education*, December 2, 2005, p. A33.
[2] Farrell, p. A34.
[3] Farrell, p. A34.

Even though the members know you well, you still must earn their trust and re-spect as a leader. Here are three suggestions:

- Involve the group in decision making as much as possible.

- Discuss ground rules for interactions with friends while assuring them of your continued friendship.

- Openly and honestly address leadership concerns with group members and seek their suggestions for resolving potential problems.[6]

Emergent Leaders

Very often, the most effective leadership occurs when a leader emerges from a group rather than being promoted, elected, or appointed. The leaders of many political, religious, and neighborhood organizations emerge. **Emergent leaders** gradually achieve leadership by interacting with group members and contributing to the achievement of the group's goal. Leaders who emerge from within a group have significant advantages. They do not have to spend time learning about the group, its goals, and its norms. In addition, leaders who emerge from within a group have some assurance that the group wants them to be its leader rather than having to accept their leadership because an election or an outside authority says it must. Such leaders usually have referent or expert power—significant factors in mobilizing members toward the group's goal.

Strategies for Becoming a Leader

Although there is no foolproof method, there are strategies that can improve your chances of emerging or being designated as a group's leader. The following strategies require a balanced approach that takes advantage of opportunities without abusing the privilege of leadership:

- Talk early and often (and listen).

- Know more (and share it).

- Offer your opinion (and welcome disagreement).

Talk Early and Often (and Listen).   Of all the strategies that can help you attain the position of group leader, the most reliable is related to when and how much you talk. The person who speaks first and most often is more likely to emerge as the group's leader.[7] The number of contributions is even more impor-tant than the quality of those contributions.

The quality of your contributions becomes more significant after you become a leader. The link between participation and leadership "is the most consistent finding in small group leadership research. Participation demonstrates both your motivation to lead and your commitment to the group."[8] Although talking early and often does not guarantee you a leadership position, failure to talk will keep you from being considered as a leader. But don't overdo it. If you talk too much, members may think that you are not interested in or willing to listen to their contributions. While it is important to talk, it is just as important to demonstrate your willingness and ability to listen to group members.

Know More (and Share It). Leaders often emerge or are appointed because they are seen as experts—people who know more about an important topic. Even if a potential leader is simply able to explain ideas and information more clearly than other group members, he or she may be perceived as knowing more.

Groups need well-informed leaders, but they do not need know-it-alls. Know-it-alls see their own comments as most important; leaders value everyone's contributions. Knowing more than other members may require hours of advance preparation. Members who want to become leaders understand that they must demonstrate their expertise without intimidating other group members.

Offer Your Opinion (and Welcome Disagreement). When groups are having difficulty making decisions or solving problems, they appreciate someone who can offer good ideas and informed opinions. People often emerge as leaders when they help a group out of some difficulty. Offering ideas and opinions, however, is not the same as having those ideas accepted. Criticizing the ideas and opinions of others runs the risk of causing resentment and defensiveness. Bullying your way into a leadership position can backfire. If you are unwilling to compromise or to listen to alternatives, the group may be unwilling to follow you. Effective leaders welcome constructive disagreement and discourage hostile confrontations. "They do not suppress conflict, they rise and face it."[9]

Implications. The strategies that are useful for *becoming* a leader are not necessarily the strategies that are needed for successful leadership. Jim Collins, author of *Good to Great*, conducted a study of successful companies in which he identified a special type of leader—someone who can take a good company and make it great. He concludes that "great" leaders are self-effacing, quiet, reserved, even shy . . . . a paradoxical blend of personal humility and professional will—more like an Abraham Lincoln than a Julius Caesar. They are ambitious for their company or organization, not for themselves.[10] The most successful leaders "channel their ego needs away from themselves and into the larger goal of building a great company."[11]

Although you may have to talk a lot, demonstrate superior knowledge, and assert your personal opinions in order to *become* a leader, you may find that the dialectic opposites—listening rather than talking, relying on the knowledge of others, and seeking a wide range of opinions—are equally necessary to *succeed* as a leader.

LEADERSHIP THEORIES

In their book *Leadership*, Warren Bennis and Bruce Nanus point out that "no clear and unequivocal understanding exists as to what distinguishes leaders from non-leaders, and perhaps more important, what distinguishes effective leaders from ineffective leaders."[12] Despite such inconclusive results, there is a lot to be learned from the many theories of leadership. Here we examine four theoretical approaches to leadership. These theories are not independent of or necessarily in conflict with one another. Rather, they are closely connected and build upon the ideas of their predecessors.[13]

Trait Theory

The trait theory is often called the "Great Man" theory. It is based on a concept that many people now believe is a myth—that leaders are born, not made. **Trait theory** identifies and prescribes individual characteristics and behaviors needed for effective leadership.

Think of the leaders you most admire. What traits do they have? In his book *Leadership*, Andrew DuBrin identifies several personality traits that contribute to successful leadership: self-confidence, humility, trustworthiness, high tolerance of frustration, warmth, humor, enthusiasm, extroversion, assertiveness, emotional stability, adaptability, farsightedness, and openness to new experiences.[14] However, just because you have most of these traits does not mean that you will be a great leader. Personality traits alone are not enough to guarantee effective leadership. For example, if you lack expertise or knowledge about the group task,

FIGURE 8.2 **Leadership Theories**

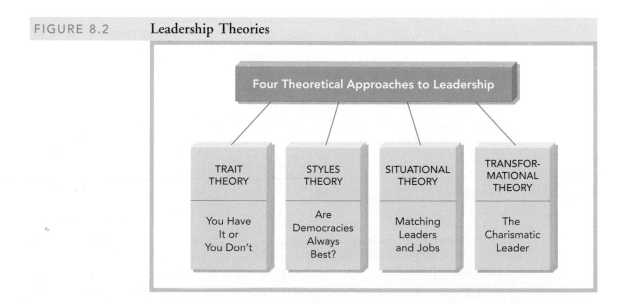

basic intelligence, and the necessary technical or work skills, personality traits will not be enough to enable you to lead a group successfully.

Although most of us would gladly follow a leader with the qualities described by DuBrin, there are many effective leaders who possess only a few of these traits. Harriet Tubman, an illiterate runaway slave, did little talking but led hundreds of people from bondage in the South to freedom in the North. Bill Gates, an introverted computer geek, became the richest man on earth as head of Microsoft, a company that all but dictates how we use personal computers.

According to proponents of the Myers-Briggs Type Indicator®, the personality measure that we discuss in Chapter 3, there is a set of traits that characterize "life's natural leaders." These "extroverted thinkers" (the ENTJ type) use reasoning ability to control and direct those around them.[15] They are usually enthusiastic, decisive, confident, organized, logical, and argumentative. They love to lead and can be excellent communicators. However, although they often assume or win leadership positions, extroverted thinkers may not necessarily be effective leaders because they may intimidate or overpower others. They may be insensitive to the personal feelings and needs of group members. Although many extroverted thinkers become leaders, they may need a less intense, more balanced approach in order to be effective leaders.

Styles Theory

As a way of expanding the trait approach to the study of leadership, researchers reexamined the traits they had identified. Rather than looking for individual leadership traits, they developed the **styles theory** of leadership—a collection of specific behaviors or styles that could be identified and *learned*. Actors work in different styles—tough or gentle, comic or tragic. Even sports teams differ in style; the South American soccer teams are known for their speed and grace, the European teams for their technical skill and aggressiveness. Different styles are attributed to leaders, too. Early attempts to describe different leadership styles yielded three categories: autocratic, democratic, and laissez-faire.[16]

Autocratic Leaders.   An *autocrat* is a person who has a great deal of power and authority, someone who maintains strict control over a group. The **autocratic leader** tries to control the direction and outcome of a discussion, makes many

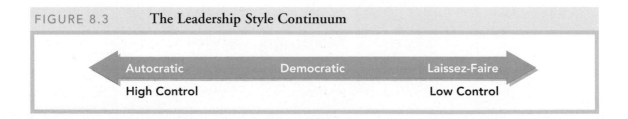

FIGURE 8.3   **The Leadership Style Continuum**

Autocratic   Democratic   Laissez-Faire

High Control   **Low Control**

of the group's decisions, gives orders, expects followers to obey orders, focuses on achieving the group's task, and takes responsibility for the results. Autocrats often use reward and coercive power to control others.

If you have a tendency to interrupt and criticize group members, to regard your way as always being the best way, or to exclude members from the decision-making process, you may be more of an autocratic than a democratic leader. There are costs to using the autocratic approach. By exerting too much control, autocratic leaders may lower group morale and sacrifice long-term productivity. Many autocratic leaders defend their actions by arguing that the group can't get the job done without the strict control of the leader.

Dr. Sandy Faber, a world-renowned astronomer, wrote about her experience as the leader of a group of six astronomers who developed a new theory about the expansion of the universe. An unfortunate back injury made her take a new look at her leadership style:

> My usual style would have been to take center stage . . . and control the process. My back problem was at its worst . . . and instead I found myself lying flat on a portable cot in Donald's office. It is very hard to lead a group of people from a prone position. My energies were at a low ebb anyway. I found it very comfortable to lie back and avoid taking central responsibility.
>
> It was the best thing that could have happened to us. The resultant power vacuum allowed each of us to quietly find our own best way to contribute. This lesson has stood me in good stead since. I now think that in small groups of able and motivated individuals, giving orders or setting up a well-defined hierarchy may generate more friction than it is designed to cure. If a good spirit of teamwork prevails, team leadership can be quite diffuse.[17]

Although many people assume that democratic leadership is always best, there are circumstances in which an autocratic style may be more effective. During a serious crisis, there may not be enough time to discuss issues or consider the wishes of all members. Think of Mayor Rudolph Giuliani's leadership immediately after the September 11 attacks in New York City. Up until that day, he had been criticized as being an autocratic bully. After September 11, he was a hero. In an emergency, a group may want its leader to take command and control of the situation.

Democratic Leaders. A **democratic leader** promotes the interests of group members and practices social equality. This type of leader shares decision making with the group, helps the group plan a course of action, focuses on the group's morale as well as on the task, and gives the entire group credit for success. Democratic leaders work to develop referent and expert power in order to motivate members and enhance group productivity. They know how to promote collaboration, manage conflict, influence others, and listen effectively.

If you have a tendency to ask open and general questions of the group as a whole, encourage participation from all members regardless of their status, and avoid dominating the group with your own opinion, you may be a democratic leader. Here, too, there are costs. Democratic leaders may sacrifice productivity by avoiding direct leadership. Many democratic leaders defend this approach by arguing that, no matter what the circumstances, the only way to make a good decision is to involve all group members. However, if they fail to take charge in a crisis or to curb a discussion when final decisions are needed, democratic leaders may be perceived as weak or indecisive by their followers.

In groups with democratic leadership, members are often more satisfied with the group experience, more loyal to the leader, and more productive in the long run. Whereas members often fear or distrust an autocratic leader, they usually enjoy working with a democratic leader. Not surprisingly, groups led by democratic leaders exhibit lower levels of stress and conflict along with higher levels of innovation and creative problem solving.[18]

Laissez-Faire Leaders. *Laissez-faire* is a French phrase that means "to let people do as they choose." A **laissez-faire leader** lets the group take charge of all decisions and actions. In mature and highly productive groups, a laissez-faire leader may be a perfect match for the group. Such a laid-back leadership style can generate a climate in which open communication is encouraged and rewarded. Unfortunately, there are laissez-faire leaders who do little or nothing to help a group when it needs decisive leadership. Laissez-faire leaders may have legitimate power, but they hesitate or fail to exert any influence on group members and

TOOLBOX 8.2

Leadership by All

According to **functional leadership theory,** any capable group member can assume leadership functions when necessary. The functional approach focuses on what a leader *does* rather than on who a leader *is*. Even more significant, the functional approach does not assume that leadership is the sole responsibility of the leader. Instead, it assumes that anyone in a group can and should help the group achieve its goal. Leadership is a job, not a person.

Although a functional approach can shift leadership responsibilities to anyone who is capable of performing them, this does not mean that leadership is unnecessary. Just the opposite may be true. If one participant is better at motivating members,

while another member excels at keeping the group on track, the group may be better off with each member assuming the leadership functions that he or she is better at than if it relies on a single person to assume all responsibilities. Rather than relying on a leader's natural traits, styles, or motivation, the functional approach concentrates on what a leader says and does in a group situation.[1]

[1] For more on functional leadership theory, see Michael Z. Hackman and Craig E. Johnson, *Leadership: A Communication Perspective*, 4th ed. (Long Grove, IL: Waveland Press, 2004), pp. 79–83; Andrea B. Hollingshead et al., "A Look at Groups From the Functional Perspective," in *Theories of Small Groups: Interdisciplinary Perspectives*, ed. Marshall Scott Poole and Andrea B. Hollingshead (Thousand Oaks, CA: Sage, 2005), pp. 21–62.

groupwork. Whether because of lack of leadership skill or lack of interest, laissez-faire leaders avoid taking charge or taking the time to prepare for complex and lengthy discussions.

Situational Theory

The situational approach assumes that leaders are made, not born, and that nearly everyone can be an effective leader under the right circumstances. Moreover, **situational theory** explains how leaders can become more effective once they have carefully analyzed themselves, their group, and the circumstances in which they must lead. One of the most influential theories of situational leadership was developed by the researcher Fred Fiedler.

Fiedler's **Contingency Model of Leadership Effectiveness** is based on his study of hundreds of groups in numerous work settings.[19] The contingency model of situational leadership suggests that effective leadership occurs only when there is an ideal match between the leader's style and the group's work situation.

Leadership Style.
Fiedler characterizes leaders as being either task-motivated or relationship-motivated. **Task-motivated leaders** want to get the job done; they gain satisfaction from completing a task, even if the cost is bad feelings between the leader and the group members. Task-motivated leaders may be criticized for ignoring group morale. Sometimes task-motivated leaders take on the jobs of other group members because they're not satisfied with the quality or quantity of the work done by others.

Relationship-motivated leaders gain satisfaction from working well with other people, even if the cost is neglecting or failing to complete a task. Relationship-motivated leaders may be criticized for paying too much attention to how members feel and for tolerating disruptive members; they may appear inefficient and weak. Sometimes relationship-motivated leaders take on the jobs of other group members because they can't bring themselves to ask their colleagues to do more.

The Leadership Situation.
Once you have determined your leadership style, the next step is to analyze the way in which your style matches the group's situation. According to Fiedler, there are three important dimensions to every situation: leader–member relationships, task structure, and power.

Fiedler claims that the most important factor in analyzing a situation is understanding the relationship between the leader and the group. Because **leader–member relations** can be positive, neutral, or negative, they can affect the way a leader goes about mobilizing a group toward its goal. Are group members friendly and loyal to the leader and the rest of the group? Are they cooperative and supportive? Do they accept or resist the leader?

The second factor is rating the structure of the task. **Task structure** can range from disorganized and chaotic to highly organized and rule-driven. Are the goals and the task clear? Is there an accepted procedure or set of steps for achieving the goal? Are there well-established standards for measuring success?

The third situational factor is the amount of power and control that the leader has. Is the source of that power an outside authority, or has the leader earned it from the group? What differences would the use of reward, coercive, legitimate, expert, and/or referent power have on the group?

Matching the Leader and the Situation. Fiedler's research suggests that there are ideal matches between leadership style and the group situation. As depicted in Figure 8.4, task-motivated leaders perform best in extremes—such as when the situation is highly controlled or when it is almost out of control. These leaders shine when there are good leader–member relationships, a clear task, and a lot of power. They also do well in stressful leadership jobs where there may be poor leader–member relationships, an unclear and unstructured task, and little control or power. Task-motivated leaders do well in extreme situations because their primary motivation is to take charge and get the job done.

Relationship-motivated leaders are most effective when there is a mix of conditions. They may have a structured task but an uncooperative group of followers. Rather than taking charge and getting the job done at all costs, the relationship-motivated leader uses diplomacy and works with group members to improve leader–member relationships. If there are good leader–member relationships but an unstructured task, the relationship-motivated leader may rely on the resources of the group to develop a plan of action. Whereas a task-motivated leader might find these situations frustrating, a relationship-motivated leader will be quite comfortable.

Implications of Situational Theory. According to the situational approach, once you know your leadership style and have analyzed the situation in which you must lead, you can begin to predict how successful you will be as a leader. If you are a task-motivated leader, you should feel confident if you are asked to take on either a highly structured or a highly unstructured task. If carrying out the group's task is your major concern and motivation, you should feel confident if you are asked to lead a group that is unable and unwilling to pursue its goal.

Relationship-motivated leaders have different factors to consider. If there is a moderate degree of structure, a relationship-motivated leader may be more successful. If people issues are your major concern, you should feel confident if you are asked to lead a group that is able but somewhat unwilling to complete its task.

You cannot always choose when and where you will lead. You may find yourself assigned or elected to a leadership situation that does not match your leadership style. In such a case, rather than trying to change your leadership style, you may find it easier to change the situation in which you are leading. For example, if leader–member relationships are poor, you may decide that your first task is to gain the group's trust and support. You can schedule time to listen to members' problems or take nonmeeting time to get to know key individuals in the group.

FIGURE 8.4   **Contingency Model of Leader Effectiveness**

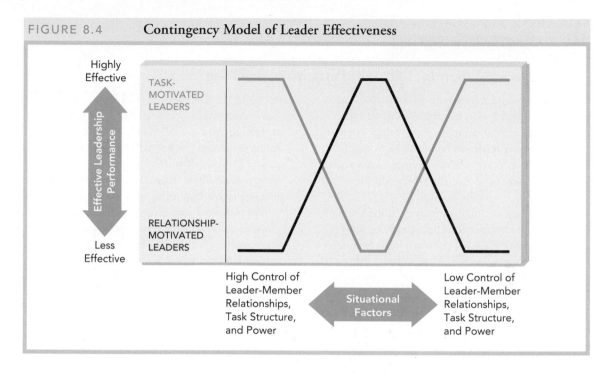

If your task is highly unstructured, you can exert your leadership by providing structure or by dividing the task into smaller, easier-to-achieve subunits. On the other hand, you may find yourself in a leadership situation where the task is so highly structured that there is almost no need for leadership. The group knows exactly what to do. Rather than allowing the group to become bored, ask for or introduce new and less structured tasks to challenge the group.

Finally, you may be able to modify the amount of power you have. If you are reluctant to use coercive power, or if you don't have enough legitimate power, you can earn referent power by demonstrating your leadership ability. If you have a great deal of power and run the risk of intimidating group members, you may want to delegate some of your duties and power.

Transformational Theory

In the late 1970s, researchers took a more sophisticated look at a special set of leadership traits. What qualities, they asked, are common to those leaders who change the world in which they live—leaders such as Abraham Lincoln, Martin Luther King Jr., Mohandas Gandhi, and the "giants" of corporate industry? The result of this investigation was the development of **transformational leadership theory,** which looks at what leaders accomplish rather than at their personal characteristics or their relationship with group members. Transformational leaders do exactly what the word *transform* implies—they bring about major, positive changes by moving group members beyond their self-interests for the good of

TOOLBOX 8.3

Decide When to Tell, Sell, Participate, or Delegate

Paul Hersey and Kenneth H. Blanchard's Situational Leadership Model explains how to match leadership style to the readiness of group members. **Member readiness** is the extent to which group members are willing (confident, committed, and motivated) and able (knowledgeable, expert, and skilled).

As a group's readiness increases, leaders should rely more on relationship behaviors and less on task behavior. Here is a summary of guidelines for leaders based on the Hersey-Blanchard model of situational leadership:[1]

Situation 1. Low Readiness—the Telling Stage. When followers are unable, unwilling, or insecure, the leader should emphasize task-oriented behavior while being very directive and even autocratic. The leader *tells* the group what to do and closely supervises the work.

Situation 2. Moderate Readiness—the Selling Stage. When group members are unable but willing or confident, the leader should focus on being more relationship-oriented. The leader *sells* by explaining the rationale for decisions and providing opportunities for member input.

Situation 3. Moderate to High Readiness—the Participating Stage. When group members are able but unwilling or insecure, the leader should provide a high degree of relationship-oriented behavior. The leader *participates* by sharing ideas, facilitating decision making, and motivating members.

Situation 4. High Readiness—the Delegating Stage. When group members are able as well as being willing and confident, they are self-sufficient and competent. The leader *delegates* by granting group members independence and trust.

[1] Paul Hersey and Ken Blanchard, *Management of Organizational Behavior: Utilizing Human Resources*, 6th ed. (Upper Saddle River, NJ: Prentice Hall, 1992).

---

the group and its goal.[20] Transformational leaders inspire members "to become highly committed to the leader's mission, to make significant personal sacrifices in the interests of the mission, and to perform above and beyond the call of duty."[21]

Attributes of Transformational Leaders. Transformational leaders are doers—they convert goals into action. With a clear and compelling goal, trust and openness among group members, confidence, optimism, and purposeful action, a leader can transform a group into a remarkable and productive team of colleagues.[22] A review of transformational leadership research reveals six attributes that transformational leaders often possess.[23]

- *Charismatic.* They present a combination of agreeableness and extroversion while earning the respect, confidence, and loyalty of group members.

- *Visionary.* They communicate a set of values that guide and motivate group members and help members go beyond their individual self-interests to look at the "big picture" and how their work contributes to a worthy and inspiring goal.

- *Supportive.* They encourage the personal development of members, provide clear directions and focus, and help members fulfill their personal and professional needs.

- *Empowering.* They involve members in decision making and help members focus on a quest for self-fulfillment, rather than on minor satisfactions.

- *Innovative.* They encourage innovation and creativity, and help members understand the need for change, both emotionally and intellectually.

- *Modeling.* They provide a model of member effectiveness and build a climate of mutual trust between the leader and group members.

The Nature of Charisma. Many researchers identify charisma as the most important quality of a transformational leader. *Charisma* is a Greek word meaning "divinely inspired gift." *The American Heritage Dictionary of the English Language* defines charisma as "a rare personal quality attributed to leaders who arouse fervent popular devotion and enthusiasm" as well as "personal magnetism or charm."[24] Andrew DuBrin, author of *Leadership*, calls attention to a unifying theme in the many definitions of charisma: "Charisma is a positive and compelling quality of a person that makes many others want to be led by him or her."[25]

Charismatic leaders develop referent and expert power (rather than relying on reward, coercive, and legitimate power) and strive to inspire and engage members in the work needed to achieve the group's goal.

- *Referent power and charisma.* Based on a leader's desirable traits and characteristics: shared beliefs with the leader, affection for the leader, seeing the leader as a role model.

- *Expert power and charisma.* Based on a leader's special knowledge, skills, and abilities: group members trust the leader's expertise and advice, and unquestionably accept and obey the leader.

- *Job involvement and charisma.* Based on a leader's ability to enhance members' involvement in their work: emotional involvement; heightened, inspiring goals; and perceived ability to contribute.[26]

THE 4M MODEL OF LEADERSHIP EFFECTIVENESS

Given the millions of words about leadership that have been published by scholars, management gurus, and popular press writers, you may have difficulty sorting out the "do's and don'ts" of effective leadership. To help you understand and balance the contributions made by these many differing approaches, we offer an integrated model of leadership effectiveness that emphasizes specific communication strategies and skills.

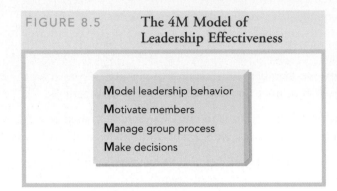

FIGURE 8.5   **The 4M Model of Leadership Effectiveness**

Model leadership behavior
Motivate members
Manage group process
Make decisions

The **4M Model of Leadership Effectiveness** divides leadership tasks into four interdependent leadership functions: (1) **m**odel leadership behavior, (2) **m**otivate members, (3) **m**anage the group process, and (4) **m**ake decisions. These strategies incorporate the features of several theories and provide a set of behaviors characteristic of effective leadership.[27]

Model Leadership Behavior

All of us have expectations about what an ideal leader should say and do. Model leaders project an image of confidence, competence, trustworthiness, and optimism while relying on referent or role model power to influence others. Leadership expert Martin Chemers refers to this function as *image management* and notes that when "image management is particularly successful, the leader may be described as charismatic."[28] Yet no matter how much you may *want* to be seen as a model leader, only your followers can grant you that honor. We recommend the following strategies for modeling effective leadership:

1. Publicly champion your group and its goals.

2. Speak and listen effectively and confidently.

3. Behave consistently and assertively.

4. Demonstrate competence and trustworthiness.

5. Study and improve your own leadership skills.

Motivate Members

Chapter 11, "Goal Setting and Motivation in Groups," emphasizes the importance of enhancing individual and group motivation. Motivating others is also a critical skill for leaders. Effective leaders guide, develop, support, defend, and inspire group members. They develop relationships that "match the personal needs and expectations of followers."[29] Five leadership skills are central to motivating members:

1. Secure members' commitment to the group's shared goal.

2. Appropriately reward the group and its members.

3. Help solve interpersonal problems and conflicts.

4. Adapt tasks and assignments to members' abilities and expectations.

5. Provide constructive and timely feedback to members.

Manage Group Process

From the perspective of group survival, managing group process may be the most important function of leadership.[30] If a group is disorganized, lacks sufficient information to solve problems, or is unable to make important decisions when they are called for, the group cannot be effective. Five leadership skills can enhance this important function:

1. Be well organized and fully prepared for group meetings and work sessions.

2. Understand and adapt to members' strengths and weaknesses.

3. Help solve task-related and procedural problems.

4. Monitor and intervene to improve group performance.

5. Secure resources and remove roadblocks to group effectiveness.

Make Decisions

A leader's willingness and ability to make appropriate, timely, and responsible decisions characterizes effective leadership. Too often we hear disgruntled group members talk about their leader's inability to make critical decisions. A high school teacher described this fatal leadership flaw as follows:

> Everyone agrees that our principal is a "nice guy" who wants everyone to like him. He doesn't want to "rock the boat" or "make waves." As a result, he doesn't make decisions or take decisive action when it's most needed. He listens patiently to a request or to both sides of a dispute, but that's all he does. Our school comes to a standstill because he won't "bite the bullet." The teachers have lost respect for him, students and their parents know that they'll get what they want if they yell loudly enough or long enough, and the superintendent has to intervene to fix the mess that results.

When you assume or are appointed to a leadership role, you must accept the fact that some of your decisions may be unpopular, and some may even turn out to be wrong. But you still have to make them. In *The New Why Teams Don't Work*, Harvey Robbins and Michael Finley contend that it's often better for a group leader to make a bad decision than to make no decision at all, "For if you are seen as chronically indecisive, people won't let you lead them."[31] The following five leadership strategies can help you determine when and how to intervene and make a decision.

1. Make sure that everyone has and shares the information needed to make a quality decision.

2. If appropriate, discuss your pending decision and solicit feedback from members.

3. Listen to members' opinions, arguments, and suggestions.

4. Explain the rationale for the decision you intend to make.

5. Make your decision and communicate it to everyone.

GROUPTECH

Leadership in Virtual Groups

Leadership is both pervasive and necessary in successful virtual groups. But, according to Jessica Lipnack and Jeffrey Stamps, authors of *Virtual Groups,* "although virtual teams may have single leaders, multiple leaders are the norm rather than the exception."[1] Why? Consider some of the added responsibilities required of someone who organizes and leads a virtual group—be it a simple teleconference, an email discussion, or an intercontinental videoconference.

Long before the actual meeting, someone must set up the unique logistics for a virtual get-together. When participants live in different cities or time zones, arranging a meeting is much more difficult than calling a regular staff meeting in a conference room down the hall. In order to make sure that members are fully prepared for a virtual meeting, a detailed agenda must be prepared and sent to all members well in advance. In addition, someone must make sure that the technology required for the conference is up and running when it's needed. Finally, someone must lead a discussion in which participants may neither see nor hear one another in real time. Effective virtual groups manage these added tasks by sharing leadership roles rather than by assuming that one superhuman leader can handle all of these complex challenges.

The 4M Model of Leadership Effectiveness also applies to the unique responsibilities of a virtual group leader. When virtual groups first "meet," they often depend on a leader to model appropriate behavior. The leader must demonstrate effective participant behavior for other virtual group members. Motivating a virtual group can be more difficult than motivating participants in a face-to-face discussion. Unmotivated members may ignore messages or respond infrequently. When this happens, a group is vulnerable to miscommunication, poor quality of work, missed deadlines, lack of cohesion, inefficiencies, and disaffected team members. Virtual groups also need leadership that reflects a compelling vision, adaptability to the challenges of virtual communication, trust in members, and the positive energy to keep the group engaged and productive.

A virtual group leader also has additional managerial duties. Resources to train group members in the use of specialized software may be needed. A leader may have to set guidelines for how and when the virtual group will do its work. Finally, making decisions in a virtual group can be difficult when group members are not communicating in real time. In virtual groups, the leader may be responsible for determining when the virtual group will "meet," the rules of interaction, and the criteria for group decision making.

By sharing leadership functions, members of virtual groups have the opportunity to become a highly cohesive and democratic team of coworkers, all of whom embrace the challenge of leading and working in groups to achieve a worthy goal.

[1] Jessica Lipnack and Jeffrey Stamps, *Virtual Teams,* 2nd ed. (New York: Wiley, 2000), p. 177.

DIVERSITY AND LEADERSHIP

For most of the twentieth century, leadership studies concentrated on the traits, styles, and functions of white male leaders. However, the global economy and the increasing diversity of the U.S. population have made a white-males-only leadership perspective a thing of the past. Today, successful organizations and groups must understand, respect, and adapt to diversity if they hope to tap the potential of their members. At the same time, female and culturally diverse leaders must understand that, even under the best of circumstances, negative stereotypes can still hamper their ability to lead.

Gender and Leadership

In the early studies of leadership, there was an unwritten but additional prerequisite for becoming a leader: Be a man. Even today, despite the achievements of exceptional women leaders, some people still question the ability of women to serve in leadership positions. These doubts are based on long-held prejudices rather than on valid evidence.

In a summary of the research on leadership and gender, Susan Shimanoff and Mercilee Jenkins conclude that "women are still less likely to be preselected as leaders, and the same leadership behavior is often evaluated more positively when attributed to a male than a female."[32] In other words, even when women talk early and often, are well prepared and always present at meetings, and offer valuable ideas, a man who has done the same things is more likely to emerge as leader. After examining the research on gender and leadership, Rodney Napier and Matti Gershenfeld conclude that "even though male and female leaders may act the same, there is a tendency for women to be perceived more negatively or to have to act differently to gain leadership."[33]

Deborah Tannen describes the difficulties that women have in leadership positions.[34] If their behavior is similar to that of male leaders, they are perceived as unfeminine. If they act "like a lady," they are viewed as weak or ineffective. One professional woman described this dilemma as follows:

> I was thrilled when my boss evaluated me as "articulate, hard-working, mature in her judgment, and a skillful diplomat." What disturbed me were some of the evaluations from those I supervise or work with as colleagues. Although they had a lot of good things to say, a few of them described me as "pushy," "brusque," "impatient," "has a disregard for social niceties," and "hard-driving." What am I supposed to do? My boss thinks I'm energetic and creative, while other people see the same behavior as pushy and aggressive.

The preference for male leaders may come down to a fear of or an unwillingness to adjust to different kinds of leaders. Because many people have worked in groups that were led by men, they may feel uncomfortable when the leadership shifts to a woman. Even though extensive research indicates that there are only slight differences between men and women leaders, stereotypical, negative expectations still persist. These expectations make it more difficult for women to gain, hold, and succeed in leadership positions.[35] Our best advice is that instead of asking whether a female leader is different from a male leader, it is more important to ask whether she is an effective leader.

Cultural Diversity and Leadership

The ways in which a leader models leadership behavior, motivates group members, manages group process, and makes decisions may not match the cultural dimensions of all group members. For example, if, as a leader, you model leadership behavior by strongly and publicly advocating group goals, you may upset members from high-context cultures who would be less direct about such matters. Your way of modeling leadership behavior may not reflect *their* view of a model leader. For example, people from Western cultures (the United States, Canada, and Europe) assume that group members are motivated by personal achievement and status. However, when group members' cultural backgrounds are more collectivist, the same motivational strategies may not work. A collectivist member may act out of loyalty to the leader and the group rather than for personal achievement or material gain.[36]

Managing group process in a group composed of culturally diverse members can be difficult if, for example, you want to give the group the freedom to decide how to structure a task. Members from uncertainty-avoidance cultures will want more structure and instruction from a leader. If your leadership style is more feminine (nurturing, collaborative, caring), you may find yourself fighting a losing leadership battle with members who are more competitive, independent, and aggressive. Your feminine leadership style may be interpreted as weakness or indecision.

Finally, the decision-making style of a leader may not match that of a culturally diverse group. If members come from a low-power-distance culture, they will not welcome an authoritarian leader who takes control of all decision making.

Many individuals emerged as leaders to help in the aftermath of the Tsunami. What behaviors increase the likelihood that a member will emerge as a group's leader? (© Julie Cumes/ The Image Works)

TOOLBOX 8.4

Two Classic and Conflicting Views of Leadership

Throughout history, cultures have developed contrasting viewpoints about the nature of effective leadership. *The Prince*, written by Italian political theorist Niccolò Machiavelli in 1531, is one of the earliest European writings on leadership. Machiavelli believes that leaders must be prepared to use craft, deceit, threat, treachery, and violence, with little or no concerns about morality. Machiavelli also warns rulers about the perils of integrity: "A certain Prince of our own days, whose name it is as well not to mention, is always preaching peace and good faith, although the mortal enemies of both; and both, had he practiced them as he preaches them, would, oftener than once, have lost him his kingdom and authority."[1] Machiavelli and his ideal prince view the politics and realities of leadership as being divorced from ethical values.

Some contemporary leaders share this 500-year-old perspective. One survey of college presidents reports that many of them find Machiavelli's advice highly useful and relevant.[2] Today, the term **Machiavellian** is used to describe someone whose thinking and behavior are characterized by the use of dishonorable and unethical means to achieve a personal goal.[3]

Whereas Machiavelli's *The Prince* discusses the need for leaders to deceive their followers in order to retain power, Lao-tzu, a sixth century B.C. Chinese philosopher, advocates a selflessness and nondirective leadership in his famous *Tao Te Ching*, a classic of Eastern philosophy. Here is a well-known excerpt:

With the best of leaders,
When the work is done,
The project complete,
The people all say
"We did it ourselves."[4]

In the *Tao of Leadership*, John Heider adapts the *Tao Te Ching* to modern leadership practices: "The wise leader . . . keeps egocentricity in check and by doing so becomes even more effective. Enlightened leadership is service, not selfishness. The leader grows more and lasts longer by placing the well-being of all above the well-being of self alone. Paradox: By being selfless, the leader enhances self."[5]

Interestingly, many contemporary leadership books, articles, and experts advocate a similar leader-as-servant approach. As Robert K. Greenleaf writes, "Becoming a servant-leader begins with the natural feeling that one wants to serve, to serve first. . . . The best test [of a servant-leader] is this: Do those served grow as persons?"[6]

[1] Niccolò Machiavelli, *The Prince,* 1513, trans. Harvey C. Mansfield, rev. (Chicago, The University of Chicago Press, 1998), p. 71.
[2] Bernard M. Bass, "Concepts of Leadership: The Beginnings," in *The Leader's Companion: Insights on Leadership Through the Ages,* ed. J. Thomas Wren (New York: The Free Press, 1995), pp. 51–52.
[3] Based on *The American Heritage Dictionary of the English Language,* 4th ed. (Boston: Houghton Mifflin, 2000), p. 1047.
[4] Diane Dreher, trans., *The Tao of Personal Leadership* (New York: HarperBusiness, 1997), p. 1.
[5] John Heider, *The Tao of Leadership* (Atlanta: Humanics Limited, 1985), p. 13.
[6] Robert K. Greenleaf, "Essentials of Servant-Leadership," in *Focus on Leadership: Servant-Leadership for the Twenty-First Century,* ed. Larry C. Spears and Michele Lawrence (New York: Wiley, 2002), pp. 23–24.

Conversely, a leader who prefers a more democratic approach to decision making may frustrate members who come from high-power-distance cultures, in which leaders make all the decisions with little input from group members.

Stereotypes about a leader from a different culture can diminish a group's effectiveness. Unfortunately, we do not have a lot of research on leaders from American ethnic minorities (such as African Americans, Latino Americans, Asian Americans,

Native Americans, Jewish Americans, or Muslim Americans). The research that is available indicates that leaders from minority groups, like women leaders, do not differ significantly from dominant-culture leaders in behavior, performance, or satisfying member expectations. Nonetheless, negative stereotypes about leaders from minority groups are prevalent, and such individuals have more difficulty moving up the leadership ladder.[37]

Culturally diverse groups and leaders from different cultures are here to stay. Effective leaders help group members work together, achieve their potential, and contribute to the group's shared goal. Balancing the needs of culturally diverse group members may be difficult, but the ability to do so is essential to providing effective leadership in the twenty-first century.

BALANCED LEADERSHIP

The leader performs the most difficult balancing act in a group. Much like a tightrope walker who juggles during a death-defying walk across open space, a group leader must juggle many dialectic interests and issues while propelling a group toward its goal. The leader must exert control without stifling creativity. The leader must balance the requirements of the task with the social needs of group members. The leader must resolve conflict without losing the motivation and energy that result from conflict and must encourage participation from quiet members without stifling the enthusiasm and contributions of active members.

Ronald Heifetz, director of leadership at Harvard's Kennedy School of Government, describes the dialectic tensions inherent in leadership as an adaptive challenge. The leader, he declares, must create a balance between the tensions required to motivate change and the need to avoid overwhelming followers.[38] Heifetz claims that effective leaders walk on a razor's edge on which they cut their feet in order to maintain balance.[39] We prefer a gentler metaphor: Effective adaptive leaders walk a tightrope between fostering interdependence and encouraging self-reliance, between unleashing conflict and building cohesion, between imposing structure and promoting spontaneity and creativity.

Effective leaders "are particularly adept at using their skills and insight to establish a balance between cooperative common action and the fulfillment of individual goals."[40] Achieving balanced leadership does *not* depend on developing a particular trait or style, but rather depends on your ability to analyze a situation and select leadership strategies that help mobilize a group to achieve its goal.

The Least-Preferred-Coworker Scale

Directions. All of us have worked better with some people than with others. Think of the one person in your life with whom you have worked least well, a person who might have caused you difficulty in doing a job or completing a task. This person may be someone with whom you have worked recently or someone you have known in the past. This coworker must be the single individual with whom you have had the most difficulty getting a job done, the person with whom you would least want to work.

On the scale below, describe this person by circling the number that best represents your perception of this person. There are no right or wrong answers. Do not omit any items, and circle a number for each item only once.

Pleasant	8	7	6	5	4	3	2	1	Unpleasant
Friendly	8	7	6	5	4	3	2	1	Unfriendly
Rejecting	1	2	3	4	5	6	7	8	Accepting
Tense	1	2	3	4	5	6	7	8	Relaxed
Distant	1	2	3	4	5	6	7	8	Close
Cold	1	2	3	4	5	6	7	8	Warm
Supportive	8	7	6	5	4	3	2	1	Hostile
Boring	1	2	3	4	5	6	7	8	Interesting
Quarrelsome	1	2	3	4	5	6	7	8	Harmonious
Gloomy	1	2	3	4	5	6	7	8	Cheerful
Open	8	7	6	5	4	3	2	1	Guarded
Backbiting	1	2	3	4	5	6	7	8	Loyal
Untrustworthy	1	2	3	4	5	6	7	8	Trustworthy
Considerate	8	7	6	5	4	3	2	1	Inconsiderate
Nasty	1	2	3	4	5	6	7	8	Nice
Agreeable	8	7	6	5	4	3	2	1	Disagreeable
Insincere	1	2	3	4	5	6	7	8	Sincere
Kind	8	7	6	5	4	3	2	1	Unkind

Scoring: Obtain your Least-Preferred-Coworker (LPC) score by adding up the numbers you circled on the scale. Your score should be between 18 and 144.

Relationship-Motivated Leader.   If your score is 73 or above, you derive satisfaction from good relationships with group members. You are most successful when a situation has just enough uncertainty to challenge you: moderate leader–member relationships, moderate task structure, and moderate power.

Task-Motivated Leader.   If your score is 64 or below, you derive satisfaction from getting things done. You are most successful when a situation has clear guidelines or no guidelines at all: excellent or poor leader–member relationships, highly structured or unstructured tasks, and high or low power.

Relationship- and Task-Motivated Leader.   If your score is between 65 and 72, you may be flexible enough to function in both leadership styles.

Source: Fred E. Fiedler and Martin M. Chemers, *Improving Leadership Effectiveness: The Leader Match Concept*, 2nd ed. (New York: Wiley, 1984), pp. 17–42.

GROUPASSESSMENT

Are You Ready to Lead?

Directions. Indicate the extent to which you agree with each of the following statements, using the following scale: (1) strongly disagree; (2) disagree; (3) neutral or undecided; (4) agree; (5) strongly agree.

Leadership Readiness Statements

1. I enjoy having people count on me for ideas and suggestions.   1   2   3   4   5

2. It would be accurate to say that I have inspired other people.   1   2   3   4   5

3. It's a good practice to ask people provocative questions about their work.   1   2   3   4   5

4. It's easy for me to compliment others.   1   2   3   4   5

5. I like to cheer people up even when my own spirits are down.   1   2   3   4   5

6. What my group accomplishes is more important than my personal glory.   1   2   3   4   5

7. Many people imitate my ideas.   1   2   3   4   5

8. Building team spirit is important to me.   1   2   3   4   5

9. I would enjoy coaching other members of the group.   1   2   3   4   5

10. It is important to me to recognize others
    for their accomplishments.   1   2   3   4   5

11. I would enjoy entertaining visitors to
    my group even if it interfered with my
    completing a report.   1   2   3   4   5

12. It would be fun to represent my group
    at an outside gathering.   1   2   3   4   5

13. The problems of my teammates are
    my problems.   1   2   3   4   5

14. Resolving conflict is an activity that I enjoy. 1   2   3   4   5

15. I would cooperate with another group with
    which my group works even if I disagreed
    with the position taken by its members.   1   2   3   4   5

16. I am an idea generator on the job.   1   2   3   4   5

17. It's fun for me to bargain whenever I have
    the opportunity.   1   2   3   4   5

18. Group members listen to me when I speak.   1   2   3   4   5

19. People have asked me to assume the
    leadership of an activity several times in
    my life.   1   2   3   4   5

20. I've always been a convincing person.   1   2   3   4   5

Scoring and Interpretation: Calculate your total score by adding the numbers circled. A tentative interpretation of the scoring is as follows:

90–100   high readiness for the leadership role
60–89   moderate readiness for the leadership role
40–59   some uneasiness with the leadership role
39 or less low readiness for the leadership role

If you are already a successful leader and you scored low on this questionnaire, ignore your score. If you scored surprisingly low and you are not yet a leader or are currently performing poorly as a leader, study the statements carefully. Consider changing your attitude or your behavior so that you can legitimately answer more of the statements with a 4 or a 5.

Source: Andrew J. DuBrin, *Leadership: Research Findings, Practice, and Skills* (New York: Houghton Mifflin, 2004), pp. 13–14. *Note:* A few words have been changed to keep the language consistent with the terminology in this textbook.

NOTES

1. Robert S. Cathcart and Larry A. Samovar, "Group Leadership: Theories and Principles," in *Small Group Communication: A Reader, 6th ed., ed.* Robert S. Cathcart and Larry A. Samovar (Dubuque, IA: Wm. C. Brown, 1992), p. 364.

2. Warren Bennis and Bruce Nanus, *Leaders: The Strategies for Taking Charge* (New York: HarperPerennial, 1985), p. 15.

3. Daniel Goleman, Richard Boyatzis, and Annie McKee, *Primal Leadership: Learning to Lead with Emotional Intelligence* (Boston: Harvard Business School Press, 2002), p. 23.

4. Michael Z. Hackman and Craig E. Johnson, *Leadership: A Communication Perspective,* 4th ed. (Prospect Heights, IL: Waveland, 2004), p. 127.

5. Hackman and Johnson, p. 132.

6. Sam R. Lloyd, *Leading Teams: The Skills for Success* (West Des Moines, IA: American Media Publishing, 1996), p. 13.

7. Edwin P. Hollander, *Leadership Dynamics: A Practical Guide to Effective Relationships* (New York: Macmillan, 1978), p. 53.

8. Hackman and Johnson, p. 191.

9. Jorge Correia Jesuino, "Leadership: Micro-macro Links," in *Understanding Group Behavior, Vol. 2, ed.* Erich H. White and James H. Davis (Mahwah, NJ: Lawrence Erlbaum Associates, 1996), pp. 93, 119.

10. Jim Collins, *Good to Great: Why Some Companies Make the Leap . . . and Others Don't* (New York: HarperBusiness, 2001), pp. 12–13, 39.

11. Collins, p. 21.

12. Bennis and Nanus, p. 4.

13. Lucy E. Garrick, "Leadership: Theory Evolution and the Development of Inter-Personal Leadership," Pacific Northwest Organization Development Network, 2004 (Copyright 2004, Lucy Garrick, North Shore Group, LLC, Seattle, WA).

14. Andrew J. DuBrin, *Leadership: Research Findings, Practice, and Skills*, 4th ed. (New York: Houghton Mifflin, 2004), pp. 51–53.

15. Otto Kroeger with Janet M. Thuesen, *Type Talk at Work: How the 16 Personality Types Determine Your Success on the Job* (New York: Dell, 1992), p. 385.

16. Kurt Lewin, Ron Lippit, and R. K. White, "Patterns of Aggressive Behaviour in Experimentally Created Social Climates," *Journal of Social Psychology, 10 (1939),* pp. 271–299.

17. Alan Dressler, *Voyage to the Great Attractor: Exploring Intergalactic Space* (New York: Alfred A. Knopf, 1994), pp. 193–194.

18. Jesuino, p. 99.

19. Fred E. Fiedler and Martin M. Chemers, *Improving Leadership Effectiveness: The Leader Match Concept,* 2nd ed. (New York: Wiley, 1984). In addition to Fiedler's Contingency Model of Leadership Effectiveness, several other situational theories offer valuable insights into the ways in which leaders must find a match between their styles and the needs of their group. See Chapter 4 in Martin M. Chemers, *An Integrative Theory of Leadership* (Mahwah, NJ: Erlbaum, 1994), for a discussion and analysis of the following theories: House's Path-Goal Directive, Vroom and Yetton's Normative Decision Theory, and Hersey and Blanchard's Situational Leadership.

20. Based on DuBrin, p. 80.

21. Martin M. Chemers and R. Ayman (eds.), *Leadership Theory and Research: Perspectives and Directions* (San Diego: Academic Press, 1993), p. 82.

22. Warren Bennis and Joan Goldsmith, *Learning to Lead: A Workbook on Becoming a Leader*, Updated Edition (Cambridge, MA: Perseus, 1997), p. xvi.

23. Sally A. Carless, Alexander J. Wearing, and Leon Mann, "A Short Measure of Transformational Leadership," *Journal of Business Psychology* (Spring 2000), pp. 389–405. Also see DuBrin, pp. 80–82.

24. *The American Heritage Dictionary of the English Language*, 4th ed. (Boston: Houghton Mifflin, 2000), p. 313.

25. DuBrin, p. 64.

26. Jane A. Halpert, "The Dimensionality of Charisma," *Journal of Business Psychology* (Summer 1990), p. 401.

27. The 4M Model of Effective Leadership is based, in part, on Martin M. Chemers's integrative theory of leadership that identifies three functional aspects of leadership: image management, relationship development, and resource utilization. We have added a fourth function—decision making—and have integrated a stronger communication perspective into Chemers's view of leadership as a multifaceted process. See Martin M. Chemers, *An Integrative Theory of Leadership* (Mahwah, NJ: Lawrence Erlbaum Associates, 1997), pp. 151–173.

28. Chemers, p. 154.

29. Chemers, p. 155.

30. Chemers, p. 160.

31. Harvey A. Robbins and Michael Finley, *The New Why Teams Don't Work: What Goes Wrong and How to Make it Right* (San Francisco: Berrett-Koehler, 2000), p. 107.

32. Susan B. Shimanoff and Mercilee M. Jenkins, "Leadership and Gender: Challenging Assumptions and Recognizing Resources," in *Small Group Communication: Theory and Practice,* 7th ed., ed. Robert S. Cathcart, Larry A. Samovar, and Linda D. Henman (Madison, WI: Brown & Benchmark, 1996), p. 327.

33. Rodney Napier and Matti Gershenfeld, *Groups: Theory and Experience (*Boston: Houghton Mifflin, 2004), p. 347.

34. Deborah Tannen, *Talking from 9 to 5: Women and Men in the Workplace: Language, Sex and Power* (New York: Avon, 1994).

35. Chemers, p. 150.

36. Chemers, p. 126.

37. Martin M. Chemers and Susan E. Murphy, *Leadership for Diversity in Groups and Organizations: Perspectives on a Changing Workplace* (Newbury Park, CA: Sage, 1995).

38. Ron Heifetz, *Leadership Without Easy Answer* (Cambridge, MA: The Belknap Press of Harvard University Press, 1994), pp. 126–128, 228.

39. Heifitz, pp. 126–127.

40. Kevin L. Freiberg, "Transformation Leadership," in *Small Group Communication: A Reader,* 6th ed., ed. Robert S. Cathcart and Larry A. Samovar (Dubuque, IA: Wm. C. Brown, 1992), pp. 526–527.

CHAPTER 9

Structured and Creative Problem Solving in Groups

CHAPTER OUTLINE

GROUP DECISION MAKING

Many group decisions are predictable and fairly easy to make—when to meet again, what to include in a monthly report, whom to assign to a routine task. Other group decisions are much more complex and difficult—whom to hire or fire, where to hold a convention, how to solve a serious problem. As difficult as making a personal decision can be, the challenges of decision making are multiplied in groups. On the other hand, while the road may be filled with obstacles, a goal reached through effective group decision making can be more satisfying and worthwhile than a decision made by an individual working alone.

Decision Making and Problem Solving

Although the terms *decision making* and *problem solving* are often used interchangeably, it is important to clarify the meaning of each term (see Figure 9.1). **Decision making** refers to the "passing of judgment on an issue under consideration" and "the act of reaching a conclusion or making up one's mind."[1] In a group setting, decision making results in a position, opinion, judgment, or action. Most groups make decisions, but not all groups are asked to solve problems. For example, hiring committees, juries, and families make decisions. Which applicant is best? Is the accused guilty? Whom should we invite to the wedding? Management expert Peter Drucker explains, "A decision is a judgment. It is a choice between alternatives."[2]

Problem solving is a more complex *process* in which groups analyze a problem and develop a plan of action for solving the problem or reducing the problem's harmful effects. For example, if student enrollment has declined significantly, a college faces a serious problem that must be analyzed and dealt with if the institution hopes to survive. Problem solving requires a group to make many decisions. Fortunately, there are decision-making and problem-solving procedures that can help a group "make up its mind."

Most groups engage in some form of decision making and problem solving. How they go about these tasks can determine whether the group achieves its goals or falls short. Rodney Napier and Matti Gershenfeld maintain that "unless well designed, a group effort at problem solving can be a colossal waste of time, money, and effort."[3] Instead of building team spirit and group morale, ineffective decision making can overwhelm and destroy a group. Even in the best of circumstances, group decisions take longer to make and run the risk of causing conflict and hard feelings among group members.

Despite these disadvantages, there are many reasons to trust group decision making and problem solving. Sheer numbers enable a group to generate more ideas than a single person working alone could. Even more important is the fact that, given a complex problem, a group is better equipped to find rational and workable solutions. As a rule, decision making in groups can generate more

FIGURE 9.1   **Decision Making and Problem Solving**

Decision Making	Problem Solving
A JUDGMENT: THE GROUP CHOOSES AN ALTERNATIVE	A PROCESS: THE GROUP DEVELOPS A PLAN
• Guilty or Not Guilty • Hire or Fire • Spend or Save	• Analyze the Problem • Develop Options • Debate Pros and Cons • Select and Implement Solution
ASKS WHO, WHAT, WHERE, AND WHEN	ASKS WHY AND HOW
• Whom should we invite? • What should we discuss? • Where should we meet? • When should we meet?	• Why doesn't our promotional campaign attract students? • How should we publicize the college's new programs?

ideas and information, test and validate more arguments, and produce better solutions to complex problems.[4]

Decision-Making Methods

There are many ways for groups to make decisions. A group can let the majority have its way, try to find a decision or solution that everyone can live with, or leave the final decision to someone else. These decision-making methods translate into voting, consensus seeking, and letting a leader or outside authority make the decision. Each approach has strengths, and the approach used should match the needs and purpose of a group and its task.

Voting.   Voting is the most obvious and easiest way to make a group decision. When a quick decision is needed, there is no method that is more efficient and decisive. Sometimes, though, voting may not be the best way to make important decisions. When a vote is taken, some members win, but others lose. A **majority vote** requires that more than half the members vote in favor of a proposal.

If a group is making a major decision, there may not be enough support to implement the decision if only 51 percent of the members agree on it. The 49 percent who lose may resent working on a project that they dislike. In order to avoid such problems, some groups use a two-thirds vote rather than majority rule. In a **two-thirds vote,** at least twice as many group members must vote for a proposal as vote against it. A two-thirds vote ensures that a significant number of group members support the decision.

Voting works best when

- A group is pressed for time.

- The issue is not highly controversial.

- A group is too large to use any other decision-making method.

- There is no other way to break a deadlock.

- A group's constitution or rules require voting on certain issues and proposals.

Consensus Seeking. Because voting has built-in disadvantages, many groups rely on consensus to make decisions. **Consensus** is reached when *all* group members agree to support a group decision or action. Julia Wood describes a consensus decision as one "that all members have a part in shaping and that all find at least minimally acceptable as a means of accomplishing some mutual goal."[5] When reached, consensus can unite and energize a group. Not only does consensus provide a way of avoiding a disruptive win/lose vote, but it also can present a united front to outsiders. The guidelines shown in Figure 9.2 should be used in seeking consensus.

TOOLBOX 9.1

 ### The Hazards of Consensus

Many groups fall short of achieving their common goal because the leader or members believe that the group *must* reach consensus on all decisions. The problem of superficial or false consensus haunts every decision-making group. **False consensus** occurs when members give in to group pressures or an external authority without really accepting the decision. Rather than achieving consensus, the group has agreed to a decision masquerading as consensus.[1]

In addition to the hazard of false consensus, the all-or-nothing approach to consensus "gives each member veto power over the progress of the whole group." In order to avoid this impasse, members may "give up and give in" or seek a flawed compromise decision. When this happens, the group will fall short of success as "it mindlessly pursues 100% agreement."[2]

In *The Discipline of Teams*, John Katzenbach and Douglas Smith observe that members who pursue complete consensus often act as though disagreement and conflict are bad for the group. Nothing, they claim, could be further from the reality of effective group performance. "Without disagreement, teams rarely generate the best, most creative solutions to the challenges at hand. They compromise . . . rather than developing a solution that incorporates the best of two or more opposing views. . . . The challenge for teams is to learn from disagreement and find energy in constructive conflict; not get ruined by it."[3]

[1] Donald G. Ellis and B. Aubrey Fisher, *Small Group Decision Making* (New York: McGraw-Hill, 1994), p. 142.
[2] John R. Katzenbach and Douglas K. Smith, *The Discipline of Teams* (New York: Wiley, 2001), p. 112.
[3] Katzenbach and Smith, p. 113.

Consensus, however, does not work for all groups. Imagine how difficult it would be to achieve genuine consensus if a leader had so much power that group members were unwilling to express their honest opinions. Consensus seeking works best in groups where members have equal status or groups that have created a climate in which everyone feels comfortable expressing their views.

Authority Rule. Sometimes a single person within or outside the group makes the final decision. When **authority rule** is used, groups may be asked to gather information for and recommend decisions to another person or a larger group.

| FIGURE 9.2 | **Consensus Guidelines** |

Consensus Guidelines

LISTEN CAREFULLY TO OTHER MEMBERS AND CONSIDER THEIR INFORMATION AND POINTS OF VIEW.

- Try to be logical rather than emotional.
- Don't be stubborn and argue only for your own position.

DON'T CHANGE YOUR MIND IN ORDER TO AVOID CONFLICT OR REACH A QUICK DECISION.

- Don't give in, especially if you have a crucial piece of information to share.
- Don't agree to a decision or solution you can't possibly support.

AVOID "EASY" WAYS OF REACHING A DECISION.

- Avoid techniques such as flipping a coin, letting the majority rule, or trading one decision for another.

IF THERE IS A DEADLOCK, WORK HARD TO FIND THE NEXT BEST ALTERNATIVE THAT IS ACCEPTABLE TO EVERYONE.

- Make sure that members not only agree but also will be commited to the final decision.

GET EVERYONE INVOLVED IN THE DISCUSSION.

- The quietest member may have a key piece of information or a brilliant suggestion that can help the group make a better decision.

WELCOME DIFFERENCES OF OPINION.

- Disagreement is natural and can expose a group to a wide range of information and opinions.

For example, an association's nominating committee considers potential candidates and recommends a slate of officers to the association. A hiring committee may screen dozens of job applications and submit a top-three list to the person or persons making the hiring decision.

Unfortunately, authority rule can have detrimental effects on a group. If a leader or an outside authority ignores or reverses the recommendations of the group, its members may become demoralized, resentful, and nonproductive on future assignments. Even within a group, a strong leader or authority figure may use the group and its members to give the appearance of collaborative decision making. The group thus becomes a "rubber stamp" and surrenders its will to authority rule.

Decision-Making Goals

Regardless of which decision-making method a group chooses, there is an immediate judgment that must be made: What is our decision-making goal? In some group settings, the decision-making goal is dictated by an outside group or authority. Yet even when a group does not choose the goal, it has an obligation to clarify that goal and determine whether the group is capable of achieving it. To assist in this process, we recommend that groups word their goal as a question that must be answered. It is useful to look at four different kinds of questions to clarify what a group must know and do in order to succeed: questions of fact, conjecture, value, and policy.

Questions of Fact.

A **question of fact** asks whether something is true or false, whether an event did or did not happen, or whether something was caused by this or that. Did product sales decrease last year? The answer to these questions is either *yes* or *no*. However, a question such as "What was the decrease in sales?" can require a more detailed answer, with possible subquestions about the sales of particular products or product sales in different regions. When a group confronts a question of fact, it must consider the best information it can find and subject that information to close scrutiny.

Questions of Conjecture.

A **question of conjecture** asks whether something will or will not happen. Unlike a question of fact, only the future holds the answer to this type of question. Instead of focusing on reality, the group must consider possibilities. If the group waits until the future happens, it can be too late to make a good decision or solve a problem. In asking a question of conjecture, the group does its best to predict what the future will bring. Will sales increase next quarter? Will there be layoffs? Who will be the next CEO? Although the answer to a question of conjecture is speculative, it should be based as much as possible on reputable facts, expert opinion, and valid data that can help decision makers establish probabilities.[6] Questions of conjecture are not answered with wild guesses; answers are developed by group members who have gathered and analyzed the best information available.

TOOLBOX 9.2

Use All Four Types of Questions

Questions of fact, conjecture, value, and policy are not isolated inquiries. Within a group discussion, all four types of questions may require consideration. For example, if your family were trying to decide how to plan a summer vacation while saving money for a new car, you might start with questions of fact and conjecture: "How much do we usually spend on a summer vacation?" "How much money will we need for a new car?" Then the discussion would move to questions of value: "How much do we value the time and place where our family vacations?" "How important is it that we buy a new car this year?" Finally, you would conclude with a question of policy: "How can we both take a summer vacation and save money for a new car?" Thus, when trying to determine the most suitable course of action, a group usually deals with all four types of questions. A group that does not consider the facts of the situation or the attitudes, beliefs, and values of its members may be headed for a poor decision.

Questions of Value. A **question of value** asks whether something is worthwhile—is it good or bad; right or wrong; moral or immoral; best, average, or worst? Questions of value can be difficult to discuss because the answers depend on the attitudes, beliefs, and values of group members. In many cases, the answer to a question of value may be, "It depends." Is a community college a better place to begin higher education than a prestigious university? The answer to this question depends on a student's financial situation, professional goals, academic achievement record, work and family situation, and beliefs about the quality of an education at each type of institution.

Questions of Policy. A **question of policy** asks whether a particular course of action should be taken to solve a problem. Many groups focus on questions of policy. How can we improve customer service? Which candidate should we support as president of the student government association? What plan, if any, should be enacted to ensure that our school system maintains a culturally diverse teaching staff? Policy questions often require answers to subquestions of fact, conjecture, and value.

THE NEED FOR PROCEDURES

In Chapter 1, we introduce the group dialectic of "structure and spontaneity" by noting that structured procedures help groups balance participation, resolve conflicts, organize discussions, and empower members. They also help groups solve problems. However, if a group becomes obsessed with rigid procedures, it misses out on the benefits of spontaneity and creativity. Whether it's just "thinking outside the box" or organizing a creative problem-solving session, groups can reap enormous benefits by encouraging innovation and "what if" thinking. Effective groups balance the need for structured problem solving with time for creative thinking.

The Need for Structured Procedures

Even if everyone understands why group decision making is valuable and appreciates the different ways in which a group makes up its mind, there is no guarantee that the group will make good decisions. Groups also need clear procedures that specify how a group should organize problem-solving tasks. Group communication scholar Marshall Scott Poole identifies structured procedures as "the heart of group work [and] the most powerful tools we have to improve the conduct of meetings."[7] Even a simple procedure such as constructing and following a short agenda enhances meeting productivity. Time and effort spent on using a well-planned, structured procedure can reap the following benefits:

- *Balanced participation.* Procedures can minimize the impact of a powerful leader or member by making it difficult for a few talkative or high-status members to dominate a group's discussion.

- *Conflict resolution.* Procedures often incorporate guidelines for managing conflict, resolving disagreements, and building genuine consensus.

- *Organization.* Procedures require members to follow a clear organizational pattern and focus on the same thing at the same time. Procedures also ensure that major discussion items are not missed or ignored.

- *Group empowerment.* Procedures provide a group with a sense of control. "This happens when members know they have followed a procedure well, managed conflict successfully, given all members an equal opportunity to participate, and as a result have made a good decision."[8]

The Need for Creative Procedures

Curiosity and creativity fuel all *great* groups. These qualities allow groups to "identify significant problems and find creative, boundary-bursting solutions rather than simplistic ones."[9] Effective group leaders understand the near-magical quality that creativity can inject into the group process. When, for example, Walt Disney "asked his artists to push the envelope of animation, he told them 'If you can dream it, you can do it.' He believed that, and, as a result, they did too."[10]

Creativity is difficult to define because it is both a process and an outcome. In Lee Towe's book on **creativity** in the workplace, he describes these two components:[11]

- *Creative thinking.* The process of searching for, separating, and connecting thoughts from many categories while limiting judgment.

- *Creative output.* The valuable combination of previously unrelated elements.

Thus, creative thinking is a process that groups can develop, and creative output is the measurable goal of creative groupwork.

Encouraging and rewarding creativity can be as important to problem solving as following any of the structured procedures described in this chapter. It is creativity and "thinking outside the box" that facilitate breakthrough decisions and solutions. For example, one of us once chaired a meeting in which the injection of creativity broke through a problem-solving logjam:

> I was chairing a meeting of graphic artists, copywriters, and public relations staff members at the college. Our assignment was to write and design a commemorative booklet for the college's fortieth anniversary. On the conference table sat a dozen such booklets from other colleges. The group had reviewed all the samples and come up with a list of common features. The problem was this: We had limited funds to print the booklet, so we had to confine ourselves to twenty-four pages. Very quickly, the group became bogged down. An uncomfortable silence settled over the group. At this point, I interjected a question: "If you hadn't seen any of these model booklets, what would you write and design to commemorate our anniversary?" The response was immediate and energizing: "You mean we can come up with something new and different?" The answer was yes. The result: A new sense of excitement and eagerness permeated the group. The "model" booklets were swept off the table. Highly creative, out-of-the-box alternatives materialized.

When groups think creatively, members share new connections and unusual possibilities. Although it is impossible to describe the creative process in precise

What procedure could help this group make decisions about the next edition of the school newspaper? (© Elizabeth Crews/The Image Works)

terms (it wouldn't be all that creative if we could), we can outline the basic stages of the process in groups. Generally, there are four stages:

- *Investigation.* Group members gather information and attempt to understand the nature and causes of a problem.

- *Imagination.* Free thinking is encouraged. Mental roadblocks are removed or temporarily suppressed. Many ideas, some of them quite unusual, are generated and discussed.

- *Incubation.* A period of time occurs during which imaginative ideas are allowed to percolate and recombine in new ways. The group may take a break or focus its attention on another topic or issue during the incubation stage.

- *Insight.* The "Aha!" moment occurs and a new approach or solution emerges. Group members recognize the breakthrough moment and may build upon or improve the idea. Many group members enjoy the fun that comes with this stage of the creative process.

Because the incubation stage is usually a prerequisite for the "Aha!" moment of insight, it may look as though the group has abandoned its task. As a result, creative problem solving is often squelched or sacrificed in the interest of following a detailed agenda or rigid procedure. For group members with strong control needs, creative problem solving may seem to divert energy from dealing with the problem to having a good time. Despite these concerns, creative thinking in groups is well worth the time and the laughter. Group members who are trained in creative problem solving participate more, criticize one another less, support new ideas more, exhibit humor, and produce more worthwhile ideas.[12]

STRUCTURED PROBLEM SOLVING

There are many structured problem-solving procedures available to groups. There are complex, theory-based models designed to tackle the overall problem facing a group. There are also decision-making methods and tools designed for subgoals of the problem-solving process. As a way of understanding the similarities and differences among these procedures, we provide a hypothetical example to illustrate how their various steps can be applied to solving a problem. Although this example does not offer many details, it can demonstrate the ways in which a group may use several of the most common structured procedures to solve problems (see Figure 9.3).

Fallingstar State College

For three consecutive years, Fallingstar State College has experienced declining enrollment and no increase in funding from the state. In order to balance the budget, the board of trustees has had to raise tuition every year. There are no

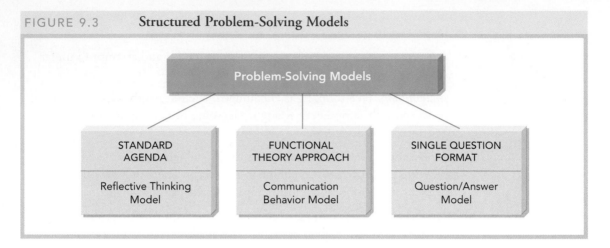

FIGURE 9.3   **Structured Problem-Solving Models**

prospects for more state funding in the near future. Even with significant tuition increases, there has been a drop in overall college revenue. The college's planning council, composed of representative vice presidents, deans, faculty members, staff employees, and students, has been charged with answering the following question: Given the severe budget constraints, what should the college do to preserve high-quality instruction and student services?

There is no "best" model or magic formula that ensures effective problem solving in groups. As a group gains experience and successfully solves problems, its members learn that some procedures work better than others and some need modification to suit the group's needs. In short, there are no hard-and-fast rules for problem solving. There are, however, well-accepted methods to help groups through this complex process.

The Standard Agenda

The founding father of problem-solving procedures is a U.S. philosopher and educator named John Dewey. In 1910, Dewey wrote a book entitled *How We Think,* in which he described a set of practical steps that a rational person should follow when solving a problem.[13] These guidelines have come to be known as Dewey's **Reflective Thinking Process.**

Dewey's ideas have been adapted to the process of solving problems in groups. The Reflective Thinking Process begins with a focus on the problem itself and then moves on to a systematic consideration of possible solutions. We offer one approach to this process—the **Standard Agenda.**[14] The basic steps in The Standard Agenda are summarized in Figure 9.4.

Task Clarification. The goal of this initial phase is to make sure that everyone understands the group's assignment. For example, Fallingstar State College's planning council could dedicate the beginning of its first meeting to making

FIGURE 9.4   **The Standard Agenda**

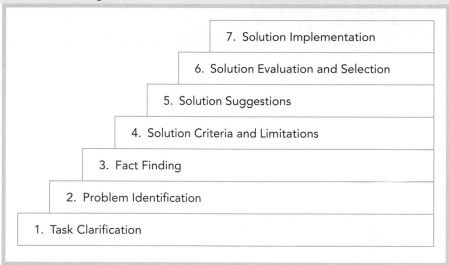

sure that everyone is aware of the time frame in which the council is working and the need to produce a written set of recommendations. During this phase, group members can ask questions about their roles and responsibilities in the problem-solving process.

Problem Identification. Overlooking this second step can send a group in the wrong direction. In the case of Fallingstar State College, there may be several different ways to define the college's problem. Is the problem declining enrollment? Some group members may consider this to be an advantage rather than a disadvantage because having fewer students can result in smaller classes, more individualized instruction, less chaos at registration, and easier parking. Is the problem a lack of money? Although lack of money seems to be a universal problem, an inefficiently run college could find that it in fact has enough money if it enhances productivity and becomes more businesslike.

The group's problem should be worded as an agreed-upon question. Whether this is a question of fact, conjecture, value, or policy determines the focus and direction of the discussion. The question "What should the college do to continue providing high-quality instruction and student services?" is a question of policy that can be answered only by also considering questions of fact, value, and conjecture.

Fact Finding. During the third step, fact finding, group members have several obligations that are reflected in the following questions of fact and value: What are the facts of the situation? What additional information or expert opinions do we need? How serious or widespread is the problem? What are the causes of the

TOOLBOX 9.3

The Role of Agendas and Parliamentary Procedure

Two important decision-making tools—meeting agendas and parliamentary procedure—can help groups make effective decisions as they solve problems. A meeting agenda is an outline of the items to be discussed and the tasks to be accomplished at a meeting. In Chapter 12, "Planning and Conducting Meetings," we provide guidelines and examples of meeting agendas.

Parliamentary procedure is a term that describes a set of formal rules used to determine the will of the majority through fair and orderly discussion and debate. For group members who are new to parliamentary procedure, it can be confusing and intimidating. Not only are there hundreds of rules, but the language of parliamentary procedure has a unique vocabulary: "Mr. Chairman, I call the previous question" or "Madam President, I rise to a point of order."

Many organizations and associations specify in their constitution or bylaws (rules governing how an organization operates) that parliamentary procedure must be used to conduct meetings. *Robert's Rules of Order*—considered the "parliamentary bible" by many organizations—provides rules that ensure reasonable and civil debate as well as timely group decisions that are accepted by supporters and opponents alike.[1]

[1] Henry M. Robert, with Henry M. Robert, III, William J. Evans, and James W. Cleary, *Robert's Rules of Order, Newly Revised,* 9th ed. (New York: Scott, Foresman, 1990). *Note*: The Houghton Mifflin web site that accompanies this textbook provides an introduction to parliamentary procedure that focuses on its basic principles as well as guidelines for making motions and requesting privileges.

Online Study Center
General Resources
Read the online chapter "Parliamentary Procedures" for more information.

---

problem? What prevents us from solving the problem? These questions require investigations of facts, conclusions about causes and effects, and value judgments about the seriousness of the problem.

Fallingstar State College's planning council could look at the rate of enrollment decline and future enrollment projections, the anticipated budgets for future years, the efficiency of existing services, the projected impact of inflation, estimated salary increases, predictable maintenance costs, and the likely causes of declining enrollment. It could take months to investigate these questions, and even then, there may not be clear answers to all of them. Failure to search for such answers, however, is much more hazardous than attempting to find them.

We offer a word of caution about this phase of The Standard Agenda. "Although analyzing the problem is important and should be undertaken before exploring potential solutions, bogging down by analyzing the problem too much can also thwart effective decision making. **Analysis paralysis** prevents a group from ever getting on with business and making a decision."[15] In other words, a college planning council could collect dozens of reports and identify ten possible causes of declining enrollment but still be unable to verify or settle on the most important reasons. Rather than spending months arguing about the issue or giving up on finding the correct answer, a group may have to move on and begin its search for solutions.

Solution Criteria and Limitations.

Solution criteria are standards that an ideal resolution of a problem should meet. The development of realistic criteria should also include an understanding of solution limitations, which can be financial, institutional, practical, political, or legal in scope. For a college planning council, criteria could include the cost of potential solutions, the goal of ensuring that all subgroups—administrators, faculty, staff, and students—accept the solution, a commitment to using fair and open procedures to assess existing programs, and considerations of the political and legal consequences of proposed actions.

Solution Suggestions.

At this point in a group's deliberations, some solutions may be obvious. Even so, the group should concentrate on suggesting as many solutions as possible. Having spent time understanding the task, identifying the problem, analyzing its consequences and causes, and establishing solution criteria, members should be able to offer numerous solutions. Later in this chapter, we describe a technique called *brainstorming* that can help a group generate creative options.

Suggestions from the college's planning council could include a wide range of options: raising tuition, embarking on a new promotional campaign, seeking additional grants and corporate donations, forgoing raises, freezing promotions, requiring additional teaching by faculty, increasing class size, reducing the number of administrators and staff, eliminating expensive programs and services, lobbying the state for more funds, and charging students fees for special services. This list could double or triple, depending on the creativity and resourcefulness of the group.

Solution Evaluation and Selection.

This stage of The Standard Agenda may be the most difficult and controversial. Here, group members discuss the pros and cons of each suggestion in light of their agreed-upon criteria for a solution. Questions of conjecture arise as the group considers the possible consequences of each option. Discussion may become heated, and disagreements may grow fierce. In some groups, members may be so tired or frustrated by the time they get to this phase that there is a tendency to jump to conclusions. If the group has been conscientious in analyzing the problem and establishing criteria for solutions, however, some solutions will be rejected quickly, while others will swiftly rise to the top of the list.

The college's planning council may hear students arguing against increased tuition and fees, whereas faculty are predicting a decline in instructional quality if they are required to teach more courses or larger classes. Administrators and staff may cringe at freezing salaries, whereas faculty may support reductions in administrative staff. In this phase, a group should remember its solution criteria and use them to evaluate the strengths and weaknesses of each suggested solution. At the end of this stage, a group should identify the solutions it wishes to endorse and implement.

Solution Implementation. Having now made a difficult decision, a group faces one more challenge: How should the decision be implemented? Should our group assume this responsibility, or will implementation be delegated to others? How will the group explain the wisdom or practicality of its decision to others? For all the time a group spends trying to solve a problem, it may take even more time to organize the task of implementing the solution. If the planning council wants a new promotional campaign to attract students, the campaign must be well planned and affordable in order to achieve its goal. If the college wants to enhance its fund-raising efforts, a group or office must be given the authority and resources to seek such funds. Brilliant solutions can fail if no one takes responsibility or has the authority to implement a group's decision.

The Functional Theory Approach

During the 1980s and 1990s, Randy Hirokawa and Dennis Gouran theorized that a set of "critical functions" can explain and predict how well a group will make decisions and solve problems. Unlike The Standard Agenda model, **functional theory** claims that "communication is the instrument by which members or groups, with varying degrees of success, reach decisions and generate solutions to problems."[16] According to this theory, effective performance of communication functions is more important than the order in which these functions are performed. If, however, groups stray too far from an agenda, the quality of the group decision may suffer.

Gouran and Hirokawa's ongoing research reveals that certain conditions explain the likelihood of a group's making good decisions and selecting appropriate solutions to a problem. We have grouped these conditions into three categories: (1) appropriate preparation, (2) appropriate procedures, and (3) appropriate precautions.

Preparation. Before a group engages in specific problem-solving tasks, the group must be well prepared for the process. There are four preparation requirements for effective decision making and problem solving. Group members must

- Make clear their interest in arriving at the best possible decision.
- Identify the resources necessary for making such a decision.
- Recognize possible obstacles to be confronted.
- Specify the procedures and ground rules to be followed.[17]

These prerequisites ensure that the group is ready, willing, and able to tackle the issue. The first task—participant interest and energy—is not sufficient to ensure success. Group members also must make sure that they have identified the sources of information they will need, the limits or constraints on their ability to make a decision, and the appropriate decision-making or problem-solving procedure.

Procedures. Once a group is ready, willing, and able to tackle an issue, an additional set of functional tasks is needed. In order for groups to satisfy fundamental task requirements, they must (1) understand the issues, (2) determine solution criteria, (3) identify possible solutions, (4) review the pros and cons of each suggested solution, and (5) select the best option.[18] These procedural tasks are the heart of functional theory. Addressing each one is critical if a group hopes to make an effective decision or solve a problem.

1. *Understand the issues.* This function combines the second and third steps in The Standard Agenda—problem identification and fact finding. Two related errors can occur in this phase. First, the group may fail to recognize or accurately define the problem. Second, it may fail to identify the causes of the problem. If, in the case of Fallingstar State College, the planning council mistakenly decides that the decrease in enrollment is caused by higher tuition, it may have ignored other factors, such as competition from other colleges, the state of the economy and its effect on students' ability to find jobs, or even a public perception that the college does not offer high-quality instruction. If, as a result, the college decides to hold the line on tuition but eliminate popular programs, the problem could be made worse.

2. *Determine solution criteria.* Once a group believes that it understands the nature and causes of a problem, it needs to establish criteria or standards for a solution. In many groups, this process is governed by specific goals or unspoken objectives. For example, a college's planning council may want to develop a plan that saves money for the college without affecting or jeopardizing anyone's job. Given such a goal, options such as reducing the number of administrators, increasing the number of teaching hours, or freezing salaries and promotions could be out of the question. In the end, such limitations could hamper the planning council's ability to solve its budgetary problem. On the other hand, when underlying goals and values match potential solutions, the final decision will be better. For example, if everyone on the planning council agrees that employee sacrifices are inevitable, the road has been cleared for a wider range of possible actions.

3. *Identify possible solutions.* With an understanding of the problem and a set of goals or standards against which to measure suggested actions, a group will identify possible solutions. This third function is similar to the solution suggestions step in The Standard Agenda.

4. *Review the pros and cons of each suggested solution.* The fourth function is the group's ability to analyze and discuss the positive and negative aspects of suggested solutions. Breakdowns at this stage of the discussion process can have serious consequences. Hirokawa points out that because it is impossible to examine *all* the positive and negative aspects of every proposed solution, a group "tends to focus on the more important or obvious positive

and negative attributes of certain attractive choices."[19] As a result, the group may overestimate a solution's strengths and fail to recognize its weaknesses.

5. *Select the best option.* At this point in the process, the group should be prepared to make a decision or choose an appropriate action to solve a problem. If a group has completed the prerequisite preparation tasks and followed the appropriate procedures, selection can and should occur. Although there may be more than one good decision or solution, the group should feel confident that its choice will be appropriate and effective.

Precautions. Although it may seem as though all of the important decision-making tasks have been completed, groups need to engage in two more functions that help ensure the quality of a decision or solution. First, the group must become aware of and overcome any constraints that prevent effective decision making and problem solving. Second, members should review the entire process that the group used to come to a decision and, if necessary, reconsider the judgments reached (even to the point of starting over).

At the very end of the decision-making process, group members may experience some uneasiness or be reluctant to finalize their decision. Reviewing the functional tasks from the very beginning and taking time to think about the potential constraints that could have influenced the group can be time well spent. It takes a brave participant to suggest that something is not right with the final product. Perhaps there has been a trace of groupthink, perhaps an early assumption was based on erroneous information, perhaps the decision failed to take into account the criteria established by the group, or perhaps a strong group member had too much influence. Once a group implements its decision, it can be difficult to undo the consequences.

Functional theory has several qualities that distinguish it from The Standard Agenda model. The first is that the competent performance of each of the functions is more important than performing the functions in a specific order. A second difference is that the functional approach recognizes that group goals and unspoken assumptions can affect the choice of solutions. Finally, this approach emphasizes the group's ability to recognize and realistically understand both the pros and the cons when considering a solution, and also understand the constraints that can undermine decision making. It is not enough for a group to follow a list of steps; it must also be well informed, realistic, and highly motivated if it hopes to solve a problem.

The Single Question Format

The **Single Question Format** is a seemingly simple problem-solving procedure that approximates the way successful problem solvers and decision makers naturally think.[20] The five basic steps in the Single Question Format provide a sharp focus on an agreed-upon question that, if thoroughly analyzed and responsibly answered, should provide the solution to a problem. The Single Question Format includes the following steps: (1) identify the problem, (2) create a collaborative setting, (3) analyze the issues, (4) identify possible solutions, and (5) answer the single question.[21]

Identify the Problem.   What is the *single* question, the answer to which is all that the group needs to know in order to accomplish its agreed-upon goal? Although reaching agreement on the single question may take many hours, the investment is essential if additional time and effort are to be well spent.[22] For example, Fallingstar State College's planning council decides to address this question: Given the severe budget constraints, what should the college do to preserve high-quality instruction and student services? In business settings, a single question might be: How should we eliminate $4 million of annual expenses without damaging the company or its customer relationships? At home you could ask: Given limited funds, how can we both take a vacation in Maine and afford to purchase another car?

Create a Collaborative Setting.   This second step is often overlooked in other problem-solving procedures. Here you ask your group to agree on a set of norms by generating a list of "we will" statements designed to foster open discussion and participation:

- We will listen to *all* points of view.
- We will ask for facts as well as opinions.
- We will be tough on issues but not on one another.
- We will put aside personal agendas.

In addition to the "we will" list, identify assumptions and biases that may influence the discussion. Ask the group: Have past approaches worked, or do we need a new approach? Do we *really* understand the problem, or do we need to take a fresh look at the situation? Are we ignoring some approaches because of personal or political biases?

Analyze the Issues.   The third step requires a group to identify and analyze relevant subquestions such as these:

- What issues must be addressed in order to answer our single question?
- Do we have accurate and relevant facts about each issue?
- Given what we know, what is the best or most reasonable response to each issue?

Completing this step helps a group "avoid arriving at a solution too early, before understanding the critical components of the problem."[23]

Identify Possible Solutions. This step asks a group to suggest two or three reasonable solutions to the overall single question *and* to discuss the advantages and disadvantages of each solution. This is a crucial step in which strong opinions and disagreements may arise. By listing advantages and disadvantages, however, a group may be able to *see* that the advantages for one solution far outweigh the disadvantages. A simple table can be used to generate the pros and cons for each option.

Possible Solution	Advantages	Disadvantages
	1.	1.
	2.	2.
	3.	3.

Answer the Single Question. After analyzing the pros and cons of each potential solution, the group selects "the best solution to the problem based on a clear, shared understanding of all the relevant issues. This clarity, in turn allows a group to proceed with sufficient confidence to their final decision and commit to it."[24]

Although the Single Question Format shares many characteristics with The Standard Agenda approach, two features make it both different and effective. First, it sharply focuses on goal clarity (a prerequisite for any work group) and issue analysis. Second, it cultivates a supportive group climate that helps members identify, raise, and resolve many interpersonal and process problems that can affect group success.

At Fallingstar State College, a single question—Given the severe budget constraints, what should the college do to preserve high-quality instruction and student services?—helps the planning council understand what it needs to know in order to avert a financial crisis caused by declining enrollment. After asking this single question, the group members spend time establishing a set of norms to determine the way in which they will discuss the problem. They may decide that the names of specific administrators will not be used when describing failed programs. Rather than assuming that the college recruitment office "ain't broke, so why fix it?" they may decide that there is room for improvement in all offices. After establishing a collaborative setting, the council can devote its attention to analyzing and responding to several critical issues, after which members can offer a limited number of reasonable solutions. A vice president might suggest efficiency moves such as increasing class size as well as a more aggressive marketing plan. A dean might propose developing new academic programs to attract more students. A student might recommend an organized protest at the state capitol in support of more funding. In the Single Question Format, the group would consider the advantages and disadvantages of every reasonable solution and determine the extent to which each suggestion could or should be incorporated into an ideal solution that answers its single question.

Figure 9.5 summarizes the main features of the three structured problem-solving procedures discussed in this chapter.

CREATIVE PROBLEM SOLVING

As is the case with structured problem solving, there are many creative problem-solving methods (see Figure 9.6). Again, there is no "best" technique. There are, however, recommended procedures for making decision making and problem solving effective by harnessing group ingenuity and creativity.

Brainstorming

In 1953, Alex Osborn introduced the concept of brainstorming in his book *Applied Imagination.*[25] **Brainstorming** is a technique for generating as many ideas as possible in a short period of time. When a group is asked to suggest the causes of or solutions to a problem, brainstorming can be used to increase the number and creativity of the suggestions. Brainstorming is a fairly simple and widely used

FIGURE 9.5   **Summary of Structured Problem-Solving Procedures**

Problem Solving Procedures		
STANDARD AGENDA	**FUNCTIONAL THEORY APPROACH**	**SINGLE QUESTION FORMAT**

1. Task Clarification
2. Problem Identification
3. Fact Finding
4. Solution Criteria and Limitations
5. Solution Suggestions
6. Solution Evaluation and Selection
7. Solution Implementation
	Preparation
	• Aim for Best Decision
	• Identify Necessary Resources
	• Recognize Possible Obstacles
	• Specify the Procedures
	
	Procedures
	• Understand the Issues
	• Determine Criteria
	• Identify Possible Solutions
	• Review Pros and Cons of Solutions
	• Select the Best Solution
		1. Identify the Problem As a Single Question
		2. Create a Collaborative Setting
		  a. Agree on Discussion Norms
		  b. Identify Assumptions and Biases
		3. Identify and Analyze the Issues
		4. Identify Possible Solutions
		5. Resolve the Single Question

FIGURE 9.6   **Creative Methods**

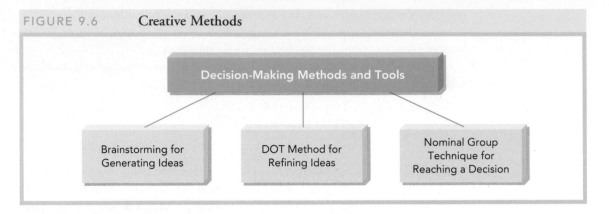

method. In fact, more than 70 percent of businesspeople claim that brainstorming is used in their organizations.[26] Unfortunately, many groups fail to use brainstorming effectively. The guidelines shown in Figure 9.7 explain the rules and nature of brainstorming.

Brainstorming is governed by two key principles: (1) Deferring judgment improves the quality of participants' input, and (2) quantity of ideas breeds quality. The idea that quantity breeds quality is based on the notion that the first ideas we come up with are usually the most obvious, and that truly creative ideas will come only after we have gotten the obvious suggestions out.[27]

There are, however, circumstances in which brainstorming can be counterproductive.[28] If, for example, a highly influential member or "the boss" is allowed to speak first, he or she can potentially influence and limit the direction of ideas. In an effort to be more democratic, some groups have members speak in turn. This approach, however, prevents the group from building momentum and results in fewer ideas. Finally, some members may try to write down all of the group's ideas. Those members end up being so focused on note taking that they rarely contribute ideas. Instead, have one person record all the ideas contributed by the group members.

Although brainstorming is often used by groups, its effectiveness depends on the nature of the group and the character of its members. If a group is self-conscious and sensitive to implied criticism, brainstorming can fail. However, if a group is comfortable with such a freewheeling process, brainstorming can enhance creativity and produce numerous worthwhile ideas.

Nominal Group Technique (NGT)

Nominal Group Technique, also known as NGT, was developed by Andre L. Delbecq and Andrew H. Van de Ven as a way of maximizing participation in problem-solving and program-planning groups while minimizing some of the interpersonal problems associated with group interaction.[29] The term *nominal* means "existing in name only." Thus, a nominal group is a collection of people

FIGURE 9.7   **Brainstorming Guidelines**[30]

BRAINSTORMING GUIDELINES

1. Sharpen the Focus
   - Start with a clear statement of the problem.
   - Give members a few minutes to think about possible ideas before brainstorming begins.

2. For All to See
   - Assign someone to write down the group's ideas.
   - Post the ideas where everyone can see them.

3. Number the Ideas
   - Numbering can motivate a group, e.g., "Let's try to get 100 ideas."
   - Numbering makes it easier to jump back and forth among ideas.

4. Encourage Creativity
   - Wild and crazy ideas are welcome.
   - Quantity is more important than quality.

5. All Input, No Putdown
   - Don't analyze, oppose, or praise another member's ideas.
   - Don't discuss, defend, clarify, or comment on your own suggestions.
   - Keep the ideas coming.
   - Ideas are evaluated only after brainstorming is over.

6. Build and Jump
   - Build on or modify ideas offered by others.
   - Combine two or more ideas into a new idea.
   - It's okay to jump back to an earlier idea or forward to a completely different line of thinking.

who, at first, work individually rather than collectively. NGT combines aspects of silent voting with limited discussion to help a group build consensus and arrive at a decision.[31]

There are two separate phases in a Nominal Group Technique session: an idea generation phase and an evaluation phase. During the idea generation phase, seven to ten individuals sit around a table in full view of one another. This first phase includes these four steps:

1. Each member writes his or her ideas on a separate piece of paper.

2. At the end of five to ten minutes, a structured sharing of ideas takes place. Each member, in turn, presents one idea from his or her private list.

3. A recorder writes each idea on a flip chart in full view of other members. There is no discussion at this point—only the recording of members' ideas.

4. Round-robin listing continues until all members indicate that they have no further ideas to share.[32]

Returning to the case of the college planning council, members could use the Nominal Group Technique to generate a list of possible causes of declining enrollment or a list of possible solutions to the budgetary shortfall. The listing of ideas in an NGT session is different from brainstorming because the ideas are generated by individuals working alone rather than emerging from group interaction.

During the second, evaluative phase of a Nominal Group Technique session, the group discusses each recorded idea and then votes to create a rank order of items as follows:

1. Discussion is structured so that each idea receives attention before independent voting.

2. Members are asked to clarify or state their support or nonsupport of each idea listed on the flip chart.

3. Independent voting then takes place. Each member privately, in writing, selects priorities by rank-ordering (or rating) the ideas.

4. The group decision is the mathematically pooled outcome of the individual votes.[33]

Nominal Group Technique can be used in a variety of group settings, particularly when individual judgments and expertise are valued. NGT can be used to rank job applicants, to select a campaign slogan, to determine which of many possible solutions receives the most support, to establish budget priorities, to reach agreement on the causes of a problem, and to make a final decision. The highly structured NGT process guarantees equal participation during the idea generation phase and also provides opportunities for discussion and critical evaluation in the second phase. NGT can also be useful when dealing with a sensitive or controversial topic on which contrary opinions and a myriad of details could paralyze the discussion.[34]

An NGT session requires a great deal of time and a skilled moderator to make it work efficiently and effectively. Given NGT's highly structured format, it is difficult to adjust or modify suggested items, and this may frustrate group members who prefer more spontaneous interaction. At the same time, NGT can curb members who dominate or block the ideas and comments of others. Because the technique begins with individual ideas, all members are able to see their suggestions discussed by the entire group.

Decreasing Options Technique (DOT)

DOT, which stands for **Decreasing Options Technique,** is a decision-making tool that helps groups reduce and refine a large number of suggestions into a manageable number of ideas. In our work as professional facilitators, we have used this technique to assist small and large groups facing a variety of decision-making tasks. We have enlisted the DOT strategy to write an identity statement for an academic discipline, to create an ethics credo for a professional association, to draft a vision statement for a college, and to create an academic curriculum for

TOOLBOX 9.4

Which Is Better: Brainstorming or Nominal Group Technique?

Several researchers have investigated the relative usefulness of brainstorming and Nominal Group Technique. It is difficult to draw absolute conclusions regarding the superiority of one method over the other because group members, group goals, and group relationships differ. Yet, there seems to be good evidence that Nominal Group Technique works better than brainstorming for generating ideas that are both numerous and creative. There are several possible reasons for this conclusion.[1]

- Waiting for a turn to speak in a brainstorming group may disrupt the thinking of group members and slow the production of ideas.
- Group members who fear negative evaluation from others may withhold ideas even though the group has been told to defer judgment.
- Some members may loaf or "free ride" and let others do all the thinking and talking.

- Some members may not believe that their contributions are important.
- Members who participate more frequently often earn higher status, which may discourage others from speaking.

Nominal Group Technique avoids most of these problems because members have time to think, write, and respond to suggestions after the idea-generating process ends. The development of electronic brainstorming may also help avoid many of these problems. In these settings, group members use networked computers programmed with groupware to generate a master list of ideas simultaneously *and* anonymously.[2]

[1] Craig E. Johnson and Michael Z. Hackman, *Creative Communication: Principles and Applications* (Prospect Heights, IL: Waveland, 1995), pp. 129–130.
[2] Johnson and Hackman, p. 131.

an emerging profession. The DOT method works best when a group must sort through a multitude of ideas and options. There are five basic steps to follow when using DOT: (1) generate ideas, (2) post the ideas, (3) sort the ideas, (4) prioritize the ideas, and (5) "dot" the ideas.

At the beginning of the DOT process, group members are asked to generate ideas or suggestions related to the topic being discussed. Ideas can be single words or full-sentence suggestions. For example, when creating an ethics credo at a National Communication Association conference, participants contributed words such as *honesty, respect,* and *truth* for inclusion in such a credo.[35] You can ask group members to generate and submit ideas *before* the group meets or ask them to contribute their ideas at the beginning of a meeting. Conference participants working on the ethics credo mailed and emailed key words to the conference chairperson several weeks in advance. These words were then sorted to avoid duplication and prepared for posting at the upcoming meeting.

Each idea should be written on a separate sheet of paper in large, easy-to-read letters—only one idea per page. Then, post the pages on the walls of the group's meeting room. When members submit their ideas in advance, the postings can be done before the meeting begins. When members generate ideas during a meeting, postings should be displayed after all members have finished writing their ideas on separate sheets of paper.

Not surprisingly, many group members will contribute similar or overlapping ideas. When this happens, sort the ideas and post similar ideas close to one another. For example, when facilitating the development of a college's vision statement, phrases like *academic excellence, quality education,* and *high-quality instruction* were posted near one another. Once everyone is comfortable with the manner in which postings have been sorted, give a title to each grouping of ideas. For example, in the vision statement session, the term *quality education* was used as an umbrella phrase for nearly a dozen similar concepts.

At this point, members must prioritize the ideas by choosing the ones they believe are most important: Which words *best* reflect the vision we have for our college? Which concepts *must* be included in our association's ethics credo? Which units are *essential* in the new curriculum? The final step requires all participants to "dot" their preferred ideas. Give every member a limited number of colored sticker dots. For example, after giving ten dots to each member of the vision statement group, we instructed them to choose the most important concepts from among the twenty-five phrases posted on the walls. After everyone has finished walking around the room and posting dots, the most important ideas are usually very apparent. Some ideas will be covered with dots; others will be speckled with only three or four; some will remain blank. After a brief review of the outcome, the group can eliminate some ideas, decide whether marginal ideas should be included, and end up with a limited and manageable number of options to consider and discuss.

When a group generates dozens of ideas, valuable meeting time can be consumed by discussing each idea, regardless of its merit or relevance. The DOT method reduces the quantity of ideas to a manageable number. Often DOT is a preface to an extended discussion of key ideas and suggestions. When the DOT approach is not employed, the number of topics to be reviewed can overwhelm a group and discourage members from participating.

Consider using DOT when

- The group is so large that open discussion of individual ideas is unworkable.
- The group has generated a significant number of competing ideas.
- The group wants to ensure equal opportunities for input by all members.
- The group wants to restrain dominant members from exerting too much influence.
- The group does not have enough time to discuss multiple or controversial ideas.

Although the examples we have used to describe the DOT process focus on face-to-face interaction, DOT also works very well in virtual settings. Instead of writing ideas on sheets of paper, posting them on walls, and dotting preferences, a virtual group can follow the same steps by using email or networked software designed for interactive groupwork. Ideas can be generated online, grouped by a moderator or

GROUPTECH

Decision Making and Problem Solving in Virtual Groups

The decision-making and problem-solving methods presented in this chapter originally were created on the assumption that group members would be meeting face to face. However, these methods also work well in virtual groups. Additionally, specialized computer software, or groupware, can facilitate group collaboration, decision making, and problem solving.

Successful virtual groups match their problem-solving or decision-making tasks to the appropriate technology. According to Deborah Duarte and Nancy Snyder, authors of *Mastering Virtual Teams*, virtual groups engage in four types of interaction: information sharing, discussion, decision making, and product producing.[1] An information-sharing meeting could include a virtual presentation or an online exchange of information among members. A discussion meeting often involves the generation of ideas or examination of issues or problems via email or bulletin boards. In a decision-making meeting, virtual groups review the important issues and make actual decisions. During product-producing meetings, virtual group members work on a project, such as developing a design or drafting a new policy.

Duarte and Snyder further suggest that different types of technology are not equally well suited to all types of group interaction.[2] For example, if your group is engaged in brainstorming, using groupware that incorporates audio, video, and text will be more effective than using email. When your virtual group has to make a decision, a videoconference will be much more useful than an electronic bulletin board. John Katzenbach and Douglas Smith remind us that "whenever teams gather through groupware to advance, they need to recognize and adjust to key differences between face-to-face and groupware interactions."[3] They also caution against approaching every virtual meeting in the same way. Group problem-solving and decision-making tasks require more opportunity for interaction than, for instance, information sharing or presentations. A virtual group should select the technology that is best suited to its problem-solving method.

[1] Deborah L. Duarte and Nancy Tennant Snyder, *Mastering Virtual Teams* (San Francisco: Jossey-Bass, 1999), p. 160.
[2] Duarte and Snyder, p. 161.
[3] John R. Katzenbach and Douglas K. Smith, *The Discipline of Teams: A Mindbookworkbook for Delivering Small Group Performance* (New York: Wiley, 2001), p. 167.

committee, and then "dotted" electronically. Sophisticated software can tally members' preferences and rank ideas based on the number of dots given to each idea.

Enhancing Group Creativity

Given the benefits of creative problem solving, we recommend four methods for enhancing group creativity: (1) control judgment, (2) encourage innovation, (3) ask "*what if,*" and (4) use metaphors.

Control Judgment. Almost nothing inhibits group creativity as much as negative responses to new ideas and innovative solutions. "That won't work." "We've tried that." "That's too bizarre." Sometimes a bizarre idea can evolve into a creative solution. "Keeping the process open and avoiding premature closure are crucially important. Because creative work is exploratory in nature, it deserves suspension of belief in the early stages."[36]

Encourage Innovation. In his book on creativity in the workplace, Lee Towe maintains that there are four sources of action that guide us through each workday.[37] These same sources of action can apply to the way groups approach problem solving.

Inertia. We've done it before.

Instruction. Someone showed us how to do it.

Imitation. We've seen how it's done.

Innovation. We have developed a new way to do it.

Think of how these sources of action could apply to the members of the group that was trying to design the commemorative booklet for the college's fortieth anniversary. Until their creativity was released, they were bogged down in inertia, instruction, and imitation. Encouraging a group to be innovative, to think outside the box, to be more imaginative may be all that is needed to spark and harness the group's creative power.

Ask "What If." One of the reasons groups are often reluctant to think creatively is that they have preconceived notions about what can and can't be done. Although there are real constraints in almost all problem-solving situations, there is no harm in removing those constraints for a discussion that asks *"what if."* John Kao, the academic director of the Managing Innovation program at Stanford University, suggests that there are two types of knowledge. The first is raw knowledge, consisting of facts, information, and data. The second type of knowledge is insight, or the "Aha!" It is "a response to the *what ifs* and *if only we coulds.*"[38] Kao points out that it is "creativity that enables the transformation of one form of knowledge to the next."[39]

Here are some questions that the commemorative booklet committee could have asked: What if we had a million dollars to design and print the commemorative booklet; what would we do? What if the "booklet" were a videotape rather than a publication? What if we had one hundred pages to work with? What if we could hire a famous author to write the copy—what would the booklet "say"? Group members could consider one more "what if" scenario: What if we do nothing?[40] In other words, what are the consequences, if any, if we don't produce a commemorative booklet? Our own experience in working with groups is that a million-dollar idea can often be implemented with a few thousand dollars. An award-winning design can be created by an artist inspired by video imagery. Rousing words can be crafted by a talented copywriter.

Use Metaphors. The answers to many problems already exist. It's just that they are hiding in other areas of our lives.[41] These hiding places can be found in common metaphors. Metaphors can help group members explain, understand, guide, and direct their creative thinking in ways they would not have thought of otherwise.[42] For example, the metaphor of an emergency room has been used to redesign the registration process at some colleges. Students who don't need any help can register online or over the telephone. Those who need help are met by a kind of "triage nurse," a college advisor who can answer simple questions, direct them to a clerk for processing, or send them to a private room where they can receive "intensive care" from a "specialist" counselor. The beauty of metaphors is that they force group members to look at a problem in new and creative ways.

Despite our enthusiasm for creativity, there is a difference between "pure" creativity and creative problem solving. A highly creative group may not be a highly productive group. Let's face it: A freewheeling creative meeting can be

ETHICAL GROUPS

 ## The Morality of Creative Outcomes

In *Organizing Genius: The Secrets of Creative Collaboration*, Warren Bennis and Patricia Ward Biederman warn that "Creative collaboration is so powerful a phenomenon that it inevitably raises moral issues."[1] They use a chilling example—the Wannsee Question—to make their point. Wannsee, in a suburb of Berlin, is where Hitler's ministers gathered to formulate plans for exterminating the world's Jews. Creative collaboration produced an evil outcome. "The men at Wannsee were no geniuses, but, united by a single, evil vision, using cutting-edge technology and working with missionary zeal, they nearly destroyed an entire people in just three years."[2]

Ethics plays an important role in the creative process. John Rawls, a contemporary ethicist, reminds us to examine the consequences of group creativity. He believes that fairness is an important consideration in creative problem solving.[3] For example, creative groups need to ask if their creative innovations have the potential to help or hurt others. Should political consulting firms help the wealthiest or the worthiest candidates?

What are the consequences when corporate executives find creative ways to "cook the books" and collect millions of unearned dollars?

Many of the creative geniuses who collaborated to create and test the atomic bomb have subsequently struggled to deal with the consequences of their work. Dr. Richard Feynman, who was to win a Nobel Prize in Physics, was one of the scientists who created and built the atomic bomb. He recalls that the group became so caught up in the frenzy and excitement of creating the bomb that they didn't stop to think about the consequences. But when a colleague of Feynman's said, "It's a terrible thing that we made," he realized that they had unleashed the greatest terror on earth.[4]

[1] Warren Bennis and Patricia Ward Biederman, *Organizing Genius: The Secrets of Creative Collaboration* (Reading, MA: Addison-Wesley, 1997), p. 216.
[2] Bennis and Biederman, p. 217.
[3] John Rawls, *A Theory of Justice* (Cambridge: Harvard University Press, 1971).
[4] James Gleick, *Genius: The Life and Science of Richard Feynman* (New York: Vintage, 1992), p. 208.

a lot more fun than routine work. Once a group releases its creative energies, it may be reluctant to return to The Standard Agenda or the Nominal Group Technique to refine a solution. In such a case, a group must work out an internal balance between creative discussions and productive research, analysis, and action.[43] Kao compares balancing creativity and group process to tending the flames of a fire. "The spark needs air, breathing room, and freedom to ignite. But let the air blow too freely, and the spark will go out. Close all the doors and windows, and you will stifle it."[44]

PROBLEM-SOLVING REALITIES

Although procedures may be the most powerful tool available to improve the conduct of meetings, there are other factors that affect the outcome of every decision and problem that a group confronts. We would be remiss if we did not acknowledge that even the best of groups can be led astray when politics, preexisting preferences, and power infiltrate the group process. Group "decision making in the real world is often messy."[45]

Politics

In organizational settings, almost all decisions have a political component. Regardless of the procedures being used, many group members come to meetings with hidden agendas and political interests. Some members may never voice their real reasons for opposing a proposed solution, whereas others may withhold valuable information as a way of influencing the outcome of a discussion.

The motives for such actions often are political. A person who wants to get ahead may be reluctant to oppose an idea supported by the boss. A member who knows why a plan won't work may remain silent in order to make sure that the person responsible for implementing the plan fails. Although most conscientious group members do not engage in such deceptive behavior, it would be naive to proceed as though all members care equally about achieving the group's common goal. Meetings can become a political arena in which individuals and special-interest groups are dedicated to meeting their own private needs. Fortunately, the use of clear procedures can minimize the influence of such members.

Preexisting Preferences

An intelligent group member is rarely a blank slate who walks into a meeting uninformed and unconcerned about the topic or issue to be discussed. When a decision must be made, most of us know how we might decide. We may even have ideas about who should be in charge, how the task should be carried out, and when it should be completed. It would be a mistake to ignore the fact that many group members have preexisting preferences about what a group should do.

Fortunately, open discussions and the use of procedures ensure that these preferences are dealt with logically and fairly. For example, the functional approach to problem solving acknowledges that groups do not always discuss issues in a predetermined order. In fact, there may be nothing wrong with members coming to a meeting with proposed solutions as long as the group engages such members in a discussion of the pros and cons of their positions and makes sure that all members understand the nature and causes of the problem. As much as we may wish that everyone would follow the order of steps in The Standard Agenda, that rarely happens. The use of procedures can ensure that all of those steps are at least considered before a group makes its final decision.

Power

The power of individual group members can have a significant effect on the outcome of any meeting. It is no secret that powerful people influence group decisions. They affect how and whether other members participate, whose ideas and suggestions are given serious consideration, and which solutions are chosen. Highly influential members can convince a group "to accept invalid facts and assumptions, introduce poor ideas and suggestions, lead the group to misinterpret information presented to them, or lead the group off on tangents and irrelevant discussion."[46] In short, one powerful but misguided member can be responsible for the poor quality of a group's decision.

One of the major advantages of using an established procedure is that it can protect a group from the debilitating effects of politics, preexisting preferences, and powerful members. Procedures make the rules of engagement clear. Anyone violating those rules or failing to carry out assigned responsibilities may justly face isolation and criticism. It is rare for a group to escape the effects of politics, preexisting preferences, and power. Yet every group can benefit when appropriate procedures are used to guide it toward its common goal.

BALANCED PROBLEM SOLVING

When group decision making works efficiently and effectively, it offers both social and task rewards to group members. Balancing independence and groupwork is one of the keys to using meeting procedures effectively, particularly when groups are making important decisions or solving significant problems. Group communication scholar Marshall Scott Poole notes:

> To be effective, a group must maintain a golden mean, a balance between independent, creative thinking and structured, coordinated work. Too much independence may shatter group cohesion and encourage members to sacrifice group goals to their individual needs. . . . Too much structured work . . . is likely to regiment group thinking and stifle novel ideas.[47]

How, then, can groups balance such extreme requirements? The answer is procedures. Procedures provide explicit instructions that let members know when they can work alone and when they must work together. Procedures also tell a group how much effort must be spent gathering and analyzing information, generating ideas, offering suggestions, and arguing for or against proposals. When procedures are used wisely and well, they maximize creative thinking and, at the same time, encourage coordination of efforts. In such a balanced climate, a group is more likely to be creative, productive, and satisfied.

GROUPWORK

Game Building[48]

Goal: To demonstrate the value of creative problem solving

Participants: Groups of five to seven members

Procedure
1. Each group receives the following items:
   - One overhead transparency sheet
   - A transparency marker
   - Game components. For example, ten large soft plastic jacks of varying colors, five marbles, one large superball or marble, and so on

2. Groups have thirty minutes to create a game using all the items and to write the rules of the game on a *single* transparency.

3. A spokesperson or spokespersons from each group present the game and its rules to the rest of the class. The written rules must fit on one transparency.

4. Discussion questions:
   - What types of creative thinking were evident in the group?
   - Were some members more skilled at creative thinking, at organizing the group task, at expressing the rules, or at making the presentation?
   - In what group situations or jobs would these skills be needed or useful?

GROUPASSESSMENT

Problem-Solving Competencies

Directions. This instrument is designed to evaluate the performance of individual group members who participate in problem-solving discussions. There are five competencies related to accomplishing the group's task and three competencies dealing with conflict, climate, and interaction. Rate individual members and the group as a whole on each item in order to assess how well an observed group solves problems and makes important decisions.

Problem-Solving Competencies	Superior	Satis-factory	Unsatis-factory
1. *Defines and analyzes the problem* Appropriately clarifies, defines, and analyzes the problem confronting the group.			
2. *Identifies criteria.* Appropriately participates in identifying criteria for assessing the quality of the group's outcome.			
3. *Generates solutions.* Appropriately identifies potential solutions or options.			
4. *Evaluates solutions.* Appropriately evaluates the potential solutions and options.			
5. *Focuses on the task.* Helps the group stay focused on the task, issue, or agenda item under discussion.			
6. *Manages conflict.* Encourages constructive disagreements and appropriately manages nonproductive conflict.			
7. *Maintains collaborative climate.* Appropriately supports other group members.			
8. *Communicates effectively.* Interacts effectively and encourages other members to participate.			

Notes

1. *The American Heritage Dictionary of the English Language,* 4th ed. (Boston: Houghton Mifflin, 2000), p. 484.
2. Peter R. Drucker, *The Effective Executive* (New York: HarperBusiness, 1967), p. 143.
3. Rodney W. Napier and Matti K. Gershenfeld, *Groups: Theory and Experience,* 7th ed. (Boston: Houghton Mifflin, 2004), p. 319.
4. See Charles Pavitt and Ellen Curtis, *Small Group Discussion: A Theoretical Approach,* 2nd ed. (Scottsdale,

AZ: Gorsuch, Scarisbrick, 1994), pp. 25–52; Robert S. Cathcart, Larry A. Samovar, and Linda D. Henman, *Small Group Communication: Theory and Practice,* 7th ed. (Madison, WI: Brown & Benchmark, 1996), pp. 102–103; Donald G. Ellis and B. Aubrey Fisher, *Small Group Decision Making: Communication and the Group Process,* 4th ed. (New York: McGraw-Hill, 1994), pp. 17–18.

5. Julia T. Wood, "Alternative Methods of Group Decision Making," in *Small Group Communication: A Reader,* 6th ed., ed. Robert S. Cathcart and Larry A. Samovar (Dubuque, IA: Wm. C. Brown, 1992), p. 159.

6. Dennis S. Gouran, "Effective Versus Ineffective Group Decision Making," in *Managing Group Life: Communicating in Decision-Making Groups, ed.* Lawrence R. Frey and J. Kevin Barge (Boston: Houghton Mifflin, 1997), p. 139.

7. Marshall Scott Poole, "Procedures for Managing Meetings: Social and Technological Innovation," in *Innovative Meeting Management, ed.* Richard A. Swanson and Bonnie Ogram Knapp (Austin, TX: 3M Meeting Management Institute, 1990), pp. 54–55.

8. Pavitt and Curtis, p. 432.

9. Warren Bennis and Patricia Ward Biederman, *Organizing Genius: The Secrets of Creative Collaboration* (Reading, MA: Addison-Wesley, 1997), p. 17.

10. Bennis and Biederman, p. 20.

11. Lee Towe, *Why Didn't I Think of That?* (West Des Moines, IA: American Media, 1996), p. 7. Also see Craig E. Johnson and Michael Z. Hackman, *Creative Communication: Principles and Applications* (Prospect Heights, IL: Waveland, 1995), pp. 12–15.

12. Roger L. Firestein, "Effects of Creative Problem-Solving Training on Communication Behaviors in Small Groups," *Small Group Research, 21* (1990), pp. 507–521.

13. John Dewey, *How We Think* (Boston: Heath, 1910).

14. Based on Kathryn Sue Young et al, *Group Discussion: A Practical Guide to Participation and Leadership,* 3rd ed. (Prospect Heights, IL: Waveland, 2001).

15. J. Dan Rothwell, *In Mixed Company: Small Group Communication,* 5th ed. (Belmont, CA: Wadsworth/Thomson Learning, 2004), p. 193.

16. See Randy Y. Hirokawa and Roger Pace, "A Descriptive Investigation of the Possible Communication-Based Reasons for Effective and Ineffective Group Decision Making," *Communication Monographs, 50* (1983), pp. 363–379; Randy Y. Hirokawa and Dirk Scheerhorn, "Communication and Faulty Group Decision-Making," in *Communication and Group Decision-Making, ed.* Randy Y. Hirokawa and Marshall Scott Poole (Beverly Hills, CA: Sage, 1986), pp. 63–80; Dennis S. Gouran and Randy Y. Hirokawa, "Functional Theory and Communication in Decision-Making and Problem-Solving Groups," in *Communication and Group Decision Making,* 2nd ed., ed. Randy Y. Hirokawa and Marshall Scott Poole (Thousand Oaks, CA: Sage, 1996).

17. Gouran and Hirokawa, p. 76.

18. Gouran and Hirokawa, pp. 76–77.

19. Randy Y. Hirokawa, "Avoiding Camels: Lessons Learned in the Facilitation of High-Quality Group Decision Making Through Effective Discussion," the Van Zelst Lecture in Communication delivered at the School of Speech, Northwestern University, 1993, p. 10.

20. Frank LaFasto and Carl Larson, *When Teams Work Best* (Thousand Oaks, CA: Sage, 2001), pp. 84–85.

21. LaFasto and Larson, p. 85.

22. LaFasto and Larson, p. 88.

23. LaFasto and Larson, pp. 89–90.

24. LaFasto and Larson, p. 90.

25. Alex F. Osborn, *Applied Imagination,* rev. ed. (New York: Scribner's, 1957).

26. Tom Kelley with Jonathan Littman, *The Art of Innovation: Lessons in Creativity from IDEO, America's Leading Design Firm* (New York: Currency, 2001), p. 55.

27. Some of the brainstorming guidelines are based on Kelley and Littman, pp. 56–59.

28. 3M Meeting Management Team with Jeannine Drew, *Mastering Meetings: Discovering the Hidden Potential of Effective Business Meetings* (New York: McGraw-Hill, 1994), p. 59.

29. Andre L. Delbecq, Andrew H. Van de Ven, and David H. Gustafson, *Group Techniques for Program Planning* (Glenview, IL: Scott, Foresman, 1975).

30. Kelley and Littman, pp. 64–66.

31. P. Keith Kelly, *Team Decision-Making Techniques* (Irvine, CA: Richard Chang Associates, 1994), p. 29.

32. Delbecq et al., p. 8.

33. Delbecq et al., p. 8.

34. Kelly, p. 29.

35. See Kenneth E. Andersen, "Developments in Communication Ethics: The Ethics Commission, Code of Professional Responsibilities, and Credo for Ethical Communication," *Journal of the Association for Communication Administration, 29* (2000), pp. 131–144. The Credo for Ethical Communication is also posted on the National Communication Association's web site (*www.natcom.org*).

36. John Kao, *Jamming: The Art and Discipline of Business Creativity* (New York: HarperBusiness, 1997), p. 87.

37. Towe, p. 14.

38. Kao, p. 8.

39. Kao, p. 8.

40. Donald J. Noone, *Creative Problem Solving,* 2nd ed. (New York: Barron's, 1998), p. 60.

41. Towe, p. 77.

42. Noone, p. 93.

43. Clay Carr, *Team Leader's Problem Solver* (Englewood Cliffs, NJ: Prentice Hall, 1996), p. 230.

44. Kao, p. 17.

45. Dirk Scheerhorn, Patricia Geist, and Jean-Claude Teboul, "Beyond Decision Making in Decision-Making Groups: Implications for the Study of Group Communication," in *Group Communication in Context: Studies of Natural Groups, ed.* Lawrence R. Frey (Hillsdale, NJ: Erlbaum, 1994), p. 256.

46. Hirokawa and Pace, p. 379.

47. Poole, pp. 73–74.

48. Special thanks to Dianne Findley, professor of psychology at Prince George's Community College, who uses a similar exercise to demonstrate human development theories to her psychology students.

CHAPTER 10

Argumentation in Groups

CHAPTER OUTLINE

Why Argue?
Arguments and Argumentation • The Value of Argumentation in Groups

Argumentativeness
Argumentativeness and Group Decision Making • Learning to Be Argumentative

The Structure of an Argument
Components of the Toulmin Model • Applying the Toulmin Model • Supporting Evidence

Presenting Your Arguments
State the Claim • Support the Claim with Valid Evidence • Provide Reasons for the Claim • Summarize Your Argument

Refuting Arguments
Listen to the Argument • State the Claim You Oppose • Give an Overview of Your Objections • Assess the Evidence • Assess the Reasoning • Summarize Your Refutation

Adapting to Argumentative Styles
Gender Differences • Cultural Differences • Argumentation and Emotional Intelligence

Balanced Argumentation

GroupWork: Got Water?

GroupAssessment: Argumentativeness Scale

WHY ARGUE?

One of the advantages of working in groups is that members can share and discuss a variety of ideas and opinions. At the same time, a group must be able to agree on a particular position or action if it hopes to achieve its common goal. In order to balance the value and consequences of diverse opinions, group members must be able to advance their own viewpoints and discuss the views of others objectively. Successful groups encourage independent thinking and the exploration of ideas to discover the best solution. "This search for a common solution is often the result of a continuous exchange of arguments and counterarguments among participants."[1] In other words, group members must be able to argue.

Brashers, Adkins, and Meyers claim that "central to group discussion . . . is the process of argumentation."[2] Whether a group meets to share information or to reach a decision, members should be able to advance and evaluate different ideas, information, and opinions.

Arguments and Argumentation

We often think of an argument as a disagreement or hostile confrontation between two people. In communication studies, we define an **argument** as a claim supported by evidence or reasons for accepting it. An argument is more than an opinion: "The Latino Heritage Club should be given more funds next year." An argument is an idea or opinion *supported* by evidence and reasoning: "The Latino Heritage Club should be given more funds next year because it has doubled in size and cannot provide the same number or quality of programs without an increase in funding." When viewed this way, an argument does not have to involve conflict or even disagreement.

Argumentation is the way in which group members advocate their own positions, examine competing ideas, and influence other members. The following example illustrates a situation in which argumentation is an important group function:

> A college's Student Finance Board is made up of elected students who are responsible for distributing funds to campus clubs and organizations. The board meets throughout the academic year to consider funding requests. Clubs usually request more money than is available. Board members evaluate all requests and argue about the significance of each club's activities and the reasonableness of its funding request. Finally, the board decides how the funds should be distributed and submits those recommendations to the vice president for student services.

In such a decision-making group, members must read funding requests and listen to oral presentations by club members who argue that their organization should receive increased funding. Then, board members share their own positions

FIGURE 10.1   **Argumentation in Groups**

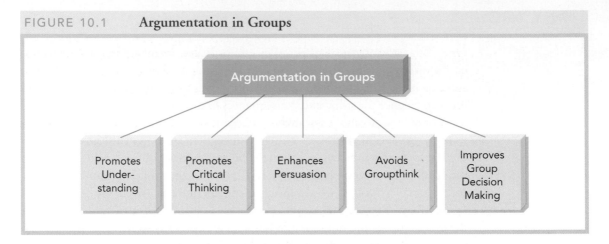

and, in many cases, find it necessary to argue for or against proposed funding levels for particular organizations. After a period of discussion and argumentation, the group makes its final decision—even though it knows that some club officers and advisors will argue that the decision was unfair or unjust.

The Value of Argumentation in Groups

Effective argumentation helps a group understand and analyze ideas, influence members, make informed and critical decisions, and achieve its goal. Thus, argumentation is a significant factor in determining how group communication influences decision making.

Promotes Understanding. Through the process of argumentation, you may discover that not all members reason in the same way. Some members may seek group goals; others may seek personal goals. Some may argue logically; others, emotionally. For example, as a member of the Student Finance Board, Charles argues in favor of funding the Philosophy Club because he is a club member. Karen supports the funding request because the club sponsored a successful forum last semester. Although both members support the same position, they do so for different reasons. Understanding how other group members reason and feel about individual issues can help you adapt your arguments to their perspectives.

Promotes Critical Thinking. Effective argumentation helps group members analyze issues and critically examine ideas. When you present your position on an issue, you may be challenged to justify that position to the rest of the group. You will need to provide strong evidence or sound reasons to support your conclusions. The process of argumentation often causes us to rethink our own positions and beliefs. Thus, the evaluation of arguments in groups encourages group members to think critically and flexibly.

Enhances Persuasion. Persuasion is communication that influences the beliefs or actions of others. Argumentation is a specific means of persuasion. As group members are exposed to different arguments, they can decide which ones are better supported and make more sense. Group members who are skilled at argumentation are often the most influential and persuasive.

Avoids Groupthink. Groupthink occurs when, as a result of an effort to discourage conflict and maintain group cohesion, a group makes flawed decisions. On the other hand, "unlike groups that engage in groupthink, groups trained to employ cooperative argumentation are able to form constructive forms of cohesion."[3] Constructive argumentation encourages the critical examination of opposing ideas without impairing group cohesion. As Chapter 7, "Conflict and Cohesion in Groups," explains, groupthink can be avoided if members ask questions, offer reasons for their positions, and seek justifications from others.

Improves Group Decision Making. As a group considers alternative ideas, argumentation helps the members examine the consequences of a potential action before making a final decision. Errors in reasoning are exposed, and weaknesses in evidence are uncovered. Argumentation in groups can also improve decision making because, unlike in one-on-one argumentation, several group members may work together to develop the same argument. In this "tag team" situation, other group members build upon the argument presented by one member by providing additional evidence or reasons to support a particular position. The result is a single comprehensive argument constructed cooperatively within the group.

Although there is strong evidence that argumentation can improve group decision making,[4] this conclusion is based on the underlying assumption that group members know how to develop and use arguments that will promote the group's goal. If argumentation is to be a constructive process, group members must know how to develop valid arguments and how to engage in cooperative argumentation with other group members.

ARGUMENTATIVENESS

In Chapter 4, "Confidence in Groups," the concept of communication apprehension is used to explain why some group members lack confidence in their ability to interact in a group. Similarly, researchers have suggested that individuals vary in how comfortable they feel about engaging in argumentation. This characteristic is referred to as **argumentativeness,** or the willingness to argue controversial issues with others.[5] Argumentativeness is a particularly constructive trait when it does not promote hostility or personal attacks. The argumentative person focuses on a discussion of the issues rather than on attacking personalities.

At the end of this chapter, there is a self-test called the Argumentativeness Scale. This questionnaire will help you identify your own level of argumentativeness.

You might want to complete the questionnaire and calculate your results before continuing with this chapter. Your score will help you understand how comfortable you are with arguing in groups.

Argumentativeness and Group Decision Making

An individual group member's level of argumentativeness provides some insight into how that group member will approach a discussion. Group members with lower levels of argumentativeness generally avoid conflict. These individuals are often viewed as not only nonconfrontational but also unskilled in argumentation. Because they are unwilling to engage in argumentation during group discussions, they have less influence in group decision making.

Group members who are highly argumentative welcome constructive conflict. They enjoy the intellectual challenge of an argument and show genuine interest in the discussion. Highly argumentative members defend their own positions confidently and challenge the arguments of others. Groups usually view their most argumentative members as dynamic and skillful arguers with high levels of credibility and influence. Argumentative members are frequently chosen as group leaders. On the other hand, they are less likely to be persuaded by others' arguments and may be perceived as inflexible and overly talkative.

Argumentative members are very influential in group decision making. In fact, argumentative group members create more arguments on *both* sides of a position.[6] When the number of choices a group can consider is thus expanded, the group is less likely to come to a biased decision or succumb to groupthink.

Learning to Be Argumentative

You can learn to argue. By practicing the skills in this chapter, you should become better able to argue your ideas and analyze the arguments of other group members. Learning to argue can also make you more influential in group decision making.

It is important to know how to achieve a balanced level of argumentativeness. Arguing too little can diminish your influence. On the other hand, members who are *extremely* argumentative can disrupt a group and its decision-making process. Effective group members know when to argue and when to acknowledge that someone else has made a good point.

THE STRUCTURE OF AN ARGUMENT

In the beginning—that is, during the time of Aristotle in ancient Greece—arguments were described as syllogisms, which have three parts:

Major premise: All men are mortal.

Minor premise: Socrates is a man.

Conclusion: So Socrates is mortal.

Stephen Toulmin, an English philosopher, believes that real-world arguments are less formal and more complex than this. He compares an argument to a living organism, with its own anatomical structure and specific physiological functions.[7] The **Toulmin Model of Argument** provides a way of both building strong arguments and refuting the arguments of others.

Components of the Toulmin Model

Before you can build or refute an argument, you need to understand the components of a complete argument. In his layout of an argument, Toulmin identifies six components: claim, data, warrant, backing, reservation, and qualifier.[8] The first three are essential in all arguments; the second three help clarify the nature and power of an argument's warrant.

Claim, Data, and Warrant.

The **claim** is the conclusion or position you are advocating. The **data** constitute the evidence you use to support your claim. For example, the statement "My group will do well on our class project" is a claim. The data for this claim might be the fact that during the first meeting, all members of the group said that they would work hard on the project. Data answer a challenger's questions: "What makes you say that?" or "What do you have to go on?"

Rather than answering the question "What have you got to go on?" a **warrant** answers the question "How did you get there?"[9] It explains how the data support and prove the claim. For example, the warrant might say that when group members are willing to work hard, a successful outcome is usually the result. The definition of the word *warrant* may help you understand this concept. A warrant can mean "justification for an action or belief" as in "Under the circumstances, the actions were warranted." A warrant is also something that provides assurance or confirmation, as in a *warrant of authenticity* or a *product warranty*. In legal terms, a warrant gives an officer the right to make a search, seizure, or arrest.[10] In argumentation, a warrant justifies your claim based on evidence. Also, as the definitions suggest, it authorizes or confirms the validity of a conclusion and gives you the right to make your claim. Here's an example of an unwarranted argument:

> Girlfriend to boyfriend: "You saw me walking to my car with your friend Dale, and you jumped to the conclusion that we were seeing each other behind your back. That inference is *unwarranted!*" In this argument, the evidence (she is walking to her car with Dale) is insufficient to make the claim (she's seeing Dale behind her boyfriend's back) because the warrant is unreasonable (if a woman is seen talking to a man, she must be dating him or having an affair with him).[11]

The relationship among these three components of the Toulmin Model is illustrated in Figure 10.2.

FIGURE 10.2   **"Basic T" of the Toulmin Model**

The argument in Figure 10.2 would sound like this: "All group members said that they would work hard. Because hard work usually results in success, the group will do well on the class project." The combined data, claim, and warrant make up the "basic T" of the Toulmin Model.

Backing, Reservation, and Qualifier.   Beyond the "basic T," there are three additional components: backing, reservation, and qualifier. The **backing** provides support for the argument's warrant. In the preceding example, backing for the warrant might be the fact that the group that worked the hardest on the last assignment received the best grade.

Not all claims are true all the time. The **reservation** is the component of the Toulmin Model that recognizes exceptions to an argument or indications that a claim may not be true under certain circumstances. At the first meeting, group members said that they would work hard. If, however, they do not attend important meetings, the group is unlikely to do well.

The final component of the model is the qualifier. The **qualifier** states the degree to which the claim appears to be true. Qualifiers are usually words or phrases such as *likely, possibly, certainly, unlikely,* or *probably.* A claim with a qualifier might be "The group will *probably* do well on the class project." The way this entire argument would look is shown in Figure 10.3.

Applying the Toulmin Model

The Toulmin Model is a way to diagram and evaluate arguments. You do not need to state each component of the argument when advancing your position. In fact, often only the claim is stated. However, understanding the model lets you know what questions to ask about an argument. If only the claim is stated, you may ask for evidence or data to support that claim. If the warrant is questionable, you may ask for backing to support it. Recognizing that situations may alter the certainty of your claim helps you advocate more reasonable positions. When you are developing your own arguments, the Toulmin Model can help you test the strength of those arguments. When you are analyzing someone else's argument, using the model helps reveal the strengths and weaknesses of the position.

FIGURE 10.3   **The Toulmin Model of an Argument**

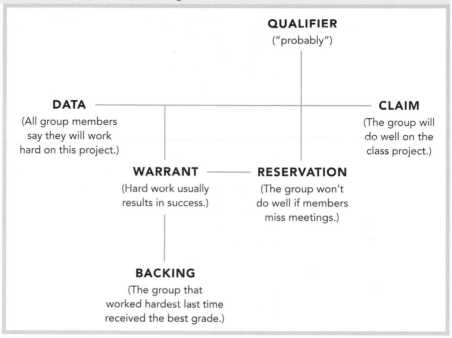

TOOLBOX 10.1

Warrants Change Claims

Warrants are the most difficult of Toulmin's components to understand and appreciate because they may not be expressed out loud. Warrants give you permission to make a claim based on evidence. They change claims in significant ways. Look at the following two arguments:[1]

Argument 1: Given that our reserves of fossil fuels are limited and will be used up in a few generations and that satisfactory alternative sources of energy are not yet available, industries must be allowed to continue using up the reserves of fossil fuel.

Argument 2: Given that our reserves of fossil fuels are limited and will be used up in a few generations and that satisfactory alternative sources of energy are not yet available, *industries may continue using up reserves of fossil fuel*

only if they accept their share of responsibility for developing alternative sources of energy.

What warrants the conclusion indicated in *italics* in Argument 2? Look at the way in which different warrants justify the claims in the two arguments:

Warrant for Argument 1: Because industry cannot function without fuel and society is dependent on industry, we must let industry go on doing what it has to do in order to keep society functioning.

Warrant for Argument 2: Because industry and society are jointly involved in a common venture, industry must adapt its activities to the broader needs of society.

[1] Based on an example in Stephen Toulmin, Richard Rieke, and Allan Janik, *An Introduction to Reasoning* (New York: Macmillan, 1979), p. 303.

Supporting Evidence

Arguments fall apart if the data used to support the claim and back the warrant are insufficient or flawed. All arguments gain strength when you research your position and use appropriate types of evidence to make your case. Data or evidence is listed first as an essential component of Toulmin's model of an argument. Evidence takes many forms: (1) facts and opinions, (2) definitions and descriptions, (3) examples and illustrations, and (4) statistics.

Facts and Opinions. Make sure that you and your group understand the differences between facts and opinions. A **fact** is a verifiable observation, experience, or event, something that is known to be true. An **opinion** is a personal conclusion regarding the meaning or implications of facts. Here is an example of a fact: In 1876, Colonel Henry M. Robert used the British Parliament's procedures and Thomas Jefferson's code of congressional rules as a basis for *Robert's Rules of Order.* Here are two disparate opinions:

- *Robert's Rules of Order* is outdated and makes a meeting more complicated than necessary.

- *Robert's Rules of Order* is time tested and ensures fair and objective decision making.

Unlike opinions, facts can usually be proved true or false. Group members should not mistake their opinions for facts.

When used as evidence, opinions usually express an authority's judgment or interpretation of facts. For example, "According to James C. McCroskey and Virginia Richmond, communication apprehension 'may be the single most important factor in predicting communication behavior in a small group.'" Keep in mind that different experts may not reach the same conclusions. Look for a variety of opinions rather than relying too heavily on claims that represent only one perspective.

Definitions and Descriptions. **Definitions** clarify the meaning of a word, phrase, or concept. A definition can be as simple as explaining what you mean by a word or as complex as an encyclopedia or unabridged dictionary entry. Here is an example:

> According to Warren Bennis and Bruce Nanus, "There is a profound difference between management and leadership, and both are important. 'To manage' means 'to bring about, to accomplish, to have charge of or responsibility for, to conduct.' 'Leading' is 'influencing, guiding in direction, course, action, opinion.'"

During an initial meeting, a group should define key terms. For example, a group dealing with sexual harassment policies should gather several definitions of sexual harassment. Groups negotiating legal contracts must carefully define their terms before an understanding can be reached between the parties.

   Descriptions go a step beyond definitions. Rather than clarifying the meaning of a word or concept, they create a mental image of a person, event, place, or object. Descriptions are more detailed than definitions. Causes, effects, historical contexts, characteristics, and operations can all be included in a description. Here is the beginning of a description of extroverts from Chapter 3: "Extroverts are outgoing, talkative, and enthusiastic; they enjoy interaction with others. Extroverts get their energy by being with people. They enjoy solving problems in groups and like to involve others in projects. . . ."

Examples and Illustrations. An **example** refers to a specific case or instance. Examples are usually brief. **Illustrations** are longer, extended examples that can take up an entire paragraph or tell a lengthy story. Here's a series of examples from the beginning of Chapter 1: "*Working in Groups* focuses on learning how to work effectively with others in many different group settings and circumstances—at school and at work, with family members and with friends, and in highly diverse arenas ranging from sports and science to courtrooms and classrooms." That same chapter opens with two illustrations—one about Dr. Peter Agre, winner of the 2003 Nobel Prize for Chemistry; the other about the Detroit Pistons winning the N.B.A. championship in 2004.

   It is important to remember that the examples and extended illustrations selected may not be typical of an entire category, situation, or group of people. If examples and illustrations are used as evidence to support a claim, you should make sure that they represent similar situations and results.

Statistics. Information presented in a numerical form is the basis for **statistics.** Statistics take various forms, including averages, percentages, rates, rankings, and so on. For example, in this textbook, you have read that according to James McCroskey and Virginia Richmond, "about 20 percent of the general population experiences very high levels of communication apprehension." You've also learned that according to the U.S. Census Bureau, "During the 1990s, the Hispanic population increased 58 percent, and the Asian population increased 48 percent."

   Many of us believe statistics, particularly when they're published by reputable sources. However, it is important to evaluate statistical findings carefully. The source and form of a statistic can result in different interpretations of the same numbers. Misinterpreting statistical information can jeopardize a group's effectiveness and success. For example, in 2005, the number of miles driven by Americans grew by just 1 percent, the smallest increase since the 1991 recession.[12] Here are some interpretations that could be claimed: (1) Health-conscious Americans are walking more and driving less, (2) Americans concerned about the environmental effects of automobile exhaust decreased their driving, and (3) record-high gas prices encouraged people to cut down on optional trips and use mass transit. Expert analysts identify the third reason as the correct interpretation.

PRESENTING YOUR ARGUMENTS

If your ideas are to be taken seriously by your group, your arguments must be well presented. Skilled arguers follow a four-step procedure for presenting arguments: state your claim, present evidence, provide reasons, and summarize.[13] This process is illustrated in Figure 10.4.

In some cases, you may not need to complete every step of the process when you present an argument. Often the evidence is sufficiently clear, and so you do not need to provide additional reasons for supporting your claim. If your argument is very brief, a summary may not be necessary. However, you should be prepared to complete all the steps if group members want further justification for your arguments.

State the Claim

The first step in the presentation of an argument is a clear statement of your claim. In Chapter 9, "Structured and Creative Problem Solving in Groups," we identify four types of discussion questions—fact, conjecture, value, and policy. Discussion questions help a group focus on its goal. Claims for arguments can be divided into the same four categories. However, when presenting arguments, group members rarely state their claims in the form of questions. A claim is a statement that identifies your position on a particular issue.

Arguments involving a **claim of fact** attempt to prove that something is true, that an event occurred, or that a cause can be identified. For example, "Sex education in schools promotes teenage promiscuity" is a claim of fact. Whether this claim is true or not depends on further analysis of the data and the warrant. A **claim of conjecture** suggests that something will or will not happen. For example, you could say, "Our profits will decrease by 10 percent by next quarter." Although your group cannot predict the future, it can make well-informed decisions

What strategies can help this union member make his argument clear and persuasive?
(© Susie Fitzhugh)

FIGURE 10.4   **Procedure for Presenting Arguments**

CLAIM ⟶ EVIDENCE ⟶ REASONS ⟶ SUMMARY

based on the best information available. **Claims of value** assert that something is worthwhile—good or bad; right or wrong; best, average, or worst. "My instructor is the best professor at the college" is a claim that places a value on someone. Arguments involving claims of value can be very difficult to resolve because each group member brings personal opinions and beliefs to the discussion. **Claims of policy** are arguments that recommend a particular course of action. "Our company should develop guidelines for dealing with inquiries from the press and the electronic media" is an example of a claim of policy.

Support the Claim with Valid Evidence

The fact that a claim is stated does not mean that it is true. In order to be convincing, you must support your claim with data. In the Toulmin Model, this means supplying the group with strong and valid evidence. Regardless of whether that evidence takes the form of facts, opinions, definitions, descriptions, examples, illustrations, or statistics, groups should continuously evaluate the quality of any evidence presented by asking several general questions:

- Is the source of the evidence reputable and credible?

- Is the evidence recent or dated?

- Does the evidence contain all the facts, or does it hide unfavorable information?

- Is it consistent with other evidence?

- Is there enough evidence?

Provide Reasons for the Claim

Sometimes it is not clear to others why a particular piece of evidence proves your claim. In such cases, reasons are needed to demonstrate the link between your evidence and your claim. In the Toulmin Model, this link is the warrant and the backing—statements that explain why the evidence is sufficient to prove the claim.

A prosecutor might argue that one of the reasons a jury should convict a murder suspect is that he lied about knowing the victim. At first, it may not be clear why or how evidence that the suspect lied is linked to his being a murderer. The prosecutor might then provide the argument's warrant by stating that unlike guilty people, the innocent have nothing to hide. Evidence of lying may weaken the defendant's claim of innocence.

TOOLBOX 10.2

Test the Validity of Statistics

Determining the validity of statistics generally requires answers to three questions. First, what is the source of the statistics? Knowing who or what organization collected and published the statistical information may alert a group to biases. For example, when tobacco company studies found no relationship between cigarette smoking and cancer rates, their results were treated with great skepticism.

Second, are the statistics accurate? Often statistics are generated by surveying or observing people. Statistical research that includes too few people or subjects who are not representative of the studied population may be invalid. For example, one study examined the effects of diet on breast cancer by studying only men.[1] Clearly, the exclusion of women from the study makes any results or conclusions suspect.

Third, how are the statistics reported? The way in which the source chooses to report the statistic can conceal or distort information. For example, group members who have been told that customer complaints have increased 100 percent over the past year may believe that they have a serious issue to address. Upon closer examination of the statistic, though, they may discover that last year only two customers complained, and this year four complaints were reported. The problem no longer appears to be as serious.

[1] Carol Tavris, *The Mismeasure of Woman* (New York: Simon & Schuster, 1992), p. 94.

Summarize Your Argument

A good summary restates the original claim and summarizes the evidence supporting it. Be brief. Do not repeat all your evidence and reasons. When the presentation of the claim and the evidence has been brief and clear, the summary can be omitted. However, lengthy and complicated arguments often need to be summarized to ensure that all members understand your argument.

REFUTING ARGUMENTS

Refutation is the process of proving that an argument is false and/or lacks sufficient support. Refutation is used to question, minimize, and deny the validity or strength of someone else's argument. Group members should be willing and able to refute claims that are unsupported or untrue. A group that is not willing to evaluate arguments risks the perils of groupthink. Six guidelines can help you refute another member's argument:

- Listen to the argument.
- State the claim you oppose.
- Give an overview of your objections.
- Assess the evidence.
- Assess the reasoning.
- Summarize your refutation.

GROUPTECH

Argumentation in Virtual Groups

The process of argumentation is the same in face-to-face and virtual groups. However, virtual groups may find that the nature of some technologies can improve the quality of their argumentation, while other forms of technology may inhibit constructive and cooperative argumentation.

In face-to-face meetings and in real-time audioconferences and videoconferences, arguments may arise spontaneously and require members to "think on their feet," with little time for thought or preparation. In online, text-based settings—email, electronic bulletin boards, and chat rooms—members of virtual groups usually have more time to develop and support their arguments. When communication is asynchronous, group members may have hours or even days to construct or respond to arguments in writing. Having more time also allows members to search for and share the best supporting evidence they can find.

There are, however, some precautions to heed when virtual groups engage in argumentation. Poorly prepared arguments, unfounded claims, and insensitive or rude criticism can become part of a permanent record. Online arguments can be saved, stored, and shared at a later date. Audioconferences and videoconferences can be recorded on tape. Thus, a thoughtless remark or foolish argument can be quoted exactly for years to come or shared with nongroup members.

As is the case in face-to-face interaction, argumentation that is characterized by personal attacks, sarcasm, or demeaning remarks has no place in virtual group discussions. Fear of rejection, personal attacks, and ridicule can inhibit interaction and group effectiveness. Fortunately, in text-based virtual groups, members can take the time to ensure that their arguments are constructive, respectful, and effective.

Listen to the Argument

First, listen for comprehension. You must fully understand an argument before you can respond to it effectively. Ask questions and take notes. Once you have comprehended the meaning of an argument, you can shift to critical listening. What type of claim is being made? Is evidence supplied to support the claim? How well does the evidence support the claim? Is the claim qualified in any way? Analyzing the argument as you listen will help you formulate a response.

State the Claim You Oppose

Different group members may have made a number of claims during an argumentative discussion. Don't try to respond to all of them at once. When you are ready, state the claim that you are opposing. Clearly stating the claim that you oppose gives you an opportunity to make sure that you understand the argument. You may think the claim was "employees are stealing supplies from the company." Instead, the claim was "the company should identify ways to use supplies more efficiently." If you have misunderstood a claim, other group members can clarify their arguments for you.

Give an Overview of Your Objections

Provide a brief overview of your objections or concerns. Letting the group know the general direction of your arguments is particularly important when your refutation will be lengthy or complicated, such as "I don't believe we should raise funds for a carnival for three reasons: the high cost, the unpredictable weather, and the undesirable location." If they have a general idea of the reasons for your refutation, group members will be better prepared to listen to and understand your objections and concerns.

Assess the Evidence

When refuting a claim, you may be able to show that the evidence supporting the claim is faulty. One way to do this is to present contradictory evidence. For example, if a group member contends that the college's tuition is high, you may present evidence from a survey showing that the college's tuition is one of the lowest in the state. You can also question the quality of the person's evidence. For example, an outdated statistic or a quotation by a discredited source can be reason enough to reject an arguer's evidence. Proving that the evidence is of poor quality does not mean that the claim is untrue, but it does show that the claim has potential weaknesses.

Assess the Reasoning

Assess reasoning by identifying fallacies. A **fallacy** is an argument that is based on false or invalid reasoning. It is not always necessary to identify the fallacy by name, particularly if group members are not familiar with the different types of fallacies. It is much more important to clearly explain why the reasoning in the argument is flawed. Figure 10.5 lists some of the most common fallacies of an argument, which are described further here.

- *Ad hominem* **attack.** In Latin, this phrase means "to the person." An *ad hominem* argument makes irrelevant attacks about a person's character rather than responding to the argument. Responding to a claim that children should attend school year-round with "What would you know? You don't have kids" is an attack on the person rather than on the real argument. Unfortunately, negative political campaigns have become little more than a series of *ad hominem* attacks that often prove false when fully investigated.

- **Appeal to authority.** Expert opinion is often used to support arguments. However, when the supposed expert has no relevant expertise on the issues being discussed, the fallacy of appeal to authority occurs. The argument that "according to a talk show host, most men cheat on their wives" commits this

FIGURE 10.5   **Fallacies of an Argument**

Fallacy	Description
AD HOMINEM ATTACK	Attacks the person rather than the argument made by that person.
APPEAL TO AUTHORITY	Relies on biased or unqualified expert opinion to support a claim.
APPEAL TO POPULARITY	Justifies an action because many others do the same thing or share the same opinion. "Everyone's doing it."
APPEAL TO TRADITION	Resists changes to traditional behavior and opinions. "We have always done it this way."
FAULTY ANALOGY	Compares two items that are not similar or comparable. "Comparing apples and oranges."
FAULTY CAUSE	Claims that an effect is caused by something that has little or no relationship to the effect.
HASTY GENERALIZATION	Uses isolated or too few examples to draw a conclusion.

fallacy. Unless the talk show host has expert credentials on issues of fidelity and marriage, the argument is vulnerable.

- **Appeal to popularity.** An argument of this nature claims that an action is acceptable or excusable because many people are doing it. During the Los Angeles riots following the Rodney King trial and the looting of stores after Hurricane Katrina hit New Orleans, some people justified their actions by claiming that everyone else was doing it. Just because a lot of people engage in an action does not make it right. Instead, it may mean that a lot of people are wrong.

- **Appeal to tradition.** Claiming that people should continue a certain course of action because they have always done so in the past is an appeal to tradition, as illustrated in the argument that "the group must meet on Monday afternoons because that is when the group has always met." Just because a course of action has been followed for a long period of time does not mean that it is the superior choice.

- **Faulty analogy.** Claiming that two things are similar when they differ on relevant characteristics is a faulty analogy. During Operation Desert Storm (the conflict before the war in Iraq), critics claimed that the United States was involving itself in another Vietnam. However, the argument was frequently refuted by pointing out critical differences between these two engagements, particularly the fact that the U.S. military action in Operation Desert Storm had a specific objective and was over in a relatively short time. Faulty analogies are often referred to as the comparison of "apples and oranges." Both are fruits, but beyond that they are very different.

- **Faulty cause.** Claiming that a particular event is the cause of another event before ruling out other possible causes is a faulty-cause fallacy. The claim that "increases in tuition have caused enrollment to decline" may overlook other explanations, such as the possibility that a decline in enrollment could be a result of fewer eligible high school graduates.

- **Hasty generalization.** An argument flawed by a hasty generalization uses too few examples or experiences to support its conclusion. This fallacy argues that if it is true for some, it must be true for all. "A Volvo is an unreliable car because I once owned one that was always breaking down" is a hasty generalization. The experience of a single car owner does not prove that all cars produced by that manufacturer are unreliable.

Summarize Your Refutation

The final step in refuting a group member's argument is to summarize your response. If your refutation has been lengthy or complex, it is helpful to restate the major points of your response. It is not necessary to review all your arguments in detail because doing so wastes valuable group discussion time. If your refutation has been short and to the point, it may not be necessary to summarize your argument.

ADAPTING TO ARGUMENTATIVE STYLES

Research suggests that men and women argue differently. There also are argumentation differences among people from different cultures. These differences appear to be a function of how we learn to argue and what values we believe are important. Effective group members recognize and try to adapt to others' ways of arguing.

Gender Differences

In a study of sex differences in group argumentation, researchers found that women and men argue differently in small group decision-making interactions.[14] Men tend to be competitive arguers; women, on the other hand, are more likely to seek consensus within a group. Men tend to view issues as only two-sided—for or against, right or wrong. Women are more likely to search out many different

ETHICAL GROUPS

 ## Ethical Arguments in Groups

Regardless of how persuasively an argument is presented, group members should also strive to be ethical arguers. Group members have four ethical responsibilities when they engage in argumentation: research responsibility, common good responsibility, reasoning responsibility, and social code responsibility.[1]

Research responsibility means that group members are expected to come to the discussion informed and prepared to discuss the issues. Information must be used honestly. To fulfill this responsibility, follow these guidelines:

* Do not distort information.
* Do not suppress important information.
* Never fabricate or make up information.
* Reveal the sources of information so that others can evaluate them.

The common good responsibility requires that ethical arguers look beyond their own needs and consider the circumstances of others. Members of a group should be committed to achieving the group goal rather than merely winning an argument. The following two principles are important for fulfilling the common good responsibility:

* Consider the interests of those affected by the decision.
* Promote the group's goal as more important than winning an argument.

The reasoning responsibility requires members to avoid presenting faulty arguments. Understanding the structure of an argument, methods of building a persuasive argument, and ways to recognize fallacies will help you fulfill this ethical responsibility, as will following these rules:

* Do not misrepresent the views of others.
* Use sound reasoning supported by evidence.
* Avoid making arguments containing fallacies.

The final ethical consideration is the social code responsibility. This requires that group members promote an open and supportive climate for argumentation. Follow these guidelines for fulfilling the social code responsibility:

* Treat other group members as equals.
* Give everyone, including those who disagree, the opportunity to respond to an argument.
* Do not insult or attack the character of a group member.
* Give the group an opportunity to review the evidence.
* Respect established group norms.

[1] Karyn Charles Rybacki and Donald Jay Rybacki, *Advocacy and Opposition: An Introduction to Argumentation*, 3rd ed. (Boston: Allyn & Bacon, 1966), pp. 10–13. Subsequent editions of Rybacki and Rybacki do not include these four responsibilities, but do discuss ethical standards for argumentation. See Karyn Charles Rybacki and Donald Jay Rybacki, *Advocacy and Opposition: An Introduction to Argumentation*, 5th ed. (Boston: Allyn & Bacon, 2004), pp. 14–21.

perspectives on a subject as well as ask questions. However, there were no differences in men's and women's production of facts, opinions, or evidence. In addition, men and women were relatively equal in their voicing of objections to others' statements. Of course, many women enjoy a direct and competitive debate. In fact, when women make up the majority of group members, they become more comfortable stating and supporting their opinions and disagreeing with others.

"In such situations, women may feel more empowered to forego communicative stereotypes, and take on interactive roles that are typically reserved for men."[15]

Although research provides generalizations about gender differences in argumentation, there are always exceptions. In her book *The Argument Culture,* Deborah Tannen cautions that "the forces of gender are far more complex than a simple male-female dichotomy suggests. Many variations exist, shaped by culture, geography, class, sexual orientation, and individual personality."[16] At the same time, it is useful to recognize that men and women may come to a group with different argumentation styles. Groups should create an environment in which everyone feels comfortable arguing.

We caution you against stereotyping the way men and women argue. Don't assume that the women in your group are more submissive and the men are more assertive. Instead we prefer a dialectic approach. Groups benefit when members value both competition and cooperation. When group members argue, they must balance "the tension between the need to agree and disagree, to challenge and reach convergence, to ask questions and make statements." Although these "tasks may be divided along gender lines . . . there is nothing inherently superior or inferior about either men's or women's communication. They may be different, but they are both necessary and equally important to the group's success in argument."[17]

Cultural Differences

Approaches to argumentation are often influenced by members' cultures. Cultural perspectives can influence the level of argumentativeness, the values that form the basis for arguments, and the approaches to evidence and reasoning. Some cultures are not as argumentative as others. For example, Asians and Asian Americans are generally less comfortable engaging in an argument. Asians may go to great lengths to preserve the harmony of a group, preferring to avoid an argument because it could jeopardize that harmony.[18] It is important, however, not to overgeneralize about the characteristics of any culture. There are significant differences among Asian cultures. For instance, in some Indian subcultures, argumentation is encouraged.

Culture also may dictate who should argue. Many cultures give enormous respect to their elders. In these cultures, a young person arguing with an older adult is viewed as disrespectful. Among several American Indian and African cultures, the elderly are viewed as wiser and more knowledgeable. The young are taught that the views of the elderly are to be accepted rather than challenged.

One of the most significant cultural differences in argumentation is the way in which people use evidence to support a claim. According to Myron Lustig and Jolene Koester,

> There are no universally accepted standards about what constitutes evidence. Among many devout Muslims and Christians, for instance, parables or stories— particularly from the Koran or bible—are a powerful form of evidence. . . . The European American culture prefers physical evidence and eyewitness

testimony, and members of that culture see "facts" as the supreme kind of evidence . . . [whereas] in certain portions of Chinese culture . . . physical evidence is discounted because no connection is seen between . . . the physical world and human actions. . . . In certain African cultures, the words of a witness would be discounted and even totally disregarded because the people believe that if you speak up about seeing something, you must have a particular agenda in mind; in other words, no one is regarded as objective.[19]

Given such different perspectives about the value of evidence, the data used to support a claim in one culture may seem irrational in another.

Argumentation and Emotional Intelligence

Daniel Goleman, author of *Emotional Intelligence*, defines **emotional intelligence** as the "capacity for recognizing our own feelings and those of others, for motivating ourselves, and for managing emotions well in ourselves and in our relationships."[20] At first, it may seem as though emotional intelligence has nothing to do with group argumentation. Yet, in many ways, emotional intelligence represents a significant aspect of effective argumentation. Think of it this way: The role of emotions in argumentation can take two forms: (1) curbing inappropriate emotions and (2) expressing appropriate emotions. Effective group members understand the need for both and learn how to balance their use. We have adapted Goleman's list of the five basic competencies of emotionally intelligent people to groups and their members:[21]

- *Self-awareness.* Group members recognize how they are feeling at the moment and use that knowledge to guide the way they communicate and make decisions. If you are aware, for example, that your voice is getting louder and you are becoming increasingly angry with someone, you may decide to lower your voice, defuse your anger, and respond to the other person with respect.

- *Self-regulation.* Group members handle their emotions responsibly, delay personal gratification to pursue group goals, and recover well from emotional distress. This does not mean suppressing your emotions; instead, self-regulation means understanding your emotions and using that understanding to deal with situations effectively.

- *Self-motivation.* Group members tap their emotional needs as sources of motivation. These feelings often enable members to be resourceful, take initiative, strive to improve group performance, and persevere in the face of setbacks and frustrations. When emotions cloud your ability to move ahead, motivation provides the energy to continue.

- *Empathy.* Group members with emotional intelligence accurately sense what other members are feeling and are able to understand and establish rapport with diverse group members. Such members analyze their relationships and emotions objectively and then have the sensitivity to respond appropriately and helpfully.

- *Social skills.* Communication skills are the foundation of social skills. Emotionally intelligent group members can read social situations and choose effective communication strategies that help them cooperate, persuade, negotiate, and lead others. These strategies require a variety of communication skills, including openness, assertiveness, listening, constructive criticism, and group communication competencies.

When group members argue about the wisdom of adopting a controversial proposal, whether to hire an unconventional applicant for an important job, or how to break bad news to colleagues, they may need emotional intelligence to help them achieve their goal. In some cases, members will have to cool down and curb their emotions. In other circumstances, they can exert more influence by heating up a discussing and displaying strong emotions.

If group members become highly emotional or aggressive during a group discussion, you may be able to cool things down by suppressing your own emotions and using the following tactics (all of which relate to a characteristic of emotional intelligence):

- *Self-awareness:* Calm down, tune in to your own feelings, and be willing to share those feelings with group members.

- *Self-confidence:* Show that you are willing to work things out by talking over the issue rather than escalating it.

- *Self-control:* State your own point of view in neutral language rather than in a combative tone.

- *Empathy:* Look for an equitable way to resolve the dispute by working with those who disagree to find a resolution that both sides can embrace.[22]

If you care about your group and its goal, you may want to express your emotions openly as a way of intensifying what you say. If, for example, your group needs motivation, you may enlist your emotions to express "infectious" enthusiasm and passion. If, however, your group is considering a decision that you see as unethical or potentially disastrous, an appropriate burst of anger and sorrow may help to underscore your arguments. Emotions are attention grabbers, operating as warnings, alarms, and motivators. They generate powerful messages by conveying crucial information without putting those data into words.[23]

BALANCED ARGUMENTATION

Effective arguers balance their own need to win an argument with the need of the group to solve a problem or make a decision. Argumentation in groups should be cooperative rather than competitive.

Josina Makau and Debian Marty define **cooperative argumentation** as "a process of reasoned interaction . . . intended to help participants and audiences

TOOLBOX 10.3

The Origins of Emotional Intelligence

Many people mistakenly believe that Daniel Goleman, author of *Emotional Intelligence*, created the concept of emotional intelligence. Goleman, who has a Ph.D. in psychology and previously reported behavioral and brain science news for the *New York Times*, does not claim this honor for himself. He fully acknowledges that fact in his books. Here's what he writes about the origins of emotional intelligence:

> A comprehensive theory of emotional intelligence was proposed in 1990 by two psychologists, Peter Salovey and John Mayer. Another pioneering model of emotional intelligence was proposed in the 1980s by Reuven Bar-On, an Israeli psychologist. . . . Salovey and Mayer defined emotional intelligence in terms of being able to monitor and regulate one's own feelings and to use feeling to guide thought and action.[1]

In addition to those whom Goleman credits, we recommend the works of Dr. Antonio Damasio, a neurosurgeon who links emotions to human consciousness and—most important for the study of communication—decision-making ability.[2] Damasio is concerned with what happens when people cannot make emotions work for them. He began his investigation by studying patients with damage to the emotional center of their brains. He notes that these patients make terrible decisions even though their IQ scores stay the same. So even though they test as "smart," they "make disastrous choices in business and their personal lives, and can even obsess endlessly over a decision so simple as when to make an appointment." Their decision-making skills are poor because they have lost access to their emotions. Damasio concludes that feelings are *indispensable* for rational decision making.[3]

Consider whether you could answer any of these questions without taking emotions into account: "Whom should I marry?" "What career should I pursue? "Should I buy this house?" Now put these kinds of questions into a group context: "What are the human consequences of our decision or solution?" "Should I let the others in my group know how uncomfortable I am with their proposed actions?" "What should I say to a bereaved colleague?"

[1] Daniel Goleman, *Emotional Intelligence* (New York: Bantam Book, 1995), p. 42.
[2] Goleman, pp. 27–28. Also see Antonio R. Damasio, *Descartes' Error: Emotion, Reason, and the Human Brain* (New York: Quill, 2000).
[3] See Damasio, *Descartes' Error*; Antonio Damasio, *The Feeling of What Happens: Body and Emotion in the Making of Consciousness* (San Diego: Harvest/Harcourt, 1999).

make the best assessments or the best decisions in any given situation."[24] Cooperative arguers focus on the group's shared goal of solving a problem or making the best decision. They recognize that the group will be better informed if there is an open exchange of ideas. Those who disagree should be viewed as resources, not rivals. Although cooperative arguers want to win arguments, they do not want to do so at the expense of the group goal.

Certainly you should present your best arguments in the hopes of persuading others. However, keep in mind that winning is not as important as helping the group make the best possible decision, which may not happen to include your ideas. Effective arguers are willing to share their views at the risk of losing the argument. Cooperative group members adhere to ethical guidelines and recognize that the arguments of all group members are potentially valid and should receive a fair hearing. "Balancing the tension between the need to agree and disagree, to challenge and reach convergence, to ask questions and make statements, is the central paradox of effective argument in decision-making groups."[25]

GROUPWORK

Got Water?

Goal: To recognize, analyze, and evaluate argumentation

Participants: Groups of five to seven members

Procedure:

1. After reading the *Got Water?* passage, each group should answer the following questions about Standage's arguments:

   a. List at least three claims made in the argument.
   b. What specific types of evidence does Standage use to support his claims?
   c. What are the implied warrants in his argument?
   d. Does he provide backing for the warrants, reservations, or qualifiers of his argument?
   e. Are there any other claims that could be added to make this argument even more persuasive?
   f. What claims would you use to refute part or all of his argument?
   g. Overall, how effective are Standage's arguments?

2. Time permitting, each group should share its answers and conclusions with the class to create a composite list of answers.

Got Water?

In the August 12, 2005, edition of the *New York Times*, Tom Standage writes that Americans squander billions of dollars on bottled water. Americans drink, on average, 24 gallons of bottled water a year; among beverages, only soda outsells it. And it's not a bargain. In fact, a gallon of Evian or Poland Spring costs more than a gallon of gasoline—which explains how we're spending $10 billion a year on the stuff. But why do we do it? Not for the taste. In blind tastings between bottled water and tap water from major municipal systems, "most people cannot tell the difference." Tests show that bottled water is just as likely as tap water to contain contaminants, while offering no nutritional advantage. And whereas tap water is nearly free, plentiful, and has no negative impact on the environment, shipping and refrigerating bottled water consumes a lot of energy and creates serious disposal problems.

Argumentativeness Scale

Directions. This questionnaire contains statements about arguing over controversial issues. Indicate how often each statement is true for you personally by placing the appropriate number in the blank. Use the following ratings to respond to each statement:

1 = almost never true
2 = rarely true
3 = occasionally true
4 = often true
5 = almost always true

_____ 1. While in an argument, I worry that the person I am arguing with will form a negative impression of me.

_____ 2. Arguing over controversial issues improves my intelligence.

_____ 3. I enjoy avoiding arguments.

_____ 4. I am energetic and enthusiastic when I argue.

_____ 5. Once I finish an argument, I promise myself that I will not get into another.

_____ 6. Arguing with a person creates more problems for me than it solves.

_____ 7. I have a pleasant, good feeling when I win a point in an argument.

_____ 8. When I finish arguing with someone, I feel nervous and upset.

_____ 9. I enjoy a good argument over a controversial issue.

_____ 10. I get an unpleasant feeling when I realize I am about to get into an argument.

_____ 11. I enjoy defending my point of view on an issue.

_____ 12. I am happy when I keep an argument from happening.

_____ 13. I do not like to miss the opportunity to argue about a controversial issue.

_____ 14. I prefer being with people who rarely disagree with me.

_____ 15. I consider an argument an exciting intellectual exchange.

_____ 16. I find myself unable to think of effective points during an argument.

_____ 17. I feel refreshed after an argument on a controversial issue.

_____ 18. I have the ability to do well in an argument.

_____ 19. I try to avoid getting into arguments.

_____ 20. I feel excitement when I expect that a conversation I am in is leading to an argument.

Scoring Instructions

1. Add your scores on items 2, 4, 7, 9, 11, 13, 15, 17, 18, and 20.

2. Add 60 to the sum obtained in step 1.

3. Add your scores on items 1, 3, 5, 6, 8, 10, 12, 14, 16, and 19.

4. To compute your argumentativeness score, subtract the total obtained in step 3 from the total obtained in step 2.

Interpretation of Scores

73–100 = high in argumentativeness

56–72 = moderate in argumentativeness

20–55 = low in argumentativeness

Source: "Argumentativeness Scale" by Dominic A. Infante and Andrew Rancer from *The Journal of Personality Assessment,* 1982. Reprinted by permission of Lawrence Erlbaum Associates and the authors.

NOTES

1. Tung Bui, Francois Bodart, and Pai-chun Ma. "ARBAS: A Formal Language to Support Argumentation in Network-Based Organizations," *Journal of Management Information Systems, 14* (Winter 1997/1998), p. 223.

2. Dale E. Brashers, Mark Adkins and Renee A. Meyers, "Argumentation and Computer-Mediated Group Decision Making," in *Group Communication in Context: Studies of Natural Groups, ed.* Lawrence R. Frey (Hillsdale, NJ: Erlbaum, 1994), p. 264.

3. Josina M. Makau, *Reasoning and Communication: Thinking Critically About Arguments* (Belmont, CA: Wadsworth, 1990), p. 54.

4. See Sandra M. Ketrow and Beatrice G. Schultz, "Using Argumentative Functions to Improve Decision Quality in the Small Group," in *Argument and the Postmodern Challenge: Proceedings of the Eighth SCA/AFA Conference on Argumentation, ed.* Raymie E. McKerrow (Annandale, VA: Speech Communication Association, 1993), pp. 218–225.

5. Dominic A. Infante and Andrew S. Rancer, "A Conceptualization and Measure of Argumentativeness," *Journal of Personality Assessment, 46* (1982), pp. 72–80.

6. Dean C. Kazoleas and Bonnie Kay, "*Are Argumentatives Really More Argumentative? The Behavior of Argumentatives in Group Deliberations over Controversial Issues,*" paper presented at the meeting of the Speech Communication Association, New Orleans, LA, 1994.

7. Stephen Toulmin, *The Uses of Argument* (London: Cambridge University, 1958), p. 94.

8. Toulmin, pp. 97–113.

9. Toulmin, p. 99.

10. *The American Heritage Dictionary of the English Language* (Boston: Houghton Mifflin, 2000), p. 1940.

11. Based on an example in Stephen Toulmin, Richard Rieke, and Allan Janik, *An Introduction to Reasoning* (New York: Macmillan, 1979), p. 45.

12. USA Today, quoted in The Week, January 6, 2006, p. 16.

13. Dominic A. Infante and Andrew S. Rancer, *Arguing Constructively* (Prospect Heights, IL: Waveland, 1988), p. 57

14. Renee A. Meyers, Dale Brashers, LaTonia Winston, and Lindsay Grob, "Sex Differences and Group Arguments: A Theoretical Framework and Empirical Investigation," *Communication Studies,* 48 (1997), p. 33.

15. Meyers et al, pp. 35–36.

16. Deborah Tannen, *The Argument Culture: Moving from Debate to Dialogue* (New York: Random House, 1998), p. 167.

17. Meyers et al, pp. 35–36.

18. Richard E. Porter and Larry A. Samovar, "Communication in the Multicultural Group," in *Small Group Communication: Theory and Practice*, 7th ed., ed. Robert S. Cathcart, Larry A. Samovar, and Linda D. Henman (Madison, WI: Brown & Benchmark, 1996), p. 311.

19. Myron W. Lustig and Jolene Koester, *Intercultural Competence: Interpersonal Communication Across Cultures*, 5th ed. (Boston: Allyn & Bacon, 2006), p. 241.

20. Daniel Goleman, *Working with Emotional Intelligence* (New York: Bantam, 1998), p. 317.

21. Based on Goleman, p. 318. Also see Henrie Weisinger, *Emotional Intelligence at Work* (San Francisco: Jossey-Bass, 1998), pp. xix–xxii.

22. Goleman, p. 182.

23. Goleman, p. 165.

24. Josina M. Makau and Debian L. Marty, *Cooperative Argumentation: A Model for Deliberative Community* (Prospect Heights, IL: Waveland, 2001), p. 87.

25. Meyers et al, p. 35.

CHAPTER 11

Goal Setting and Motivation in Groups

CHAPTER OUTLINE

Goal Setting
Goal Theory
Setting Motivating Goals

Member Motivation
Motivating by Meeting Needs
Motivating Diverse Personality Types

Group Motivation
A Sense of Meaningfulness
A Sense of Choice
A Sense of Competence
A Sense of Progress

Assessment and Feedback
The Role of Assessment
The Role of Feedback

Rewards and Punishment
Extrinsic and Intrinsic Rewards
Objective Rewards
Effective Rewards
The Role of Punishment

Balancing Mission and Motivation

GroupWork: Your Guiding Motive

GroupAssessment: Group Motivation Inventory

GOAL SETTING

Although effective communication is an absolute prerequisite for group success, it does not guarantee that a common goal will be achieved or that the group experience will satisfy the group members' needs and expectations. An additional ingredient, motivation, is necessary to fuel group performance.

An effective group has *both* a clear understanding of its goal *and* a belief that its goal is meaningful and worthwhile.[1] The Apollo Moon Project is a good example. Which goal is more motivating: "To be leaders in space exploration" or "To place a man on the moon by the end of the 1960s"? Fortunately, NASA adopted the second goal, and its simple words were both clear and inspiring.[2] In Carl Larson and Frank LaFasto's three-year study of characteristics that explain how and why effective groups develop, they put "a clear and elevated goal" at the top of their list.[3] Any old goal is not enough.

Clear, elevated goals create a sense of excitement and even urgency. They challenge group members and give them the opportunity to excel—both as individuals and as a group. Here is how Larson and LaFasto describe what happens when groups work to achieve such goals:

> [Groups] lose their sense of time. They discover to their surprise that it's dark outside and they worked right through the supper hours. The rate of communication among team members increases dramatically, even to the point that individuals call each other at all hours of the night because they can't get something out of their minds. There is a sense of great excitement and feelings of elation whenever even minor progress is made toward the goal.[4]

Effective goal setting in groups is critical to all major theories of group motivation. First and foremost, motivated group members know what the goal is, understand what actions are needed to accomplish the goal, agree upon the criteria for judging whether the goal has been reached, and are aware of how their own behavior contributes to achieving the goal.[5]

Goal Theory

Edwin Locke and Gary Latham's **goal theory** examines the value of setting group goals and the methods needed to accomplish those goals. They conclude that groups function best when their goals have the following characteristics. Effective goals (1) are specific, (2) are hard but realistic, (3) are accepted by members, (4) are used to evaluate performance, (5) are linked to feedback and rewards, (6) are set by members and groups, and (7) allow for member growth.[6]

Locke and Latham conclude that effective goal setting does more than raise group productivity and improve work quality. It also clarifies group and members' expectations, increases satisfaction with individual and group performance, and enhances members' self-confidence, pride, and willingness to accept future

TOOLBOX 11.1

Is Our Goal a Mission or a Vision?

What is the difference between a *goal*, a *mission*, and a *vision*? Our definition of group communication emphasizes the importance of establishing and working toward achieving a common *goal*. In Chapter 1, we define a **goal** as a group's purpose or objective. We note that without a common goal, groups would wonder: Why are we meeting? Why should we care or work hard? Where are we going? Thus, a goal embodies a worthwhile or important result that the group hopes to achieve. In one sense, a *mission* or *vision* may be viewed as an exalted word for a goal. Understanding how these terms are used can help clarify your group's goal and elevate its purpose.

- *Mission.* In business management literature, a **mission** expresses a group's ultimate goal *and* what the group must do to motivate its members to achieve that goal. Peter Drucker, a renowned business management expert, states that group members want to know what their group "is here for and how they can contribute." A mission, he notes, doesn't have to be fancy or snobby, but it has to be clear and concrete, as in the mission of the Coca-Cola company: "Beat Pepsi."[1] In this chapter, the word *mission* is used to describe the overall and motivating goal established by a group.

- *Vision.* Whereas a mission describes what a group does, a **vision** describes a view of the future when the group has achieved its goal. Warren Bennis and Joan Goldsmith write that "a vision is a picture that can be seen with the mind's eye." They prefer the term *vision* because it "can be pictured—it has substance, form, and color."[2] In a general sense, vision statements are more inspiring and future-focused than mission statements. Bennis and Goldsmith contend that a successful vision engages your heart and spirit by tapping embedded concerns and needs.[3]

[1] Paul Cohen, "Peter F. Drucker: The Shape of Things to Come," in *Leader to Leader*, ed. Frances Hesselbein and Paul M. Cohen (San Francisco: Jossey-Bass, 1999), p. 118.
[2] Warren Bennis and Joan Goldsmith, *Learning to Lead: A Workbook on Becoming a Leader*, updated edition (Cambridge, MA: Perseus, 1997), p. 105.
[3] Bennis and Goldsmith, p. 106.

challenges. Difficult or challenging goals can lead to greater effort and persistence than easy goals, assuming that a group accepts the difficult goals as worthwhile.[7]

Think of your own accomplishments. If you set out to earn a passing C in your courses, you may not work hard or feel proud of the results if you succeed. If, however, you strive for As, you will work harder, be proud of your work, and, if you succeed, enjoy the reward of achieving an enviable grade-point average.

Setting Motivating Goals

If your group is given what someone else thinks is a clear and elevated goal, group members may not be impressed or inspired. However, if your group is involved in developing a goal, the motivation of members to work for the achievement of that goal is heightened.[8] This increase in motivation comes about because group-based goal setting produces a better match of member and group needs, a better understanding of the group actions needed to achieve the goal, and a better appreciation of how individual members can contribute to group action. Moreover, when group members set the group's goals, the process can create a more interdependent, cooperative, and cohesive environment in which to work.[9]

Group goals should be both specific and challenging. Specific goals lead to higher performance than do generalized goals. For example, telling a group to "do your best" in choosing someone for a job is a generalized goal. A specific goal would be for the group to review the candidates for the job, recommend three top candidates, and include a list of each top candidate's strengths and weaknesses.

Think of the difference between a specific, challenging class assignment and one that is vague and undemanding. "Be prepared to discuss the questions at the end of the chapter" doesn't give you much direction, whereas "Choose one of the discussion questions at the end of the chapter, outline your answer with references to textbook content, and turn in your outline on Monday" gives both clear and (hopefully) thought-provoking directions.

Setting a clear and elevated goal benefits *every* group. You don't have to be a NASA scientist or a corporate executive to set impressive goals. Even if your only task is to participate in a graded classroom discussion, your group should take the time to develop a set of appropriate goals. For example, in many group communication classes, instructors require students to participate in a problem-solving discussion. The group usually chooses its topic, creates a discussion agenda, and demonstrates its preparation and group communication skills in class. This is nothing like "putting a man on the moon." Yet, even a classroom discussion can be more effective if the group establishes a clear, elevated goal, such as "Our group and every member of it will earn an A on this assignment." In order to achieve this goal, your group will have to do many things: Choose a meaningful discussion topic, prepare a useful agenda, research the topic thoroughly, make sure that every member is well prepared and ready to contribute, and demonstrate effective group communication skills during the discussion. A clear, elevated goal does more than set your sights on an outcome; it helps your group decide how to get there.

Regardless of the circumstances or the setting, your group will benefit by asking the following six questions about your goals:

1. *Clarity.* Is the goal clear, specific, and observable if achieved?

2. *Challenging.* Is the goal difficult, inspiring, and thought-provoking?

3. *Commitment.* Do members see the goal as meaningful, realistic, and attainable?

4. *Compatible.* Can both group and individual goals be achieved?

5. *Cooperative.* Does the goal require cooperation among group members?

6. *Cost.* Does the group have adequate resources, such as time and materials, to achieve the goal?[10]

Routine goals can be boring. Clear and elevated goals can be powerful motivators. When President John F. Kennedy declared that the United States would put a man on the moon and bring him back safely, no one doubted the magnificence of the challenge, even if they had reservations about whether it could be achieved.

MEMBER MOTIVATION

In Chapter 1, we introduce the engaged–disengaged group dialectic. In some situations, a group's high-energy action is unstoppable because group members are extremely motivated and personally committed. At the other end of the dialectic spectrum, groups may have little enthusiasm for their work because they are not motivated or personally rewarded for it. In this chapter we focus on strategies for motivating group members, but we also recognize that, even in the most energetic groups, members may need to pause, recharge, and relax in order to see a project through.

The word *motivate* comes from a French word, *motif,* which means "causing to move." Thus, if you motivate someone, you give that person a reason to act. When we use the term **motivation,** we refer to the reasons that move a person or group to do something. **Group motivation** provides the inspiration, incentives, and reasons that move group members to work together in order to achieve a common goal. Without motivation, we may know what needs to be done, and we may even have the skill to perform the work, but we lack the will and energy to do it. Motivation is the power that moves us to work in groups.

Group success depends on a unified commitment by *all* group members. Part of that commitment is "team spirit," as well as a sense of loyalty and dedication.[11] Taking the time and effort to ensure that a group is highly motivated can mean the difference between its success and its failure.

What motivates you to work in groups? Will the same things that motivate *you* also motivate other group members? If there were universal motivators, group motivation would be easy. You could list all the motivators that work for you and then apply them to other members of the group. Unfortunately, that's exactly what some leaders and groups do. And it doesn't work. What works is a concerted effort to match motivators to members' needs, personality types, and cultural differences.

Motivating by Meeting Needs

In Chapter 2, "Group Development," we describe two psychological theories—Maslow's Hierarchy of Needs and Schutz's Fundamental Interpersonal Relationship Orientation. These theories help explain the variety of reasons why individuals join, stay in, and leave groups. Here we return to these theories as ways of understanding how to motivate individual group members.

Maslow's Hierarchy of Needs. The same needs that motivate us to join groups can also motivate us to achieve our group's shared goal. For the purpose of discussing motivation in groups, Maslow's five needs can be divided into two categories: satisfiers and motivators.

Satisfier (also called *deficiency needs*) include Maslow's most basic needs—physiological and safety needs. Many groups and the people who create those groups have the power to satisfy members' material needs—money for food and shelter, job security, health-care and life insurance benefits, and opportunities to advance in a career that will earn them even more money. Money can satisfy deficiency needs, but it will not necessarily motivate a person or group to work harder or better.

Motivators (also called *fulfillment needs*) include Maslow's higher-level needs—belongingness, esteem, and self-actualization needs. The ability of groups to satisfy belongingness needs is obvious. Group communication scholar Ernest Bormann describes many of these social functions:

> The group furnishes refuge from loneliness. It provides members with friends and enemies, either within their own or within competing groups. Members gain a sense of belonging from the group. They learn to know other people and to find that they like and respect others.[12]

Groups can also motivate their members by satisfying esteem needs. When a group that you belong to succeeds, you may experience personal pride and gain esteem in the eyes of others. Effective group members often gain immense satisfaction from mastering difficult skills and completing ambitious projects. Group members with high achievement needs will set challenging but realistic goals. However, when esteem needs are not satisfied, members may feel inconsequential and lack self-worth.[13] Psychologist Douglas Bernstein and his colleagues describe people with high achievement needs as follows:

> They actively seek success, take risks when necessary, and are intensely satisfied with success. But if they feel they have tried their best, people with high achievement motivation are not too upset by failure. . . . They select tasks with clear outcomes, and they prefer feedback from a harsh but competent critic rather than from one who is friendlier but less competent.[14]

When members satisfy high achievement needs by working in groups, they are highly motivated. Some members, however, may not have high achievement needs; instead, they may be preoccupied with meeting other needs. For example, in collectivist cultures, success and member satisfaction are often derived from groupwork, not from individual achievement. In addition, gender differences in achievement motivation often appear at an early age. Research suggests that some women fear success because they feel that they may be seen as unfeminine or because they believe that their personal achievements may threaten their male colleagues.[15] Effective groups understand, respect, and adapt to cultural and gender differences in member motivation.

In the best groups, members have opportunities for personal growth and self-actualization. Some of us are lucky enough to love the work we do. Ernest Bormann maintains that "the desire to do a good job, to make a contribution to other people, to feel that life has meaning over and above the satisfying of [basic] needs" can be met by groups. "If members do important and difficult tasks and see opportunities for additional training and competence, they can gratify some of their desire for self-actualization."[16] Figure 11.1 presents a view of Maslow's Hierarchy of Needs that illustrates the connection between need satisfaction and group motivation.

Schutz's Theory of Interpersonal Needs. Schutz's theory does more than explain why members participate in groups. It also provides some of the tools needed to motivate individual group members.[17] As we explain in Chapter 2, Schutz describes three interpersonal needs that affect why we work in groups.

FIGURE 11.1   **Maslow's Hierarchy of Needs**

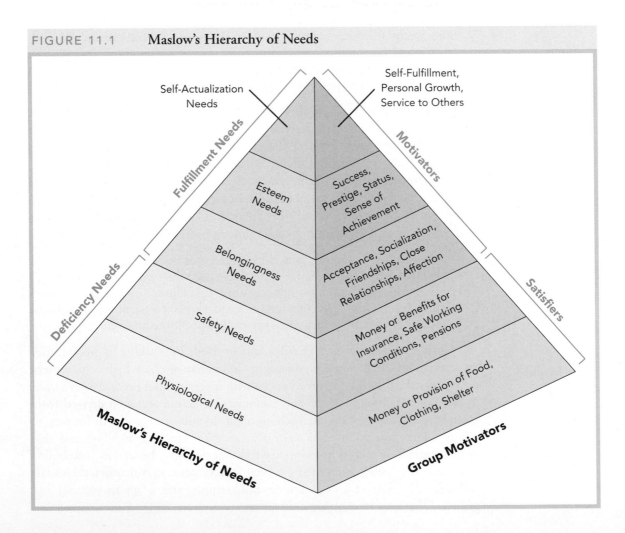

- *Need for inclusion:* The need to belong and be accepted

- *Need for control:* The need to take charge, direct, and have power

- *Need for affection:* The need to feel liked and have close personal relationships

Certainly a group can satisfy these individual needs. Just belonging to a group can satisfy inclusion needs. Developing friendships within a group can satisfy affection needs. Groups can provide leadership opportunities that satisfy control needs.

Schutz's theory also suggests ways to motivate individual members. If you know that some group members have unmet inclusion needs, invite them to participate more actively. Tell them how valuable they are to the group. Ask for their opinions, and listen carefully to their answers. If some group members have strong affection needs, spend time with them in nonwork settings. Be open with these members, and listen carefully when they talk. If you do, they will feel well liked and highly motivated. If some group members have high control needs, you don't have to appoint or elect them as leaders to satisfy those needs. You can make them chairs of subcommittees or see that they get special assignments in which they have full control over their work.

Expectancy-Value Theory. **Expectancy-Value Theory** contends that motivation results from a combination of individual needs and the value of the goals available in the environment. This theory stresses the idea that the probability of motivated behavior depends not only upon the value of the goal to the individual, but also upon the expectation of obtaining the goal.[18] Thus, even when a goal is highly valued (becoming a Hollywood star, inventing the next computer operating system, captaining a spaceship), you may not be highly motivated to pursue that goal if your chance of reaching it is very small. If a group has a shared goal that everyone values, and if the chances of achieving that goal are good, group motivation should provide the level of commitment and energy needed to achieve it.

Expectancy-Value Theory claims that motivation is a function of three perceptions: expectancy, instrumentality, and valance.

- *Expectancy.* This measures the probability that effort will produce a desired outcome. (If I study harder than everyone else, I will learn more and know more.)

- *Instrumentality.* This measures whether achieving a desired result will result in a reward or benefit. (If I know more than anyone else in the class, I will earn an A.)

- *Valence.* This measures the value you place on the reward. (Do I really want an A? Is it worth the effort?)

If any of these three perceptions is missing, motivation will also be missing. For example, even if you have the time to study harder and you believe that studying harder will earn you an A, you may not think that earning an A is worth the effort—and thus, you may not be motivated to study.[19]

In order to be motivated, group members must value the reward or possible outcome, believe that they have the skills or resources to achieve the outcome, and have reasonable expectations that their behavior will lead to a valued reward.[20] The following guidelines can help you use Expectancy-Value Theory principles to motivate group members:

- Make sure that group members understand and accept a realistic, but challenging group goal.

- Make sure that rewards are attainable and are sufficient to motivate group members.

- Recognize individual differences or preferences. For example, whereas one group member might be motivated by a risky or complex assignment, another may prefer routine tasks. In collectivist cultures, recognizing someone in front of the group could be insensitive and embarrassing.[21]

Motivating Diverse Personality Types

The Myers-Briggs Type Indicator® theory explains that every person has preferences of thought and behavior that can be divided into four categories, each with opposite preferences: extrovert or introvert, sensor or intuitive, thinker or feeler, and judger or perceiver. Each type responds to different motivators. Understanding the different personality types in a group can help you choose the most appropriate motivational strategies. Figure 11.2 provides a brief look at the many ways in which different personality types call for different approaches to motivation.[22]

You can motivate both extroverts and introverts by providing all group members with meeting agendas well in advance. Introverts need the time to prepare materials and develop their thoughts in advance. Extroverts may need time to collect information that supports their already formed ideas.

Motivating sensors and intuitives requires respect. Sensors will remain motivated if they are allowed to share information and observations. Intuitives will remain motivated if their creative and big-picture ideas are given serious consideration by other group members. During a discussion, give sensors uninterrupted time to share relevant information. Then let the intuitives "loose" to use that information as a springboard for new ideas or innovative solutions.

Motivating thinkers and feelers requires a balance between task and social dimensions. Thinkers should be thanked for their analyses, but also reminded that logical decisions affect real people. Feelers should be given time to discuss personal perspectives, but also reminded that disagreements can help a group reach good, people-focused decisions.

Motivating both judgers and perceivers requires patience, skill, and balance. Judgers may see perceivers as flaky and undisciplined. Perceivers may see their

TOOLBOX 11.2

Motivating Culturally Diverse Members

What motivates you may not motivate the other members of your group, particularly if they come from diverse cultural backgrounds. In Chapter 3, we present six cultural dimensions, each of which has implications for group members' motivation. Here we suggest ways to adapt motivational strategies to culturally diverse members.

- *Individualism–Collectivism.* Individualistic members may need and seek public recognition and praise for personal achievement. A member with a collectivist perspective might be embarrassed by public praise and prefer being honored as a member of an outstanding group.
- *High power distance–low power distance.* Members from high-power-distance cultures value recognition by a leader and take pride in following instructions accurately and efficiently. Members from low-power-distance cultures prefer compliments from other group members and enjoy working in a more independent and collaborative environment.
- *High uncertainty avoidance–low uncertainty avoidance.* Members who avoid uncertainty and change are motivated when a group follows tried and true ways of doing things. Something that is new and different may frighten and even *de*motivate them. Members with low uncertainty avoidance view uncertainty and change as stimulating and energizing. What is new and different is motivating.[1]
- *Masculine–feminine.* Members—both male and female—with a masculine perspective are moti-

vated by competitive goals, opportunities for leadership, and tasks that require assertive behavior. Members with more feminine values may be extremely effective and supportive of group goals but have difficulty achieving a real voice or influence in the group. Such members may be motivated by taking on group maintenance roles, such as encourager-supporter, harmonizer, compromiser, or tension releaser.
- *High context–low context.* Group members from high-context cultures do not need to *hear* someone praise their work—they are highly skilled at detecting admiration and approval because they are more sensitive to nonverbal cues. Members from low-context cultures often complain that they never receive praise or rewards when, in fact, they are highly respected and valued by others. Low-context members need to hear words of praise and receive tangible rewards.
- *Monochronic–polychronic.* Members from monochronic cultures take pride in and are motivated by groups that concentrate their energies on a specific task and meet deadlines. Members from polychronic cultures often find the single-mindedness of monochronic members stifling rather than motivating. Giving polychronic members the opportunity to work on multiple tasks with flexible deadlines can motivate them to work more effectively.

[1] Lee Gardenswartz and Anita Rowe, *Diverse Teams at Work: Capitalizing on the Power of Diversity* (New York: McGraw-Hill, 1994), p. 133.

judging colleagues as rigid and intolerant. Neither type deserves such harsh labels. Both types take their responsibilities seriously and will get a job done. You can motivate judgers by assuring them that a decision will be made and will include a detailed implementation plan. You can motivate perceivers by assuring them that they will be given opportunities to reconsider decisions and make midcourse adjustments if needed.

FIGURE 11.2   **Personality Type and Motivation**

Personality Type	Type-Based Beliefs About Groups	Type-Based Motivational Strategies
Extrovert	Groups get work done and create useful relationships.	1. Encourage interaction. 2. Allow time for "talking out" ideas. 3. Provide frequent feedback.
Introvert	Groups can waste time, make decisions too quickly, and create more work.	1. Set clear and valued goals. 2. Provide thinking time before and during discussions. 3. Provide opportunities to speak.
Sensor	Groups need to gather and use facts but often get bogged down in vague and unrealistic discussions.	1. Set realistic goals. 2. Keep meetings short and relevant. 3. Request real, practical information. 4. Make sure decisions are made.
Intuitive	Groups uncover possibilities and can make inspired decisions.	1. Develop an engaging goal. 2. Encourage visioning and creativity. 3. Encourage brainstorming.
Thinker	Groups must test ideas and possible solutions if they want to make good decisions.	1. Focus on task dispassionately. 2. Encourage debate on substantive issues. 3. Encourage logical decision making.
Feeler	Groups provide opportunities for cooperation and growth.	1. Discuss impact of decisions on people. 2. Encourage cooperation and harmony. 3. Recognize members' contributions.
Judger	Groups get the task done when they're structured and task-focused.	1. Encourage closure on issues. 2. Provide an agenda and deadlines. 3. Set standards and expectations.
Perceiver	Groups examine possibilities during the discussion process.	1. Focus on a variety of alternatives. 2. Keep the time frame open. 3. Let a decision gradually emerge from discussion.

GROUP MOTIVATION

In addition to theories on how to motivate individual group members, there are theories, methods, and tools for motivating groups as a whole. In *Intrinsic Motivation at Work,* Kenneth Thomas describes four categories of motivators needed to energize and reinforce an entire group.

- *A sense of meaningfulness*—the feeling that the group is pursuing a worthy task
- *A sense of choice*—the feeling that the group has the power and ability to make judgments about doing the task
- *A sense of competence*—the feeling that you are doing good, high-quality work on the task
- *A sense of progress*—the feeling that you are accomplishing something[23]

A Sense of Meaningfulness

Groups are more likely to find a goal meaningful and, as a result, be motivated if their members believe that the goal can be achieved through their efforts. Members also need to receive feedback that lets them know immediately whether their efforts are contributing to the group's goal.[24] In short, and as Expectancy-Value Theory suggests, highly motivated groups believe that the job is worth doing *and* that they are capable of getting it done.[25]

Whether your group is setting out to climb Mt. Everest, planning a homecoming rally, or establishing a new product line, your goal should be clear and should be supported by every member of the group. History teaches us that

What factors motivate Habitat for Humanity volunteers to donate their free time and effort? (© Sonda Dawes/ The Image Works)

groups will expend enormous amounts of energy in pursuit of a worthy goal. People have guarded secrets, endured hardships, worked tirelessly, and fought and died for causes when they believed that those causes were worthwhile. The point is this: Group members must be committed to a shared goal before they can be motivated to support it.[26] You can help promote a sense of meaningfulness in your group by

- Expressing enthusiasm; don't be cynical about the group's work

- Learning what motivates you as an individual and what motivates the other members of the group

- Understanding what the group is capable of accomplishing and discussing those capabilities with your group

- Volunteering for group tasks that interest you

Motivated members believe that the group's work is meaningful. They become even more motivated when they have the power to influence their own work. No one likes being micromanaged. A sense of meaningfulness is especially important in volunteer groups. Here's what one student wrote after participating in a service-learning project with members of his class:

> This project went well because the cause was such a great one; everyone was willing to work equally hard on it, despite his or her busy schedule. There were a few times when some were more motivated than others were, but when it came time to actually collect the canned foods, our group jelled so solidly that it became one of the great experiences that some only dream about. We felt purposeful and became satisfied with each other and with ourselves; we were extremely proud of our group and individual efforts.

A Sense of Choice

In addition to sharing a worthy goal, motivated groups develop a structured plan for getting to that goal. They engage in critical thinking and choose agreed-upon strategies for achieving their goal. Every member knows what she or he is expected to do. Members communicate frequently in an effort to share information, discuss issues, and make decisions.[27] Throughout this textbook, we have offered theories, methods, and tools for helping a group achieve its goal. Whether they are working with a theory of conflict resolution, a method of solving problems, or tools for increasing participation, highly motivated teams select appropriate strategies for achieving worthwhile and attainable goals. You can help promote a sense of choice within your group by

- Letting members make decisions about how the group does its work

- Demonstrating that the group can exercise authority responsibly

- Accepting the inevitability of making mistakes when exploring innovative approaches

TOOLBOX 11.3

Dealing with Apathy

Apathy is the most visible symptom of an un-motivated group. **Apathy** is the indifference that occurs when members do not consider the group or its goal important, interesting, or inspiring. Intrinsic motivators—meaningfulness, choice, competence, and progress—are minimal or missing. As Expectancy-Value Theory predicts, members exhibit signs of apathy when their personal needs and expectations are not met. If your best ideas are blocked or if too much time is taken up with the demands of self-centered recognition seekers or with what seem to be meaningless tasks, you can easily become turned off. If you experience high levels of communication apprehension, you may feel more comfortable playing a passive role rather than an active one. If it appears that a worthy goal cannot be reached or requires an unreasonable expenditure of your valuable time and energy, it can be easier to disengage than to tackle a seemingly impossible task.

Finding a cure for group or member apathy depends on correctly diagnosing its cause. If a group's goal does not meet members' expectations,

spend time reexamining the goal itself. Does the goal meet member and group needs? Is the goal meaningful, inspiring, visionary? Is there a reasonable plan for achieving the goal? Is the group capable of achieving it?

Assigning appropriate tasks to group members is a second strategy that can decrease apathy. Often members are unsure of how they can contribute. Assigning specific responsibilities and tasks to members based on their needs, interests, and skills can increase their commitment to and involvement in the group. Apathetic members may not necessarily be uninterested or lazy; they may be intimidated or frustrated. Help them by finding something that they are ready, willing, and able to do.

Sometimes confronting apathy head-on is the only way to deal with apathetic members or an apathetic group. Bring up the issue and talk about it. For example, asking an entire group why it seems bogged down or talking privately with an apathetic member can uncover causes and generate solutions.

- Seeking and taking advantage of new opportunities
- Becoming well informed about the group's work

When group members have the power to make decisions, they are motivated by a greater sense of personal control and responsibility.

A Sense of Competence

Once a group has a clear goal and has selected strategies for achieving that goal, a third motivating element should be addressed: Are members ready, willing, and able to perform the tasks necessary to achieve the goal? Does your group have the expertise needed to achieve the goal? If not, how can the group recruit or secure the experts needed to implement its well-informed decisions? If group discussions are disorganized, is there someone who can function as a facilitator, procedural technician, or gatekeeper? If enthusiasm is flagging, will someone assume the role of energizer or encourager-supporter? If conflict among some members begins to erode motivation, can other group members function as harmonizers, compromisers, and tension releasers?

Group members who feel incapable of adequately performing the tasks required in the group may become overwhelmed and feel defeated before they begin. You can help promote a sense of competence within your group by

- Encouraging everyone to seek the information needed to complete the group's tasks

- Providing constructive feedback to group members and listening to feedback from others

- Recognizing rather than minimizing the value of your skills

- Complimenting other group members' abilities and achievements

- Setting high standards for yourself and others

Group members can create a sense of competence by recognizing one another's abilities and contributions. Groups that feel confident about the value of their abilities will be motivated to put their skills to work.

A Sense of Progress

"How are we doing?" is an important question for all groups. It's difficult for members to stay motivated throughout the life of a group if they do not have any notion of whether the group is making progress toward its goal. A well-chosen, structured goal should be measurable. Motivated groups "create good, objective measurements that people can relate to their specific behavior."[28] In the upcoming section on assessment and feedback, we offer ways of measuring a group's effectiveness and progress.

Groups must feel a sense of progress in order to be motivated to continue their work. Official employee performance evaluations rarely provide a group with a sense of progress. Instead, you and your group can provide a sense of progress by

- Developing a group method of tracking and measuring progress

- Looking for collaborative ways to resolve group difficulties

- Recognizing and celebrating group accomplishments

- Monitoring and, if needed, finding ways to sustain group motivation at various points in the work process

The realization that the group is making progress motivates members to pursue the group's goal with persistence. Although leaders and managers should accept the challenge of creating environments that promote highly motivated teams, the most successful groups take responsibility for motivating themselves.

GROUPTECH

Motivation in Virtual Groups

Motivating "real" groups is complicated and challenging. Motivating virtual groups doubles the complications and the challenges. Group members who are new to virtual interaction may struggle with new technologies, new behaviors, and new work relationships. Yet, as we indicate in Chapter 6, "Listening in Groups," some group members communicate more confidently and effectively in virtual groups, while others find involvement in virtual groups either intimidating or an easy way to avoid participating. For example, in a teleconference, you can engage a speakerphone and do other work while half-listening to a less-than-exciting discussion. By making an occasional supportive comment, you may sound as though you're involved in the inter-action, even though your attention is a million miles away. In computer-mediated discussions—whether synchronous or asynchronous—you can ignore comments made by other group members, withhold your own comments, or not respond at all. When other group members aren't present and looking at you, you can easily disengage and disappear with impunity. If members aren't motivated, a virtual group cannot expect to achieve its shared goal.

Here we offer several methods and tools designed to make working in virtual groups a rewarding and motivating experience:[1]

- If possible, schedule a face-to-face orienta-tion meeting with all members of the virtual group—even if it means spending time and money. Use the orientation meeting to agree upon or to clarify the group's goal, to develop mutual respect and trust, to explain how and when technology will be used, to agree upon norms for interaction, and to build a motivated team.

- Provide a detailed agenda well in advance of a scheduled virtual meeting, along with any resources and online documents needed to prepare for the meeting.
- Make a special effort to adapt to members' needs, personality preferences, and cultural dif-ferences. Do members who prefer to focus on facts become lost in wide-ranging online discus-sions? Are members given enough time to think about information before being asked to com-ment or make decisions? Are nonnative speakers given enough time to listen, read, and respond?
- Make sure that everyone contributes. Go "around the room" virtually. Ask each person for his or her opinion. Assign specific tasks and/or roles to group members to stimulate interaction and motivation.
- Use technology such as group editing, colla-borative writing, bulletin boards, and online voting to obtain "buy-in" from everyone. If someone isn't giving verbal or written responses, ask that person for an opinion, a piece of information, or an action.
- Structure the meeting so that members can come in and out of it according to their need to obtain information or offer input. Don't make members endure prolonged discussions that have little or nothing to do with their interests or talents unless there is a genuine need for everyone to know and respond to the information being presented.
- Allow members to develop and nurture "virtual" friendships, inject a bit of humor and fun into meetings, and keep the group focused on its shared, valued, and achievable goal.

[1] D. L. Duarte and N. T. Snyder, *Mastering Virtual Teams: Strategies, Tools, and Techniques That Succeed,* 2nd ed. (San Francisco: Jossey-Bass, 2001), pp. 172–174.

ASSESSMENT AND FEEDBACK

How do you know whether your group is both motivated and making progress? At times, a highly motivated group may do a job enthusiastically but still not achieve its goal. Groups need regular assessment and constructive feedback to determine whether they are doing good work and making progress.

The Role of Assessment

Assessment is a mechanism for monitoring group progress and a way of determining whether a group has achieved its goals. Rather than viewing assessment negatively as an evaluation system designed to determine or withhold group rewards, members can use assessment to answer questions about how well the group is doing and how it can improve its performance.

Regardless of whether you are evaluating a group of community volunteers or a management team in a multinational corporation, assessment can serve a variety of purposes:[29]

- To motivate work performance

- To inform individual members about their job performances

- To clarify the job to be done

- To encourage increased competence and growth

- To enhance and improve communication

- To correct problems

- To encourage responsibility

Throughout this textbook, we include assessment instruments at the end of every chapter. Many of these instruments measure variables related to group motivation. Figure 11.3 summarizes selected instruments that can be used to assess various aspects of group motivation.

Assessment instruments can help determine how well a group is progressing toward its goal and whether interpersonal or procedural problems are impeding its effectiveness. Using assessment instruments, however, is not the only way in which a group can determine whether it is making progress. Face-to-face discussions about a group's progress can be just as effective.

The Role of Feedback

Group and member motivation can increase productivity and member satisfaction when a group receives useful feedback about its progress. In *Encouraging the Heart*, James Kouzes and Barry Posner note, "Goals without feedback, and feedback without goals, have little effect on motivation."[30] Feedback "requires us to get close to people, show that we care about them, and demonstrate that we are

FIGURE 11.3   **Group Assessment Instruments**

Chapter	Instrument	Types of Motivational Assessment
CHAPTER 1	Essential Group Elements	Assesses the extent to which a group has the five basic elements needed to work efficiently and effectively in groups.
CHAPTER 2	Group Attraction Survey	Assesses the motivation of members to join and stay in a group.
CHAPTER 5	Auditing Team Talk	Assesses the extent to which members engage in productive team talk.
CHAPTER 7	Ross-DeWine Conflict Management Message Style Instrument	Assesses group members' message style during conflict situations.
CHAPTER 9	Problem-Solving Competencies	Assesses the extent to which a group and its members perform essential problem-solving competencies.
CHAPTER 10	Argumentativeness Scale	Assesses how group members' levels of argumentativeness can affect group productivity and member satisfaction.
CHAPTER 12	Post-Meeting Reaction (PMR) Form	Assesses how well a group conducts its meetings.
CHAPTER 14	Virtual Meeting Rating Scale	Assesses how well a group conducts three types of virtual meetings.

interested in others."[31] Constructive feedback serves two purposes: It encourages groups and provides evidence of their progress.

Feedback can motivate or discourage a group, depending on the way in which it is presented. Feedback can be controlling or informative. **Controlling feedback** tells people what to do, whereas **informative feedback** tells people how they are doing. Although both forms of feedback can be positive or negative, informative feedback works much better.[32] For example, a manager who reminds group members that their performance evaluations will affect their job security is providing controlling feedback. In effect, the manager is saying, "If you don't do better, you may lose your job." Controlling feedback can also be stated in positive terms: "If you continue to make such good progress, you may earn a bonus." Even so, controlling feedback, whether negative or positive, imposes a leader's or outside authority's will on the group instead of tapping factors that intrinsically motivate group members.

Informative feedback is any feedback that tells a group how well it's doing and to what extent it's achieving the group's goal.[33] Whereas controlling feedback emphasizes the power to reward or punish performance, informative feedback focuses on the group's work and how further progress can be achieved.

Using "It" Statements.   You can learn to provide constructive, informative feedback by giving up "you" statements, which imply "You messed up" or "You failed." Instead, provide feedback using "it" statements. "You" statements suggest a personal opinion about a person or the members of a group, while "it" statements talk about how the group is working and progressing, not about how members are doing or what you feel about them.[34] Which of the following statements would you rather hear: "You're way behind schedule," or "It seems as though the group will miss its deadline"? The following guidelines can help you use "it" statements to provide informative feedback.

- "It" statements avoid using the word *you* when describing individual or group behavior.

- "It" statements focus on the task rather than on individual group members.

- "It" statements are based on objective information about the group's work.

- "It" statements answer the question "How is *it* going?" rather than "How am *I* doing?"[35]

Certainly group members can benefit from individual feedback regarding their behavior. Informative feedback, however, has the advantage of motivating the group as a whole because it focuses on the group's goal rather than on individuals.

Using Reprimands.   Sometimes positive and informative feedback fails to motivate group members or to correct a problem. Rather than punishing a group or an individual member, you may want to consider using a reprimand. **Reprimands** are not punishments; they are a form of feedback that identifies work-related problems or deficiencies. Think of it this way: A reprimand is similar to a driver's warning ticket. Before reprimanding a group member or a group as a whole, be sure that you can answer the following questions:[36]

- Are you certain that you have all the facts concerning the situation?

- Has the group or member been reprimanded previously for the same problem?

- Are group members aware of the rules or standards that have been violated?

- Will the reprimand benefit the group or be counterproductive?

- Were other groups or group members involved in the incident?

- Was the infraction intentional, an honest mistake, or a matter beyond the member's or group's control?

- Was this a personal problem or a group-based problem?

Depending on how you answer these questions, you may discover that a reprimand is not necessary or that it must be used as the first step toward correcting a serious problem. If a reprimand is appropriate, make sure that you follow the guidelines for constructive feedback. Your comments should be informative and should be phrased as "it" statements rather than as "you" statements. Most important of all, ensure that the reprimand is fair and impersonal. Regardless of the infraction, you should make it perfectly clear that the reprimand involves something a member *did,* not who the member *is.*

REWARDS AND PUNISHMENT

Rewards and motivation are not the same thing. A **reward** is something that is given or received in recompense for some service or worthy behavior. Rewards are bestowed when a group progresses toward or achieves its shared goal. Certainly, the *prospect* of receiving a reward can motivate individual group members and the group as a whole. However, in many cases, motivation may have little or nothing to do with external rewards.

Extrinsic and Intrinsic Rewards

Why do you go to work? One obvious answer is that you work to earn money. The money you earn allows you to live comfortably and securely. If you earn a lot of money, you can live a luxurious life. There's a second answer to this question, though. Many of us work because we like what we do, get satisfaction from

TOOLBOX 11.4

The Power to Reward

Power is the ability or authority to influence and motivate others. Chapter 8, "Group Leadership," discusses the various sources of a leader's power: reward power, coercive power, legitimate power, expert power, and referent power. A leader may use one or more of these sources of power to motivate a group to complete a goal. A leader may reward members for their good work or punish them for not performing well. However, leaders who think that they can rely on rewards to motivate group members may be in for a rude awakening. The group, not the leader, must see the reward as appropriate and worthwhile.

A leader with legitimate power can order groups to perform tasks but may not be able to rely on the team to accept those tasks with dedication and enthusiasm. Leaders with referent and expert power can motivate many groups. In such cases, the leader is either a role model for the group or an expert and has earned the admiration of other members. When coercive power is used to punish, discipline, demote, or dismiss group members, groups may do nothing more than work hard to "keep out of trouble."

our accomplishments, and enjoy the company and friendship of colleagues. These two answers represent the extrinsic and intrinsic rewards for working.

Extrinsic rewards come from the "external environment in which we live."[37] They include both the money we earn and the benefits and perks that come with the job. Most extrinsic rewards don't come from groups; they are doled out by supervisors to ensure that work is done and that rules are followed. Money and work benefits are extrinsic rewards that satisfy our most basic needs—physiological and safety needs. Depending on the size of the extrinsic rewards, they can even satisfy esteem needs. Extrinsic rewards, however, do not motivate groups to work together in pursuit of a shared goal. They do not appeal to members' passions, nor do they demand much of members' collective intelligence and expertise.[38]

In the opinion of many researchers and human relations managers, we put too much emphasis on extrinsic rewards and not enough emphasis on their counterpart—intrinsic rewards. R. Brayton Bowen gives us a broad definition of intrinsic rewards. An **intrinsic reward,** he writes, is "anything that is satisfying and energizing in itself."[39] Completing a challenging project that encouraged personal growth can provide intrinsic rewards. So can participating in a retreat with respected colleagues or representing your organization at a professional or public event. In most groups, intrinsic rewards have more power than do extrinsic rewards.

The research on employee effectiveness emphasizes the power of intrinsic rewards. One survey examining employee turnover found that the chief reason people give for leaving a job has nothing to do with salaries and benefits. When asked why they are leaving, the need for praise and recognition rises to the top. Employees rate "the ability to recognize and acknowledge the contributions of others as the skill their managers need to develop."[40] In *Recognizing and Rewarding Employees,* Bowen describes motivation as an "inside" job—no one can make you do something against your will. The decision to act is yours. Bowen also notes that "you can't buy motivation. It has to come from within."[41]

How, then, do you reward an individual or a group? It's not a simple process or decision. Rewards must be attractive to group members.[42] Thus, a person who is given a bonus of $500 when she is expecting $5,000 may greet the reward with disgust and anger. A person who is rewarded with the prestigious assignment of chairing a major work team may not be grateful for the assignment if his archenemies are appointed to the group he must lead. Given that most of us enjoy receiving rewards and sincere appreciation from others, groups face the challenge of finding the right rewards and reward system for the right reasons.[43]

Rewards are meaningless and even resented if "who you know" is more important in determining them than the quantity and quality of the work you do. At the same time, rewards are just as meaningless and resented when everyone receives the same rewards—both those who deserve them and those who don't. Rewards are something given for worthy behavior. They should be determined fairly if they are expected to keep groups and their members motivated.

Objective Rewards

Effective rewards reflect well-conceived, objective criteria. Four criteria should be considered when developing a reward system for groups: The rewards should be fair, equitable, competitive, and appropriate.[44]

Fair.   The reward should be fair given the effort and risk; more work and more risk deserve more rewards. A person who exerts little effort and takes few risks should not receive the same reward as the most productive, risk-taking member. Because we don't like to disappoint or upset group members, we often extend rewards to everyone when, in fact, only a few members did most of the work responsible for the group's success. Fairness requires us to give rewards to those who have earned them.

Equitable.   The reward system should be equitable for all; everyone should have an equal opportunity to receive rewards. If the group's leader is the only one who receives a reward for the group's performance, members will lose their motivation. If each member is not given an equal opportunity to earn rewards, group morale may deteriorate. The group may become less productive or, even worse, counterproductive. Being equitable does not mean giving rewards to everyone. Being equitable means giving everyone an equal opportunity to earn rewards.

Competitive.   The rewards should be competitive and similar to the rewards given to others who do the same kind of work; intergroup competition should be fair and based on objective standards. If your group achieves the same goal as another group, the reward should be the same. If the group next door earns an all-expenses-paid vacation to a fancy resort and your group gets a $50 Wal-Mart coupon, the reward system will not work.

Appropriate.   The rewards should be appropriate for the achievement. A simple thank-you note for a job well done may be an appropriate reward for a simple task. A thank-you note will not work if the task was complex, difficult, stressful, and critical to the success of a company or organization. Think of it this way: What potential reward would you offer as a pretask motivator: "If you finish this eighteen-month project on time, I'll send you a thank-you note," or "If you finish this eighteen-month project on time, I'll make sure that each of you receives a bonus that equals 10 percent of your salary"?

Effective Rewards

Rewards range from taking the time to shake a colleague's hand to offering valuable stock options. The list of potential rewards is almost endless, given the many different ways in which you can compensate or show your appreciation to fellow group members.[45] However, rewards may not accomplish anything if they are not fair, equitable, competitive, and appropriate. Moreover, a reward that satisfies one group member or group may be meaningless to another. Just like motivators, rewards should be selected to match member and group needs.

Here we've divided rewards into two forms: personal recognition and material compensation. No matter what rewards you use, make sure that they are meaningful and appropriate for the individual or group that you are rewarding.

Personal Recognition. Most of us crave recognition for a job well done. Unfortunately, few of us receive the encouragement we need. One study found that about 40 percent of North American workers report that they *never* get recognized for outstanding individual performance.[46]

Individual members and groups as a whole want and need recognition. The following suggestions are only a few of the many ways in which you can reward a team and its members:

- Letters of praise, thanks, and recognition

- Public recognition at a major event or meeting

- Individual and group awards for achievement

- Public display of a group's product or accomplishment

- Video or newsletter articles about the group and its achievements

- A personal visit or meeting with top management

- Giveaway rewards such as team T-shirts, pen sets, or achievement pins

- Public signs announcing group achievement, such as "Team of the Month"

- A prize for group achievement, such as "Most Valuable Team Member," "Best Team Spirit," or "Best Customer Service"

- Appointment as a representative to a top-management task force or committee

- Recognition luncheon or dinner

- Time or days off

- Special party for all group members

All of these suggestions celebrate individual and group achievements. In their book *Corporate Celebration,* Terrence Deal and M. K. Key argue that "celebration is an integral element of culture, and . . . provides the symbolic adhesive that welds a community together.[47] In one study, researchers found that high-performing groups participated in a wide variety and frequency of celebratory events where recognition and appreciation were expressed.[48] Take time to celebrate. It's fun, and it can help motivate your group to new heights of achievement.

TOOLBOX 11.5

The Reward of Affection

What quality separates highly effective, best-performing leaders from less effective leaders? A study conducted by the Center for Creative Leadership found that a high score on Schutz's affection scale was the one and only factor differentiating top managers from those rated as least effective. "Contrary to the myth of the cold-hearted boss who cares very little about people's feelings, the highest-performing managers show more warmth and fondness towards others than do the bottom 25 percent."[1]

James Kouzes and Barry Posner put it this way: We all really do want to be loved.[2] Very few of us doubt the importance of this need in our most personal relationships. Then why should we doubt it with regard to our relationships in groups? When we believe that our colleagues like us, we feel better about ourselves. We also look forward to working with people who like us. Sharing your affection with other group members is not about hugging, dating, or intimacy. Sharing your affection involves a willingness to be open with other group members—to share your feelings with them. At the same time, we recognize that expressing affection must be balanced with task-focused work. Rewards that appeal to both the head and the heart can make a significant contribution to group motivation and productivity.

[1] James M. Kouzes and Barry Z. Posner, *Encouraging the Heart: A Leader's Guide to Rewarding and Recognizing Others* (San Francisco: Jossey-Bass, 1999), p. 9.
[2] Kouzes and Posner, p. 11.

Material Compensation. Personal recognition and affection serve as intrinsic rewards, but most employers provide extrinsic rewards as well. These rewards take the form of material compensation for a job well done. Some of these rewards are costly, whereas others need only limited resources to implement. Here are some examples:

- Salary bonuses
- Promotions
- Larger and better-equipped offices
- Paid attendance at professional seminars and meetings
- Funds for special supplies, software, books, or subscriptions
- A group "retreat" devoted to anything but work
- Office parties with award presentations
- Lunch or dinner with staff and spouses
- Mini-bonuses for reaching interim milestones
- Improved working conditions (furniture, lighting, décor)
- Tickets to theater and sporting events

- Cell phone
- Home computer, printer, or email service

Many companies offer special perks to high-achieving individuals and teams. We extend our list of forms of material compensation by offering a "perk buffet."[49]

- Memberships in professional associations
- Company car
- Free subscriptions to professional and technical journals
- Exclusive membership in social, business, or country clubs
- Free coffee, snacks, or meals
- Free child care
- Subsidized transportation
- A reserved parking place
- Free tuition and scholarships
- Flextime

Always keep in mind that a group member's needs have a significant impact on the extent to which material rewards can motivate that person's behavior. For example, a new parent may value free child care more than membership in a country club. An individual may feel that working with friends is more important than working in a highly competitive, work-obsessed group.

The Role of Punishment

So far, we have not discussed the use of punishment as a motivational tool—and for a good reason: Punishment does not motivate. In fact, it *de*motivates. If the threat and use of punishment were effective ways to motivate people to behave properly and to do their jobs, our prison population would be low, students would never break rules, and parents would merely have to threaten punishment to transform unruly kids into perfect angels.

Punishment is the opposite of motivation. When group members are punished (denied advancement, recognition, resources, perks, and so on), they may spend more of their energy complaining, getting even, pursuing outside interests, or even sabotaging the work of others. The world's great animal trainers use positive reinforcement, not whippings and denials. Our human colleagues deserve the same humane treatment.

There are some situations, however, in which a group member—despite multiple constructive feedback sessions and reprimands—is so disruptive or nonproductive that the group would be much better off without that person. Also, when a serious rule has been broken, this cannot be overlooked or minimized. In such cases, the exclusion of a member from the group may be the "punishment that fits the crime." For example, John Sortino, the founder of the Vermont Teddy Bear Company, posts only three rules, but they are strictly enforced: No stealing, no lying, and all employees must follow the laws regarding discrimination, sexual harassment, and so forth. If a worker breaks one of these rules, that person is out of a job.[50]

When students are selected to work as interns at Walt Disney World, they are greeted with three no-exceptions rules: (1) You cannot miss more than a specified number of mandatory training sessions, (2) a person of the opposite sex may not be in your Disney apartment after a specified hour at night, and (3) you may not use illegal drugs. Interns who break any of these rules are sent home immediately.

The three rules at the Vermont Teddy Bear Company and at Walt Disney World set expectations and standards, but they do not motivate. All workers know that crossing these lines of behavior will result in the ultimate punishment: immediate dismissal.

ETHICAL GROUPS

Using Power and Punishment

The decision to punish a group member has ethical consequences. Punishing a member is unethical if it is done to suppress differences of opinion or penalize opponents. A group is behaving unethically if it refuses to listen to, understand, and respect other members before judging and punishing them. Ethical groups promote a communication climate of caring and mutual understanding that respects the unique needs and characteristics of individual communicators rather than punishing or excluding members who are different or disagreeable.

If you and your group decide that someone deserves to be punished, the punishment should be predictable (everyone should know the rules/expectations), immediate (applied as soon as possible after notice of the violation), consistent (applied equally to all), and

impersonal.[1] The following short checklist may help you apply these four standards:

1. Make sure that everyone has the same understanding of the rules. Don't punish someone who is unaware of the group's norms and policies.
2. Make sure that the rules apply to everyone and are enforced equally.
3. Make sure that a policy is in place for dealing with those who violate the rules. Don't make up a policy and assign punishments as you go along.
4. Make sure that you enforce all the rules that you create—all the time. To not do so is to risk losing respect among group members.[2]

[1] Michael Ramundo with Susan Shelly, *The Complete Idiot's Guide to Motivating People* (Indianapolis, IN: Alpha Books, 2000), p. 187.
[2] Ramundo, p. 183.

BALANCING MISSION AND MOTIVATION

Not only is a motivated group more committed to achieving its goals, but its members also enjoy the experience of working together. Highly motivated groups create optimal group experiences for all members. An **optimal experience** is an experience "where people are totally caught up in what they are doing, wholly focused on it, and able to perform at a very high level with ease."[51] Groups that provide optimal experiences can be exhilarating. Creative thinking comes easily, and working on the task is pleasurable. Hard work is energizing rather than exhausting. Some group members may find the optimal experience so pleasurable that they see working in the group as preferable to relaxing or socializing.[52]

To achieve this optimal level of motivation, groups must balance a number of factors. They must have a worthy mission that motivates both individual members and the group as a whole. They must use motivational strategies that appeal to the needs and personality types represented in the group. Assessments and rewards must be carefully balanced to ensure that evaluations are informative rather than controlling. Finally, although extrinsic rewards are common and useful, intrinsic rewards are often more powerful. Ultimately, members of motivated groups discover that working together in pursuit of a worthy goal is its own greatest reward.

GroupWork

Your Guiding Motive

Goals
- To identify the major intrinsic factors that motivate group members
- To demonstrate the diversity of motivators within a single group

Participants: Groups of five to seven members

Procedure
1. Each class member should have seven blank index cards. Write each of the following six categories on a different card: Achievement, Recognition, Work Itself, Responsibility, Advancement, and Personal Growth.

2. Consult the Guiding Motives Information Sheet.

3. If you believe that you are motivated by something other than these six guiding motives, write your additional motive on the seventh index card, along with a few words explaining the motive's unique qualities.

4. Think about the six or seven guiding motives, and discard the three that are least important to you. Then think about the remaining motives and discard another one or two, so that you are left with only two motive cards.

5. Form groups of five to seven members. Each member of the group should choose the less important of his or her final two cards and, one by one, answer the following questions:

   - Why is this motive important to you?
   - How does this motive affect your participation in groups?
   - How can groups use this motivator to motivate your behavior?
   - Do differences in motives reflect member diversity?

6. Do a second round in which members discuss their final and most important personal motives. Again, answer the previous four questions.

7. After all participants have discussed their most important motives, the group should discuss the following questions:

   - Which, if any, of the motives were most frequently chosen by group members?
   - How can the group enlist the most frequently chosen motives to enhance group productivity and member satisfaction?
   - If one or two members have unique motives, how can the group enlist these motives to enhance groupwork?

8. Depending on time availability, groups may share their top motives with the rest of the class and discuss similarities and differences.

Source: The motives on the Guiding Motives Information Sheet are derived from Herzberg's research. From "Groupwork: Your Guiding Motive" from *The Motivation to Work* by F. Herzberg, B. Mausner, and B. Snyderman. Copyright © 1993. Reprinted by permission of Transaction Publishers.

Guiding Motives Information Sheet

Achievement

Contributions to goals	Knowledge and expertise
Abilities and skills	High standards for work
Self-created, personal goals	

Recognition

Regular, constructive feedback	Praise for accomplishments
Awards and celebrations	Status and job titles
Salary increases and bonuses	

The Work Itself

Challenging and interesting work	Involvement in group decisions
Freedom to work in your own way	Measurable standards of
Clear, relevant, and worthy goals	performance/improvement

Responsibility

Authority to act	Involvement in planning
Less supervision	Access to information and experts
Trust in your ability and loyalty	

Advancement
Leadership assignments   Job prestige and status
Promotion   Career plans and objectives
Management responsibilities

Personal Growth
Self-knowledge   Continuous learning and improvement
Long-term personal goals   Personal confidence
Creativity and invention

Additional Category:

GROUPASSESSMENT

Group Motivation Inventory

Directions. This instrument can be used to measure the motivation level of a group of which you are currently a member or in which you have worked in the past. Complete the instrument on your own. Use the following scale to assign a number to each statement:

(5) strongly agree
(4) agree
(3) neutral
(2) disagree
(1) strongly disagree

_____   1. I work very hard in my group.

_____   2. I work harder in this group than I do in most other groups.

_____   3. Other members work very hard in this group.

_____   4. I am willing to spend extra time on group projects.

_____   5. I try to attend all group meetings.

_____   6. Other members regularly attend group meetings.

_____   7. I often lose track of time when I'm working in this group.

_____   8. Group members don't seem to mind working long hours on our project.

_____   9. When I am working with this group, I am focused on our work.

_____   10. I look forward to working with the members of my group.

_____   11. I enjoy working with group members.

_____ 12. Group members enjoy working with one another.

_____ 13. I am doing an excellent job in my group.

_____ 14. I am doing better work in this group than I have done in other groups.

_____ 15. The other members are making excellent contributions to this group.

_____ 16. I am willing to do whatever this group needs in order to achieve our goal.

_____ 17. I trust the members of my group.

_____ 18. The other group members are willing to take on extra work.

_____ 19. I am proud of the work my group is doing.

_____ 20. I understand the importance of our group's work.

_____ 21. Everyone is committed to successfully achieving our goal.

_____ 22. I am proud of the contributions I have made to this group.

_____ 23. This group appreciates my work.

_____ 24. I am proud to be a member of this group.

_____ 25. This group really works well together.

Scoring and Interpretation: Add your ratings for all of the statements. A score below 75 indicates a low level of group motivation. Scores between 76 and 99 represent a moderate level of motivation. Any score above 100 suggests that the group is highly motivated. Compare your score to those of other members of your group. You may discover that you share similar feelings about your group and its tasks.

If all the members of the group are highly motivated, the group can proceed and expect positive results. Otherwise, the group should discuss why some members are more motivated than others. Is there disagreement about the goals of the group, the way the task is structured, or the expectations of members? Are some members doing most of the interesting work, while others are relegated to routine assignments? Do some members feel left out or ignored?

If most group members lack motivation, the group may need to discuss its reason for being. Has the group been assigned a task but not given clear directions or a justification for doing the assignment? Is the task too difficult or too complex for the group to handle? Are the expectations unclear or unreasonable? Are some members making it difficult for others to participate?

Source: The Team Motivation Inventory acknowledges the contributions of other inventories, including the JML Inventory in Alexander Hiam, *Motivating and Rewarding Employees* (Holbrook, MA: Adams Media, 1999), and the Encouragement Index in James M. Kouzes and Barry Z. Posner, *Encouraging the Heart: A Leader's Guide to Rewarding and Recognizing Others* (San Francisco: Jossey-Bass, 1999).

NOTES

1. Carl E. Larson and Frank M. J. LaFasto, *TeamWork: What Must Go Right/What Can Go Wrong* (Newbury Park, CA: Sage, 1989), p. 27.
2. Larson and LaFasto, p. 28.
3. Larson and LaFasto, pp. 27–38.
4. Larson and LaFasto, p. 33.
5. David W. Johnson and Frank P. Johnson, *Joining Together: Group Theory and Group Skills*, 2nd ed. (Englewood Cliffs, NJ: Prentice Hall, 1982), pp. 170–171.
6. Edwin A. Locke and Gary P. Latham, *Goal Setting: A Motivational Technique That Works!* (Englewood Cliffs, NJ: Prentice Hall, 1984); also see Andrew J. DuBrin, *Leadership: Research Findings, Practice, and Skills*, 4th ed. (New York: Houghton Mifflin, 2004), pp. 297–298.
7. Locke and Latham, pp. 18–19.
8. Johnson and Johnson, p. 174.
9. Johnson and Johnson, p. 174.
10. Based on Locke and Latham, pp. 27–40; Johnson and Johnson, pp. 173–174.
11. Larson and LaFasto, p. 73.
12. Ernest G. Bormann, *Small Group Communication: Theory and Practice* (Edina, MN: Burgess International Group, 1996), p. 86.
13. Herbert L. Petri, *Motivation: Theory, Research, and Applications,* 4th ed. (Pacific Grove, CA: Brooks/Cole, 1996), p. 320.
14. Douglas A. Bernstein et al., *Psychology* (Boston: Houghton Mifflin, 2001), p. 378.
15. Bernstein et al., p. 380; Petri, pp. 257–259.
16. Bormann, p. 90. See also Petri, pp. 321–328.
17. See Will Schutz, *The Human Element* (San Francisco: Jossey-Bass, 1994).
18. See Martin Fishbein and Icek Ajzen, *Belief, Intention, and Behavior* (Reading, MA: Addison-Wesley, 1975); Julien B. Rotter, "Generalized Expectancies for Internal Versus External Control of Reinforcement," *Psychological Monographs, 80* (1966), pp. 1–28; Petri, pp. 245–254.
19. Fishbein and Ajzen; Rotter, pp. 1–28; Petri, pp. 245–254. See also "Expectancy Theory," *Quick MBA,* available at *http://www.quickmba.com/mgmt/expectancy-theory*; "Expectancy Value Theory," University of Twente (The Netherlands), *http://wwww.tcw.utwente,nl/theorieenoverzicht*, last modified on 9/06/04.
20. DuBrin, p. 291.
21. DuBrin, pp. 293–296. DuBrin lists eight skills for enhancing motivation by applying Expectancy-Value Theory as well as an exercise for estimating the value of rewards.
22. The following resources were used to develop the table of personality type motivators: Larry Damerest, *Looking at Type in the Workplace* (Gainesville, FL: Center for Applications of Psychological Type, 1997); Jean M. Kummerow, Nancy J. Barger, and Linda K. Kirby, *Work Types* (New York: Warner Books, 1997).
23. Kenneth W. Thomas, *Intrinsic Motivation at Work* (San Francisco: Berrett-Koehler, 2000), p. 44.
24. Alexander Hiam, *Motivating and Rewarding Employees: New and Better Ways to Inspire Your People* (Holbrook, MA: Adams Streetwise, 1999), p. 152.
25. Eric Klinger, *Meaning and Void: Inner Experiences and the Incentives in People's Lives* (Minneapolis: University of Minnesota Press, 1997). Klinger provides a discussion of *meaningfulness* as a motivator. He claims that people pursue objects, events, and experiences that are emotionally important for them. However, individuals are not necessarily willing to work to obtain everything that has incentive value when the time and effort needed to obtain the goal are more than the individual is willing or able to expend.
26. Michael Ramundo with Susan Shelly, *The Complete Idiot's Guide to Motivating People* (Indianapolis, IN: Alpha Books, 2000), p. 79.
27. Larson and LaFasto, pp. 39–58.
28. Ramundo, p. 86.
29. Deborah Harrington-Mackin, *The Team Building Tool Kit* (New York: AMACOM, 1994), pp. 118–119.
30. James M. Kouzes and Barry Z. Posner, *Encouraging the Heart: A Leader's Guide to Rewarding and Recognizing Others* (San Francisco: Jossey-Bass, 1999), pp. 54–55.
31. Kouzes and Posner, p. 59.
32. Hiam, p. 170.
33. Hiam, p. 178.
34. Hiam, p. 183.
35. Hiam, p. 183.
36. Based on strategies in Ramundo.
37. R. Brayton Bowen, *Recognizing and Rewarding Employees* (New York: McGraw-Hill, 2000), p. 179.
38. See Thomas, pp. 6–7.
39. Bowen, p. 163.
40. Kouzes and Posner, p. 13.
41. Bowen, p. 30.

42. Bormann, pp. 83–84.

43. Daniel Goleman, "In New Research, Optimism Emerges as the Key to a Successful Life," *New York Times,* December 24, 1991, p. 81.

44. For a discussion of reward criteria, see Bowen, p. 29; Bob Nelson and Dean R. Spitzer, *The 1001 Rewards and Recognition Fieldbook: The Complete Guide* (New York: Workman, 2003).

45. Many books offer long lists and numerous examples of rewards. See Bob Nelson and Dean Spitzer, *The 1001 Rewards and Recognition Field Book* (New York: Workman, 2003) and Bowen.

46. Kouzes and Posner, p. 4.

47. Terrence E. Deal and M. K. Key, *Corporate Celebration: Play, Purpose, and Profit at Work* (San Francisco: Berrett-Koehler, 1998), p. 11.

48. Quoted in Kouzes and Posner, p. 114, from M. O. James et al., *Performing Well: The Impact of Rituals, Celebrations, and Networks of Support,* paper presented at the Western Academy of Management Conference, California.

49. Hiam, pp. 245–247.

50. Ramundo, p. 182.

51. Hiam, p. 17.

52. Hiam, p. 17.

Participation Tools

© Spencer Grant/Photo Edit

CHAPTER 12

Planning and Conducting Meetings

CHAPTER OUTLINE

MEETINGS, MEETINGS, MEETINGS

Approximately 11 million business meetings take place in the United States every day. The typical employee spends almost fifteen hours a week in meetings and may attend sixty formal or informal meetings a month.[1] Odds are that you've spent your share of time in meetings. Certainly you will be attending meetings in the future. Unfortunately, many of these meetings will not be productive or rewarding group experiences. One study suggests that "there is a direct correlation between time spent each week in meetings and an employee's desire to find another job."[2] A new member of a group describes the effect of poor meetings:

> I was appointed to replace a member of an organization's board of directors. Apparently, the departing member had been asked to resign because she stopped attending meetings. Well, no wonder she lost interest! During the first meeting I attended, several people were no-shows, most of those attending arrived late, and the president of the board provided little leadership. We often postponed voting on important issues because members hadn't read the background material.

Many meetings fail to achieve their goal. Our own observations as well as studies and expert conclusions suggest the following explanations for why so many people criticize and dread meetings:

- The meeting was unnecessary and wasted time.

- The meeting's goal was unclear.

- The meeting failed to use or follow an agenda.

- There was not enough prior notice or time to prepare.

- The right people did not attend or were not invited.

- The meeting was held at the wrong time or place.

- The chairperson was ineffective.

- There was too much political pressure to conform or take sides.

Meetings also fail because we take them for granted. Too often we resign ourselves to attending unproductive meetings rather than trying to improve the meetings we must attend. In one study, workers rated 69 percent of the meetings that they attended as "ineffective."[3]

If a group of people get together in the same room at the same time, you have a meeting, right? Wrong. You merely have a gathering of people in one place. We define a **meeting** as a scheduled gathering of group members for a structured discussion guided by a designated chairperson.

You can better understand the unique nature of a meeting by examining the three elements of the definition: schedule, structure, and chairperson. First, a

FIGURE 12.1   **Three Essential Elements of a Meeting**

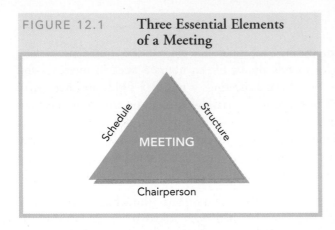

meeting is usually scheduled in advance for a particular time and place; a coincidental gathering of group members does not constitute a meeting.

Second, meetings can be formal and highly structured or informal and loosely structured. A meeting using parliamentary procedure is an example of a formally structured meeting, whereas an emergency staff meeting would be less structured. The third element of a meeting is a designated chairperson. A **chairperson** is a group member who has been appointed or elected to conduct the meeting. The chairperson is not necessarily the group leader but is the person responsible for guiding the group through discussion topics or tasks in an orderly manner.

Note that two of the elements represent the dialectics of structure–spontaneity and leadership–followership. Effective groups understand that the amount of structure and spontaneity must be appropriate for the meeting's goal and for the group's norms and level of formality. Effective groups also understand that effective leadership should match the characteristics of group members as well as the nature of the group's task.

PLANNING THE MEETING

The success or failure of a meeting largely depends on proper planning. Careful planning can prevent at least twenty minutes of wasted time for each hour of a group's meeting.[4] Answering the questions in Figure 12.2 can help you begin the process of planning an effective group meeting.

FIGURE 12.2   **Meeting Planning Questions**

Meeting Planning Questions

- **Why** are we meeting?
- **Who** should attend the meeting?
- **When** should we meet?
- **Where** should we meet?
- **What** materials do we need?

Why Are We Meeting?

The best way to ensure that your meeting does not waste time or frustrate members is to make sure that the meeting is really needed. Answering the following questions can help you decide whether to meet or not to meet:

- Is an immediate decision or response needed?

- Are group input and interaction critical?

- Are members prepared to discuss the topic?

TOOLBOX 12.1

Using Parliamentary Procedure

Many associations and organizations use parliamentary procedure to conduct their official meetings. Their constitution or bylaws may even require it. As we note in Chapter 9, parliamentary procedure is a systematic method for conducting a decision-making meeting in an orderly manner. The chief purpose of parliamentary procedure is to protect the rights of minority members while ensuring majority rule. Parliamentary procedure requires that members be called upon by the chairperson to speak, that voting follow set procedures, and that issues be discussed and debated in the order determined by the rules. Basic parliamentary procedure includes rules for making a motion, seconding a motion, amending a motion, and voting.

- *Main motion.* A new proposal is presented to the group: "I move that the search for a new marketing director be reopened."
- *Seconding a motion.* A main motion must be seconded before it can be discussed: "I second the motion."

- *Amendments.* A main motion can be amended by any member: "I move that the search for a new marketing director be reopened and that previous applicants be invited to reapply."
- *Voting.* After a motion has been discussed, it can be accepted or rejected: "All those in favor say *aye.* All those opposed say *nay.*"

Most groups do not use parliamentary procedure to conduct their meetings. However, it is useful to know its basic principles and rules when making decisions about how to guide any group discussion. The Houghton Mifflin web site for this textbook includes a chapter that summarizes the principles, basic rules, and primary motions of parliamentary procedure.

Online Study Center
General Resources
Read the online chapter "Parliamentary Procedures" for more information.

In many situations, alternative forms of communication can prevent unnecessary group meetings. A memo, fax, email, voice-mail message, or one-to-one conversation may be sufficient. Yet, sometimes, calling a meeting is the fastest way to inform and interact with a group of people.

The most important step in planning a meeting is defining its goal as clearly as possible. A meeting's goal is not the same as the meeting's subject. The subject is the topic of the discussion. The goal identifies the desired outcome of the meeting. For example, if an executive calls her assistant and says, "Call a staff meeting next Thursday at 2:00 p.m.," the assistant may ask, "What will the staff meeting be about?" "Employer-provided day care," the executive replies. Has the executive revealed the goal of the meeting? No. We know only that the subject of the meeting is employer-provided day care. If the executive had said, "We need to determine whether our employer-provided day-care system needs to be expanded," we would know the purpose or goal of the meeting.

It is important to ensure that a group can achieve the goal by the end of the meeting. If this cannot be done during a single meeting, the purpose statement should be rewritten to focus on a more specific outcome. If necessary, a series of meetings should be scheduled in order to achieve the final goal.

Who Should Attend the Meeting?

The membership of many groups is predetermined. However, if a task does not require input from everyone or needs the expertise of only certain people, you should select participants who can make a significant contribution. When selecting meeting participants, try to include those members who will be directly affected by the outcome of the meeting. In addition, choose participants with special expertise, different opinions and approaches, and the power to implement decisions. Although you may be tempted to invite only those people who agree with your point of view, individuals who disagree or who represent minority opinions can provide a more balanced and realistic discussion of issues.

Make sure that your group is a manageable size. The larger the group, the more difficult it will be to manage. Try to limit a small group meeting to fewer than twelve participants; a group of five to seven members is ideal. In many situations, the size of the group is predetermined. For instance, an organization's bylaws may require that a majority of the board members attend in order to conduct a vote.

How would this meeting room affect a group's ability to interact and achieve a common goal?
(© Photonica/Getty Images)

When Should We Meet?

The next step is deciding what day and time are best for the meeting. Should the meeting be in the morning, in the afternoon, after work hours, or during lunch? Avoid scheduling group meetings near holidays or at the beginning or end of the week when members may be less focused on working. Determine both what time the meeting should begin and what time it should end. For a time-consuming and difficult goal, you may decide that more than one meeting will be necessary.

Contact group members to find out when they are available, and schedule the meeting at a time when the most essential and productive participants are free. A meeting that only a few members can attend will not be very productive and will waste the time of those who do show up.

Where Should We Meet?

Choose a location that is appropriate for the purpose and size of the meeting. The room should be large enough, clean, well lit, not too hot or too cold, and furnished with comfortable chairs. Although you may have little control over such features, do your best to provide an appropriate and comfortable setting. Working in an attractive meeting room can make a group feel more important and valued. Also, the meeting room should be located away from distractions such as ringing phones and noisy conversations.

What Materials Do We Need?

A meeting agenda is the most important item to prepare and distribute to a group prior to the beginning of a meeting. The agenda tells the group what topics will be discussed and in what order. In addition to the agenda, you may need to distribute reports or other reading material that group members must review in order to contribute to a productive discussion. Distribute all materials far enough in advance of the meeting so that everyone has time to prepare. In addition, make sure that needed supplies and equipment, such as markers, paper, flip charts, projectors, or computers, are available to the participants.

TOOLBOX 12.2

Choose an Appropriate Meeting Site

The setting of a meeting can mean the difference between attentive members who are comfortable and able to fully participate in a discussion and distracted members who must contend with disruptions or an uncomfortable room. Groups often have several possible choices of meeting location. Typically, meetings occur in four types of locations:[1]

- Your office
- Another person's office
- An on-site meeting room
- An off-site meeting room

There are advantages and disadvantages to each type of meeting site.[2] Your office may be convenient for you and may provide easy access to important reference materials. But if you are the boss, it may create an atmosphere in which members feel more like guests than like group members. In addition, distractions and interruptions can frustrate both you and other group members. Meeting in another group member's office can prove equally distracting but could serve to boost the morale and status of that group member.

On-site meeting rooms, such as conference rooms in your organization's building, can avoid many of the distractions that occur in an individual's office. However, nongroup members may interrupt a group member with questions about other work issues. Off-site meeting rooms, such as space provided by a hotel or conference center, eliminate most distractions and have the added advantage of creating a neutral territory for everyone to come together. On the other hand, off-site meeting sites can be expensive and require travel time.

Business consultants Robert Heller and Tim Hindle point out that "the choice of location is vitally important to the success of a meeting. It is not only a question of comfort; participants must feel that the place is appropriate for the occasion."[3]

[1] Robert Heller and Tim Hindle, *Essential Manager's Manual* (New York: DK Publishing, 1998), p. 445.
[2] Heller and Hindle, p. 445.
[3] Heller and Hindle, p. 444.

PREPARING THE AGENDA

An **agenda** is an outline of the items to be discussed and the tasks to be accomplished at a meeting. A well-prepared agenda can serve many purposes. First and foremost, the agenda is an organizational tool—a road map for the discussion that helps group members remain focused on their task. When used properly, an agenda helps participants prepare for a meeting by telling them what to expect and even how to prepare. An agenda also provides a sense of continuity for a group—it tracks members' assignments and provides status checks for work in progress. After a meeting, the agenda can be used to assess the meeting's success by determining the extent to which all items on the agenda were addressed.

When you are very busy or when a meeting is routine and predictable, writing up an agenda for a future meeting may seem like a waste of time. Just the opposite is true. Failure to plan and prepare an agenda denies a chairperson and a group one of the most powerful tools in meeting management.

Elements of an Agenda

Although the chairperson is responsible for preparing and distributing an agenda in advance of the meeting, group input can ensure that the agenda covers the topics that are important to the entire group. Figure 12.3 summarizes the elements of a traditional business meeting agenda.

Not all meetings will follow the traditional sequence of agenda items. The norms of a group and the goal of a meeting should determine the format of the agenda. For example, if a meeting is called to solve a problem, the agenda items may be in the form of questions rather than the key word format of a more formal agenda, as illustrated in Figure 12.4.

The questions will be determined by the problem-solving method that the group decides to use. In addition to identifying topics to be addressed during the meeting, agenda items should include any information that will help group members prepare for the meeting. The following guidelines can improve meeting productivity:

- Note the amount of time it should take to complete a discussion item or action. This will let the group know the relative importance of the item and help to manage the time available for discussion.

- Identify how the group will deal with each item by noting whether information will be shared with the group, whether the group will discuss an issue, or whether a decision must be made. The phrases *For Information, For Discussion,* and *For Decision* can be placed next to appropriate agenda items.

- Include the name of any person responsible for reporting information on a particular item or facilitating a portion of the discussion. Such assignments remind members to prepare for a specific topic or action item.

FIGURE 12.3	Elements of a Business Agenda	
Purpose of the Meeting	A clear statement of the meeting's objective and topic for discussion helps members prepare.	
Names of Group Members	A list of all participants lets members know who will be attending.	
Date, Time, and Place	The agenda clearly indicates the date, time, duration, and precise location of the meeting.	
Call to Order	This is the point at which the chairperson officially begins the meeting.	
Approval of the Agenda	This gives members an opportunity to correct or modify the agenda.	
Approval of the Minutes	The minutes of the previous meeting are reviewed, revised if necessary, and approved by the group as an accurate representation of the last meeting's discussion.	
Reports	Officers, individuals, or subcommittees report on the progress of their activities.	
Unfinished Business	The agenda lists topics that require ongoing discussion or issues that the group was unable to resolve during the last meeting.	
New Business	New discussion items are outlined and discussed in this section.	
Announcements	Any items of information that the group needs to know but that do not require any discussion are announced.	
Adjournment	The chairperson officially dismisses the participants and ends the meeting.	

Determining the Order of Items

After you have identified all the agenda items, carefully consider the order in which the topics should be discussed. When several different topics must be addressed during a single meeting, they should be put in an order that will maximize productivity and group satisfaction. The following guidelines should help you determine how to balance the sequence of discussion topics in an agenda:

- Begin the meeting with simple business items and easy-to-discuss issues.

- Reserve important and difficult items for the middle portion of the meeting.

- Use the last third of the meeting for easy discussion items that do not require difficult decisions.

This sequence provides the group with a sense of accomplishment before it launches into more complex, controversial issues. If a difficult but important

FIGURE 12.4   **Sample Discussion Meeting Agenda**

Recycling Task Force
November 20, 2006, 1:00 P.M. – 3:00 P.M.
Conference Room 352

Purpose: To recommend ways to increase the effectiveness and participation in the company's recycling program.

I.   What is the goal of this meeting? What have we been asked to do?

II.   How effective is the company's current recycling effort?

III.   Why has the program lacked effectiveness and full participation?

IV.   What are the requirements or standards for an ideal program?
A. Level of Participation
B. Reasonable Cost
C. Physical Requirements
D. Legal Requirements

V.   What are the possible ways in which we could improve the recycling program?

VI.   What specific methods do we recommend for increasing the recycling program's effectiveness and level of participation?

VII.   How should the recommendations be implemented? Who or what groups should be charged with implementation?

decision is taking more time than anticipated, the group may be able to deal with the less important discussion issues scheduled for the last third of the meeting at the next meeting. For example, suppose Ron is preparing an agenda for the next meeting of his local school district's Library Resources Committee. He anticipates a lengthy and controversial discussion of several new sex education books, but there are other items that must also be discussed at the meeting. Ron decides to begin the meeting by reviewing the budget and reporting on the effort to update media technology, then devote a significant amount of meeting time to discussing the sex education books. The last item on the agenda will be a discussion of plans to purchase foreign-language books, which can be addressed at another meeting if the group runs out of time. Sequencing the order of items in this way should allow the group to achieve its goals for this particular meeting.

Double-Checking the Agenda

Once you have determined what items need to be included in the agenda, check them against the meeting's stated goal.

• Are there any items that don't relate to the overall goal and that can be delayed until another meeting? If so, they should be eliminated from the agenda.

- Can all of the items on the agenda be addressed within the allotted meeting time? If there isn't enough time to cover all of the items, rephrase the meeting's goal to be more specific and eliminate some items.

Avoid overloading agendas by trying to do too much in a single meeting.[5] For example, the group may not have time to both discuss the causes of a problem and start identifying possible solutions in the same meeting. You may need to reconsider the number of meetings and their goals.

THE CHAIRPERSON'S RESPONSIBILITIES

If you are the chairperson of a meeting, you have a tremendous amount of influence over, and responsibility for, the success of the meeting. Although you may or may not be responsible for planning the meeting, you must conduct the meeting, and you are often responsible for following up on decisions after the meeting is over. Effective chairpersons facilitate productive discussions by making sure that they have fulfilled their responsibilities prior to, during, and after the meeting (see Figure 12.5).

Prior to a meeting, the chairperson must notify everyone who should attend, preferably in writing. The announcement should include a clear statement of the meeting's goal, what is expected of participants, and the time, location, and duration of the meeting. After the meeting has been announced, all the materials needed by participants, including the agenda, should be distributed in advance. As the chairperson, you should check with all members to confirm that they are planning to attend and, if necessary, send a brief reminder before the meeting. Also, you should be fully prepared for the discussion.

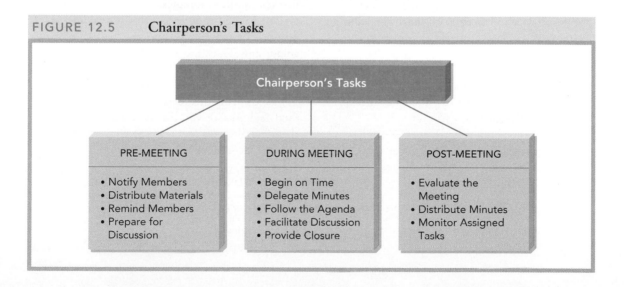

FIGURE 12.5   **Chairperson's Tasks**

Chairperson's Tasks

PRE-MEETING	DURING MEETING	POST-MEETING
• Notify Members • Distribute Materials • Remind Members • Prepare for Discussion	• Begin on Time • Delegate Minutes • Follow the Agenda • Facilitate Discussion • Provide Closure	• Evaluate the Meeting • Distribute Minutes • Monitor Assigned Tasks

During the meeting, effective chairpersons "balance strength with sensitivity; they balance knowing where they want the meeting to go with allowing the group to sometimes take it way off course; they balance having something to say with the restraint to say nothing; they assume the role of traffic cop in discussions without coming across with stifling authority."[6]

The agenda will be your guide to keeping the discussion moving in an orderly way. The meeting should begin at the scheduled time. Make sure all members have a copy of the agenda, and determine who will take the minutes of the meeting. Attendance should then be taken and noted in the minutes. Ask the group to review the agenda and make any revisions that may be needed. After the completion of these preliminary tasks, you can proceed through the agenda items as planned. As chairperson, you should refrain from dominating the meeting. Your first priority is facilitating the group's discussion.

Finally, the chairperson should provide a sense of closure to the meeting by briefly summarizing what has been accomplished and what still needs attention and action. If work has been delegated to different members of the group during the meeting, those responsibilities should be reviewed. If the group plans to schedule another meeting, ask for suggestions for agenda items and, if possible, set the date, time, and place of the next meeting.

TOOLBOX 12.3

Pace the Meeting

There is nothing worse than sitting through a meeting that moves too slowly, strays from the agenda, or lasts too long. A good chairperson allows enough time for everyone to participate but still ends the meeting on time. The following strategies can help keep your meetings moving at a comfortable pace:[1]

• Start the meeting on time.
• Don't waste time reviewing things for latecomers.
• Stick to the agenda.
• Place a time limit on each agenda item.
• Stay focused on the meeting's goal.
• Schedule another meeting to discuss unfinished items.

As many as 73 percent of meeting participants admit to having done other work during a meeting. Almost all of us have probably daydreamed during a boring meeting.[2] Group members are usually most attentive during the first ten to fifteen minutes of a meeting. Their attention tends to decline during the middle portion of a meeting, then increase again before adjourning. Thus, the optimal meeting length is forty-five minutes.[3] If your meeting must run longer, schedule breaks at least every ninety minutes. Giving members time to stretch, get food or drinks, or visit the restroom will make them more relaxed and ready to work when the meeting reconvenes.[4]

[1] Robert Heller and Tim Hindle, *Essential Manager's Manual* (New York: DK Publishing, 1998), pp. 470–471.
[2] Jeff Davidson, *The Complete Idiot's Guide to Getting Things Done* (New York: Alpha Books, 2005), p. 232.
[3] Heller and Hindle, p. 471.
[4] Heller and Hindle, p, 471.

If you are the chairperson, you should distribute the minutes of the meeting and any reports that were prepared. A chairperson's job does not end when a meeting adjourns; it may continue right up to the minute when a subsequent meeting is called to order. After the meeting is over, take time to evaluate its success and determine what should be done to improve the next meeting.

DEALING WITH DIFFICULT PEOPLE

A carefully planned meeting can fail if the chairperson or the group allows individuals to persist in behavior that disrupts the group process. All group members should address such behavior rather than assuming that the chairperson can or will resolve the problem. In their book *How to Make Meetings Work*, Michael Doyle and David Straus write that "dealing with these problem people is like walking a tightrope. You must maintain a delicate balance between protecting the group from the dominance of individual members while protecting individuals from being attacked by the group."[7] Although there can be as many potential problems as there are group members, there are a few particular types of behavior that cause most of the headaches.

Nonparticipants

You don't need full participation from all members all the time; the goal is to have a balanced group discussion over the course of the entire meeting. The group should be concerned, however, about members whose participation is always minimal. Are they anxious, unprepared, or uninterested?

Apprehensive or introverted participants should not be forced to contribute before they are ready to do so. At the same time, though, make sure you provide opportunities for reluctant members to become involved in the discussion. When nonparticipants do contribute, respond positively to their input to demonstrate that you see the value in their ideas.

Loudmouths

A member who talks more than the others is not necessarily a problem. However, when a person talks so much that no one else gets a chance to speak, the group has a loudmouth problem. At first, allow loudmouths to state their ideas, and acknowledge that you understand their positions. It may be necessary to interrupt them to do so. Then shift your focus to other members or other issues by asking for alternative viewpoints. If a loudmouth continues to dominate, remind him or her of the importance of getting input from everyone. The next time the group meets, you may want to assign the loudmouth the task of taking minutes as a way of shifting her or his focus from talking to listening and writing.

Interrupters

Sometimes group members are so preoccupied with their own thoughts and goals that they interrupt others when they have something to say. Although most interrupters are not trying to be rude, their impatience and excitement cause them to speak out while other members are still talking. When a group member continually interrupts others, it is time to interrupt the interrupter. Invite the previous speaker to finish making her or his point. A more aggressive option is simply not to allow the speaker to be interrupted—to intervene and say, "Let Mary finish her point first, and then we'll hear other viewpoints."

Whisperers

A person who carries on a confidential conversation with another group member during a meeting can distract everyone else. The interference caused by members who are whispering or snickering makes it hard for people to concentrate and listen to other members. Directing eye contact toward such sideline conversations can make the offenders more aware of their disruptive behavior. If the behavior persists, ask the talkers to share their ideas with the group. This will probably stop the behavior and may uncover issues that deserve discussion.

Latecomers and Early Leavers

People who arrive late and leave early can distract those who have managed their time well enough to arrive on schedule and stay through the entire meeting. If you are the chairperson, start the meeting at the scheduled time, and avoid wasting meeting time by stopping to review what has already been accomplished for the benefit of latecomers. Let latecomers sit without participating until they have observed enough of the meeting to contribute to the discussion. We don't recommend that you publicly reprimand or embarrass latecomers or early leavers, but you may want to talk to them after the meeting about what can be done to enable them to attend the entire meeting.

Members who come in and out of the meeting in order to do other work at the same time cannot be full participants. Such behavior is distracting; it communicates to the rest of the group that the meeting is not very important. These members should be asked politely either to stay for the entire discussion or to take care of other work in advance.

When you have to confront a dysfunctional member, be sensitive and focus on the behavior rather than making personal attacks. Point out the behavior and suggest an alternative, and also indicate the consequences if the alternative is not followed. Don't overreact; your intervention can be more disruptive than the problem member's behavior. It is best to begin with the least confrontational approach and then work toward more direct methods as necessary.

GROUPTECH

Virtual Group Meetings

Deborah Duarte and Nancy Snyder point out that "technology cannot make up for poor planning or ill-conceived meetings. In fact, it can make the situation worse."[1] Fortunately, the same principles that apply to planning a productive face-to-face meeting apply equally well to planning virtual meetings. Just as for any meeting, the goal of the meeting must be clear, and all participants should receive an agenda in advance. If your virtual meeting will involve several technological applications, your agenda might indicate which items will rely on which technology. For example, if brainstorming is planned, the agenda might indicate that an anonymous input feature will be used. This knowledge will give group members the opportunity to prepare for the discussion and to make sure that they can use the necessary technology adequately.

When deciding who should attend a virtual meeting, avoid the temptation to include too many participants. Virtual meetings take place electronically. Thus, they typically are not limited in size because of the number of seats in a conference room. However, including too many participants is a mistake. It is easier for members to become nonparticipants in virtual meetings than in face-to-face meetings. Furthermore, opportunities to participate become more limited when too many members are involved. Include only people who actually need to attend the virtual meeting, and keep the group small enough to allow everyone to contribute actively.

Determining when your group should meet can be simplified through the use of technology. If you work for a company or organization with a computer network, you may have access to a calendar program with a group scheduling feature. Such a program can provide an instant list of times and dates when all members will be available. The program will schedule the meeting,

notify the participants by email, and enter the meeting on their calendars.

When planning a face-to-face meeting, you need to determine where your group should meet. When planning a virtual meeting, you should decide which technology can best serve the meeting's goal. Should your group meet via an audioconference or a videoconference? Can the group accomplish its goal during an online text-only meeting? You also may need to determine what specific technology will be required to accomplish specific tasks. For example, how will the group brainstorm ideas, organize those new ideas, and vote during its virtual meeting? The answers to these questions will depend on the goal of your meeting, the specific tasks on the agenda, and your group's access to technology.

In addition to distributing the agenda and any other documents, make sure that the participants have access to the technology and can use it adequately. If necessary, your group should schedule a separate training session at which participants can learn how to use any equipment or programs that will be needed during your virtual meetings. If group members are able to use the many devices and applications that are available, communication technologies can enhance your group's ability to work together from remote locations. However, if group members are uncomfortable with or unable to take advantage of such technologies, they will find your virtual meetings frustrating and unproductive. The group will end up focusing on technical problems rather than addressing its agenda. Finally, always test the technology that you will be using prior to meeting with the group. Careful planning can ensure that your virtual meetings are productive and efficient.

[1] Deborah L. Duarte and Nancy Tennant Snyder, *Mastering Virtual Teams: Strategies, Tools, and Techniques That Succeed*, 2nd ed. (San Francisco: Jossey-Bass, 2001), p. 157.

ADAPTING TO DIFFERENCES

Very often, group members from different cultural, ethnic, and age groups do not share similar expectations about group roles and individual behavior in meetings. In some cultures, it would be considered disrespectful for a young group member to interrupt an older one or for a new group member to challenge a veteran member. In such cases, it may be tempting to interpret lack of participation as inattention or lack of interest, when, in fact, the group member is demonstrating a high degree of respect for the group and its leader.

At one college, the president appointed an advisory council to coordinate activities designed to improve the racial climate on campus. One member of the group reported the following observation:

> One council member was a former diplomat from a West African country. He rarely spoke, but when he did, he always began with a very formal "Madam Chairman." After that, he would deliver a three- to five-minute speech in which he would summarize what had been said and offer his opinion and recommendations. When he was finished, he would thank everyone for listening. At first we didn't know how to respond. It was so formal, so complex. Eventually we learned to expect at least one "speech" from this member. We learned to listen and respond to a very different style of participation. This member defined his participant role very formally and acted accordingly. Patience on the part of other participants helped the group accept and adapt to his custom of formality.

Group members may represent different ages, genders, educational and work backgrounds, religions, political viewpoints, and cultures. All of these elements can affect how a meeting is conducted and how well a meeting accomplishes its goals. Adapting to the diversity of group members involves understanding and accommodating differences while pursuing shared goals.

PREPARING THE MINUTES

The **minutes** of a meeting are the written record of a group's discussion and activities during the meeting. The minutes record discussion issues and decisions for those who attended a meeting and provide a way to communicate with those who did not attend. By looking through a group's minutes over a period of time, you can learn about the group's activities, measure how productive the group has been, learn about individual members' contributions to the group, and know whether group meetings tend to be formal or informal. Of most importance, however, the minutes help prevent disagreement over what was decided in a previous meeting and what tasks individual members agreed to do.

Select a Recorder

The chairperson is ultimately responsible for the accuracy and distribution of the minutes. However, during the meeting, the chairperson must be free to facilitate the group's discussion. Therefore, the task of taking minutes should be delegated to another group member. The group may designate a recorder or secretary to take minutes at every meeting, or members can take turns volunteering to do the minutes. Regardless of who takes the minutes, however, the chairperson is responsible for checking their accuracy and distributing copies to all group members.

Determine What Information to Include

For the most part, the format of the minutes should follow the format of the agenda. If you are assigned to take minutes, you will probably include much of the following information:

- Name of the group
- Date and place of the meeting
- Names of those attending
- Name of the person who chaired the meeting
- Names of absent members
- The exact time the meeting was called to order
- The exact time the meeting was adjourned
- Name of the person preparing the minutes
- Summary of the group's discussion and decisions, using agenda items as headings
- Specific action items

Action items are tasks that individual members have been assigned to do after the meeting. An action item includes the person's name, the assignment, and the deadline. For example, an action item might look like this: "Action: Mark Smith will review the prices charged by competing companies by the next meeting." It is helpful to underline action items in the minutes to make it easier to refer back to them when reviewing the group's progress.

CLOSE TO HOME   JOHN McPHERSON

© 1994 John McPherson/Dist. by Universal Press Syndicate

As soon as Mrs. Felster began to read the minutes of the last meeting, the board members knew she was not going to work out as the new secretary.

FIGURE 12.6   **Sample of Informal Minutes**

> **Domestic Violence Class Discussion Group Meeting**
> **February 10, 2006, in Library Conference Room 215**
>
> Present: Gabriella Hernandez (chairperson), Eric Beck,
> Terri Harrison, Will Mabry, Tracey Tibbs
>
> Absent: Lance Nickens
>
> Meeting began at 2:00 P.M.
>
> **Group Topic:** The group discussed whether emotional and verbal abuse should be included in the project. Since we don't have much time to do our presentation, we decided to limit the topic to physical abuse only.
>
> **Research Assignments:** Since the assignment is due in two weeks, we decided to divide the issue into different topics and research them on our own.
>   *Action: Eric will research why people stay in abusive relationships.*
>   *Action: Gabriella will research the effects on the children.*
>   *Action: Terri will find statistics and examples of the seriousness of the problem.*
>   *Action: Will is going to find out why and how the abuse happens.*
>   *Action: Tracey will find out what resources are available in the area for victims.*
> Members will report on their research at the next meeting.
>
> **Absent Members:** Lance has not been to the last two class meetings. We don't know if he is still going to participate in the group. *Action: Gabriella will call Lance.*
>
> **Class Presentation:** We need to think of creative ways to make a presentation to the class. The group decided to think about this and discuss it at the next meeting.
>
> **Next Meeting:** Our next meeting will be at 2:30 on Tuesday, February 14th, in the same place. *Action: Terri will reserve the room.*
> The meeting ended at 3:15 P.M.
>
> (Meeting notes taken by Tracey Tibbs)

Taking Minutes

Well-prepared minutes are brief and accurate. When summarizing a group's discussion, remember that the minutes are not a word-for-word record of everything that every member has said. To be useful, they must briefly summarize the discussion. The following guidelines should be used when taking minutes:

- Instead of describing the discussion in detail, write clear statements that summarize the main ideas and actions.

- Make sure to word decisions, motions, action items, and deadlines exactly as the group makes them in order to avoid future disagreements and misunderstandings.

- If there is any question about what to include in the minutes at any point during the meeting, ask the group for clarification.

- Obtain a copy of the agenda and any reports that were presented to attach to the final copy of the minutes. These documents become part of the group record along with the minutes.

Immediately after the meeting, you should prepare the minutes for distribution. The longer you delay, the more difficult it will be to remember the details of the meeting. In some meetings, minutes may be taken on a laptop computer. Once the minutes have been prepared, they should be given to the chairperson for review. When a group has officially approved the minutes, they are final and become the official record of the meeting.

ETHICAL GROUPS

 ## Use Discretion When Taking Minutes

The person charged with taking minutes has an ethical obligation to exercise good judgment when deciding what to include in the minutes and what to omit. Everything that is included in the minutes must accurately reflect the major discussion issues and decisions. At the same time, you must make decisions about what would be inappropriate or harmful to include in the official record of the group's meeting.

There are times when a group does not want portions of its discussion recorded in the minutes. For instance, groups that are discussing sensitive legal or personnel issues often must keep information confidential. Confidentiality is compromised if the minutes are made available to individuals outside of the group. If the meeting agenda will include some confidential items, make sure that all group members understand that some information is not to leave the group and should not be recorded in detail in the minutes.[1]

During a meeting, group members may make comments that would not be wise to include in the minutes. For example, a group that vents its frustration with a boss that the members don't like will not want to read in the minutes that "The group agreed that Dan is unreasonable and insensitive." Groups often express frustrations and complaints within the confines of a meeting. Including such comments in the minutes can stifle open communication and is not necessary for making the meeting minutes useful.

The group's recorder must balance the need for accuracy with discretion. The following guidelines can help you determine when to include information and when to leave it out:

- Report the facts and all sides of a discussion accurately.
- Never insert your own personal opinions.
- Be discreet. If the group determines that a portion of the discussion should be "off the record," you should honor that decision.
- When in doubt, ask the group if an issue should be included or how it should be worded in the minutes.
- Always keep in mind that the minutes are often the only record of the meeting and may be read by individuals outside of the group.

[1] Robert Heller and Tim Hindle, *Essential Manager's Manual* (New York: DK Publishing, 1998), p. 429.

EVALUATING THE MEETING

To determine the effectiveness of meetings and identify areas for improvement, chairpersons and participants should evaluate their meetings. There are a number of ways to determine the success of a meeting:

- Throughout the meeting, the chairperson may ask for comments and suggestions before moving on to the next item. This feedback allows the group to modify its behavior and improve its interaction when discussing the next item.

- At the end of the meeting, the chairperson can briefly summarize his or her perceptions of the meeting and ask for comments and suggestions from the group before adjourning.

- After the meeting, participants can be approached individually for their comments and suggestions for improving the group's next meeting.

- A Post-Meeting Reaction Form can be distributed to members before adjourning.

A **Post-Meeting Reaction (PMR) Form** is a questionnaire designed to assess the success of a meeting by collecting written reactions from participants. The chairperson should prepare the form in advance of the meeting, distribute it at the meeting, and collect it before participants leave. Regardless of the format of the questions, a PMR form should ask questions about the issues being discussed, the quantity and quality of group interaction, and the effectiveness of meeting procedures. The feedback from the group should then be used to improve the next meeting. The sample PMR form in the assessment section at the end of this chapter contains many of the typical questions asked to evaluate a group's meeting.

BALANCED MEETINGS

Just as every group is unique, every meeting is different. Planning and conducting effective meetings require balanced decision making. On the one hand, the group should strive for an ideal meeting, but, at the same time, it should understand and adapt to what can realistically be accomplished in a single meeting. Even in a short meeting, effective groups and group members attempt to balance the competing components of groupwork by taking a *both/and* approach to resolving dialectic tensions.

The 3M Meeting Management Team describes the critical role of the chairperson as "a delicate balancing act" in which chairpersons must

... influence the group's thinking—not dictate it. They must encourage participation but discourage domination of the discussion by any single member.

They must welcome ideas but also question them, challenge them, and insist on evidence to back them up. They must control the meeting but take care not to overcontrol it.[8]

Effective meetings achieve a balance between the different needs of individual members and the necessity of accomplishing the group's goal. Balanced meetings result in greater productivity and member satisfaction.

GROUPWORK

Meet the People Problems

Goal: To understand the principles and apply textbook suggestions to other common people problems that arise during meetings

Participants: Groups of five to seven members

Procedure

1. Read the descriptions of the five additional people problems that often arise in meetings.

2. As a group, prepare at least two strategies for dealing with each type of people problem.

3. Groups should share their strategies with the entire class and discuss the following question: What general, overriding principles emerge as effective strategies for dealing with difficult members?

People Problems

- The *Broken Record* keeps bringing up the same point over and over.
- The *Headshaker* nonverbally disagrees in a dramatic and disruptive manner. Headshakers shake heads, roll eyes, cross and uncross legs, slam books shut, push chairs back, or madly scribble notes after someone has said something.
- The *Attacker* launches personal attacks on another group member or on you as facilitator.
- The *Know-It-All* uses credentials, age, length of service, or professional status to argue a point: "Well, I'm the one who has a Ph.D. in physics, and I know it doesn't work that way"; "I have been working in this business longer than anyone else here, and I know that will never fly.
- The *Backseat Driver* keeps telling you what you should be doing: "I would have let people discuss the issue more before brainstorming"; "I would move on to the next issue if I were you."

Source: Based on "How to Be a Good Facilitator," from *How to Make Meetings Work* by Michael Doyle and David Straus, copyright © 1976 by Michael Doyle and David Straus. Used by permission of Berkley Publishing Group, a division of Penguin Group (USA) Inc.

Post-Meeting Reaction (PMR) Form

Directions. After a selected meeting, complete the following PMR form by circling the number that best represents your answer to each question. After compiling the answers from all participants, including the chairperson, use the results as a basis for improving future meetings.

1. How clear was the goal of the meeting?

unclear	1	2	3	4	5	clear

2. How useful was the agenda?

useless	1	2	3	4	5	useful

3. Was the meeting room comfortable?

uncomfortable	1	2	3	4	5	comfortable

4. How prepared were group members for the meeting?

unprepared	1	2	3	4	5	well prepared

5. Did everyone have an equal opportunity to participate in the discussion?

limited opportunity	1	2	3	4	5	ample opportunity

6. Did members listen effectively and consider different points of view?

ineffective listening	1	2	3	4	5	effective listening

7. How would you describe the overall climate of the meeting?

hostile	1	2	3	4	5	friendly

8. Were assignments and deadlines made clear by the end of the meeting?

unclear	1	2	3	4	5	clear

9. How would you rate this meeting overall?

unproductive	1	2	3	4	5	productive

Additional Comments:

NOTES

1. Jeff Davidson, *The Complete Idiot's Guide to Getting Things Done* (New York: Alpha Books, 2005), p. 232.

2. Matthew Gilbert, *Communication Miracles at Work: Effective Tools and Tips for Getting the Most from Your Work Relationships* (Berkeley, CA: Conari Press, 2002), p. 173.

3. *The Week*, April 2, 2005, p. 35. Study reported in CNNmoney.com.

4. Karen Anderson, *Making Meetings Work: How to Plan and Conduct Effective Meetings* (West Des Moines, IA: American Media Publishing, 1997), p. 17.

5. Charlie Hawkins, "First Aid for Meetings," *Public Relations Quarterly* [online], 42 (1997), p. 2. Available at *http://db.texshare.edu/ovidweb/ovidweb.cgi.* Accession Number: 03528854.

6. Bobbi Linkemer, *How to Run a Meeting That Works* (New York: American Management Association, 1987), p. 42.

7. "How to Be a Good Facilitator," from *How to Make Meetings Work* by Michael Doyle and David Straus, copyright © 1976 by Michael Doyle and David Straus. Used by permission of Berkley Publishing Group, a division of Penguin Group (USA) Inc.

8. 3M Meeting Management Team, with Jeannine Drew, *Mastering Meetings: Discovering the Hidden Potential of Effective Business Meetings* (New York: McGraw-Hill, 1995), p. 78.

CHAPTER 13

Making Presentations in Groups

CHAPTER OUTLINE

PRESENTATIONS IN GROUPS

The spontaneous, give-and-take nature of group discussions enhances a group's ability to share information and solve problems. There are circumstances, however, in which groups may set aside time for less spontaneous and more structured communication. Individual members or a selected spokesperson may be asked or required to make an oral presentation. The following related scenarios illustrate how such presentations become part of the group process:

- *Debating the tuition proposal.* The student government association has been asked to discuss the college's proposal to increase tuition by 10 percent. In order to ensure that everyone has an equal chance to speak at the meeting, student representatives are limited to three-minute statements.

- *Opposing the tuition proposal.* The student government association selects a spokesperson to make an oral presentation opposing the proposed tuition increase at the monthly meeting of the college's board of trustees.

- *Appealing for state funding.* The college president asks the student government association's spokesperson to be part of a group presentation to the state legislature's appropriations committee in which a team of administrators, faculty, staff, and students will be given thirty minutes to present a request for increased state funding.

Whether it is within a group, on behalf of a group, or by an entire group, a **presentation** occurs when a member is given the opportunity to speak, uninterrupted, to a group of people. During the course of any group discussion or meeting, a presentation by one or more group members may be required. In other situations, a group member may be asked to make an oral presentation to an outside group or audience. In such situations, the reputation of a group may be judged by how successful its members are as speakers.

This chapter offers specific guidelines that can help you prepare and give a successful presentation that is adapted to the needs and characteristics of a group and its goals. These guidelines can also be used in the event that you or your group has to make a presentation to an outside audience.

PRESENTATION GUIDELINES

Most experienced speakers do not follow a strict set of rules. Instead, they use a set of guidelines to direct them through critical decision-making steps. The guidelines shown in Figure 13.1 represent essential decision-making points and questions that should be addressed when developing an oral presentation.[1]

FIGURE 13.1   **Presentation Guidelines**

Order	Guideline	Key Question
1	Purpose	What is the goal of your oral presentation?
2	Audience	How will you adapt to the members of your audience?
3	Logistics	How will you adapt to the occasion and setting of your presentation?
4	Content	What ideas and information should you include?
5	Organization	How will you organize and support your ideas?
6	Credibility	How can you enhance your believability and perceived competence?
7	Performance	How should you practice and deliver your presentation?

Purpose

The first and most important step in developing a successful presentation is identifying your purpose—much like the need for groups to identify and agree upon a common goal. Your purpose is not the same thing as your topic. Your purpose is what you want your listeners to know, think, believe, or do as a result of your presentation. For example, the proposed tuition increase is the discussion topic for the student government association. A student speaker's purpose, however, may be to support or oppose the increase. When someone is making a presentation in a group setting, the general topic is usually predetermined by the group and its agenda. Thus, when a student rises to speak for or against higher tuition, everyone is well aware of the topic but may be unable to predict the speaker's position or arguments. Having a clear purpose does not necessarily mean that you will achieve it. Without a purpose, though, little can be accomplished and much can be lost.

Dr. Terry Paulson, psychologist and author of *They Shoot Managers, Don't They?*, cautions speakers against making a presentation without a purpose:

There are so many messages and memos being hurled at today's business professionals [that] they are in information overload. It's like sipping through a fire hydrant. Don't unnecessarily add to the stream by including unnecessary fill, fact, and fluff. Volume and graphs will not have a lasting impression: having a focus will. Ask yourself early in the process: What do I

want them to remember or do three months from now? If you can't suc-
cinctly answer that question, cancel your presentation.[2]

Know your purpose, drop what is unimportant, and focus on the essentials.

Audience

If the first and most important guideline in developing a presentation is identifying your purpose, the next most important is to analyze and adapt to your
listeners—the members of your group or the people in an outside audience. This
process begins by seeking answers to two questions: What are your listeners' characteristics? What are their opinions?

Characteristics.
Two characteristics to consider when analyzing a group of
listeners are demographic traits and individual attributes. **Demographic traits**
include age, gender, race, ethnicity, religion, and marital status. If you have been
working in a group for a long time, it will be easy for you to catalog the demographic traits of group members. For a presentation to a new or a large audience,
however, the task is more difficult. Take a good look at your listeners to note visible demographic traits, such as age, gender, and race. At the same time, assume
that there is more diversity than similarity among your audience members.

Within a group, **individual attributes** take into account the distinctive features
of particular group members, such as job title and status, special interests, personality traits, relationships with other members, and length of group membership. Demographic traits and individual attributes can affect how your listeners
react to you and your message. For example, students who support themselves on
limited incomes may oppose a tuition increase more strongly than students who
can afford the increase.

Opinions.
There can be as many opinions in an audience as there are members. Some members will agree with you before you begin your presentation,
whereas others will disagree with you no matter what you say. Some listeners
will have no opinion about an issue and will be quite willing to accept a reasonable point of view or proposal. Effective presenters try to predict who or how
many listeners will agree, disagree, or be undecided (see Figure 13.2).

If most of your listeners agree with you, are undecided, or have no opinion,
your presentation should focus on introducing new information or summarizing the most important ideas and arguments. When people share the same opinions and goals, the presentation should update listeners who are in need of
information and motivate them to work as a cohesive group. For example, if the
members of the student government are universally opposed to a tuition increase, a speaker could focus on motivating the audience to take political action.

If audience members disagree with you, make sure that you have set realistic
goals. Asking students to storm the president's office may get the administration's

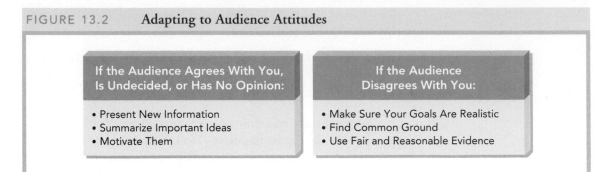

FIGURE 13.2   **Adapting to Audience Attitudes**

If the Audience Agrees With You, Is Undecided, or Has No Opinion:

- Present New Information
- Summarize Important Ideas
- Motivate Them

If the Audience Disagrees With You:

- Make Sure Your Goals Are Realistic
- Find Common Ground
- Use Fair and Reasonable Evidence

attention but may be too radical an action for most students to support. A second strategy is to work at getting audience members to listen to you. You can't do that by telling them that you're right and they're wrong. You can't change their minds if they won't listen. Instead, try to find **common ground.** Find a belief or value that you share with those who disagree with you. Emphasizing shared ideas, feelings, history, and hopes can help you overcome resistance. For example, if a student speaker tells the board of trustees that the student government wants to help it find a solution to the financial crisis, the board may be more willing to listen to student concerns about the proposed tuition increase. Finally, when you address a controversial issue, make sure you support your arguments with fair and reasonable evidence. If your arguments and evidence are weak, your opponents are likely to use those weaknesses against you.

Logistics

Deciding how to adapt to the occasion and setting of a presentation requires more than taking a quick look at the seating arrangements for a meeting. Ask questions about *where* and *when* you will be speaking.

Where? Where will you be delivering your presentation—in a large conference room, an auditorium, a classroom? What are the seating arrangements? Are there any distracting sights or sounds? Can the lighting be changed? Will you need a microphone? Will special equipment be needed for presentation aids? Once you have the answers to such questions, the next step is figuring out how to adapt to where you will be delivering your presentation. For example, a request for a microphone would be in order if a student government spokesperson learns that several hundred students plan to attend the board of trustees meeting.

When? Will you be speaking in the morning or in the afternoon? Are you scheduled to speak for five minutes, twenty minutes, or an hour? What comes before or after your presentation—other presentations, lunch, a question-and-answer session? The answers to questions about timing may require you to make major adjustments to your oral presentation. If you are given a time limit for your presentation, that

TOOLBOX 13.1

Adapt to Key Audience Members

Sometimes an audience may be so varied that it's impossible to find one best way to reach everyone. In such cases, it helps to identify and concentrate on key audience members—the people who have the authority or ability to make things happen. They may be opinion leaders or other respected audience members. Other audience members may take their cues from the ways in which these people react to a presentation or speaker. If the key people seem interested and responsive, others will mimic their behavior. If they seem bored or annoyed, others will be too.

If you cannot reach everyone in the audience, try to reach those who have influence. How do you identify these key individuals? Observe the nonverbal behavior of audience members: Who gets the most handshakes? Who is given a prominent seat or is accompanied by an entourage? Who commands attention? If you can't tell who is most important by observing the audience, ask the person who invited you or your group.[1]

[1] Isa N. Engleberg and John A. Daly, *Presentations in Everyday Life: Strategies for Effective Speaking,* 2nd ed (Boston: Houghton Mifflin, 2005), p. 106.

limit should be respected. Whether you are scheduled to speak for five minutes or one hour, never add more than 5 percent to your allotted time. Even better, aim for 5 percent less. Most people lose patience with someone who speaks too long.

Content

As soon as you know you have to make a presentation, start collecting ideas and information. Gathering materials can be as simple as spending a few hours thinking about the purpose of your presentation or as complicated and time-consuming as spending days doing research on the World Wide Web and in the library. Regardless of the topic or your purpose, research multiple sources and include more than one type of information in your presentation. Houghton Mifflin Company, the publisher of this textbook, provides an online web site that includes a chapter titled "Informed Groups." This Web-based chapter provides models and advice for doing effective and ethical research. These recommendations also apply to gathering and assessing content for a presentation.

Online Study Center General Resources
Read the online chapter "Informed Groups" for more information.

Organization

Planning a presentation requires organizing your ideas and supporting material in a way that will help you achieve your purpose. Ask yourself whether there is a natural structure or framework for your message. What common ideas have appeared in most of your materials? What information seems most interesting, important, and relevant to the purpose of your presentation?

Organizational Patterns. Fortunately, there are many organizational patterns that can help you put your ideas and information in order. Figure 13.3 summarizes some common patterns.

Regardless of whether you choose one of the patterns shown in Figure 13.3 or create a different organizational structure that is better suited to your needs, you should always focus on your purpose. Consider whether a pattern lends itself to achieving the purpose of your presentation. If it does, you can move on to connecting your supporting material to the organizational pattern you have chosen.

Outlining Your Presentation. Outlines for a presentation start with a few basic building blocks. The following outline can be used as a model to organize almost any kind of presentation.

I. Introduction
II. Central Idea or Purpose (Preview of Main Points)
III. Body of Presentation
   A. Main Point 1
      1. Supporting Material
      2. Supporting Material
   B. Main Point 2
      1. Supporting Material
      2. Supporting Material

FIGURE 13.3   **Organizational Patterns**

Organizational Pattern	Example
REASON GIVING	Three reasons why we should increase the dues are…
TIME ARRANGEMENT	The college's hiring steps must be complied within the following order…
SPACE ARRANGEMENT	The following membership increases occurred in the east, south, west, and central regions…
PROBLEM–SOLUTION	This research method avoids the problems we encountered last time…
CAUSES AND EFFECTS	Here's what could happen if we fail to increase our dues…
STORIES AND EXAMPLES	I've contacted four community associations in this county and here's what I found…
COMPARE–CONTRAST	Let's take a look at the two research methods we considered…

TOOLBOX 13.2

Order the Main Points

In many cases, the organizational pattern you have chosen will dictate the order of your key points. If, for example, you are using time arrangement, the first step in a procedure should come first. If you are discussing a historical event, you can begin at the beginning and work your way forward to the finish. In other instances, your format may not suggest an order. In these cases, identify your strongest ideas and place them in strategic positions. Do you "put your best foot forward"? Or, do you "save the best for last"? Your answer to these questions depends on many factors, such as the audience's attitude toward you, your group, and your message. The following strategies can help you make the right decision:

- *Strength and familiarity.* If one of your ideas is not as strong as the others, place it in the middle position. This sequence avoids beginning or ending the presentation with a weaker point.

- *Audience.* Consider what you know about your audience and what it expects from the presentation. For example, if your audience is not very interested in your topic, don't begin with detailed technical information. Instead, begin by explaining why the topic is important.
- *Logistics.* If you are one of a series of speakers, you may end up having less time to speak than you expected. Plan on discussing your most important points first. That way, if you have to shorten your presentation, your audience will have still heard your key points.

There are no absolute rules about ordering your main points. Just make sure that they follow a logical progression and are ordered in a way that helps your audience to understand and remember them.[1]

[1] From Isa N. Engleberg and John A. Daly, *Presentations in Everyday Life: Strategies for Effective Speaking,* 2nd ed. (Boston: Houghton Mifflin, 2005), p. 206.

      C. Main Point 3
          1. Supporting Material
          2. Supporting Material
  IV. Conclusion

Naturally, every outline will differ, depending on the number of main points you want to make and the amount and type of supporting material you use. Once you have outlined your presentation, the major sections should be filled in with more specific ideas and supporting material.

The introduction of a presentation should be used to gain the audience's attention and interest. An effective beginning should direct the audience's attention toward you and your message. An interesting example, statistic, quotation, or story at the beginning of a presentation can "warm up" your audience and prepare it for your message.

The "central idea or purpose" section of a presentation lets you explain your basic purpose and gives you an opportunity to preview your main points. This section should be brief, no more than a few sentences. It simply reveals your purpose and, in some cases, the organizational plan you will use in the body of the presentation.

The heart of your presentation is the "body" section. Here you add your supporting material to each main point. No matter how many main points there are, each should be justified or backed up with at least one type of supporting material. If you can use several different types of material, your presentation will be more interesting and impressive.

The end of a presentation should have a strong and well-planned conclusion. An effective conclusion can help listeners remember the most important parts of your message. A quick summary, a brief story, a memorable quotation, or a challenge to the group can leave a strong final impression. Figure 13.4 shows the organizational structure and notes that could be used for a presentation by a student spokesperson to a college's board of trustees.

Credibility

In a presentation, your personal credibility depends on how well the audience can identify with you and your message. No matter how much you know about the subject or how sincere you are about your purpose, it is your audience that determines whether you are perceived as qualified and believable. Your **credibility** as a speaker represents the extent to which an audience believes you and the things you say.[3] This guideline may sound simple—improve your credibility and the audience will believe you—but it depends on many factors. Two important factors that have been identified by researchers are competence and character.

Competence refers to your expertise and abilities.[4] If you are not a recognized expert on a subject, you must demonstrate that you are well prepared. There is nothing wrong with letting your group or the members of your audience know how much time and effort you have put into researching the topic or with sharing your surprise at discovering new ideas and information. In both cases, you would be demonstrating that you have worked hard to become a qualified and competent speaker.

Character reflects your goodwill and your honesty. Are you trustworthy and sincere? Do you put the group's goal above your own? "Do you make a special effort to be fair in presenting evidence, acknowledging limitations of your data and opinions, and conceding those parts of opposing viewpoints that have validity?"[5] If your audience or the members of your group don't trust you, it won't matter what you say.

Performance

By the time you start asking questions about your delivery, you should know what you want to say and have given some thought to how you want to say it. David Zarefsky writes that "*how* a speaker says something affects *what* is really being said, and it also affects what listeners actually hear and understand"[6]

Forms of Delivery. In many group and public audience settings, you will be asked to speak **impromptu**—a form of delivery without advance preparation or

FIGURE 13.4   **Sample Presentation Outline**

SAMPLE PRESENTATION OUTLINE

Hold the Line on Tuition

I.   Introduction

Story: Student who had to choose between buying shoes for her children and paying tuition for her nursing courses.

II. Central Idea or Purpose

Because a tuition increase will have a devastating effect on many students, we ask you to search for other ways to manage the college's financial crisis.

III. Body of Presentation

A.   Another tuition increase will prevent students from continuing or completing their college education on schedule.

1.   More students are becoming part-time rather than full-time students. (College statistics)

2.   Students are taking longer to complete their college degrees. (College statistics)

3.   Students are sacrificing important needs to pay their tuition bills.
(Quotations and examples from college newspaper)

B.   There are better ways to manage the college's financial crisis.

1.   Consolidate areas and reduce the number of administrators and support staff.
(Compare to college of same size that has less staff)

2.   Seek more state and grant funding.
(Statistics from national publication comparing funding levels and grants at similar types of colleges)

3.   Re-evaluate cost and need for activities and services such as athletic teams, the off-campus homecoming and scholarship balls, intersession courses, and full staffing during summer sessions. (Examples)

IV. Conclusion
Money is a terrible thing to waste when students' hearts and minds are at stake. Let's work together to guarantee that all of our students become proud and grateful alumni.

practice. For example, a member of the board of trustees may ask a student spokesperson a question after an oral presentation. The student must respond impromptu. Being well informed and anticipating such requests is the best way to be prepared for impromptu speaking.

When you do have advance notice, you will be more effective if you speak extemporaneously. **Extemporaneous speaking**—the most common form of delivery—involves using an outline or a set of notes to guide you through your presentation. Your notes can be a few key words on a single small card or a detailed outline that includes supporting materials. These notes will reflect the decisions you have made during the preparation process, but they will also give you the flexibility to quickly adapt your presentation to the audience and the occasion.[7]

Unless the situation is very formal or your words are intended for publication, avoid reading a manuscript version of your presentation. Even though your manuscript may be well written and well read, such a delivery is too formal for most settings. Moreover, reading from a script prevents you from observing listeners' reactions and modifying your presentation as a result of those reactions. If you must use a manuscript, write it as though you are speaking; that is, avoid long sentences, complex words, and formal term-paper grammar. Also, do not memorize your manuscript and try to deliver it without any notes. What if you forget or go blank? Unless you have the skills of a professional actor and can memorize a script and make it sound as if you just came up with the wording, forget about memorizing a presentation.

Vocal and Physical Delivery.   The key to a successful performance is practice. After you have begun your presentation is much too late to make delivery decisions. Moreover, the only way to predict the length of your presentation accurately is to practice it out loud and time it. The place to work on how you sound and look is during rehearsal sessions.

Vocal characteristics such as volume, rate, pitch, articulation, and pronunciation can be controlled and practiced. Rehearse your presentation in a voice loud enough to be heard, but without shouting. Even in a small-group setting, an oral presentation requires a bit more volume than you would use in a normal conversation. Also, monitor the rate at which you speak. Many listeners have difficulty following someone who speaks at a rate that exceeds 180 words per minute. The most tolerable and useful all-purpose rate is 140 to 180 words per minute.[8]

Sometimes speakers are difficult to understand because their articulation is not clear. Poor articulation is often described as sloppy speech or mumbling. Generally, it helps to speak a little more slowly and a little louder and to open your mouth a little wider than usual. Similar problems can occur when words are mispronounced. Because it can be embarrassing to mispronounce a word or a person's name, look up any words you are not sure of in a dictionary or ask someone how to pronounce them correctly.

The single most important physical characteristic in an oral presentation is eye contact. Look directly at the individual members of your audience, eye to eye. Even before a large audience, "the only kind of eye contact that successfully establishes the feeling of connection with members of the audience is a reasonably long, in-focus look at specific individuals."[9]

There is more to body movement than thinking about how you sit in a chair or stand before a group. Your gestures, appearance, and actions can add to or detract from your presentation. If you are well prepared and have practiced, your gestures and movements should be natural. At the same time, try to avoid distracting gestures such as pushing up eyeglasses, tapping the table with a pencil, or pulling on a strand of hair. Such annoying movements can draw attention away from the content of your presentation.

GROUP PRESENTATIONS

The seven guidelines discussed so far—purpose, audience, logistics, content, organization, credibility, and performance—apply to any presentation you might make to your small group or to external audiences. If, however, you are asked to make a presentation as a member of a public group or as part of a team presentation, there are additional factors to consider.

GROUPTECH

Presentations in Virtual Groups

Presentations are no longer the sole domain of people who speak, uninterrupted, to an audience that they can see and hear in real time. Groups use technology to communicate across time, distances, and organizational boundaries. Learning how to prepare and deliver a virtual presentation is an essential skill for anyone working in a virtual group. The following suggestions can strengthen your ability to "perform" effective presentations in audioconferences, teleconferences, and text-based computer conferences.

In audioconferences, you must use your voice to communicate your meaning and emotions. Speak as clearly as you can. Use changes in rate, pitch, and inflection to emphasize particular ideas and communicate your feelings. When video is added to the virtual mix, your appearance sends a powerful message to those who are watching. Dress appropriately. Avoid busy patterns, noisy jewelry, and stark white or black clothing. If someone asks you a question during a video-

conference, look at that person as if he or she were in the room with you. If the question comes across the television screen, look at the camera (not at the person's image) when you respond. If you are the only person in a room talking to an audience at another location, speak directly to the camera as though it were a group member instead of a machine. Try to keep your delivery natural and sincere. This isn't prime time live; it's a group at work.

If you have to make a "presentation" in a text-only computer conference, you have two options: You can write a report and send it to all members, or you can write minipresentations to make your point. Think of your writing as a substitute for speech. Also, remember that the basic requirements of any good presentation still apply— you need a clear purpose, audience analysis, logistical planning, thorough preparation, good organization, personal credibility, and a well-rehearsed delivery.

Public Group Presentations

Chapter 1 describes four different types of public groups: panel discussions, symposia, forums, and governance groups. In all these settings, group members are speaking to a public audience. In addition to following the presentation guidelines described in this chapter, make sure you have considered the unique requirements of a presentation by a public group for a public audience. As a member of a public group, you have a responsibility to yourself, your group, and your audience.

When you are participating in a public group, remember that you are "on stage" all the time—even when you are not speaking. If you look bored while another member is speaking, the audience may wonder whether what that speaker is saying is worth sharing. During a presentation by a public group, an attentive audience will notice other group members' "gestures, facial expression, and posture. They deliberately look for unspoken disagreements or conflicts."[10] For example, if a member of the college's board of trustees rolls his eyes every time another board member speaks in support of student concerns, the audience will receive a mixed message about the board's commitment to serving student needs. Try to look at and support the other members of your group when they speak, and hope that they will do the same for you.

Team Presentations

When a solitary group member prepares an oral presentation, dozens of decisions must be made. When an entire group is charged with preparing a presentation, the task becomes enormously complex. Unlike a panel discussion, symposium, forum, or governance group, a team presentation is not necessarily designed for a general audience; its goal is to inform and influence a very special audience. A **team presentation** is a well-coordinated, persuasive presentation by a cohesive group of speakers who are trying to influence an audience of key decision makers. Team presentations are common in nonprofit agencies and international corporations. They are seen in marketing presentations, contract competitions, and organizational requests for funding.

- A professional football team seeking backing for a new stadium brings a well-rehearsed group of executives and players to a public meeting, at which they explain how the stadium will enhance the economic development and prestige of the community without adversely affecting the surrounding neighborhoods.

- Companies making the "shortlist" of businesses being considered for a lucrative government contract are asked to make team presentations to the officials who will award the final contract.

- In a presentation to the state legislature's appropriations committee, a state college's board chairperson, college president, academic vice president, and student representative are given a total of thirty minutes to justify their request for more state funding.

Team presentations are used to decide whether a group or a company is competent enough to perform a task or take on a major responsibility. They are also used to present a united front when organizations are seeking support and endorsements. Thomas Leech describes how significant a team presentation can be:

> Team presentations are important; the stakes are often high. There generally has to be a significant reason to gather a diverse, highly paid, and often influential group together to hear a team of presenters. And whether the presentation involves the company president or a junior designer, the presenting team has to put forth a great deal of time and money in getting ready, reflecting the importance an organization places on team presentations.[11]

A team presentation is not a collection of individual speeches; it is a team product. Although a symposium is a coordinated presentation, symposium speakers do not necessarily present a unified front or have a strategic goal as their purpose. In many ways, the team presentation is the ultimate group challenge because it requires both efficient and effective decision making and a coordinated performance. Groups that work well in the conference room may fall apart in the spotlight of a team presentation.

Fortunately, the oral presentation guidelines described in this chapter can direct a group through the critical decision-making steps needed to develop an effective team presentation. Much like an individual speaker, a team should:

- Determine the team presentation's overall purpose or theme.

- Adapt the presentation to a specific group of decision makers.

- Adjust to the place where the team presentation will be delivered.

- Prepare and share appropriate content and supporting materials.

- Plan the introduction, organization, and conclusion for each team member's presentation as well as for the entire team's presentation.

- Enhance the team's credibility by demonstrating its expertise and trustworthiness.

- Practice until the team's performance approaches perfection.

In addition to these guidelines, a team must make sure that everyone, including management, knows what the team is going to do and that every detail has been considered. Marjorie Brody, author of *Speaking Your Way to the Top*, writes:

> To be effective, team presentations must be meticulously planned and executed. They must be like a ballet, in which each dancer knows exactly where to stand, when to move, and when to exit from the stage. . . . If a team works like a smooth, well-oiled machine, if one member's presentation flows into

the next presentation, and if all members present themselves professionally and intelligently, the impression left is one of confidence and competence.[12]

Team presentations require a great deal of time, effort, and money to prepare and present. The payoffs, however, are high. For instance, following team presentations by several companies, the Department of Energy awarded a $2.2 billion contract for environmental cleanup to a team headed by Fluor Corporation. Fluor made the best impression. "All the firms had capabilities, but how the team works as a team in the oral presentations is a key determining factor."[13] The awarding of a $2.2 billion contract should convince anyone who doubts the value of effective team presentations.

QUESTIONS AND ANSWERS

Once you or your team has completed a well-prepared presentation, you may not be finished; group or audience members may have questions or comments. The key to making a question-and-answer session a positive experience for everyone is to be prepared to answer a variety of questions and to know what to do when you don't have an answer.

If there is a single rule, it is this: Answer the question. One way to practice for a question-and-answer session is to follow these guidelines:

- *Be brief.* Respond to questions with no more than three sentences.

- *Be honest.* If you don't know the answer to a question, admit it. Don't change the subject. The audience will know if you are avoiding the issue.

How can group members prepare to answer audience questions efficiently and effectively? (© Michelle Gabel/Syracuse Newspapers/The Image Works)

- *Be specific.* Provide appropriate information. Have some ready-made remarks, including interesting statistics, stories, examples, and quotations, that you can use in your answers.

If you run into difficult or hostile questions, remember that just because one listener disagrees with you doesn't mean that everyone is against you. If you encounter an antagonistic question, remember the listening guideline "listen before you leap." Take your time before answering, and do not strike back in anger. Try to paraphrase the question to make sure you understand what the person is asking. If you are prepared and ready for questions, you should have little difficulty dealing with the unexpected.

PRESENTATION AIDS

Presentation aids are supplementary audio and/or visual materials that help an audience understand and remember what is said in a discussion or oral presentation. Effective presentation aids can make a dull topic interesting, a complex idea understandable, and a long presentation endurable. Studies sponsored by the 3M Corporation found that group "presenters who use visual aids are perceived as

TOOLBOX 13.3

 ### Encourage Questions

Effective presenters use a variety of techniques to encourage audience members to ask questions. Never open a question-and-answer session with "Are there any questions?" This requires only a *yes* or *no* response. If audience members do not have any questions in mind, they may just sit there. Instead, begin by asking a question that assumes that there are questions, such as "What are your questions?" or "Who has the first question?"

If no one answers at this point, pause and wait. Inexperienced presenters often feel uncomfortable waiting the several seconds it takes for audience members to come up with questions. Keep in mind that just as you may need a few seconds to organize your thoughts for an answer, the audience members may need time to frame their questions. If you still don't get any questions after a significant pause, be prepared

with some of your own. For example, "One of the questions our group often hears after our presentation is . . ." or "If I were in the audience, I'd want to know. . . ."

Once an audience member asks the first question, you may find yourself facing the opposite situation: You may get an overwhelming number of questions and not have enough time to answer them all. As you near the end of your allotted time, or when you determine that the question-and-answer session has gone on long enough, bring the questioning to an end by saying, "I have time for two more questions." Then do just that: Answer two more questions and thank the audience for its participation.[1]

[1] Isa N. Engleberg and John A. Daly, *Presentations in Everyday Life: Strategies for Effective Speaking*, 2nd ed. (Boston: Houghton Mifflin, 2005), p. 499.

better prepared, more professional, more highly credible, and more interesting than those who do not."[14] At first, these findings may be difficult to believe. Can something as simple as an overhead transparency make that much difference? The answer is *yes*.

Creating Presentation Aids

Only a dozen years ago, a hand-drawn poster would have been an acceptable presentation aid in most situations. This is no longer the case. The availability of presentation software makes it possible for speakers to create more professional-looking presentation aids. You are probably familiar with some presentation software. The most popular product is Microsoft's PowerPoint®. **Presentation software** is a computer program that is used to create slides that can be displayed on an overhead projector, on a computer monitor, or directly from a computer onto a screen. Most presentation software packages also contain features for printing a speaker's notes and handouts.

The first question you should ask yourself is whether you even need a slide to make a particular point. Sometimes a message can be communicated more effectively through words alone. Many listeners complain that even the simplest presentations have become dull displays of unnecessary slides that waste everyone's time. Although we cannot provide comprehensive instruction on how to use presentation software, we suggest that you follow some basic design principles (see Figure 13.5) regardless of what software you use.

Restraint. Presentation software offers such a dazzling array of graphics, fonts, colors, and other visual elements that one's first inclination is to use them all. Resist the temptation. More often than not, a simple slide will be much more effective than a complex one.

Two recommendations can help you decide how much is "just right" for a presentation using computer-generated slides: (1) Make only one point on each

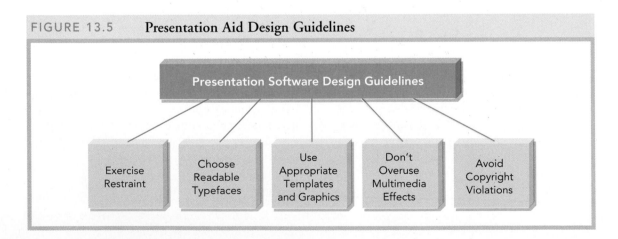

FIGURE 13.5   **Presentation Aid Design Guidelines**

Presentation Software Design Guidelines

Exercise Restraint · Choose Readable Typefaces · Use Appropriate Templates and Graphics · Don't Overuse Multimedia Effects · Avoid Copyright Violations

slide, and (2) follow the six-by-six rule. Each slide should make only one point, and the title of the slide should state that point. Everything else on the slide should support the main point. It takes less time to present two well-structured slides than to load up one slide with a muddled message.[15] In addition, aim for no more than six lines of text with six words per line. This rule of thumb allows your slide to contain the main heading and several bullet points below without bloating or information overload.[16] These recommendations also apply to other types of presentation aids, including hand-drawn posters and flip charts.

Remember that an aid is only an aid; slides are not a presentation. They are not meant to be a script that is read word for word. Useful presentation aids balance "tersity" and diversity. In other words, make slides compact and concise, while using them to add variety and interest. Finding this balance depends on understanding the value of presentation aids and the pitfalls to avoid when adding technical "sizzle" to your presentation.[17]

Type. After deciding what you want to put on a slide, you will need to select a typeface or font. "Users of presentation software have instant access to a veritable candy store of typefaces with tempting names like Arial, Calypso, Gold Rush, and Circus."[18] Again, exercise restraint. Using too many typefaces looks amateurish. As a general rule, never use more than two different fonts on a single slide. As much as you may be tempted, avoid the fancy, but difficult-to-read, fonts. You are better off choosing common typefaces such as Helvetica, Arial, or Times Roman.

The size of type is as important as the selection of font. The best way to determine if your type is large enough is to prepare a few sample slides and project them in the room where your group will be meeting. Generally, you should try to avoid type that is smaller than 24 points. If you find that you have more text than will fit on a slide, don't reduce the size of the type. Doing so is an indication that you are trying to put too much text on one slide. Textual slides should contain just a few key words. Reducing the size of the type to include more text not only makes for a poor presentation aid, but also makes the aid less legible.

Templates and Graphics. On a slide-by-slide basis, use a consistent style and background. From within your presentation software, you can select any of several dozen backgrounds or templates. Here, too, it is important to exercise restraint. In most cases, it is better to choose a modest background that will spruce up your slide but not compete with your words, charts, or graphics.

In choosing graphics, the first question you must ask yourself is whether group members really need to see the picture you want to use. If, for example, you are making a presentation about a new medical device, it may be useful to show the actual device or a picture of the device. On the other hand, showing a picture of a doctor during the presentation would probably not be useful. A picture of a doctor does not help explain the medical device.

Artwork that doesn't have a specific purpose can get in the way of your presentation. Presentation software often comes with numerous clip-art images that you may be tempted to use. Resist the temptation to use graphic elements just because you can. More often than not, clip-art graphics get in the way of messages when the graphic is not the reason for displaying the slide.

Multimedia. **Multimedia** technology allows you to use words, charts, graphics, sounds, and animation in a single presentation. It is possible to create presentation aids so dazzling that group members remember more about the slides than about you or your message. Although there are times when animation or sound may enhance understanding, these multimedia components are frequently no more than window dressing. They can be extraneous items that get in the way of the message rather than increase understanding. The last thing you want is for your audience to leave a presentation wondering how you got the *Tyrannosaurus rex* to eat the pie chart instead of discussing the data that were represented in the pie chart.

Multimedia effects are often misused by presenters. Some such effects are so overused that they have become clichés. Beginning a presentation with the theme from *Rocky* or *2001: A Space Odyssey* is not only unnecessary, but also tired. If you decide to include multimedia effects in a presentation, you should be able to articulate a reason for doing so other than "it's neat." The fine line between "adding

ETHICAL GROUPS

 ### Respect Copyrights

Technology not only makes it easier to create professional-looking presentation aids, but it also makes it easier to appropriate the creative work of others in a presentation. When the creation of visual or audio images is a person's livelihood, the uncompensated use of such images raises ethical questions. Such unfair use may even be a violation of federal copyright laws. A discussion of whether a particular use of an image is illegal is far beyond the scope of this book; however, you should be aware of the legal and ethical implications of using unlicensed images.

A whole industry has developed to provide clip art and clip audio to computer users. A user who purchases such a package has the right to make copies of the images and use them in presentations. Likewise, the visual and audio images that are included with presentation software can be used in your presentations. On the other hand, if you create a computer image by scanning an image from another source or if you obtain an image from the Internet, your conscience and your knowledge of copyright law must act as your guide.

enough to spice up the presentation" and "overpowering your listeners" is often trampled by enthusiastic presenters.[19] Multimedia presentations may be fun to put together, but they must be well designed, well rehearsed, and well presented.

Pitfalls of PowerPoint

PowerPoint is everywhere. Unfortunately, many presenters use PowerPoint (or other brands of presentation software such as Lotus Freelance® or Corel Presentations®) without thoroughly investigating whether it enhances the listeners' comprehension and helps the speaker accomplish her or his purpose. Some corporations have even banned PowerPoint presentations by employees who have not had extensive training in visual design and its relationship to audience comprehension and reasoned analysis. The 3M Corporation discourages the use of PowerPoint because "it removes subtlety and thinking."[20]

Edward Tufte, the writer of several books on graphic design, notes:

> Presentations largely stand or fall on the quality, relevance, and integrity of the content. . . . If your numbers are boring, then you've got the wrong numbers. If your words or images are not on point, making them dance in color won't make them relevant. Audience boredom is usually a content failure, not a decoration failure. . . . PowerPoint cognitive style routinely disrupts, dominates, and trivializes content. PowerPoint presentations too often resemble a school play: very loud, very slow, and very simple.[21]

A survey of college students concluded that students like technology when it is used well, but some gave professors failing grades when it came to using PowerPoint. They complained that many professors cram slides with text and then recite the text during class, which some students say makes the delivery flatter than if the professor did not use the slides.[22] As one student put it, "The majority are taking their lectures and just putting them on PowerPoint. . . . With a chalkboard, at least the lights were on and you didn't fall asleep." One professor reported a 20 percent drop in attendance when he posted his PowerPoint slides on the Web. Now his slides are "riddled with blanks and missing information, which he fills in aloud during lecture."[23]

In many cases, paper handouts can show text, numbers, data, graphics, and images more effectively than slides can. Images on paper have a higher resolution. Content can include more words and numbers. Thoughtfully planned, well-written handouts tell your audience that you are serious and thorough, that your message has consequences, and that you respect their attention and intelligence.[24]

Using Presentation Aids

Presentation aids can take many forms: handouts, posters, flip charts, overhead transparencies, computer-generated slides, and videos. The following list of do's and don'ts can help you avoid some of the common pitfalls that speakers encounter when using any type of presentation aid.

- *Explain the point.* A presentation aid does not speak for itself. You may need to explain why you have chosen it and what it means.

- *Wait until it's time.* Prepare listeners for a presentation aid so that they will want to see it. Give them enough time to look at it so that they don't mind turning their attention back to you.

- *Don't talk to your aid.* You control the presentation aid; it shouldn't control you. Talk directly to the people in your audience, not to the poster, flip chart, or slide.

- *Be prepared to do without.* Presentation aids can be lost or damaged; equipment can malfunction. Have a backup plan. Be prepared to make your presentation without your aids.

Above and beyond these do's and don'ts, there is one more piece of advice that should not be ignored: practice, practice, practice. Not only can practice improve your overall performance, but it can also alert you to problems with your presentation aids. For example, we once watched a consultant put almost everything in her talk on transparencies. As soon as she projected something onto the screen, she would turn around and point out the numbers that she thought were important. Unfortunately, she stood right between the screen and the projector, so that most of the information was projected onto her back. If she had practiced in front of others before making the presentation, the problem could have been avoided.

TOOLBOX 13.4

Don't Leave Them in the Dark[1]

Although adjustable lighting has considerable advantages over simple on/off switches, use it carefully. If you are going to display videotapes, overhead transparencies, or computer-generated slides, turn the lights down, but don't leave your audience in the dark. You never want the lights any dimmer than they need to be. If the room is too dark, your audience may drift off to dreamland in the glow of your beautiful slides.

If you intend to turn off your projector when you are not displaying slides, remember that the room will become even darker without that light source. Another problem may occur if you dim the lights sufficiently to let everyone see your slides or overheads: The room may become too dark for you to read your notes.

Obviously, you need to find a middle ground. Dimming the lights only partially is one solution. Getting a lectern with a light might be another option. The more you know about the lighting system in a room, the better you can plan how to speak and how to use your presentation aids effectively.

[1] Isa N. Engleberg and John Daly, *Presentations in Everyday Life: Strategies for Effective Speaking*, 2nd ed. (Boston: Houghton Mifflin, 2005), p. 151.

BALANCED PRESENTATIONS

"Having the floor" in a group discussion is not the same as "being on stage" for a public presentation. When you are preparing and delivering an oral presentation, you should adapt to the needs and expectations of the audience. In an oral presentation, listeners may expect to hear accurate information but not a long-winded technical report; that can be made in writing. In an oral presentation, listeners may want to understand every word but not be exposed to a dramatic performance; that should be done on the stage. Finally, an audience may expect to hear a well-developed argument but not an impassioned plea; that should be made in court.

The guidelines outlined in this chapter cannot produce a successful presentation—only *you* can. Regardless of whether you are talking to a group of friends or to the state legislature, you should try to make informed decisions about your purpose, audience, logistics, content, organization, credibility, and performance. Understanding and balancing these factors will guide you toward an effective and impressive oral presentation.

GROUPWORK

A Practice Presentation

Goal: To practice your delivery skills and gain experience in impromptu, extemporaneous, manuscript, and memorized speaking

Participants: All members of the class

Procedure

1. Each student should prepare a short presentation in which four forms of delivery are used as follows:

   - *Memorized.* Recite thirty seconds of something you have memorized—a poem, the Pledge of Allegiance, song lyrics, or something else.
   - *Manuscript.* Read thirty seconds of any piece of prose—for example, a book or a newspaper or magazine article.
   - *Extemporaneous.* Spend sixty seconds talking to the audience about a personal experience or opinion—what hobbies you have, what you think about a campus or political issue, or some other topic.
   - *Impromptu.* After you have completed these presentations, someone in the audience should ask a question. Answer the question in thirty seconds or less.

2. Assess each speaker's performance and answer the following questions about all of the oral presentations: Which forms of delivery

- Were the most natural?
- Had the most eye contact?
- Were the most interesting to look at?
- Were the easiest to listen to?

GROUPASSESSMENT

Presentation Rating Scale

Directions. Use the following presentation guidelines to assess how well a group member, group spokesperson, or team makes an oral presentation to the group or a public audience. Identify the speaker's strengths and also make suggestions for improvement.

Presentation Guidelines	Superior	Satis-factory	Unsatis-factory
Purpose: Sets clear and reasonable goal			
Audience: Adapts to listeners			
Logistics: Adapts to occasion and setting			
Content: Uses a variety of effective supporting materials to support main points			
Organization: Uses clear organization and an effective introduction and conclusion			
Credibility: Demonstrates competence and character			
Performance: Uses voice, body, and presentation aids effectively			

Comments
Strengths of Oral Presentation:

Suggestions for Improvement:

NOTES

1. Based on Isa N. Engleberg and John A. Daly, *Presentations in Everyday Life: Strategies for Effective Speaking*, 2nd ed. (Boston: Houghton Mifflin, 2005), and Isa N. Engleberg and Ann Raimes, *Pocket Keys for Speakers* (Boston: Houghton Mifflin, 2004).

2. Quoted in Lilly Walters, *Secrets of Successful Speakers* (New York: McGraw-Hill, 1993), pp. 3–4.

3. Engleberg and Daly, p. 129.

4. Engleberg and Daly, p. 130.

5. Jo Sprague and Douglas Stuart, *The Speaker's Handbook,* 6th ed. (Belmont, CA: Wadsworth, 2003), p. 255.

6. David Zarefsky, *Public Speaking: Strategies for Success, 4th ed.* (Boston: Pearson Education, 2005), p. 302.

7. Engleberg and Daly, p. 321.

8. Authors of voice and articulation textbooks generally agree that a useful, all-purpose speaking rate is around 145 to 180 words per minute. See Lyle V. Mayer, *Fundamentals of Voice and Articulation*, 13th ed. (Boston: McGraw-Hill, 2004); Jeffrey C. Hahner, Martin A. Sokoloff, and Sandra L. Salisch, *Speaking Clearly: Improving Voice and Diction,* 6th ed. (New York: McGraw-Hill, 2002); Ethel C. Glenn, Phillip J. Glenn, and Sandra Forman, *Your Voice and Articulation,* 4th ed. (Boston: Allyn & Bacon, 1998).

9. Marya W. Holcombe and Judith K. Stein, *Presentations for Decision Makers: Strategies for Structuring and Delivering Your Ideas* (Belmont, CA: Wadsworth, 1983), p. 169.

10. Holcombe and Stein, p. 178.

11. Thomas Leech, *How to Prepare, Stage, and Deliver Winning Presentations* (New York: AMACOM, 1993), p. 278.

12. Marjorie Brody, *Speaking Your Way to the Top: Making Powerful Business Presentations* (Boston: Allyn & Bacon, 1998), p. 81.

13. Leech, p. 288.

14. 3M Meeting Management Team, with Jeannine Drew, *Mastering Meetings: Discovering the Hidden Potential of Effective Business Meetings* (New York: McGraw-Hill, 1994), p. 140.

15. RAND, *Guidelines for Preparing Briefings* [online] (1996). This document is available at *http://www.rand.org/publications/electronic/.*

16. William J. Ringle, *TechEdge: Using Computers to Present and Persuade* (Boston: Allyn & Bacon, 1998), p. 125.

17. Ringle, pp. 125 and 135.

18. S. Hinkin, "Designing Standardized Templates: First You Choose It, But How Do You Get Them to Use It?" *Presentations, 8* (August 1994), p. 34.

19. Ringle, p. 132.

20. "Microsoft PowerPoint®," *Wikipedia, http://en.wikipedia.org/wiki/PowerPoint.*

21. Edward R. Tufte, *The Cognitive Style of PowerPoint* (Cheshire, CT: Graphics Press, 2003), p. 24.

22. Jeffrey R. Young, "When Good Technology Means Bad Teaching," *Chronicle of Higher Education*, November 12, 2004, pp. A31–32.

23. Young, p. A32.

24. Tufte, p. 24.

Technology and Virtual Groups

TECHNOLOGY AND GROUP COMMUNICATION

Both small and large corporations use virtual teams to develop products, deliver services, and solve problems. According to Deborah Duarte and Nancy Snyder, "they use electronic collaboration technologies and other techniques to lower travel and facility costs, reduce project schedules, and improve decision-making time and communication. For many teams, traveling and having continual face-to-face meetings is not the most efficient or effective way of working."[1] Major corporations such as Boeing Company and IBM report that special computer software has reduced their meeting time by more than 50 percent.[2] In higher education, computer-assisted instruction, faculty web sites, and online classes have become an integral part of the learning process.[3]

Group members who look forward to the latest technological innovation are eager to enlist the power of technology to enhance group effectiveness. However, for members who fear that virtual interaction will erode group morale and productivity, the parade of new technologies can be overwhelming and threatening. Regardless of your perspective, there is no question that technology has become an inevitable and, in some cases, indispensable component of groupwork. These technologies are tools, not toys. Embracing a new technology simply because it's "new and nifty" can have just as negative an effect on groupwork as would rejecting a new technology for fear that it could erode group morale and productivity. Group members must keep in mind that the "convenience of electronic communication does not diminish the importance of face-to-face meetings. Relying totally on electronic communication sacrifices the bonding and synergy that happens when team members meet and work face-to-face."[4]

In this chapter, we provide information about communication technologies that can help you make informed decisions about the use of these technologies in groups. We also provide technical advice for communicating more effectively when using these technologies. We cannot describe or recommend specific hardware and software, because such information is guaranteed to be obsolete by the time this textbook is published. We do, however, encourage you to explore the potential of both old and new technologies as tools for enhancing and improving your ability to communicate and work in virtual groups.

Virtual Groups

Virtual groups rely on technology to communicate, often across time, distance, and organizational boundaries. This definition recognizes that members of some virtual groups may be separated by thousands of miles and several hours of time, while others may work in the same room but use computer technology and software to enhance their interaction and problem solving.

Virtual groups have the potential to be more effective, efficient, and flexible—and often less expensive—than face-to-face groups. Some virtual work groups rarely meet face to face. IBM has an entire unit in which employees telecommute. They do not work in a traditional office, nor do they meet with one another in a face-to-face setting. At PeopleSoft, telecommuting is the dominant style of work throughout the entire company. Corporations are increasingly providing laptop computers, dedicated phone lines, software support, fax-printer units, help lines, and full technical backup at the nearest corporate facility. As a

TOOLBOX 14.1

The Dialectics of Virtual Groups

Virtual groups experience the same dialectic tensions as face-to-face groups. The nature of virtual groups, however, can intensify dialectic tensions. Here we use two dialectics to illustrate some of the unique tensions in virtual groups: (1) conformity and nonconformity and (2) conflict and cohesion.

Conformity and nonconformity. This dialectic is represented in the concept of **group polarization**, a tendency for members of groups to express more extreme opinions and take more extreme actions. This tendency is intensified in virtual groups because members cannot see one another's reactions and because they may feel more independent when contributing online.[1] Effective virtual groups understand that group polarization can lead to *both* strong group agreement (conformity) *and* fruitful risk taking (nonconformity).

Psychologist Patricia Wallace explains that group interaction seems to intensify the viewpoints of individual group members and moves them toward extremes.[2] This tendency is quite strong in virtual groups because there are fewer nonverbal cues to moderate opinions and behavior. Thus, although the potential for flocking with "birds of a feather" in virtual groups has advantages, it also "can lead to a false sense of security in one's point of view."[3]

Conflict and cohesion. On the one hand, you may find it easier and more comfortable to express disapproval or disagreement online than in a face-to-face situation. On the other hand, virtual groups are often more successful in balancing conflict and cohesion because members feel more independent and are physically removed from the "dangers" of face-to-face conflict. Researchers note that the content of messages in virtual groups tends to be "less controversial than is popularly believed: Conversations are more helpful and social than competitive. Interactive messages seem to be more humorous, contain more self-disclosure, display a higher preference for agreement and contain many more first-person plural pronouns."[4] In short, virtual groups provide an environment that encourages *both* constructive conflict *and* genuine cohesion.

[1] Crispin Thurlow, Laura Lengel, and Alice Tomic, *Computer Mediated Communication: Social Interaction and the Internet* (London: Sage, 2004), p. 63.

[2] Patricia Wallace, *The Psychology of the Internet* (Cambridge: Cambridge University Press, 1999), p. 75.

[3] Thurlow et al., p. 63.

[4] Sheizaf Rafaeli and Fay Sudweeks, "Networked Interactivity," *Journal of Computer-Mediated Communication*, 2 (1997), available online at *http:www.december.com/cmc/mag/current/toc.html,* October 23, 2003, cited in Thurlow et al., p. 67.

result, employees work almost exclusively in virtual groups.[5] The technologies available for virtual communication are growing rapidly and include

- Internet technologies, including email, listservs, newsgroups, bulletin boards, chat rooms, blogs, metaworlds, personal home pages, and webcams

- Meeting facilities with sophisticated electronic and technical support as well as interactive capacities

- Electronic meeting rooms augmented by computer graphics, faxes, printers, and whiteboards that enable participants to utilize organizational databases, distant experts, and the World Wide Web

Synchronous and Asynchronous Communication

When group members use technology to interact simultaneously in real time, they are engaged in **synchronous communication**. Conference calls, videoconferences, and Internet chat rooms are examples of synchronous communication.

Because synchronous communication requires real-time group interaction, it allows group members to work together as a cohesive unit and thus promotes synergy. Synchronous communication is spontaneous and dynamic; it can enhance group processes such as brainstorming or solution development and analysis. Unfortunately, some of the advantages of synchronous communication are lost online because most of us type more slowly than we speak. Consequently, there can be significant lag time between a comment and a response.

Another problem that can disrupt synchronous online communication is that the message sequence can become confused. Statements and responses may not arrive in the order in which they were sent. Consequently, some group members may be addressing a new topic, while others are still composing responses to a prior issue.

Asynchronous communication is the opposite of synchronous communication. Asynchronous communication is linear and not interactive. Immediate feedback is not received when a message is sent. During asynchronous communication, one person makes a statement and posts it for the group to see. Group members, often at their convenience, look at the message and then post responses. Asynchronous communication does not require group members to hold a meeting. Instead, members read and respond to messages as their schedules permit. Email and bulletin boards are examples of asynchronous communication.

Asynchronous communication is more deliberate than synchronous communication. Group members can take the time to give serious consideration to one another's messages and offer carefully thought-out responses. It is particularly useful for completing certain types of group tasks, such as developing and editing written reports. Sending out a document to an entire group via email may require no more effort or expense than sending it to a single person.

The advantages and disadvantages of these two types of computer-based group communication are summarized in the table shown in Figure 14.1.

Synchronous Communication	Asynchronous Communication
ADVANTAGES	**ADVANTAGES**
• Group Cohesion and Synergy • Spontaneous and Dynamic Interaction	• More Time to Compose Responses • Facilitates Document Review and Editing
DISADVANTAGES	**DISADVANTAGES**
• Typing Speed Is Slower Than Speaking Speed • Messages Might Be Received Out of Order	• Lacks Spontaneity • Linear Rather Than Interactive

GROUP COMMUNICATION MEDIA

Throughout this textbook, we describe various ways in which groups interact and solve problems in face-to-face settings. Groups can also perform these functions virtually. Here we offer more specific guidelines for using voice-, video-, and text-based media in virtual group settings.[6]

Audioconferences

When virtual groups use voice-only media to communicate, they engage in an **audioconference.** Audioconferences take two forms: teleconferences and computer-based voice links. The teleconference is the most familiar and easiest type of electronic meeting to convene. A computer-based voice link functions just like a teleconference, but it uses computers rather than telephones. Frequently referred to as a "conference call," a **teleconference** is a coordinated phone call involving three or more group members. All it requires is a telephone with service that supports conference calling. Almost all business telephone services and some residential phone services have teleconference capabilities.

Participating in Audioconferences. Audioconferencing is the easiest type of virtual group interaction to understand because we are familiar with the basic technology—the telephone. However, author and business executive Clyde Burelson offers the following advice: "Do not think of teleconferencing as talking on the telephone. This is a meeting."[7] A group should plan for an audioconference just as it would for a face-to-face meeting. This means developing an

TOOLBOX 14.2

Internet Addiction Can Sidetrack Groups

The phrase *Internet addiction* is no joke, although it began as one. In 1995, psychiatrist Ivan Goldberg lightheartedly posted a diagnosis for **Internet Addiction Disorder** (IAD), which he described as "a maladaptive pattern of internet use, leading to clinically significant impairment or distress."[1] Although Goldberg intended his "diagnosis" as a joke, it quickly became a popular term and a serious topic for study by mental health professionals. Today, researchers shun the word *addiction* and instead use labels such as "problematic" or "pathological" to describe excessive or disturbed patterns of Internet use, with symptoms that include mood alteration, inability to fulfill major role obligations, guilty feelings, and cravings for more.[2] Here are a few symptoms that can help identify group members with problematic Internet use:

- They feel a strong need to use the Internet and spend increasing amounts of time doing so to achieve satisfaction.
- They feel restless, moody, depressed, or irritable when attempting or forced to cut down or stop Internet use.
- They stay online longer than they originally intended.
- They have lied about or concealed the amount of time they spend on the Internet.
- They use the Internet as a way of escaping problems or relieving feelings of anxiety or depression.[3]

In terms of group communication, recognizing problematic Internet use can help explain a member's nonproductive or antisocial behavior. For example, are any of these behaviors characteristics of one or more group members?

- They prefer Internet interaction to face-to-face communication.
- They eagerly volunteer to do an Internet search for the group when, in fact, the issue does not require extensive research.

- They are reluctant to leave their computers for a meeting and may even bring a wireless laptop to meetings so that they have access to the Internet.

If these behaviors are common among some group members, your group may be sidetracked by computer-dependent members whose attention and effort are consumed by the Internet and its resources. However, we urge you to be cautious about drawing unwarranted conclusions about problematic Internet use or about discouraging members from using the Internet. Instead, we advocate a balanced, dialectic approach. As Andrew Goodman put it, "For every story about Internet addiction leading victims to ignore their families and become withdrawn, antisocial, and depressed, there is an [opposite] example of a person who has found a support group, employment prospects, or a community of like-minded topical enthusiasts through the 'net."[4] To that list, we would add group members who use the Internet effectively and responsibly to help a group achieve its common goal.

[1] For a summary discussion of Internet addiction issues, see Crispin Thurlow, Laura Lengel, and Alice Tomic, *Computer Mediated Communication: Social Interaction and the Internet* (London: Sage, 2004), pp. 148–154. Also see the following web sites: Anne Federvisch, "Internet Addiction?" *Nurseweek/ Healthweek, http://www.nurseweek.com/features/97-8/iadct.html*; Ivan Goldberg message posted to the *Psychology of the Internet*, available at *www.rider.edu/suler/psychberg/psycyber.html*; Leonard Holmes, "Internet Addiction—Is it Real?" *http:// mentalhealth.about.com/cs/sexaddict/a/interaddict.html*, March 10, 1997; Leonard Holmes, "What Is 'Normal' Internet Use?" *http://mentalhealth.about.com/cs/sexaddict/a/normalinet.htm*, March 10, 1997.
[2] Janet Morahan-Martin and Phyllis Schumacher, "Incidence and Correlates of Pathological Internet Use Among College Students," *Computers in Human Behavior*, 16 (2000), p. 14.
[3] Kimberly S. Young, "Internet Addiction: The Emergence of a New Disorder," *CyberPsychology and Behavior*, 1 (1998), pp. 237–244.
[4] Andrew Goodman, "Online Communities Endure as Platforms Come and Go," *http://www.traffick.com/story/2001-04/online_community.asp*, April 28, 2001.

agenda and making all other preparations appropriate for the meeting. The following methods and tools can make audioconferences easier to conduct:

- Limit participation to no more than seven active participants.

- Prepare and distribute an agenda and any necessary documents well in advance. Phone calls don't require agendas; audioconferences do.

- Take the "roll" and make introductions at the beginning of the meeting so that everyone knows who is participating.

- Identify yourself by name when you speak.

- If someone must "sign off" before the end of the meeting, ask that member to inform the group when she or he is leaving.

- At the end of the meeting, summarize the discussion and describe the next step or announce the date and time for a subsequent meeting. Then distribute the minutes of the meeting as soon as possible.

The most obvious difference between a voice-only conference and a traditional meeting is the fact that the participants cannot see one another. Consequently, it can be difficult to determine who is speaking. Burelson emphasizes that "not knowing who is speaking affects how you perceive the messages. It's like sitting in a regular meeting blindfolded, trying to guess who is making what point. That is bound to impact your judgment."[8] A simple introduction is usually sufficient: "This is Deidre, and I think we should . . ." As we explain in Chapter 5, "Verbal and Nonverbal Communication in Groups," a significant portion of your meaning during face-to-face communication is expressed nonverbally. For example, you might make a sarcastic remark in a meeting that everyone knows is a joke because you smile when you say it. However, in a voice-only environment, no one can see you smile. Your joke could be taken seriously.

Pros and Cons of Audioconferences. The primary advantage of the telephone version of a voice-only conference is that it is quick and easy to set up and use. In order to conduct a computer-based, voice-linked audioconference, all members must have compatible equipment and software. Once everyone is familiar with the technology and the conferencing procedures, however, the rest of the process is relatively simple. In general, audioconferences provide an effective means for a group to discuss and solve problems. They are less effective as a medium for sharing data, generating ideas and plans, or negotiating technical or interpersonal conflicts.[9] However, if an issue or an emergency arises that must be addressed immediately, audioconferencing may be the best method for getting a group together. And for virtual groups without immediate access to computers, a teleconference may be the only way to communicate and collaborate.

Audioconferencing does have some drawbacks. Because members may feel isolated, the quantity and quality of their participation may suffer. For example,

FIGURE 14.2   **Advantages and Disadvantages of Audioconferences**

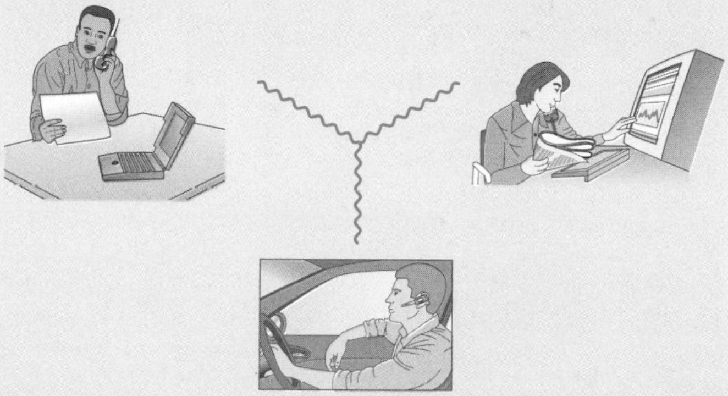

Advantages of Audioconferences	Disadvantages of Audioconferences
• Easy to Set Up and Use • Can Be Used to Discuss and Solve Problems • Have Fewer and Less Expensive Equipment Requirements • Can Be the Best Way to Reach Group Members In an Emergency	• May Make Group Members Feel Isolated • Can Reduce Group Cohesion • Difficult to Share and Edit Documents • Allow Members to Tune In and Out of a Meeting

group members who would never think of bringing nongroup work to a face-to-face meeting may be tempted to work on other matters during an audioconference. Sharing, editing, revising, and finalizing written documents can be extremely difficult when a group is working in a voice-only medium. Group members may feel less a part of the group when they don't meet with one another face-to-face. Thus, although audioconferences are convenient, it is best to avoid using them as your only form of group interaction.

Videoconferences

A **videoconference** is much like an audioconference except that a visual component is added. Thus, videoconferences permit both oral and visual communication. The visual element of a videoconference eliminates many of the drawbacks associated with audioconferences. In its most general sense, videoconferencing is audioconferencing with pictures. However, videoconferences rely on much more sophisticated and expensive equipment than do audioconferences.

Setting up a videoconference is more complicated than setting up an audioconference. The most sophisticated videoconferences take place in specially

What are the advantages and disadvantages of a virtual meeting between colleagues in New York and San Diego? *(© Gloria Wright/ Syracuse Newspapers/The Image Works)*

designed studios equipped with professional lighting, cameras, and a crew. It is also possible to conduct videoconferences using less expensive digital cameras connected to personal computers. As technology improves, the cost of videoconferencing will continue to drop, the equipment will become easier to use, and the picture quality will improve.

The high cost of videoconferencing must be balanced against the costs of a face-to-face meeting. If group members have to travel from various parts of the country, the time lost in traveling must be taken into account, as well as the cost of airfare, hotel accommodations, meals, and other expenses associated with the face-to-face meeting. When the right technology is available, a videoconference can be highly productive while saving both time and money.

Participating in Videoconferences. Here are a number of methods and tools to use when preparing for and conducting a videoconference:

- Brief all members about the operation of the videoconferencing system.
- Make sure that everyone has an agenda and any necessary documents well in advance.
- If you want to interact with participants at other sites, look directly at the camera, not at their images on a television monitor.
- Use the microphone discreetly.
- Dress appropriately.

Although videoconferences are becoming more popular, they can produce anxiety in participants. For many people, the thought of being "on television" during a videoconference generates a great deal of communication apprehension. If an effective meeting is to take place, this anxiety should be addressed before the videoconference. All group members should be fully briefed on how the videoconference works and what to expect. The more group members know about the process, the more comfortable they will be during the meeting.

Always be aware of the microphone. In videoconferences, a microphone will be attached to your clothing, set on a table in front of you, or suspended above you. Regardless of how the microphone is set up, remember that it is always listening. Avoid the temptation to lean over and whisper something to the person sitting next to you. Although the people across the room may not be able to hear you, everyone at the other end of the videoconference will.

Consider what you are going to wear to a videoconference. If your clothing is distracting, you will create a barrier to effective communication. Narrow, contrasting stripes should be avoided because video monitors can make striped clothes appear to pulsate. Also avoid wearing shiny or reflective clothing. Finally, clothes that fit poorly will appear to fit even less well when your image is magnified on the screen.

Pros and Cons of Videoconferences. The primary advantage of videoconferencing is that it allows group members to see and hear one another much as they would during a face-to-face discussion. Once participants' apprehension about being on camera passes, a videoconference can operate as efficiently and

---

FIGURE 14.3   **Advantages and Disadvantages of Videoconferences**

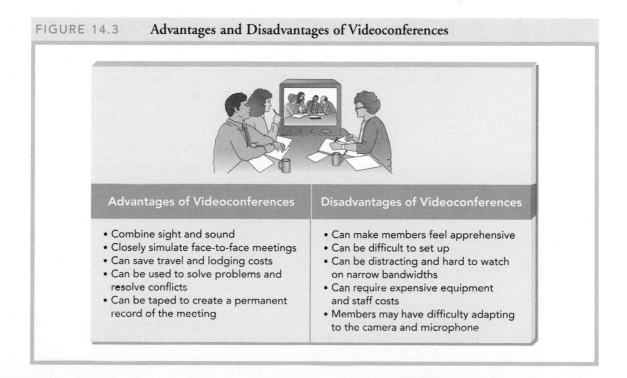

Advantages of Videoconferences	Disadvantages of Videoconferences
• Combine sight and sound • Closely simulate face-to-face meetings • Can save travel and lodging costs • Can be used to solve problems and resolve conflicts • Can be taped to create a permanent record of the meeting	• Can make members feel apprehensive • Can be difficult to set up • Can be distracting and hard to watch on narrow bandwidths • Can require expensive equipment and staff costs • Members may have difficulty adapting to the camera and microphone

effectively as a traditional meeting. Like audioconferences, videoconferences are an effective means for a group to discuss and solve problems. Of all the virtual group formats, videoconferences are the best suited for negotiating technical or interpersonal conflicts.

Videoconferencing, however, may not be as effective when a group needs to spend time brainstorming, prioritizing, outlining, or reaching consensus about complicated issues.[10] Compared to audioconferences, videoconferences require more effort to plan and set up and are likely to be much more expensive. Furthermore, if your video equipment lacks sufficient bandwidth, or if you are using video via the Internet or desktop videoconferencing, the visual distortions and poor quality can become very annoying. If you've ever endured the jerkiness of narrow-bandwidth video transmissions, you can well imagine the increasing agony of watching these motions during a long meeting.

Text-Based Computer Conferences

Text-based computer conferencing is the third and fastest-growing type of medium used by virtual groups. Unfortunately, there is no simple definition of text-based computer conferences because they cover a wide range of activities that can be combined with audioconferencing and videoconferencing. It is probably best to think of **text-based computer conferencing** as using a computer keyboard (and, in some cases, an accompanying voice link) to communicate and collaborate with a group. Today, more and more people are using their computers as communication tools. Linked together via local area networks and the Internet, computers provide a "place" for groups to communicate and work together.

Participating in Text-Based Computer Conferences. If you use networked computers at work or use the Internet to communicate with friends, family, and colleagues, you know that this is a very different communication medium. In text-only conferences, there is no spoken or nonverbal component—no vocal tone, no inflection, and no physical gestures or facial expressions to add meaning to the communication. The focus is solely on words and visual displays. In most cases, particularly in synchronous conferencing, there is an informality and an immediacy in computer-based, text-only conferencing that separates it from the other kinds of writing that we do.

Because we tend to communicate interpersonally in computer conferences, there is a tendency to write down the same words that we would speak. The quick turnaround time necessary during computer conferences all but requires that we write in an informal style. Some researchers have suggested that when computer conference participants haven't met or don't know one another very well, this abbreviated and personal writing style helps create stereotypical impressions of the participants.[11] If you write something amusing, you are more likely to be perceived by the receivers of your message as a person with a good sense of humor. If you provide much-needed information, you are more likely

TOOLBOX 14.3

Learning Netlingo and Netspeak

David Crystal, who writes about language, writes that "Netspeak is a development of millennial significance. A new medium of linguistic communication does not arrive very often in the history of the [human] race."[1] Savvy Internet users are fluent in netlingo and netspeak. Some of us, however, are confronted with new words and typographic strategies when we read our email. Here we offer a brief description of these language features.[2]

Netlingo refers to a variety of language forms used in Internet communication, such as the familiar FYI (for your information) and FAQ (frequently asked questions):

- *Compounds and blends.* Examples: shareware, netiquette, e- and cyber-anything.
- *Abbreviations and acronyms.* Examples: BTW = by the way; THX = thanks; IRF = in real life; F2F = face-to-face; IMHO = in my humble opinion; GMTA = great minds think alike; BBL = be back later; WDYT = what do you think?
- *Less use of capitalization, punctuation, and hyphenation.* Examples: internet and email.
- *Less use of traditional openings and closings.* Examples: *Hi* or *hello* instead of *dear* or using no greeting phrase at all.

Netspeak includes common typographic strategies used to achieve a more sociable and interactive communication style.

- *Letter homophones.* Examples: RU (are you); OIC (oh, I see); CYL8R (see you later)
- *Capitalization or other symbols used for emphasis.* Examples: YES, *yes*
- *Onomatopoeic and/or stylized spelling.* Examples: cooooool, hahahahahah
- *Keyboard-generated emoticons.* Examples: ☺ = smiley; @>—;— = rose; ;-) = winking; ;-o = shocked, uh-oh, oh-no

Be careful when using these strategies. Many readers won't "get it" and may be left confused and frustrated. Moreover, you can get carried away with using symbols. Too many in one message can make reading difficult, confusing, and annoying as well as make you and your writing appear immature.[3]

[1] David Crystal, *Language and the Internet* (Cambridge: Cambridge University Press, 2001), pp. 238–239, cited in Crispin Thurlow, Laura Lengel, and Alice Tomic, *Computer Mediated Communication: Social Interaction and the Internet* (London: Sage, 2004), p. 123.
[2] For definitions as well as several categories and examples of netlingo and netspeak, see Thurlow et al., pp. 124–125.
[3] For additional examples and warnings about overuse of symbols, see Deborah Jude-York, Lauren D. David, and Susan L. Wise, *Virtual Teams: Breaking the Boundaries of Time and Place* (Menlo Park, CA: Crisp Learning, 2000), pp. 91–92.

to be seen as an expert. If you help edit a working document, the group may turn to you for advice about report writing. All this happens because readers have nothing but the text to rely on in making judgments about those sending messages. Remember, however, that although the communication style may be more informal than in traditional writing, errors in spelling and grammar may create a negative impression.

Because nonverbal elements such as vocal tone, inflection, facial expressions, and gestures are missing from a text-only message, some people who communicate frequently via computers use a set of symbols to convey an emotional subtext to written messages. As we've indicated in previous chapters, these symbols are referred to as **emoticons.** In addition to the overused "smileys," there are a number of convenient and easily understood emoticons that can be employed. Bracketing a word with asterisks gives emphasis to *important* words and often takes the place of underlining. Using all capital letters can indicate forcefulness or ANGER. Thus, a message typed in all capital letters may be perceived as rude, even if the Internet user's only intention was to improve the readability of the type.

Whenever you are participating in a text-based computer conference, read your messages carefully before you send them and rewrite them if you think they might be misunderstood. Consider the real-life example of a group that received an important report via the Internet. One member responded to the group email with the concluding sentence, "I resent the report." What she meant was that she had *re-sent* the report to someone who, because of a computer glitch, hadn't received it the first time. For days, however, committee members assumed that she resented (was offended by) what was written in the report, and no one could figure out why. The more frequently you engage in computer conferencing, the more comfortable you will become communicating in a text-only environment.

The following methods and tools can help you take full advantage of text-based computer conferences:

- Make sure that all members have access to the technology *and* have the ability to use that technology.

- Prepare and distribute an agenda and any necessary documents well in advance when using technology to conduct a meeting.

- Appoint a facilitator or moderator to keep the discussion on track.

- Monitor members' participation. Identify and deal with nonparticipants and members who assume negative roles (e.g., blocker, dominator, and so on).

- Make sure that all group members know the schedule for participation and the deadlines for contributions.

Pros and Cons of Text-Based Computer Conferencing. Text-based computer conferences are very effective when a group needs to collect and share information and when members must collaborate to generate ideas and plans. A text-based conference also has permanence because members' contributions can be saved. And, of all the media available to virtual groups, this type allows text-based messages to be sent at any time from any place for future reading. The pervasiveness of email has made text-based computer conferencing both easy and available to just about everyone.

One of the biggest drawbacks to text-only conferences is the misunderstandings that can occur when participants must rely on words alone to understand the meaning of a message. Unless group members know one another well, text-based communication makes it difficult to establish strong personal connections with other group members. Face-to-face meetings and videoconferences are

FIGURE 14.4   **Advantages and Disadvantages of Text-Based Computer Conferences**

Advantages of Text-Based Computer Conferences	Disadvantages of Text-Based Computer Conferences
• Save time, travel, and expenses • Can create a permanent record of interactions • Can enhance honesty and participation by members due to distance or anonymity • Are highly efficient and effective means of collecting, sharing, and discussing data and documents	• Can lead to misunderstandings because they lack visual and oral cues • Provide fewer opportunities for effective participation by poor typists and writers • Can be frustrating for members who like or need to talk through ideas and debate issues • Decrease social support for members

more lively, social, and warm than are bulletin boards and email, "mostly because they enable the spontaneous, back-and-forth exchange that we associate with normal conversation." [12]

GROUPWARE

The term **groupware** refers to computer-mediated methods and tools designed to support group collaboration, even though participants may not be together in either time or space.[13] Groupware combines two basic ideas: *group* + *ware,* or people + technology.[14] Although groupware may sound as though it's a type of software, sophisticated groupware often requires special equipment, a designated server, and a moderator or facilitator to serve as a procedural technician or gatekeeper. In the realm of virtual groups, the accelerated development and adoption of groupware is dramatically altering the manner in which groups interact across a variety of tasks and settings.[15]

The most common type of groupware is email. However, more sophisticated types of groupware, such as electronic meeting systems, are becoming more available, affordable, and widely used. As a way of explaining the many options available to virtual groups, we offer guidelines for using four of the most common types of groupware: email, bulletin boards, electronic chat, and electronic meeting systems.

Email

As a worldwide, text-based medium, email provides a way for group members to interact from great distances and across time. When voice and video features are added to email, the medium can also simulate face-to-face discussion. In most corporate and professional settings, group members may communicate via email more than they do on the phone or in person. In fact, some group members are able to express themselves better through email than in face-to-face meetings.[16]

One way of reaching every member of a virtual group with email is by using a **listserv,** a program that delivers messages to everyone in the group. You may have worked on a committee or had a course in which the chairperson or instructor used a listserv to send messages to the entire group. Listserv messages are often more general than bulletin board or email messages. An email message or monitored bulletin board message can be highly targeted to specific group members, while a listserv message is often written as a public rather than a personal message.[17]

Participating in Email Discussions. Email is asynchronous. You receive a message that may have been sent days, hours, or just seconds ago. You respond to it when you can or by a designated deadline and hope that other members will do the same. If you are going to participate in an email discussion, the following special guidelines can help your group achieve its purpose efficiently and effectively:

- Make sure that all participants know what is expected of them. They should know the group's specific purpose, the deadlines and schedule for returning email, and the amount of time expected for the task.

- Ask for confirmation that your email was received. In many cases, your software system can tell you whether the email was received and opened.

- Develop a common system for editing documents (underlining, strikeovers, colors, or the track changes feature in your software), and make sure that these features are available on everyone's computer.

- Provide training for members who are unfamiliar with a computer system's email features.

- Contact and encourage members who are not participating. You may have to telephone them or meet with them in person to find out why they are not responding to the group's email messages.

TOOLBOX 14.4

Cueless in Virtual Groups

Virtual groups are usually cueless. *Cuelessness* simply means the "absence of all nonverbal cues (e.g., gestures, facial expressions, tone of voice, appearance) *and* identity markers (e.g., status, occupational role, age, and gender)." Usually these cues and markers communicate a range of social and emotional information, including the way members react to the topic of discussion and to other group members.[1] As in all communication, a dialectic is at work. The absence of visual and vocal cues in virtual groups can increase "psychological distance," which leads to more impersonal communication. For example, whereas you might not tell

a group member "I don't like this idea at all" in a face-to-face meeting, you might be willing to write it in an email exchange to which other members contribute. Crispin Thurlow and colleagues suggest that cuelessness can be a good thing because it means that we're less prejudiced by status and physical appearance.[2] But it also can have negative effects because communication can be more clumsy, less spontaneous, and certainly subject to misinterpretations.

[1] Crispin Thurlow, Laura Lengel, and Alice Tomic, *Computer Mediated Communication: Social Interaction and the Internet* (London: Sage, 2004), p. 49.
[2] Thurlow et al., p. 49.

- Observe good grammatical form. Don't abandon the rules of capitalization, spelling, grammar, and formatting. Good grammatical form is more professional and much easier to read.

- Include a context for your reply. A message that says only, "I disagree" may leave other members unsure about what you oppose.

Pros and Cons of Email. Email is a terrific way to discuss ideas and plans, to share information, and to revise documents. When group participation is active, email can be used to define and solve problems. Members can take time to reflect and write their responses carefully. One of the great advantages of email is that it produces a written record that can be analyzed, edited, and voted on.

Even though email has become as common as regular mail, telephone conversations, and face-to-face meetings, it still has drawbacks. Because—at least in most cases—you cannot see or hear other group members, you must rely on text and text only. As we indicated earlier in this chapter, text-only communication can lead to misunderstandings and decreased member involvement.

Given the limitations of email, it can be difficult to debate complex issues and to make far-reaching decisions using this technology. If there is an interpersonal conflict intruding on the process, email is not well suited to resolving the problem. And, unfortunately, email is easy to ignore. Nonparticipants can be *loafers* (infrequent and detached members), *lurkers* (members who are present but offer no comments or contributions), or *newbies* (inexperienced or apprehensive email users).[18] An effective group will make sure that every member is an active participant.

FIGURE 14.5   **Advantages and Disadvantages of Email**

Advantages of Email	Disadvantages of Email
• Easy to use, inexpensive, widely used, and available	• Content subject to misinterpretation because it lacks visual and oral cues
• Makes it easier to discuss subjects that people are reluctant to discuss face to face	• Easy to ignore messages, fake participation, or avoid difficult conversations and decisions
• Good for discussing and revising ideas, plans, and documents as well as for defining and discussing problems	• Poor for brainstorming and prioritizing as well as for debating issues and reaching consensus
• Easy to transmit files and documents	• Too many messages waste time and discourage use
• Can include many people in a discussion	• Not well suited for interpersonal conflict resolution
• Provides access to people and resources across time and distances	

Bulletin Boards

Like email, bulletin boards are an asynchronous, text-based communication medium. What distinguishes bulletin boards from email is the size of the audience they attempt to reach and the manner in which messages are written and read. If you subscribe to a bulletin board, you send your message to a single address. The program or a designated moderator then sends your message to everyone else on the bulletin board. But unlike a real bulletin board, a computer-mediated bulletin board organizes incoming materials so that subsequent messages are posted as responses to specific messages, one right after the other.[19] This system is called a *thread,* and it can continue and extend for as long as participants send submissions. Thus, a **threaded discussion** occurs when a series of email messages about a specific issue is posted on a bulletin board. On some organizational web sites, there are opportunities to join a threaded discussion or visit a bulletin board.

Participating on Bulletin Boards. Generally, bulletin boards make fewer demands on participants than email does. Good bulletin boards become a source of information and a means of following the development of an argument, plan, or report. Being a loafer or a lurker on a bulletin board can be perfectly acceptable. If, however, you want to post messages or respond to others, there are several guidelines to follow:

- Determine whether the bulletin board will be moderated or whether the program will accept and post all messages. If it is moderated, the program should not permit anonymous input, particularly if virtual group members will be held responsible for the outcome.

- Organize your thoughts before you contribute to a bulletin board. State your point clearly. No one wants to read your ramblings.

- Be careful of being highly critical. Your comments are being made in writing and will become part of a permanent record.

- If you want to pursue an issue with only one or two members, contact them by email. Don't take up bulletin board space with a private conversation.

Pros and Cons of Bulletin Boards. Bulletin boards allow many conversations to occur at once, and, as a result, they are time savers.[20] Bulletin boards allow you to think before sharing your ideas, to evaluate the ideas of others, and to word your response carefully. They can be used for brainstorming as well as for generating and commenting on ideas. They provide a useful work space for collecting information and discussing the implications of that information.

But participating in a bulletin board can also be a dreadful experience. A bulletin board can become a free-for-all, with participants venting their frustrations and criticizing others. Mean-spirited members can do a lot of damage to a group if they are allowed to run wild or to express themselves anonymously. Many bulletin boards are moderated to ensure that the comments made are relevant and appropriate.

FIGURE 14.6   **Advantages and Disadvantages of Bulletin Boards**

Advantages of Bulletin Boards	Disadvantages of Bulletin Boards
• Easy to use, usually inexpensive	• Content subject to misinterpretation because it lacks visual and oral cues
• Provide space for shared messages, displays, and documents	• Easy to ignore
• Good for brainstorming; discussing ideas, plans, and documents; collecting and sharing information	• Poor for debating, voting, prioritizing, and outlining; difficult to organize, debate, and analyze data and issues
• Enable threaded discussions that allow complex interaction with many participants	• Not an effective decision-making tool
• Can create synergy and increased collaboration	• High volume of messages can waste time, discourage users, and result in information overload
• Effective way to communicate with many participants	• Discussions can degenerate into nonproductive personal arguments

Group Blogs and Wikis

Virtual groups are beginning to recognize the potential of blogs and wikis as researching, information-sharing, problem-solving, editing, and coordinating tools. When the first edition of this textbook was published, blogs did not exist. The term *weblog* was coined in 1997. The short form, *blog*, appeared in 1999 when a blogger divided the word *weblog* into the phrase "we blog" as a sidebar on his own weblog. A **blog**—short for *weblog*—is a web site on which text, images, Web links, and other files are posted on a regular basis. Unlike open-ended chat rooms, bulletin boards, forums, or newsgroups, only the author or authoring group can create new subjects for discussion on a blog. Blogs can be personal online diaries; political blogs that post personal opinions, essays, and relevant Web links; and topical blogs that focus on narrow topics ranging from community issues to stock market discussions.[1]

Multiuser and group blogs are a new, rapidly emerging phenomenon. In fact, team-based blogs can support a project by giving all members input into the decision-making process. Group blogs can be a very effective means for updating a group, facilitating project input, developing goals and milestones, solving problems, and writing reports. Group blogs are not a simple compilation of individual comments; they are a mesh of ideas that intercept, overlap, and complement one another. Group blogs allow for collaborative interaction and inspiration. They also make access and use as easy as possible and even provide intrinsic rewards for individual members who make valuable contributions.[2]

A **wiki** is a type of web site that allows users to add and edit content and is particularly well suited for constructive collaborative writing. The *WikiWikiWeb* was established in 1995 and is based on the Hawaiian word *wiki*, meaning "quick, fast, or to hasten."[3] Wikipedia, a free English-language encyclopedia, is the world's largest wiki. Wikipedia is managed by a non-profit parent company that allows anyone to edit its content. An expert-led investigation by *Nature* found Wikipedia's content more current and close to the prestigious *Encyclopedia Britannica* in accuracy.[4] *Wikipedia* also demonstrates the power of groups in that biased, out of date, or incorrect information is quickly corrected by participants.[5]

Group wikis have many of the same features as group blogs. Wikis, however, function primarily as sites for editing documents. A group can use a wiki to identify and codify key issues, recommend solutions to problems, or write reports and publishable materials. Much like the track changes feature in word-processing software, a wiki allows group members to edit and change copy over time, while keeping track of all changes so that a page can be restored to any of its previous states.[6]

[1] Wikipedia, "Blog," *http://en.wikipedia.org/wiki/blog*. Updated on November 14, 2005.

[2] Wikipedia, "Blog."

[3] Wikipedia, "Blog."

[4] Wikipedia, "Wiki" and "Wikipedia," *http://en.wikipedia .org/wiki*; *http://en.wikipedia.org/wikipedia*. Modified January 3, 2006.

[5] George Johnson, "Commentary: The Nitpicking of the Masses vs. the Authority of Experts," *New York Times*, p. F2, January 3, 2006.

[6] Wikipedia, "Wiki" and "Wikipedia."

Electronic Chat

Chat rooms go by many titles: desktop conferencing, real-time conferencing, and Internet relay chat (IRC), to name a few. There are chat rooms all over the Internet. They are places where participants can discuss a wide range of topics, from current events and hobbies to professional issues. In this chapter, we look at the ways in which virtual groups use electronic chat to achieve their purposes.

Electronic chat is real-time, synchronous communication in which members have text-based conversations with one another. The questions, responses, concerns, and comments of all members are visible on each participant's computer monitor. Technological advances are now making electronic chat a multimedia experience. By adding audio links, full-motion video, and sophisticated whiteboard technology, chat rooms are becoming as well equipped as videoconference facilities—all through one's own computer.

Participating in Electronic Chat. At first glance, an electronic chat session may *look* confusing. Because people read faster than they type, written comments may overlap, be highly repetitive, or seem irrelevant. Yet despite the presence of these multiple messages, chat room participants "seem to be able to keep track of their particular thread in the conversation because of the textual record that is preserved as contribution after contribution is displayed on the screen."[21] Several guidelines can help a virtual group take advantage of the freewheeling nature of electronic chat:

- Extended electronic chat sessions should be well planned. Participants should have an agenda and have access to relevant information or documents well before the interchange begins.

- When a situation arises that requires immediate interaction, electronic chat should be highly focused.

- Someone should facilitate an electronic chat session in order to maintain focus and order.

- Group size should be kept small in order to keep the process under control.

- Participants should avoid getting sidetracked by irrelevant threads of conversation.

Pros and Cons of Electronic Chat. The advantages and disadvantages of electronic chat vary, depending on the kind of technology supporting the system. Compared to face-to-face interaction and audioconferencing, electronic chat provides a synchronous environment in which members have more time to compose and edit their contributions. And whereas a domineering member can monopolize a face-to-face conversation or a telephone call, you don't have to wait your turn in order to contribute in a chat room. Kenneth Graetz and his colleagues note that "although members of electronic chat groups are not isolated, they are not necessarily bound by the traditional rules of conversation and are free to enter statements at any time."[22] For members who experience high levels of communication apprehension, a chat room may reduce their anxiety.

Despite their popularity and advantages, text-only electronic chat rooms can be confusing places. Under some circumstances, it can be difficult to organize information, analyze data, and make decisions, particularly if the group is large. If a chat room comes "fully loaded" with audio links, video, and whiteboard capabilities, the medium has the potential to simulate a face-to-face meeting. Yet even in the most sophisticated chat rooms, inexperienced and reticent participants can become lost in a technology-rich environment. Moreover, electronic chat may not be as effective a medium as other forms of groupware. Research by Graetz and his colleagues indicates that group members in electronic chat environments have more difficulty coordinating input and verifying information, take longer to make decisions, and may experience greater difficulty solving complex problems. As a result, when comparing electronic chat with other communication media, participants report higher levels of frustration in virtual chat groups.[23]

Electronic Meeting Systems

Electronic meeting systems (EMS) include a wide range of communication and decision-making tools available to virtual groups through the use of computers and communication technology. Compared with email, bulletin boards, and electronic chat, electronic meeting systems require much more planning, coordination, and focus. By combining specialized software and hardware, meeting participants can perform many group tasks, such as brainstorming, problem

---

FIGURE 14.7   **Advantages and Disadvantages of Electronic Chat**

Advantages of Electronic Chat	Disadvantages of Electronic Chat
• Easy to use, available, and inexpensive • Effective in small, active groups • Good for brainstorming, sharing data, discussing issues, and sharing opinions • Freewheeling discussions can lead to creative ideas and solutions	• Content subject to misinterpretation because it lacks visual and oral cues • Easy to ignore • May need designated facilitator to keep the group focused and disciplined • Poor for debating, explaining opinions, reaching consensus, and making decisions • Discussion can evolve into irrelevant, nonproductive conversations

ETHICAL GROUPS

Ten Commandments for Computer Ethics

The following ten commandments of computer ethics were first presented by Dr. Ramon C. Barquin in a paper titled "In Pursuit of a 'Ten Commandments' for Computer Ethics." In this paper, Dr. Barquin concludes "that the time is ripe to enter into a normative phase as we attempt to pursue a 'ten commandments' for computer ethics."[1] In discussing the need for a set of standards to guide and instruct people in the ethical use of computers, he calls for the use of the following "Ten Commandments for Computer Ethics" by today's computing professionals:

1. Thou shalt not use a computer to harm other people.

2. Thou shalt not interfere with other people's computer work.

3. Thou shalt not snoop around in other people's computer files.

4. Thou shalt not use a computer to steal.

5. Thou shalt not use a computer to bear false witness.

6. Thou shalt not copy or use proprietary software for which you have not paid.

7. Thou shalt not use other people's computer resources without authorization or proper compensation.

8. Thou shalt not appropriate other people's intellectual output.

9. Thou shalt think about the social consequences of the program you are writing or the system you are designing.

10. Thou shalt always use a computer in ways that ensure consideration and respect for your fellow humans.[2]

These "ten commandments" are a useful starting point for computer ethics, but they are short on details and practical guidelines. Although Barquin's commandments have been widely adopted by the computing industry as a starting point for ethics standards, most professionals recognize that keeping within the ten commandments does not mean that everything you are doing is proper. Individual situations must be evaluated based on specific circumstances.[3]

Take a few minutes to review Barquin's commandments. Do they make sense? Are they difficult to understand? Is something missing? For example, consider the third commandment, "Thou shalt not snoop around in other people's computer files." "What if the 'other people' are using the computer to do harm? Should we still refrain from interfering? Should computer files be private even if they are being used as part of a criminal conspiracy?"[4]

As is the case with many ethical issues, there are no easy answers to the questions that arise from reviewing these commandments. At the same time, Barquin's code is widely accepted and forms the basis for developing useful guidelines about the ethical use of computers, whether they are being used by individuals or by virtual groups.

[1] Copyright: 1991 Computer Ethics Institute. Author: Dr. Ramon C. Barquin. Reprinted with permission.
[2] Copies of the Ten Commandments for Computer Ethics can be obtained by e-mailing the Brookings Institute at *cei@brookings.edu*. Also available at *http://www.cpsr.net/oldsite/externalSiteView/program/ethics/cei.html*.
[3] Ben N. Fairweather, "Commentary on the 'Ten Commandments for Computer Ethics,'" available at *http://www.ccsr.cse.dmu.ac.uk/resources/professionalism/codes/cei_command_com.htm*.
[4] Fairweather.

solving, and decision making, at individual work stations.[24] Whether they are in the same room or miles apart, participants using electronic meeting systems can collaborate on a variety of group tasks. Most electronic meeting systems include several capabilities:[25]

- *Generating ideas and brainstorming.* Electronic meeting systems can resemble a chat room in which virtual group members present ideas and are able to see the ideas contributed by all other members on their monitors or on a projection screen. In most cases, a member can develop ideas in private before sharing them with other group members.

- *Grouping and analyzing issues.* Collectively, virtual group members can move ideas into different categories, identify ideas that merit further discussion, outline a plan, and finalize a list of ideas or issues for further development.

- *Creating and editing documents.* Members of virtual groups can write assigned sections of documents and comment on or revise material written by other members.

- *Voting.* In a virtual meeting, special voting features can be used to assess the degree of consensus on ideas and decisions without pressuring members to make a final decision. Electronic meeting system software also can display voting results in total, graphic, or tabular form.

In order to appreciate this type of groupware, consider the following examples in which electronic meeting systems helped two very different groups reach important and far-reaching decisions:

- Nine senior executives of a $2.5 billion transportation leasing company took less than four hours to brainstorm about fifty-two risks to the corporation and then to identify the ten that presented the greatest risk to the company's achieving its strategic objectives and the ten that should receive the highest priority for an internal audit. After six months, the results of this four-hour meeting were still guiding the focus of both the senior executives and the internal audit staff.[26]

- The members of the congregation filed into the church sanctuary, filling every seat in every pew. The top ten priorities of each of the five church task forces were projected on five screens along the side wall. The task of the 467 people in the sanctuary was to choose, from among all fifty priorities, the ones on which the church should spend its limited resources. By using 467 keypads (a combination of hand-held numeric keypads, computer software, and a projection screen), the members took only three hours to reach agreement on thirteen priorities for the coming year.[27]

Participating in Electronic Meeting Systems. In addition to the usual requirements for effective participation, electronic meeting systems require the use of specialized software, compatible and sometimes specially networked hardware, and computer expertise to make the process work. In addition to having someone who can make sure that all of the equipment is up and running, a virtual meeting of this kind usually requires a facilitator to keep the group moving through the process, a coach or trainer to help inexperienced or nonparticipating members, and a technician who is prepared to solve technical problems. The best advice we can offer to participants in such a complex virtual group is this: Follow instructions carefully and leave the rest to the hardware and software.

Pros and Cons of Electronic Meeting Systems.   Depending on the system and a group's technical expertise, members can move back and forth from the EMS to other computer-based applications, such as word processing, spreadsheets, presentation software, and project-management software. The EMS can also be integrated with other systems, such as desktop video, so that the interpersonal dynamics of a meeting can be captured.[28] Both of us have participated in several virtual meetings using sophisticated electronic meeting systems, and we have been impressed with the process and the results. Projects that would otherwise have taken months to complete were finished in weeks or days.

FIGURE 14.8   **Advantages and Disadvantages of Electronic Meeting Systems**

Advantages of Electronic Meeting Systems	Disadvantages of Electronic Meeting Systems
• Result in shorter and more productive meetings	• Expensive and complex systems requiring special software, equipment, and networking
• Efficient and effective way to tap expertise and opinions	• Require training, facilitation, and technical assistance
• Facilitate collaboration, preparation, discussion, and editing of plans and documents	• Less effective for complex analysis and resolving conflict
• Can reorganize and prioritize ideas and issues in a variety of ways	• Can remove accountability for decisions
• Good for brainstorming; displaying data; discussing and debating ideas and issues; offering and evaluating options	• Members can comment on their own proposals as if they were someone else's
• Anonymity increases participation and promotes honesty; inhibits groupthink	• Discussions can degenerate into nonproductive debate if meeting is not well facilitated
• All members have equal opportunities to contribute ideas, voice opinions, and vote	

The ideas flowed, the posting of results led to highly targeted discussions, and the final product was of the highest quality.

As much as we wish that every business, professional organization, civic association, and meeting facility had the capacity to use electronic meeting systems, the cost of installing and maintaining such systems is still high. Even renting an EMS facility can be prohibitive for many groups. In addition, a staff member is often needed to make the process work. At the very least, a skilled facilitator is necessary to keep the group moving and to ensure that group members are using the software and hardware properly.

Fortunately, sophisticated EMS services have become available and affordable via the World Wide Web. After downloading a peer-to-peer collaboration platform, groups pay a user fee to establish direct, instant communication and collaboration with other group members. Groove.net, chatspace.com, and cogos.com are just three examples of providers offering this type of electronic collaboration service.

COLLABORATIVE PRESENTATION TECHNOLOGY

When you see the term *presentation technology,* PowerPoint presentations may come to mind. We have added the word *collaborative* to this phrase in order to move beyond individual PowerPoint presentations and into the realm of technology-enhanced, interactive group presentations. **Collaborative presentation technology** projects an idea or graphic onto a screen, wall, or whiteboard so that both face-to-face and virtual participants can interact with the presentation.[29] Collaborative presentation tools make it possible to display information without being physically present with other group members. The use of these technologies also allows members to review, revise, edit, and finalize documents.

Sophisticated meeting rooms now come fully equipped with the tools necessary for collaborative presentations: projection screens, computer slide projectors, whiteboards, video cameras and monitors, laptop computers, and even old-fashioned flip charts and overhead projectors. One of the most useful collaborative presentation technologies is the **electronic whiteboard.** Computer-based electronic whiteboards allow members to work on the same document or drawing simultaneously. Anything written on the whiteboard is instantly digitized. This means that it can be stored, printed, and displayed in both the location where it is created and remote locations. Thus, group members can sketch a flow chart or draw a design on an electronic whiteboard, and it can be seen and altered by other group members, regardless of whether they are in the same room or located thousands of miles away. Group members can pose ideas, suggest modifications, draw links among ideas, edit text, and format documents. The primary advantage of using whiteboards is that they build on the team members' existing skills and meeting behaviors while also providing some sense of social presence. They are very useful for groups that need to share ideas and concepts graphically. The primary disadvantage is that team members must have access to specially equipped conference rooms or desktop systems in order to participate.[30]

When electronic whiteboards are used in virtual or face-to-face settings and are combined with audio and video capabilities, the potential for effective collaboration increases significantly. State-of-the-art electronic whiteboards offer a great deal of flexibility and choice in sharing ideas, building presentations, and creating documents. Whether a group is presenting a full-fledged multimedia production or preparing simple text and graphics to be discussed at a staff meeting, electronic whiteboards make interaction and collaboration more efficient and effective.

GROUP DIVERSITY AND THE DIGITAL DIVIDE

Technical diversity affects virtual groups as much as differences in culture, gender, and personality type. In terms of interactive audio, visual, and computer technologies, there are "haves" and "have nots" as well as "know a lots" and "not know a lots." Those of you who rely on computers and Internet access at home, work, or school for a wide range of tasks may assume that everyone has the same opportunities and skills. Certainly members of virtual groups must have access to compatible technology and possess comparable abilities in order to achieve a common goal. Those who "have" and "know a lot" about technology may work in groups in which other members do not "have" and do "not know a lot."

The Digital Divide

Virtual groups frequently encounter the digital divide and its consequences. The phrase **digital divide** refers to inequalities in access to, distribution of, and use of information technology between two or more populations. For example, surveys of Internet use in many countries provide a profile of the typical user as young, urban, male, and relatively well educated. This profile leads to discrepancies in use based on factors such as age, gender, socioeconomic variance, and culture.[31]

Age. If you have grown up during the personal computer and Internet age, you are probably relatively comfortable, confident, and competent when using these technologies. Many children know more about computers and the Internet than their parents do. Many senior citizens in advanced, industrialized countries do not have easy access to the Internet or do not use it frequently. Fortunately, Internet use by "senior surfers" is increasing and is becoming a popular pasttime for those who have the time and money to go online.[32]

In terms of virtual groups, older members vary significantly—from those who have embraced computer technology and excel in its use to those who fear or have avoided learning and using computer technology. Such disparities in attitude and ability have consequences for virtual groups. A valuable and conscientious group member who is older than most of the members may lack computer skills and not be able to contribute to and benefit from Internet interactions among members.

Gender. The digital divide often separates men from women, particularly given that most Internet users are well-educated, urban males. Only in countries where Internet use is well developed, such as Scandinavia and the United States, has the gender gap begun to close. Even so, a study by the American Association of University Women concludes that

- Girls consistently rate themselves significantly lower on computer ability than boys do, and boys exhibit higher self-confidence and more positive attitudes about computers than do girls.

- Software programs (and gaming) often reinforce gender bias and stereo-typed gender roles.

- Girls use computers less often outside of school. Boys enter the classroom with more prior experience with computers and other technology than girls have.[33]

Socioeconomic Factors. Income level is a strong determinant of a person's access to computer technology and the Internet. Here are highlights of a government study on Internet use in the United States:

- Urban households earning incomes over $75,000 are over *twenty times* more likely to have home Internet access than rural households at the lowest income levels.

- Those earning $20,000 and using the Internet outside the home are twice as likely to get access through a public library or community center.

- People earning under $25,000 generally cite cost as the primary reason for not using the Internet at home, while those earning more than $25,000 are more likely to say that they "don't want to."[34]

In international terms, nearly 90 percent of all Internet users are in industrialized countries, with the United States and Canada alone accounting for 57 percent of the worldwide total. In contrast, Internet users in Africa and the Middle East together account for only 1 percent of global Internet users.[35]

Think of the practical and technical barriers facing certain populations. People who live in communities that have only sporadic electricity or that have no telephone lines or mobile network connections will also lack computers and access to the Internet.[36] There are also huge cost factors involved. For example, the national average monthly wage of farm workers in South Africa is less than

$50. Most workers earning that wage can't afford transportation into the village to buy groceries, let alone afford to use technology at current prices. While Internet access represents 1.2 percent of the average monthly income in the United States, it would represent 278 percent of the average annual income in Nepal, 614 percent in Madagascar, and 191 percent in Bangladesh.[37]

Cultural Dimensions. Language differences are an obvious, but often overlooked, cultural difference among computer and Internet users. For a group member whose native language is different from that of the majority of the group, communicating online can be difficult and frustrating. Members should "forgive" nonnative speakers for any spelling or grammar errors and encourage their active communication.[38]

In terms of cultural dimensions, individuals from high-context cultures may want to hear and see group members in person rather than relying on written words to interpret meaning. Moreover, group members who come from strongly networked cultural minorities or nonliterate communities may have difficulty learning, using, and understanding the necessary skills and gaining the resulting benefits of working in virtual groups.

Implications for Virtual Groups

Effective groups understand, respect, and adapt to the many ways in which group diversity and the digital divide affect groupwork and group success. They also develop strategies for fully integrating all group members into the virtual group environment. Here are several challenges to working in virtual groups that groups should address and resolve:

- Diverse technical skills

- Diverse writing skills because of differences in cultural background, language, and education

- Diverse writing styles because of differences in gender, cultural background, and personality

- Diverse attitudes toward technology, such as technophobia or online shyness

- Diverse hardware, software, and technical support

- Diverse experiences using technology and the Internet

- Diverse languages and computer-related vocabularies

By their very design and function, virtual groups include people from different locations, organizations, lines of work, ages, genders, socioeconomic backgrounds, and cultures. Although there are challenges, virtual groups can offer a rich diversity of members seeking to achieve a common goal.

BALANCING TECHNOLOGY IN GROUPS

In the preface to *CyberMeeting: How to Link People and Technology in Your Organization,* James Creighton and James Adams emphasize the need to balance the advantages and disadvantages of using technology for working in groups. On the one hand, they note that organizations will spend billions of dollars "connecting their employees through technology that will permit collaboration and electronic participation in meetings." On the other hand, "hundreds of millions of those dollars will be wasted chasing fads and installing technology that people will use to work the same way they worked before the technology was installed."[39] As important as it is to understand how to use technology in group settings, it is even more important to understand why and when to choose technology as a tool for enhancing group efficiency and effectiveness. In the end, the real issue is collaboration; technology is simply a valuable tool for helping to bring it about.[40]

Groups with access to every modern technology are not necessarily better groups. A nubby piece of chalk in the hands of a conscientious group member can do more to help a group achieve its goal than can a team of graphic designers. Harvey Robbins and Michael Finley observe that a "team is still a team, no matter how much hardware and software it drags behind it. A computer will not impose clarity on a fuzzy notion or vice versa. That is something only we can do."[41]

Technology is only a tool. Like any of the other tools used by groups, it is "a means to pursue particular objectives."[42] In our eagerness to grab the latest piece of software, hardware, or groupware, we may seize the wrong tool—one that neither addresses the group's goal nor stretches the group's thinking in important new directions. Effective groups take advantage of technology but do not substitute technology for the effort and wisdom of their members. Perhaps the most important balance that groups must achieve is the balance between the marvels of technology and the untapped potential of their members. Just like face-to-face groups, virtual groups must "communicate in ways that provide guidance and structure—shared control over why and how a group orients itself—in what is likely to be a relatively unfamiliar, and often unstructured, group context."[43]

GROUPWORK

Computer and Teleconference Simulation

Goal: To demonstrate the advantages and disadvantages of computer conferences and audioconferences

Participants: Four groups of at least three members

Procedure

1. Each group will simulate a different type of conferencing.

   - Group 1 will simulate audioconferencing. The group members will sit with their backs to one another and communicate orally. Group members should not look at one another.
   - Group 2 will simulate synchronous, text-based computer conferencing. The group members will sit with their backs to one another and communicate by writing messages on index cards. Group members are encouraged to send messages whenever they choose. Messages should be passed to all members of the group and can be passed to the left or the right. Group members should not look at one another.
   - Group 3 will simulate an asynchronous, text-based computer conference. Group members will sit with their backs to one another and communicate by writing on a piece of paper. One individual will start the conference by writing an initial message. The paper will be passed to the left. The next group member will respond by writing a message on the same piece of paper and then will pass the paper to the left. The process continues in this fashion. Group members should not look at one another.
   - Group 4 will engage in a face-to-face discussion.

2. Each group should address the following question: How can technology be used to enhance student learning? Members should discuss the various ways in which technology should (or should not) be used to enhance instruction and learning. The group's suggestions should be listed in order of priority.

3. After the groups have completed their discussion, the class should discuss the following questions:

   - How did each group's conference method help or hinder the discussion?
   - What communication problems did each group experience? Can these problems be resolved by using the group's conference method?
   - What types of tasks were easiest to accomplish using each group's conference method?
   - Which tasks were the most difficult?

GROUPASSESSMENT

Virtual Meeting Evaluation

Directions. When you participate in an audioconference, videoconference, or computer conference, use the following criteria to evaluate how well these types of virtual meetings were planned and conducted. Circle the number that best represents your assessment of each statement.

Audioconference

1. An audioconference was appropriate for this meeting.
   Disagree   1   2   3   4   5   6   7   Agree

2. The sound quality was satisfactory.
   Disagree   1   2   3   4   5   6   7   Agree

3. A meeting agenda was provided and followed.
   Disagree   1   2   3   4   5   6   7   Agree

4. Members introduced themselves before speaking.
   Disagree   1   2   3   4   5   6   7   Agree

5. Members adapted to the oral-only medium.
   Disagree   1   2   3   4   5   6   7   Agree

Videoconference

1. A videoconference was appropriate for this meeting.
   Disagree   1   2   3   4   5   6   7   Agree

2. A meeting agenda was provided and followed.
   Disagree   1   2   3   4   5   6   7   Agree

3. The video quality was satisfactory.
   Disagree   1   2   3   4   5   6   7   Agree

4. Members used the microphones effectively.
   Disagree   1   2   3   4   5   6   7   Agree

5. Members dressed appropriately.
   Disagree   1   2   3   4   5   6   7   Agree

Computer Conference

1. A computer conference was appropriate for this meeting.
   Disagree   1   2   3   4   5   6   7   Agree

2. A meeting agenda was provided and followed.
   Disagree   1   2   3   4   5   6   7   Agree

3. Members typed clear and succinct messages.
   Disagree   1   2   3   4   5   6   7   Agree

4. Members interacted frequently and met deadlines.
   Disagree   1   2   3   4   5   6   7   Agree

5. Delays between messages were reasonable.
   Disagree   1   2   3   4   5   6   7   Agree

Comments:

NOTES

1. Deborah L. Duarte and Nancy Tennant Snyder, *Mastering Virtual Teams: Strategies, Tools, and Techniques That Succeed*, 2nd ed. (San Francisco: Jossey-Bass, 2001), p. 4.

2. Scott Ober, *Contemporary Business Communication*, 2nd ed. (Boston: Houghton Mifflin, 1995), p. 503.

3. Zane L. Berge, "Electronic Discussion Groups," *Communication Education, 43 (1994)*, pp. 102–111.

4. Fran Rees, *How to Lead Work Teams* (San Francisco: Jossey-Bass/Pfeiffer, 2001), pp. 114–115.

5. Mahlon Apgar IV, "The Alternative Workplace: Changing Where and How People Work," *Harvard Business Review*, May/June 1998, pp. 121–139.

6. Throughout this chapter, we cite several resources that we consulted to assess the value of and to provide guidelines for the use of various media and tools by virtual groups. In addition to our own experiences, we relied on the following excellent references: David Coleman (ed.), *Groupware: Collaborative Strategies for Corporate LANs and Intranets* (Upper Saddle River, NJ: Prentice Hall, 1997); James Creighton and James W. R. Adams, *CyberMeeting: How to Link People and Technology in Your Organization* (New York: AMACOM, 1998); Deborah L. Duarte and Nancy Tennant Snyder, *Mastering Virtual Teams: Strategies, Tools, and Techniques That Succeed* (San Francisco: Jossey-Bass, 1999); Jessica Lipnack and Jeffrey Stamps, *Virtual Teams: People Working Across Boundaries with Technology*, 2nd ed. (New York: Wiley, 2000); Andrew F. Wood and Matthew Smith, *Online Communication: Linking Technology, Identity, and Culture* (Mahwah, NJ: Erlbaum, 2001); Fran Rees, *How to Lead Work Teams* (San Francisco: Jossey-Bass/Pfeiffer, 2001).

7. Clyde Burelson, *Effective Meetings: The Complete Guide* (New York: Wiley, 1990), p. 168.

8. Burelson, p. 171.

9. Duarte and Snyder, p. 28.

10. Duarte and Snyder, pp. 28 and 40.

11. Joseph B. Walther, "Group and Interpersonal Effects in International Computer-Mediated Collaboration," *Human Communication Research, 22* (1997), p. 452.

12. Duarte and Snyder, p. 26.

13. For a brief history and explanation of the term *groupware*, see Coleman, pp. 1–2.

14. Gerald O'Dwyer, Art Giser, and Ed Lovett, "Groupware and Reengineering: The Human Side of Change," in *Groupware: Collaborative Strategies for Corporate LANs and Intranets*, ed. David Coleman (Upper Saddle River, NJ: Prentice Hall, 1997), p. 566.

15. K. A. Graetz, "Information Sharing in Face-to-Face, Teleconferencing, and Electronic Chat Groups," *Small Group Research, 29* (1998), p. 714.

16. Andrew F. Wood and Matthew J. Smith, *Online Communication: Linking Technology, Identity, and Culture* (Mahwah, NJ: Erlbaum, 2001), p. 80.

17. Wood and Smith, p. 12.

18. Michael F. Hauben, "The Netizens and Community Networks," *CMC Magazine,* February 1997. Available at *http://www.december.com/cmc/mag/1997/feb/hauben.html*. We have substituted the term *loafers* for the term *surfers*, which was originally used in this 1997 article.

19. Wood and Smith, p. 11.

20. Duarte and Snyder, p. 45.

21. Wood and Smith, p. 13.

22. Graetz et al., p. 718

23. Graetz et al., pp. 714–743.

24. Creighton and Adams, p. 86.

25. Duarte and Snyder, p. 36.

26. W. A. Flexner and Kimbal Wheatley, in *Groupware: Collaborative Strategies for Corporate LANs and Intranets*, ed. David Coleman (Upper Saddle River, NJ: Prentice Hall, 1997), p. 193.

27. Flexner and Wheatley, p. 194.

28. Duarte and Snyder, pp. 36–37.

29. Coleman, p. 266.

30. Duarte and Snyder, pp. 38–39.

31. Wikipedia, "Digital Divide," available at *http://wiki.media-culture.org.au/index.php/Digital Divide*. Major revisions by Adam Margerison, October 28, 2005.

32. Crispin Thurlow, Laura Lengel, and Alice Tomic, *Computer Media Communication: Social Interaction and the Internet* (London: Sage, 2004), pp. 216–217.

33. Cynthia Lanius, "Girls and Technology," available at *http://math.rice.edu/~lanius/pres/cwac99.html,* April 24, 1999.

34. "'Digital Divide' Widening at Lower Income Levels." Available at *http://www.clickz.com/stats/sectors/geographics/article.php/5911_569351.*

35. "Digital Divide Widening."

36. Thurlow et al., p. 83.

37. Thurlow et al, p. 83. Also see Bridges.org, "Spanning the Digital Divide: Understanding and Tackling the

Issues," available at *http://bridges.org/spanning/ summary.html,* March 28, 2003.

38. Deborah Jude-York, Lauren D. Davis, and Susan L. Wise, *Virtual Teaming: Breaking the Boundaries of Time and Place* (Menlo Park, CA: Crisp Learning, 2000), p. 50.

39. Creighton and Adams, p. ix.

40. Creighton and Adams, p. 226.

41. Harvey Robbins and Michael Finley, *The* New *Why Teams Don't Work: What Went Wrong and How to Make It Right* (San Francisco: Berrett-Koehler, 2000), p. 250.

42. Peter M. Senge, Art Kleiner, Charlotte Roberts, Richard Ross, and Bryan Smith, *The Fifth Discipline Fieldbook: Strategies and Tools for Building a Learning Organization* (New York: Doubleday, 1994), p. 29.

43. Edward A. Mabry and Fay Sudweeks, "Oracles and Other Digital Deities: Using Expert Teams as 'Leaders' in an Online Collaborative Research Project," in *Facilitating Group Communication in Context: Innovations and Applications with Natural Groups,* ed. Lawrence R. Frey (Cresskill, NJ: Hampton Press, 2006), p. 254.

Glossary

Abdicrat. A group member whose need for control is not met; an abdicrat is submissive and avoids responsibility.

Abstract Word. A word that refers to an idea or concept that cannot be perceived by your five senses.

Accent. The sound of one language imposed upon another language.

Accommodating Conflict Style. An approach to conflict in which a person gives in to other group members, even at the expense of his or her own goals.

Achievement Norm. A norm that determines the quality and quantity of work expected from group members.

Action Item. An item in the written minutes of a meeting that identifies the individual responsible for an assigned task.

Ad Hoc Committee. A committee that is formed for a specific purpose and disbands once it has completed its assignment or task.

Ad Hominem **Attack.** An irrelevant attack against a person's character rather than a substantive response to an issue or argument.

Adjourning Stage. The group development phase in which the group has achieved its common goal and begins to disengage or disband.

A-E-I-O-U Model. A conflict resolution model with five steps: *A*ssume that other members mean well, *E*xpress your feelings, *I*dentify your goal, clarify expected *O*utcomes, and achieve mutual *U*nderstanding.

Affection Need. The need to express and receive warmth or to be liked.

Affective Conflict. A type of conflict that reflects the emotions stirred by interpersonal disagreements related to a member's self-concept, feelings, personality traits, or communication style.

Agenda. An outline of the items to be discussed and the tasks to be accomplished at a meeting.

Aggressiveness. Critical, insensitive, combative, or abusive behavior that is motivated by self-interest at the expense of others.

Aggressor. A group member who puts down other members to get what she or he wants (a self-centered role).

Analysis Paralysis. A situation in which group members become so focused on analyzing an issue or problem that they are reluctant or unable to make a decision.

Analytical Listening. A type of listening that focuses on evaluating and forming opinions about the content of a message.

Apathy. The indifference that occurs when members do not consider the group or its goal to be important, interesting, or inspiring.

Appeal to Authority. The fallacy of using the opinions of a supposed expert when in fact the person has no particular expertise in the area under consideration.

Appeal to Popularity. The fallacy of claiming that an action or belief is acceptable because many people do it or believe it.

Appeal to Tradition. The fallacy of claiming that people should continue a certain course of action because that is the way it has always been done.

Appreciative Listening. A type of listening that focuses on valuing or enjoying how an idea, opinion, or act is expressed.

Arbitration. A conflict resolution method that involves a third party who, after considering all sides in a dispute, decides how to resolve the conflict.

Argument. A claim supported by evidence or reasons for accepting it.

Argumentation. A process used to advocate a position, examine competing ideas, and influence others.

Argumentativeness. The willingness to argue with others and take public positions on controversial issues.

Assertiveness. Speaking up and acting in your own best interests without denying the rights and interests of others.

Assessment. A mechanism for monitoring group progress and determining whether a group has achieved its goals.

Asynchronous Communication. Electronic communication that does not occur simultaneously or in real time; communication that is linear and not interactive.

Audioconference. A voice-only communication medium that usually takes one of two forms: a teleconference or a computer-based voice link.

Authority Rule. A situation in which a leader or an authority outside a group makes final decisions for the group.

Autocrat. A group member whose need for control is not met; an autocrat tries to dominate and control the group.

Autocratic Leader. A leader who uses power and authority to strictly control a group and its discussion.

Avoidance Conflict Style. A passive and nonconfrontational approach to conflict.

Backing. The component of the Toulmin model of argument that provides support for an argument's warrant.

Balance. A state in which groups effectively assess communication theories, methods, and tools and adapt them to group goals and member needs.

Basic Term. A word that immediately comes to mind when observing an object.

Blocker. A group member who stands in the way of progress and uses delaying tactics to derail an idea or proposal (a self-centered role).

Blog. A web site on which text, images, web links, and other files are posted on a regular basis by an individual or organized group.

Brainstorming. A technique that encourages group members to generate as many ideas as possible in a nonevaluative atmosphere.

Bypassing. A form of miscommunication that occurs when people have different meanings for the same words or phrases and miss each other with their meanings.

Chair or **Chairperson.** A person who has been appointed or elected to conduct a group meeting.

Channel. A medium through which group members share messages.

Character. A speaker's goodwill and honesty; a factor in determining credibility.

Charismatic Leader. A leader who uses expert and referent power to inspire and engage members as they work to achieve a common goal.

Claim. The component of the Toulmin model of argument that states the proposition or conclusion of an argument.

Claim of Conjecture. An argument suggesting that something will or will not happen.

Claim of Fact. An argument stating that something is true or false or that something did or did not occur.

Claim of Policy. An argument advocating a specific course of action.

Claim of Value. An argument evaluating whether something is good or bad, right or wrong, worthwhile or worthless.

Clarifier-Summarizer. A group member who explains ideas, reduces confusion, and sums up group progress and conclusions (a task role).

Climate. The group atmosphere, characterized by the degree to which members feel comfortable interacting.

Clown. A group member who injects inappropriate humor into the discussion and seems more interested in goofing off than in working (a self-centered role).

Co-Culture. A group of people who coexist within the mainstream society, yet remain connected to one another through their cultural heritage.

Codeswitching. The ability to change from the language or dialect of your own culture and adopt the language or dialect of another cultural group.

Coercive Power. The ability or authority to pressure or punish group members if they do not follow orders and directions.

Cognitive Restructuring. A technique for reducing communication apprehension that analyzes worrisome, irrational, and nonproductive assumptions about speaking to and with others (cognitions) and seeks to modify those thoughts (restructuring).

Cohesion. The mutual attraction that holds the members of a group together.

Collaborative Conflict Style. An approach to conflict emphasizing the search for solutions that satisfy all group members and that also achieve the group's common goal.

Collaborative Presentation Technology. Technology that enhances interactive group presentations by allowing members to project ideas or graphics onto a screen, wall, or whiteboard.

Collectivism. A cultural value or belief in interdependence that places greater emphasis on the views, needs, and goals of the group than on the views, needs, and goals of individuals.

Committee. A group given a specific assignment by a larger group or by a person in a position of authority.

Common Ground. An identifiable belief, value, experience, or point of view shared by all group members.

Communication Apprehension. An individual's level of fear or anxiety associated with either real or anticipated communication with another person or persons.

Competence. A speaker's expertise and abilities; a factor in determining credibility.

Competitive Conflict Style. An approach to conflict that is focused on achieving a person's own goals rather than the group's goals, even if this upsets the group and its members.

Comprehensive Listening. A type of listening that focuses on accurately understanding the meaning of spoken and nonverbal messages.

Compromiser. A group member who helps minimize differences among group members and helps the group reach consensus (a maintenance role).

Compromising Conflict Style. An approach to conflict that involves the concession of some goals in order to achieve others.

Concrete Word. A word that refers to something that can be perceived by the senses.

Confessor. A group member who inappropriately reveals personal feelings and problems and constantly seeks emotional support rather than promoting the group's goal (a self-centered role).

Conflict. The disagreement and disharmony that occurs in groups when differences regarding ideas, methods, and/or members are expressed.

Conflict↔Cohesion. A group dialectic in which the value of constructive conflict is balanced with the need for unity and cohesiveness.

Conforming↔Nonconforming. A group dialectic in which a commitment to group norms and standards is balanced with a willingness to accept differences and change.

Conformity. The choice of behaviors that are socially acceptable and favored by a majority of group members.

Connotation. The personal feelings connected to the meaning of a word.

Consensus. A situation in which all group members accept and are willing to support a group decision.

Constructive Conflict. An approach to disagreement in which group members express differences in a way that values everyone's contributions and promotes the group's goal.

Constructive Nonconformity. The act of resisting conformity to group norms and expectations while still working to achieve the group's goal.

Context. The physical and psychological environment in which group communication takes place.

Contingency Model of Leadership Effectiveness. A leadership theory claiming that effective leadership depends upon an ideal match between the leader's style and the group's work situation.

Control Need. The need to feel competent, confident, and free to make your own choices.

Controlling Feedback. Positive or negative feedback used to influence member behavior by telling them what to do.

Cooperative Argumentation. A process of reasoned interaction intended to help members make the best assessments or decisions in a given situation.

Creativity. The process and outcome of searching for, separating, and connecting thoughts from many categories while limiting judgments.

Credibility. The extent to which others believe you and your messages.

Culture. The learned set of shared expectations about beliefs, values, and norms that affect the behaviors of a relatively large group of people.

Data. The component of the Toulmin model of argument that provides evidence to support a claim.

Decision Making. The act of reaching a conclusion; a group selects an option from among possible alternatives.

Decreasing Options Technique (DOT). A procedure for reducing and refining a large number of ideas or suggestions into more manageable categories.

Definition. A statement that clarifies the meaning of a word, phrase, or concept.

Democratic Leader. A leader who practices social equality and shares the decision-making process with group members.

Democratic Member. A group member whose need for control is met and who has no problems dealing with power in groups.

Demographic Traits. Audience traits such as age, gender, race, ethnicity, religion, and marital status.

Denotation. The objective, dictionary-based meaning of a word.

Description. A reference that creates a mental image of a person, event, place, or object.

Deserter. A group member who seems bored or annoyed with the discussion and stops contributing (a self-centered role).

Designated Leader. A leader selected by a group or an outside authority.

Destructive Conflict. Disagreement expressed through behaviors that create hostility and prevent achievement of the group's goal.

Destructive Nonconformity. Resistance to conforming to group norms and expectations without regard for the best interests of the group and its goal.

Dialect. The distinct regional and cultural variations in vocabulary, pronunciation, syntax, and style that differ from the commonly accepted form of a particular language and that characterize speakers from different ethnic groups, geographic areas, and social classes.

Dialectics. Theories that explore the methods of argument or exposition that systematically weigh contradictory facts or ideas with a view of resolution of their real or apparent contradiction.

Digital Divide. Inequalities in access to, distribution of, and use of information technology among different groups or populations.

Discrimination. Acting out and expressing prejudice by excluding groups of people from the opportunities and rights granted to others.

Discriminative Listening. The ability to distinguish auditory and/or visual stimuli.

Dominator. A group member who tries to assert authority and prevents others from participating (a self-centered role).

Electronic Whiteboard. A writing board fully linked to a computer system that allows information written on the board to be stored, printed, and displayed.

Emergent Leader. A person who gradually achieves leadership status by interacting with group members and contributing to the achievement of the group's common goal.

Emoticon. Typographical characters used to express emotion when communicating via computer.

Emotional Intelligence. Daniel Goleman defines emotional intelligence as the capacity for recognizing your own feelings and those of others, for motivating yourself, and for managing emotions in yourself and in various interpersonal relationships.

Empathic Listening. A type of listening that focuses on understanding and identifying with a person's feelings, motives, and situation.

Encourager-Supporter. A group member who praises and agrees with others, provides recognition, and listens empathetically (a maintenance role).

Energizer. A group member who motivates others and helps create enthusiasm for the task (a task role).

Engaged↔Disengaged. A group dialectic in which members' loyalty and labor are balanced with the group's need for rest and renewal.

Ethics. An understanding of whether group members' communication behaviors meet agreed-upon standards of right and wrong.

Ethnocentrism. A mistaken belief that your culture is a superior culture with special rights and privileges that are or should be denied to others.

Evaluator-Critic. A group member who assesses ideas and diagnoses problems (a task role).

Example. A reference to a specific case or instance.

Expectancy-Value Theory. A theory that motivation results from a combination of individual needs and the value of the goals available in the environment.

Expert Power. The ability to motivate and persuade others by demonstrating special skills or knowledge.

Explicit Norm. A norm that is written or stated verbally.

Extemporaneous Speaking. A form of presentation delivery in which the speaker has done prior preparation but uses limited notes.

Extrinsic Rewards. Rewards that come from the external environment, such as money, benefits, and job perks.

Extrovert. A Myers-Briggs personality type who is outgoing, usually talks more than others, and is often enthusiastic and animated during a discussion.

Face. The positive image that a person tries to create or preserve that is also appropriate to a particular culture.

Fact. A verifiable observation, experience, or event, something that is known to be true.

Fallacy. An argument that is based on false or invalid reasoning.

False Consensus. A situation in which members succumb to group pressure and accept a decision that they do not like or support.

Family. A self-defined group of intimates who create and maintain themselves through their own interactions and their interactions with others.

Faulty Analogy. The fallacy of claiming that two things are similar when they actually differ with regard to relevant characteristics.

Faulty Cause. The fallacy of identifying the cause of an event before ruling out other possible causes.

Feedback. The verbal or nonverbal response or reaction to a message.

Feeler. A Myers-Briggs personality type who wants everyone to get along and who will spend time with other group members to achieve harmony.

Feminine Society. A culture in which gender roles overlap: Both men and women are supposed to be modest, tender, and concerned with the quality of life.

Follower. A cooperative group member who is willing to accept group decisions and carry them out (a maintenance role).

Forming Stage. The group development phase in which member and group goals are explored and interpersonal relationships are tested.

Forum. A public meeting in which audience members express their concerns and address questions, often to public officials and experts.

4M Model of Leadership Effectiveness. An approach to leadership that divides leadership tasks into four interdependent functions: (1) *M*odeling leadership behavior, (2) *M*otivating members, (3) *M*anaging the group process, and (4) *M*aking decisions.

4Rs Method. A conflict management method that allows groups to analyze conflicts based on *R*easons, *R*eactions, *R*esults, and *R*esolution.

Functional Leadership Theory. An approach to leadership that claims that any capable group member can assume leadership functions when necessary.

Functional Theory. A problem-solving theory claiming that a set of critical communication functions can explain and predict how well a group will solve problems.

Fundamental Interpersonal Relationship Orientation (FIRO). William Schutz's theory that examines the extent to which the satisfaction of inclusion, control, and affection needs affects why people join groups and how well group members communicate and behave toward one another.

Gatekeeper. A group member who monitors participation and tries to regulate the flow of communication in a discussion (a maintenance role).

Goal. The purpose or objective toward which a group's efforts are directed.

Goal Theory. A theory that examines the value of and techniques for setting group goals and the methods needed to accomplish those goals.

Golden Listening Rule. The principle that you should listen to others as you would have them listen to you.

Governance Groups. State legislatures, city and county councils, and governing boards of public agencies and educational institutions that conduct decision-making meetings in public.

Group Communication. The interaction of three or more interdependent people working to achieve a common goal.

Group Dialectics. The several complex and competing components of groupwork that require an appropriate level of balance to maximize group effectiveness.

Group Motivation. The inspiration, incentives, or reasons that move group members to work together in order to achieve a common goal.

Group Polarization. A tendency for group members (and especially virtual groups in which there are no visible nonverbal cues) to express more extreme opinions and take more extreme actions.

Grouphate. An intense aversion to working in groups.

Groupthink. The deterioration of group effectiveness that can result from in-group pressure.

Groupware. Computer-mediated methods and tools, such as email, bulletin boards, electronic chat, and electronic meeting systems, that are designed to support group collaboration.

Habit. A form of effective communication that requires knowledge, skills, and desire.

Harmonizer. A group member who helps resolve conflicts and promotes teamwork (a maintenance role).

Hasty Generalization. The fallacy of using too few examples or experiences to support a conclusion.

Heterogeneous Group. A group composed of members who are different from one another.

Hidden Agenda. An individual member's private motives and goals that differ from a group's common goal.

High Context Culture. A culture in which very little meaning is expressed through words; gestures, silence, facial expression, and relationships among communicators are more reliable indicators of meaning.

High Context–Low Context. A cultural dimension that reflects the directness of communication in specific circumstances.

High Power Distance. A cultural norm of accepting major differences in power; assuming that all people are *not* created equal.

High Uncertainty Avoidance. A cultural characteristic of members who feel a need for predictability and are threatened by uncertain or unknown situations.

Homogeneous Group. A group composed of members who are all the same or very similar.

Homogeneous↔Heterogeneous. A group dialectic in which member similarities are balanced with member differences in skills, roles, personal characteristics, and cultural perspectives.

Hyperpersonal Communication. An increase in confidence and decrease in communication apprehension that occur in computer-mediated rather than face-to-face communication.

Illustration. An extended or detailed example.

Implicit Norm. A norm that is rarely discussed or openly communicated.

Impromptu. A form of presentation delivery in which a person speaks without prior preparation or practice.

Inclusion Need. The need to be accepted and affiliated with a group; the need to belong or be involved.

Individual Attributes. Distinctive features of particular group members, such as personality traits, job titles, status, special interests, relationships with other members, and length of membership.

Individual Goals↔Group Goals. A group dialectic in which members' personal goals are balanced with the group's common goal.

Individualism. A cultural value or belief that the individual is important, that independence is worth pursuing, that personal achievement should be rewarded, and that individual uniqueness is an important value.

Individualism–Collectivism. A cultural dimension that reflects whether people prefer to act independently or interdependently.

Information Giver. A group member who provides and organizes relevant information (a task role).

Information Seeker. A group member who asks for needed information, requests explanations and clarifications, and makes the group aware of information gaps (a task role).

Informative Feedback. Feedback that provides a group with an assessment of its performance and the extent to which a goal is being achieved.

Initiator. A group member who proposes ideas and suggestions, provides direction for the group, and gets the group started (a task role).

Interaction. Communication among group members who use verbal and nonverbal messages to generate meaning and establish relationships.

Interaction Norm. A norm that determines how group members communicate with one another.

Intercultural Dimension. An aspect of a culture that can be measured relative to other cultures.

Interdependence. The extent to which group members are affected and influenced by the attitudes and behaviors of other members.

Internet Addiction Disorder (IAD). A maladaptive pattern of Internet use that results in clinically significant impairment or distress.

Interpersonal Space. The psychological space surrounding each person that expands and contracts in different contexts.

Intimate Distance. Interpersonal space ranging from zero to eighteen inches, typically reserved for close friends, family, and lovers.

Intrinsic Rewards. Rewards that are satisfying and energizing in themselves.

Introvert. A Myers-Briggs personality type who needs time to think before speaking and who may prefer to work alone rather than in a group.

Intuitive. A Myers-Briggs personality type who likes to make connections and formulate big ideas but who may become bored with details.

Jargon. The specialized or technical language of a profession.

Judger. A Myers-Briggs personality type who is highly structured and likes to plan ahead.

Kinesics. The study of body movement and physical expression.

Laissez-Faire Leader. A leader who lets the group take charge of all decisions and actions.

Leader–Member Relations. A situational leadership factor that assesses how well a leader gets along with group members.

Leadership. The ability to make strategic decisions and use communication to mobilize a group toward achieving a common goal.

Leadership↔Followership. A group dialectic in which effective and ethical leadership is balanced with loyal and responsible followership.

Learning Group. A group that meets to help its members acquire knowledge and develop skills by sharing information and experience.

Legitimate Power. The power that resides in a job, position, or assignment rather than in a person; the power to make decisions as an authorized or elected representative of a group.

Listening. The process of receiving, constructing meaning from, and responding to spoken and/or nonverbal messages.

Listserv. An email option that delivers messages to everyone in a group.

Low-Context Culture. A culture in which meaning is expressed primarily through language; people from a low-context culture tend to speak more, speak louder, and speak more rapidly than people from a high-context culture.

Low Power Distance. A cultural perspective in which power distinctions are minimized.

Low Uncertainty Avoidance. A cultural characteristic of members who accept change, tolerate nonconformity, take risks, and view rules and regulations as restricting and counterproductive.

Machiavellian. A term used to describe a leader who is willing to use dishonorable and unethical means in order to achieve a personal or group goal.

Maintenance Role. A positive role that affects how group members get along with one another while pursuing a common goal.

Majority Vote. The results of a vote in which more than half the members vote in favor of a proposal.

Masculine↔Feminine. A cultural dimension that reflects concerns for self and success (masculine) or a focus on caring and sharing (feminine).

Masculine Society. A culture in which men are supposed to be assertive, tough, and focused on material success, whereas women are supposed to be more modest, tender, and concerned with the quality of life.

Maslow's Hierarchy of Needs. A specific sequence of needs (physiological, safety, belongingness, esteem, and self-actualization) that can explain why people are attracted to particular groups.

Mediation. A facilitated negotiation that employs the services of an impartial third party for the purpose of guiding, coaching, and encouraging disputants to a successful resolution and an agreement.

Meeting. A scheduled gathering of group members for a structured discussion guided by a designated chairperson.

Member. Any individual whom other members recognize as belonging to the group.

Member Readiness. The extent to which a member is willing and able to contribute to achieving the group's goal.

Messages. Ideas, information, opinions, and/or feelings that generate meaning.

Method. A strategy, guideline, procedure, or technique for dealing with the issues and problems that arise in groups.

Minutes. The written record of a group's discussion and activities during a meeting.

Mission. The overall and motivational goal established by a group.

Monochronic–Polychronic. A cultural dimension that describes how people organize and value time.

Monochronic Time (M Time). An approach to time that favors clear deadlines and the scheduling of one thing at a time.

Motivation. The reasons that encourage, move, or inspire a person or group to do something.

Motivators. Extrinsic and intrinsic factors that encourage and inspire group members to work together to achieve a common goal.

Multimedia. Technology that enables you to combine words, charts, graphics, sounds, and animation in a single presentation.

Muted Group Theory. A theory that claims that some female members' discomfort with expressing themselves assertively affects their ability to effectively participate in a group.

Myers-Briggs Type Indicator®. A widely used inventory that identifies specific personality types based on the ways in which people perceive the world around them and make judgments.

Negotiation. A process of bargaining for the purpose of settling differences or reaching solutions.

Netlingo. Language forms common to communication via the Internet, such as abbreviations, acronyms, and less use of punctuation.

Netspeak. Typographical strategies common to communication via the Internet that are used to achieve a more sociable and interactive style.

Noise. Anything that interferes with or inhibits communication.

Nominal Group Technique (NGT). A procedure in which members write and report suggested ideas, after which discussion and multiple votes are used to decide the priority or value of the listed suggestions.

Nonconformity. A member's behavior that does not meet the norms or expectations of the group.

Nonverbal Communication. The behavioral elements of messages other than the actual words spoken.

Norm. An expectation held by group members concerning what kinds of behavior or opinion are acceptable or unacceptable.

Norming Stage. The group development stage in which members resolve conflicts and work as a cohesive team to develop methods for achieving the group's goal.

Observer-Interpreter. A group member who monitors other members' feelings and behaviors and who paraphrases others' ideas, opinions, and emotions (a maintenance role).

Offensive Language. Terminology that demeans, inappropriately excludes, or stereotypes people.

Open System↔Closed System. A group dialectic in which external support and recognition are balanced with internal group solidarity and rewards.

Opinion. A personal conclusion regarding the meaning or implications of facts.

Opinion Giver. A group member who states personal beliefs and interpretations and offers analysis and arguments (a task role).

Opinion Seeker. A group member who asks for others' opinions (a task role).

Optimal Experience. An experience in which all group members are caught up in the group's work and are performing at a high level of achievement.

Overpersonal Member. A group member whose affection needs are not met and who is too talkative and overly personal.

Oversocial Member. A group member whose inclusion needs are not met and who seeks attention as a way of compensating for feelings of inadequacy.

Panel Discussion. A group discussion in which participants interact with one another on a common topic for the benefit of an audience.

Paraphrasing. A form of feedback that uses different words to restate what a person has said as a way of indicating that the listener has understood what the speaker means and feels.

Parliamentary Procedure. A systematic method and set of formal rules used to determine the will of the majority through fair and orderly discussion and debate.

Passive-Aggressive. Uncooperative and obstructive behavior that appears to be cooperative.

Passivity. Nonassertive behavior characterized by a lack of confidence and a reluctance to communicate.

Perceiver. A Myers-Briggs personality type who is less rigid about deadlines and time constraints and who is flexible and willing to try new options.

Performing Stage. The group development stage in which group members focus their energy on doing the work needed to achieve group goals.

Personal Distance. Interpersonal space ranging from eighteen inches to four feet, typically used for friends and acquaintances.

Personal Member. A group member whose affection needs are met and who is comfortable interacting with group members.

Polychronic Time (P Time). An approach to time that allows many things to be done at once; schedules are flexible, and deadlines may be missed.

Post-Meeting Reaction (PMR) Form. A questionnaire designed to assess the success of a meeting by collecting written reactions from participants.

Power. The ability or authority to influence and motivate others.

Power Distance. A cultural dimension that reflects the distance between those of different status.

Prejudice. A negative attitude about other people that is based on faulty and inflexible stereotypes.

Presentation. A relatively uninterrupted talk or speech to a group of people.

Presentation Aids. Supplementary audio and/or visual materials used in a discussion or oral presentation.

Presentation Software. Computer programs used to design and present visual aids.

Primary Group. A group of family members or friends who provide affection, support, and a sense of belonging.

Primary Tension. The social unease and inhibitions experienced by group members during the getting-acquainted phase of a group's development.

Problem Solving. A complex process in which groups analyze a problem and develop a plan for reducing the harmful effects of the problem.

Procedural Conflict. A disagreement over what method or process a group should follow to accomplish its goal.

Procedural Norm. A norm that dictates how a group will operate.

Procedural Technician. A group member who assists with preparations for meetings, including suggesting agenda items, making room arrangements, and providing needed materials and equipment (a task role).

Proxemics. The study of how people perceive and use personal space and distance.

Public Distance. Interpersonal space beyond eight feet, typically reserved for large audiences.

Public Group. A group that discusses issues and makes presentations in front of or for the benefit of a public audience.

Qualifier. The component of the Toulmin model of argument that states the degree to which a claim is thought to be true.

Question of Conjecture. A decision-making question that asks whether something will or will not happen.

Question of Fact. A decision-making question that asks whether something is true or false, or whether something did or did not occur.

Question of Policy. A decision-making question that asks whether and how a specific course of action should be taken to solve a problem.

Question of Value. A decision-making question that asks the group to decide whether something is good or bad, right or wrong, or worthwhile or worthless.

Race. A socially constructed concept that classifies people into separate value-based categories.

Recognition Seeker. A group member who boasts about her or his accomplishments and tries to become the group's center of attention (a self-centered role).

Recorder-Secretary. A group member who keeps and provides accurate written records of a group's major ideas, suggestions, and decisions (a task role).

Referent Power. The personal power and influence held by a person who is admired and respected.

Reflective Thinking Process. A set of practical steps that a rational person should follow when solving a problem.

Refutation. The process of proving that an argument is false and/or lacks sufficient support.

Relational Dialectics Theory. A theory that examines how relationships are characterized by ongoing, dialectic tensions between the multiple contradictions, complexities, and changes in human experiences.

Relationship-Motivated Leader. A leader whose major satisfaction comes from establishing close personal relations with group members.

Reprimand. A form of feedback that identifies and discusses a person's work-related problems or deficiencies.

Reservation. The component of the Toulmin model of argument that recognizes the conditions under which a claim would not necessarily be true.

Reward. Something that is given or received as recompense when a group member or the entire group progresses toward or achieves its common goal.

Reward Power. The authority to give group members something that they value.

Role. A group member's unique set of skills or behavioral patterns that serve specific functions within the group.

Satisfiers. Actions or compensations that meet group members' basic deficiency needs—money for food and shelter, job security, insurance—but do not necessarily motivate members to work harder or better.

Secondary Tension. The frustrations and personality conflicts experienced by group members as they compete with one another for acceptance and achievement.

Self-Actualization Need. The need to fulfill one's own human potential; the personal reward of becoming the best that is possible.

Self-Centered Role. A negative role in which individual needs are put ahead of the group's goal and other members' needs.

Self-Help Group. A group that offers assistance and encouragement to members who need support with personal problems.

Sensor. A Myers-Briggs personality type who focuses on details and prefers to concentrate on one task at a time.

Service Group. A group dedicated to worthy causes that help people both inside and outside the group.

Single Question Format. A problem-solving procedure that focuses group analysis on answering a single agreed-upon question in order to arrive at a solution.

Situational Theory. An approach to leadership that helps leaders improve by carefully analyzing themselves, their group, and the circumstances in which they must lead.

Social Dimension. A group's focus on the interpersonal relationships among group members.

Social Distance. Interpersonal space ranging from four to eight feet, typically reserved for new acquaintances and strangers.

Social Group. A group in which members share common interests in a friendly setting or participate in common leisure activities.

Social Member. A person whose inclusion needs are met and who enjoys working with other people but is comfortable working alone.

Solution Criteria. The standards that the ideal resolution of a problem should meet.

Special Interest Pleader. A group member who tries to influence others to support nongroup interests (a self-centered role).

Standard Agenda. A procedure that guides a group through problem solving by using the following steps: clarify the task, understand and analyze the problem, assess possible solutions, and implement a decision or plan.

Standing Committee. A committee that remains active in order to accomplish an ongoing task.

Statistics. Information presented in a numerical form.

Status Norm. A norm that identifies levels of influence among group members.

Stereotype. A generalization about a group of people that oversimplifies their characteristics and results in erroneous judgment about the entire group of people.

Storming Stage. The group development stage in which members compete with one another to determine individual status and to establish group goals.

Structure↔Spontaneity. A group dialectic in which the need for structured procedures is balanced with the need for innovative and creative thinking.

Styles Theory. An approach to leadership that identifies specific behaviors or styles that can be learned; these can be put into three categories: autocratic, democratic, or laissez-faire leadership.

Subordinate Term. A concrete and specialized term.

Substantive Conflict. A disagreement over ideas, issue analysis, and potential solutions or actions.

Superordinate Term. A word in which objects and ideas are grouped together very generally.

Symposium. A group presentation in which participants give short, uninterrupted speeches on different aspects of a topic for the benefit of an audience.

Synchronous Communication. Communication that occurs simultaneously and in real time, either face to face or electronically.

Synergy. The interaction of two or more agents or forces in which the effect of their combined efforts is greater than the sum of their individual efforts.

Systematic Desensitization. A technique for reducing communication apprehension that requires learning relaxed responses to increasingly anxiety-producing situations.

Task Dimension. A group's focus on achieving its goal.

Task Dimension↔Social Dimension. A group dialectic in which the responsibility and motivation to complete tasks are balanced with promoting relationships among members.

Task Force. A type of committee appointed to gather information and make recommendations regarding a specific issue or problem.

Task-Motivated Leader. A leader whose major satisfaction comes from successfully completing the group task rather than from promoting positive interpersonal relationships with group members.

Task Role. A positive role that affects a group's ability to do the work needed to achieve its goals.

Task Structure. A situational leadership factor that assesses how a group must organize or plan a specific task.

Team Presentation. A coordinated presentation by a group of speakers who are trying to influence an audience of decision makers.

Team Talk. The nature of the language that group members use as they work together.

Teleconference. A coordinated phone call involving three or more group members.

Tension Releaser. A group member who alleviates tension with friendly humor and tries to relax other group members (a maintenance role).

Territoriality. The sense of personal ownership attached to a particular space.

Text-Based Computer Conferencing. A conference in which group members use their computer keyboards to communicate and collaborate with one another.

Theory. A principle that tries to explain or predict events and behavior.

Thinker. A Myers-Briggs personality type who takes pride in thinking objectively and making difficult decisions.

Thought Speed. The speed (in words per minute) at which most people can think compared to the slower speed at which most people speak.

Threaded Discussion. A series of email messages about a specific issue posted on an electronic bulletin board.

Tool. A resource, rule, or skill that helps a group carry out or achieve its common goal.

Toulmin Model of Argument. A model developed by Stephen Toulmin that represents the structure of an argument.

Trait Theory. An approach to leadership that tries to identify common characteristics and behaviors of effective leaders.

Transformational Leadership Theory. An approach to leadership that examines the ways in which leaders inspire followers to move beyond self-interest and become a unified group.

Two-Thirds Vote. The results of a vote in which at least twice as many group members vote in favor of a proposal as oppose it.

Uncertainty Avoidance. A cultural dimension that reflects the extent to which people within a culture are uncomfortable in unstructured, unclear, or unpredictable situations.

Underpersonal Member. A group member whose affection needs are not met and who has only superficial relationships with other group members.

Undersocial Member. A group member whose inclusion needs are not met and who may withdraw from the group or feel unworthy.

Verbal Communication. The use of words to generate meaning.

Videoconference. A form of communication that combines audio and video media to provide both voice communication and video images.

Virtual Group. A group that relies on technology to communicate synchronously and/or asynchronously, often across time, distance, and organizational boundaries.

Vision. A view of the future that will result when a group achieves its goal.

Visualization. A technique for reducing communication apprehension that encourages positive thinking about communicating in groups by relaxing and imagining yourself succeeding.

Warrant. The component of the Toulmin model of argument that provides the justification for how the data support a particular claim.

Wiki. A web site that allows users to add and edit content.

Word Stress. The degree of vocal prominence given to a syllable within a word or to a word within a phrase or sentence.

Work Group. A group responsible for achieving specific tasks or performing routine duties on behalf of a company, organization, association, agency, or institution.

Work Team. A group given full responsibility and resources for achieving a goal.

Index

Online Study Center web chapters A and B are indicated by page references preceded by an A or B.